GRASSROOTS
RESISTANCE

The only people whose names are
recorded in history are those who did
something. The peaceful and indifferent
are forgotten; they never know
the fighting joy of living.

ELIZABETH GURLEY FLYNN
January 28, 1917

GRASSROOTS RESISTANCE

Social Movements in
Twentieth Century
America

ROBERT A. GOLDBERG
University of Utah

Wadsworth Publishing Company
Belmont, California
A Division of Wadsworth, Inc.

History Editor: Peggy Adams
Editorial Assistant: Cathie Fields
Production Editor: Angela Mann
Designer: Andrew Ogus
Print Buyer: Barbara Britton
Copy Editor: Stephanie Prescott
Technical Illustrator: Susan Breitbard
Compositor: Omegatype
Cover: Laurie Anderson

Chapter 2 Two lines from "Where Everybody Knows Your Name" by Gary Portnoy and Judy Hart Angelo. Copyright © 1982 by Addax Music Co., Inc. Reprinted by permission of Famous Music Publishing Companies.
Chapter 3 Lyrics from *Songs of the Workers.* Reprinted by permission of the Industrial Workers of the World, 3435 N. Sheffield, Chicago, IL 60657.
Chapter 4 Sections from *Hooded Empire: The Ku Klux Klan in Colorado* by Robert A. Goldberg. Copyright © 1981 by the Board of Trustees of the University of Illinois. Reprinted by permission of the University of Illinois Press.

Printed in the United States of America 49
1 2 3 4 5 6 7 8 9 10—95 94 93 92 91
Library of Congress Cataloging in Publication Data
Goldberg, Robert Alan,
    Grassroots resistance : social movements in twentieth century
America / Robert A. Goldberg.
        p.   cm.
    Includes bibliographical references.
    ISBN 0-534-12906-4
    1. Social movements—United States—History—20th century.
I. Title.
HN57.G58   1991   90-34246
303.48'4'09730904—dc20   CIP

For David, Michael, Erin,
Seth, Joshua, Brooke, and Anna. . .
remain rooted to your pasts,
but open before change

CONTENTS

Preface   xi

1 An Introduction to Social Movements   **1**

What Is a Social Movement?   2
Social Movements and the Theorists: The Classical Tradition   4
Social Movements and the Theorists: The Resource
    Mobilization Approach   7
Up from the Grass Roots   11
Eight Movements   16

**2 The Death of John Barleycorn:
The Anti-Saloon League**   **18**

Nineteenth-Century Roots   19
The Challenge of the Saloon   21

The Prohibitionist Response   23
   Competing in a Crowded Field   26
Building a Consensus   27
The Momentum of Protest   30
   The Wet Counterattack   32
On to Washington   34
Victory and Defeat   35
Aftermath   39

3 One Big Union: The Industrial Workers of the World   41

"Conditions They Are Bad"   42
   "Outcast and Starving"   44
"Workingfolk Unite"   46
"Commonwealth of Toil"   49
"Are You a Wobbly?"   51
   "All Hell Can't Stop Us"   53
   "They Go Wild . . . Over Me"   55
"Dump the Bosses off Your Back"   57
"Hold the Fort"   60
   "Now the Final Battle Rages"   62
"Still Ain't Satisfied"   64

4 Invisible Empire: The Knights of the Ku Klux Klan   65

The Kluxing of America   66
   Selling the Klan   68
   Imperial Rule, Klavern Power   70
Denver: Queen City of the Colorado Realm   73
   The Klan Program   74
   Reaching for Influence   77
Beneath the Hood and Robe   78
Triumph at the Polls   82
Fall of the Invisible Empire   85
   Beyond Denver   87
Evolving Reincarnations   89

5 Throw Off Your Chains:
The Communist Party   **91**

"Acute Revolutionary Crisis"   92
The Limits of Authority   95
  Bolshevizing the American Party   *97*
The Crisis of Capitalism   99
The Popular Front   101
  Allegiance to the Party   *104*
  The Communist Cocoon   *106*
Changes in the Party Line   107
  Postwar Fallout   *109*
  Retreat and Ruin   *112*
Passing of the Old Left   114

6 Bridging McCarthyism and Reaganism:
The John Birch Society   **116**

McCarthyism   117
Robert Welch's Creation   120
  Portrait of an Anticommunist   *123*
Return of the Right   124
Confronting the Conspiracy   126
  Opinion Makers' Response   *128*
A Choice Not an Echo   130
  Profile of the Membership   *131*
Veering Farther Right   133
Toward Reaganism   136
  After Welch   *139*

7 "We Shall Not Be Moved": The Student
Nonviolent Coordinating Committee   **141**

"Freedom's Comin' and It Won't Be Long"   142
  "Get on Board"   *144*
"Fighting for My Rights"   147
  "We'll Never Turn Back"   *148*
  "I'm Gonna Sit at the Welcome Table"   *150*
"Been Down in the South"   152
  "I've Got a Hammer"   *155*

"Ain't Gonna Let Nobody Turn Me Round"   156
   "Eyes on the Prize"   159
"Hard Travelin' "   162
   "We've Been 'Buked and We've Been Scorned"   163

8 The Campus Revolt: The Berkeley Free Speech Movement   167

The "Multiversity" Setting   168
   A New Activism   170
Disputed Ground   173
   Confrontation   174
Taking Stock   178
   The Powers That Be   179
A Joining of Adversaries   181
Endgame   183
   Who Was There?   185
   Resolution   186
Changing Times   188

9 Never Another Season of Silence: The National Organization for Women   193

Rising Opportunities   194
Higher Consciousness   197
   From Civil Rights to Women's Rights   198
   The Emergence of NOW   200
Women's Liberation   203
   NOW Evolves   206
Equal Rights Now   208
The ERA   211
   Stalemated   213
Present and Future   214

10 The Challengers' Legacy   218

Movement Members   219
The Protest Present   220

Change and Continuity   223
    The More Things Change . . .   224
    . . . The More They Stay the Same   227
Challenging Outcomes   229
    Four Critical Variables   230
Pluralism Revised   234

Notes   **236**

Bibliography   **282**

Index   **304**

PREFACE

Both historians and sociologists have long been interested in social movements. But the search for knowledge in the academic world is a fragmented undertaking: as scholarship has become more specialized, even members of the same discipline may sense a lack of common ground. Such circumstances makes the union of two disciplines an especially difficult marriage to arrange. When the two are sociology, a social science, and history, one of the humanities, the relationship becomes particularly awkward. Historians and sociologists may speak the same language, but words of importance have different meanings and values. Scholars in these fields collect and analyze data in different ways. Similarly, they are far apart in conceptualization and their sense of the past. Still, to study collective action effectively, to illuminate an issue that has intrigued both sociologists and historians, the analyst must draw insights from both.

Sociologists have spent much time and effort seeking to understand social movements and the world that spawns them. They have constructed theories to account for the appearance of protest, the kinds of people who participate, and the outcomes of protest activity. The conceptual frameworks they have created have enhanced our knowledge and stimulated additional insights. But sociologists' models, in attempting to explain the recurrence of certain types of events, blur the backdrops of time and place—the fabrics of society and history are never so smooth or seamless as sociologists suggest. Historians, on the other hand, have traced the activities of movements of reform, revolution, and reaction. They have focused on the particular to explain the specific. Such a perspective tends to isolate and fix events in time rather than conceptualize them as elements of patterns and trends. This study seeks to moor sociological insights to a historical framework. It offers sociologists the necessary dimensions of time and human involvement while providing historians a theoretical lens through which to look at pieces of the past.

I wrote this book to serve as a teaching tool. It crosses academic specializations to offer students an interdisciplinary synthesis to study social movements and social change in twentieth century America. It views the century as a whole and provides a change-over-time perspective without neglecting the different contexts of the past. Ordinary men and women occupy the foreground as movers of events rather than observers of history. This book also specifically addresses the lack of available books for courses about social movements and collective behavior. Students in more general courses will find grassroots activities a necessary supplement to a national focus.

Like any work of synthesis, this study is built upon the research that has come before. A quick scan of its pages reveals how much I have borrowed and owe to other scholars. Also providing mortar for the book is my own research on social movements. My studies of the Ku Klux Klan, the Jewish agrarian movement, and the civil rights movement have enabled me to test, discard, and verify hypotheses concerning collective action. Not least, the students in my classes on American social movements have made a vital contribution to the construction of my ideas. In the arena of the classroom, they have shown little mercy in probing inconsistencies and pointing out missteps. Their interest and enthusiasm have provided the intellectual and emotional adrenaline that energizes all scholarship.

All authors know that the debts accumulated during research and writing are actually mushrooming assets. I thank my friends and colleagues Dale Erikkila, David Green, Tom Lund, Dean May, Duane Shrontz, and Stephen Tatum for their scholarly insights and personal encouragement. Reviewers Leonard Dinnerstein, University of Arizona; William A. Gamson, Boston College; Professor Robert Ingalls, University of South Florida; David L. Johnson, Portland State University; Glenna Matthews, Stanford University; Roy Rosenzweig, George Mason University; and Melvin I. Urofsky, Virginia Commonwealth University, all provided helpful comments. Peggy Adams, senior editor at Wadsworth, eased the transition from the Dorsey Press and could not have been more professional or supportive. Angela Mann and Stephanie Prescott guided the book through the production process and enhanced its meaning and value.

As did my other books, this one drew me closer to my father. During my research, he revealed his youthful flirtations with activism, a revelation that gave me a greater understanding of his constant refrain during the 1960s: "Whatever you do, don't sign anything!" My brother, long a political role model, first introduced me to the concepts of social movement mobilization. Once again, my work draws deeply from Susan's intelligence, humanity, and love. There is no measure of her influence. This book is dedicated to those who form the next link in a chain that ties the generations—past, present, and future.

1

AN INTRODUCTION TO

SOCIAL MOVEMENTS

It is required of a man that he share the action and passion of his time at the peril of being judged not to have lived.

OLIVER WENDELL HOLMES, JR.

How do Americans modify the political, economic, and social rules that govern their lives? Why do some efforts toward change succeed and others fail? Who, in America, are the agents of change?

To answer these questions, we may look in different directions. Most of us turn to the formal mechanisms of government, to the electoral process, congressional measures, presidential directives, and Supreme Court decisions. Or, we may single out specific people, like Theodore Roosevelt, Franklin Roosevelt, Samuel Rayburn, Earl Warren, Lyndon Johnson, and Ronald Reagan as the shapers of twentieth-century America. We may also look to impersonal forces to understand changing times, discerning in depression, war, and technology the innovators of thought and behavior.

However, concentrating upon the leaders of a society ignores other engines of change and results in an incomplete picture. Similarly, the environment and the sometimes cataclysmic events of life may establish conditions, but they do not determine responses, whether individual or collective.

To answer these questions from the perspective of individuals and the groups they form, we must look to the grass roots. Far from Washington, D.C., attuned to the daily rhythms of their communities, come other carriers of reaction, reform, and revolution. In the streets, in the workplace, or on the town square, they interpret and react to events in a manner that fits their needs and interests. It is this mobilization of common people for change, through the social movement, that is the subject of this book.

In exploring the vital impact of social movements on twentieth-century American society, we need to establish a common ground of definitions and terms. Then we can describe the people, events, and conditions that give rise to social movements; the shape these movements take; and their relationship to other vehicles of change on the American landscape.

WHAT IS A SOCIAL MOVEMENT?

A social movement is a formally organized group that acts consciously and with some continuity to promote or resist change through collective action. Let us dissect this working definition into its component parts.

A social movement is an "organized group" having a coherent internal structure, leadership, a written statement of purpose, membership, and a logistical base. Using sociologist Roberta Ash Garner's concept of a social movement organization, it is the action agent of larger and more generalized waves of protest and ferment. Thus, our definition focuses upon individual organizations like the Berkeley Free Speech Movement, the Ku Klux Klan, and the Student Nonviolent Coordinating Committee to help us understand more effectively such phenomena as the youth rebellion, the rise of the Right, or even the civil rights movement. The internal structure of social movements varies greatly. Some are highly centralized and bureaucratically structured groups with a single nucleus of leaders and a strict chain of command; others are organizations of semiautonomous locals with a minimal division of labor. Movement leaders direct their organizations by planning strategy, devising tactics, and gathering resources. They derive their authority through election, birth, or dictation. Like other groups, social movements demand men and women who possess a variety of skills and styles to sustain the operation, maintain its direction, and motivate the membership.[1]

A movement's "consciousness" exists in its statement of purpose or ideology. This set of beliefs and values about society serves a group in three ways. First, an ideology offers members and leaders a blueprint for change.

This guide for action proclaims the movement's goals and dreams for a better life and world. Second, an ideology explains the reasons for the movement's emergence and fixes targets of blame for the difficulties or setbacks that have occurred and that led to the rise of the movement. By interpreting the past and its interaction with the present, the movement brings understanding and the opportunity to act. Activists inspire effort with an explanation that not only decries conditions but points out those culpable. In this way, the movement is able to justify its existence to potential recruits as well as the community at large and, at the same time, negatively to spotlight those intent upon defending the status quo and quelling opposition. Finally, a movement must justify and glorify itself by appealing to its culture's sacred articles and persons. An ideology evokes those symbols that provide inspiration and whose name or meaning will be perpetuated through collective action. Thus, God, the Founding Fathers, the Declaration of Independence, the Constitution, or Karl Marx may be summoned to testify to the justice, morality, or patriotism of the cause. In sum, by espousing an ideology, the movement acts to raise consciousness, integrate members, generate community acceptance, and guide action with a uniting and energizing call to defend and advance the cause of right.[2]

A movement's organizational base, internal structure, leadership, and ideology enable it to act with intent and "continuity." A formal membership—which further distinguishes a movement from such ephemeral phenomena as fads, riots, and crowds—also provides stability. Often recruited along established lines of group interaction and communication, members officially join, carry cards, and pay dues to support their movement. Members are expected to contribute time, funds, skills, and wisdom to the effort. Movements may have a large base of followers with a small leadership core, they may be composed of a cadre of professional activists with an inactive membership, or they may reflect any combination of these two extremes. In any case, because membership is voluntary, leaders must continuously strive to insure the commitment and resources of their followers.

Finally, a social movement seeks to "promote or resist change." Unlike a fraternal order or an inward-looking commune, it contends with other groups for control of the present and the future. But the social movement's challenge is more than one of ideas. It also draws fire for its chosen paths to power. As a newcomer to the political arena, the social movement can not easily attain access to the established and traditional avenues of influence. Aware of power realities, movement leaders mobilize recruits to pursue goals in unorthodox and innovative ways. Their choice of tactics, depending upon conditions, may range from lobbying and electoral efforts to parades, boycotts, sit-ins, demonstrations, threats, and violence. Through such means, activists attempt to mobilize sufficient resources to prod decision makers toward change.

SOCIAL MOVEMENTS AND THE THEORISTS:
THE CLASSICAL TRADITION

Why do social movements arise? What makes men and women susceptible to their message? Who joins? The social theorist's responses to these questions are, to a considerable extent, the product of one's location in history. Dramatic historical events intertwined with personal experiences have shaped profoundly the research methods and insights of the students of social movements. For the generation of theorists, writing in the 1940s and 1950s, the dark shadows of nazism and the cold war had cast a pall over all forms of collective behavior. In this section we will survey the classical tradition of these theorists and their approach to social movements.

In the aftermath of World War II, with the death of Adolf Hitler a recent event and the threats of Stalinism and McCarthyism prevalent concerns, there was an understandable apprehension of social movement activism. Theorists portrayed social movements as symptoms of social pathology. Like rising crime and suicide rates, social movements were interpreted as society's red flags of distress: These movements housed the emotional, the fanatical, and the violent. They appealed to those segments of the population most eager to embrace contrived symbols and simplistic ideologies.

Those who view the social movement as an abnormality trace the roots of collective action to large-scale disruptions in a nation's economy and social structure.[3] In this view, rapid industrialization and urbanization, war, and depression weaken community ties, discredit authority, and dissolve the bonds of social control. Such widespread and unsettling change upsets traditional beliefs and makes accepted norms irrelevant. Uprooted, cut off from those institutions that had provided support and meaning, the isolated individual finds escape from fear and powerlessness in submission to a new authority.

Although conservative social critics first erected the scaffolding for this theory in the eighteenth and nineteenth centuries, full-scale construction was not completed until the middle decades of the twentieth century. Psychoanalyst Erich Fromm, writing when nazism was still a viable threat, diagnosed allegiance to mass movements as an attempt to escape from freedom. Since the Middle Ages, he argued, men and women have experienced a gradual loosening of ties to authorities and a continuous expansion of economic, political, and social freedoms. But, as people became more independent, they shed their anchors of security. Modern life exacerbated these feelings of personal precariousness and insignificance. Fromm saw the anonymity induced by cities, the mechanization of life, and sensory overload from the media as "expressions of a constellation in which the individual is confronted by uncontrollable dimensions in comparison with which he is a small particle.

All he can do is fall in step like a marching soldier or a worker on the endless belt."[4] Frightened and confused, the pawns of unconscious needs, people in a world ruled by chaotic change grasp for a psychic haven in the "new idolatry" of a social movement.[5]

Like Fromm, social philosopher Eric Hoffer traces participation in social movements to feelings of inadequacy and purposelessness rather than to the rational pursuit of an objective. In his best-selling book, *The True Believer*, Hoffer maintains that a mass movement "attracts and holds a following not by its doctrine and promises but by the refuge it offers from the anxieties, barrenness and meaninglessness of an individual existence."[6] The social movement meets the needs of its recruits by stripping them of their distinctiveness and autonomy and transforming them into anonymous specks without will and judgment. "The result," concludes Hoffer, "is not only a compact and fearless following but also a homogeneous plastic mass that can be kneaded at will."[7]

The most systematic presentations of this orientation appear in the works of William Kornhauser, Neil Smelser, Hannah Arendt, and Seymour Lipset. While Fromm and Hoffer concentrate upon the psychology of the recruit, these analysts investigate the deficiencies in society that prove conducive to the growth of mass action. They maintain that society faces its greatest danger when its members are held together only by their common allegiance to the state authority and lack the cross-cutting ties and loyalties produced through association in civic, religious, occupational, and fraternal organizations and communities. Social distress in the shape of industrialization, war, or depression may fray and even tear the fabric of these integrating arrangements and communal bonds. "Alienation," writes Kornhauser in 1959, "heightens responsiveness to the appeal of mass movements because they provide occasions for expressing resentment against what is, as well as promises of a totally different world. In short, *people who are atomized readily become mobilized.*"[8] Neil Smelser, writing in 1963, stresses the irrationality and deviance of participation in movements. Participants mobilize on the basis of a "generalized belief" that "short-circuits" or compresses the normal processes of problem solving. Like magic and superstition, these beliefs shift attention to imaginary conspiracies, endow followers with unlimited power, and foster unrealistic expectations of movement outcomes. According to Smelser, the social movement, like the panic, craze, or riot, "is the action of the impatient" who mobilize in response to simplistic and extreme explanations of society's strains.[9]

In this traditional view of social movements, then, mass behavior sharply contrasts with practical and conventional political action. Unlike members of other groups, movement participants are unconcerned with real community tensions and problems. Their gaze, instead, is fixed upon abstract issues and symbols far removed from personal experience and the affairs of daily life.

In social movements, traditional controls on conduct and proper behavior offer few restraints. Democratic procedures are readily discarded, orders are obeyed with little hesitation, and great stress is placed upon coercion and violence as means to ends. This is not surprising, for men and women enlist not to further their concrete interests but to express their "resentment and hostility against the established order and in response to the pseudo-authority and pseudo-community provided by the totalitarian movement."[10]

Who are the "mere particles of social dust,"[11] those eager to trade isolation and anxiety for the security of a movement? Eric Hoffer finds movements peopled by "the failures, misfits, outcasts, criminals, and all those who have lost their footing, or never had one in the ranks of respectable humanity."[12] For Kornhauser, those shorn of all but their links to family and friends are the most receptive to demands for change. Hannah Arendt goes even further. The most active and loyal recruit is "without any other social ties to family, friends, comrades, or even mere acquaintances, [and] derives his sense of having a place in the world only from his belonging to a movement, his membership in the party."[13] Similarly, Seymour Lipset finds the potential activist among "the disgruntled and the psychologically homeless, . . . the personal failures, the socially isolated, the economically insecure, the uneducated, unsophisticated, authoritarian persons at every level of the society."[14] While discovering joiners in all socioeconomic ranks, these theorists specifically delineate the unemployed, recently discharged war veterans, minorities, the young, marginal members of the middle class, the unskilled, and unattached intellectuals as disproportionately represented in movement ranks. Such people find a new meaning in their common sense of estrangement and dispossession.

Underlying this multidisciplinary interpretation is a conception of American society and the distribution of power within. According to this conception, collective action is illegitimate and unnecessary because American political, social, and economic structures are permeable to dissenters and flexible in responding to demands for change. Such a view, often labeled Pluralism, assumes a nation in which all groups have access to decision makers and, if they play by the rules of the game, may achieve influence. In this nation, government is an impartial judge mediating between petitioners and ruling in favor of the common interest. In contrast, social movements, by gathering resources in improper ways and engaging in unsanctioned collective behavior outside established power channels, are the creations of the unruly and the erratic. Rather than real and legitimate change, participants seek only noninstrumental goals like identity, belonging, and status.

Collaterally, within this perspective can be discerned a social control and a conflict management orientation. Established authorities and traditional institutions must be protected and the disease of protest cured. It is a view from the mansion balcony rather than the street. This orientation has led

Michael Harrington to call sociology the "house nigger" of the ruling classes. [15] But sociologists are not alone in this indictment; many historians, psychologists, and political scientists have also taken up residence in the mansion on the hill.

SOCIAL MOVEMENTS AND THE THEORISTS: THE RESOURCE MOBILIZATION APPROACH

The classical conception of social movements continued to reign during the 1960s. Its proponents wrote college textbooks, sat on presidential commissions, and transmitted the word on television and radio. The equation of the social movement with deviancy was, for many, popular wisdom. Yet it was also during the 1960s that scholars, inspired by their participation in activist politics or contact with students and friends involved in social movements, began to revise and move beyond the accepted interpretation. They realized that not all groups in American society shared equal access to decision makers, and that, as a result of this uneven distribution of power, the government was selective in its response to challenges. These observers judged attempts to portray collective action as deviant as part of the strategy of control used to isolate movements from potential supporters. In this revised view, the mass movement was seen as the lever by which the powerless, the ignored, the invisible, and the poor could move a nation. Rather than a creation of the dark side of human nature, the movement represented a just and necessary attempt to attain the promise of American life. [16]

According to these new theorists, the atomized and irrational were noticeable by their absence from the civil rights, student, antiwar, and women's movements. Protesters were angry and, at times, bitter, yet unconscious psychic drives offered less explanation of their motivation than real grievances and legitimate programs of change. They interpreted violence, too, in a different light, seeing disruption not necessarily as an act of desperation but as a tactic in social conflict. Violence was seen, moreover, as a means that established authorities seemed more likely to employ in a systematic and brutal fashion than movement members. "The appropriate image for this political interaction," concludes William Gamson, "is more a fight with no holds barred than it is a contest under well-defined rules." [17]

The emerging approach, known as *resource mobilization theory*, stresses the continuity that exists between social movements and more conventional groups. According to this theory, social movements, like other organizations, gather, trade, use, and occasionally waste resources in their efforts to achieve power. These resources, including money, members, votes, information, trust, jobs, guns, and image, are the tools used to gain influence. Resource mobilization theorists assume that movement participants make decisions, as do those in government agencies and corporate boardrooms, on the basis of a rational assessment of options. Sociologist Anthony Oberschall observes that activists "weigh the rewards and sanctions, costs and benefits, that alternative courses of action represent for them. In conflict situations, as in all other choice situations, their prior preferences and history, their predispositions, as well as the group structure and influence processes they are caught up in, determine their choices."[18]

According to these theorists, accepting the message of a social movement does not strip the individual of mind or will. The hypnotic gaze of the charismatic leader does not hold men and women captive or force them to perform deviant acts. In other words, as Michael Schwartz writes, "People who join protest organizations are at least as rational as those who study them."[19] This emphasis on rationality does not preclude the possibility that movement activists, like all organizational players, are liable to errors in analysis and mistakes in strategy. While they act to ensure the greatest return to the group, leaders have imperfect knowledge of the intentions and resources of their competitors and may be forced to make decisions on the basis of incomplete or even faulty information.[20]

In essence, the focus of these theorists is on the group and on the resources that shape its efforts to lay claims to influence. They reject the traditional theorists' correlation of collective action with societal breakdown and individual psychological trauma. Instead, they consider discontent and grievance to be relatively constant and pervasive in history and, therefore, not the triggers of social movements. Some even argue that discontent is unimportant because movement activists are able to create and manipulate it whenever necessary. With grievance at best a necessary, not a sufficient, cause of protest, the resource mobilization school looks to those factors that affect the availability of resources and a movement's ability to organize them. They are especially concerned with the balance of resources among groups, the relationships of established groups to the social movement and each other, the extent of the social control powers of authorities, the leadership and organizational structure of the movement, and issues and groups in competition with the movement for scarce resources.[21]

Since resource mobilization theorists see social movements differing in degree rather than in kind from other organizations, they assign economically and socially marginal men and women minor roles in activist politics. Their research indicates that society's fabric of groups, rather than restraining individuals from joining social movements, has a mobilizing effect. "The presence of numerous organizations," writes Oberschall, "ensures a pre-established communications network, resources already partially mobilized, the presence of individuals with leadership skills, and a tradition of participation among members of the collectivity."[22] Using this organizational structure as a launching pad, social movements are able to build more rapidly a stock of recruits, funds, knowledge, and good will from which they may draw to withstand attack. Friendship and family supports are likewise transferred to the cause. Participation in movements thus merges smoothly with the rituals and routines of everyday life. According to William Gamson, "Rebellion, in the resource mobilization perspective, is simply politics by other means."[23]

Historian and sociologist Charles Tilly suggests a resource mobilization model that is helpful in understanding the interplay and relationships among protagonists in political and social conflict. Based upon his research on collective violence and revolution, Tilly delineates three sets of players in the struggle for power. The central role in a system is played by government, which serves as an arbiter of disputes and makes the key decisions about the distribution of benefits in a society. As a result, the decision-making authorities are positioned to accept, reject, or modify a group's claim for influence. Government is, as well, the prime defender of the established order and controls the means of coercion, such as police and troops, necessary to enforce its decisions and silence dissenters. In the United States, government is not a monolithic entity; power is distributed among local, state, and federal levels of authority. The American political party system and the separation of powers within state and federal governments further diffuse the locus of control. Any or all levels or branches of government may be the targets of a group's demand for influence. Thus, while power may be centered in government, a variety of opportunities for conflict or cooperation within and between its component parts will affect a movement's chances of bringing change.[24]

In Tilly's model, those seeking influence with decision makers are the "contenders for power." These are groups that bring their resources to bear on the determination of policy. Contenders are of two sorts. The first, which Tilly labels "polity members," are contenders who enjoy routine access to government officials, whose views on issues are solicited, and who successfully influence the direction of decisions. Depending upon the political climate, such organizations as General Motors, the AFL-CIO, the National Association of Manufacturers, and the American Medical Association represent the polity, the "establishment," the "inner circle," or the "power brokers." These members also have a voice in deciding which groups may become polity insiders. Outside of this select circle are the "challengers," or social movement organizations, making claims on government in irregular and not necessarily successful ways. The goal of any challenger is to secure favored status and gain the advantages of membership in the polity.[25]

Tilly's model is a fluid one. Position in the polity is not fixed, and groups attempting to join or remain within must undergo "tests of membership."

These tests involve the organization's ability to muster resources, the keys to the doors to power. The store of resources is far from static or secure. Large-scale social change or short-term fluctuations in political or economic fortunes cause variations in the opportunity for protest, the strength of contending groups, the power of social control forces, and the availability of resources. The impact, whether negative or positive, of these factors on a group's ability to mobilize and act is profound. Thus, a contender may find the credibility of its message enhanced, the possibilities of building a coalition dimmer, or the determination of authorities to defuse protest strengthened.[26]

There are two main strategies in the application of resources. First, resources can be used to induce authorities to change policy. By providing information, offering financial support, marshalling votes, or generating a persuasive media image, a contender may convince decision makers to accept its program. A group may also, in combination with or apart from a persuasive strategy, disrupt its targets through the power of boycotts, strikes, demonstrations, and violence. A test of any leadership, regardless of the type of organization, is in the use of resources, in fine-tuning the timing, target, and dose of their application. If the rise to power is paved with resources, so too is the fall. The loss of control over resources, or demobilization, spells the end of influence and, for social movements, decline and death.[27]

The reaction to a challenger may take many forms. Polity members may choose to ally with, resist, or ignore the protest carrier. Although alliances often bring the social movement financial support and an easier reception, they also generate disadvantages. Coalition with a stronger partner may make a challenger vulnerable, and too heavy a dependence destroys the independence of action and thought of the social movement. A challenger may also become embroiled in the rivalry and testing among insiders. If other power brokers perceive the challenger as a threat because its sponsor is a rival, they will mobilize resources against the movement or solicit authorities to act as their proxies. Similarly, challengers interact with other challengers by competing, cooperating, or remaining neutral. A movement may also spawn new organizations by providing a role model in deed and ideology.[28]

Finally, in Tilly's model, the authorities do not stand above the system as impartial or passive spectators. The social control power of government spans a continuum of responses from facilitation to tolerance to repression. Officials do not often deal with a movement in a consistent or exclusive manner, but vary actions with circumstances. Governments have funded, publicized, and legitimized movements, allowing them routine access to decision making. This may lead to a redirection or rechanneling of other protest movements into more acceptable outlets. At different times and with different movements, authorities have pursued a strategy of reform and preemption by which the challenger's proposals were adopted, but it was denied a place among the influential. Co-optation absorbs activists into government or elite groupings, yet blunts the thrust for change by robbing the movement of its leadership and denying the validity of its platform. Repression has also been an effective strategy in turning aside a challenge. Governments may infiltrate, wiretap, leak fabricated information, encourage internal conflict, freeze assets, jail activists, and provoke violence to suppress collective action.[29]

The results of movement challenges vary. William Gamson, in his study of "challenging groups" in American history, measures outcomes in terms of "acceptance" and "new advantages." In gaining acceptance, the movement obtains rights of negotiation and consultation with the authorities and established groups. If protest goals are attained, regardless of how or by whom, Gamson judges that a movement has secured advantages. He concludes that almost four in ten of the groups he studied achieved complete success and were able to find acceptance and new advantages. Twenty percent of the organizations experienced outcomes of preemption or co-optation. The rest (42 percent) found the system unyielding and were defeated without securing change or acceptance.[30]

UP FROM THE GRASS ROOTS

Resource mobilization theory provides a valuable reassessment of collective action. The research of Oberschall, Tilly, Gamson, and others demonstrates the appropriateness of seeing social movements and conventional groups as members of the same species. Their work dispels notions that movement members are irrational, and marginal members of society; they portray participants as thinking, caring, and reasonable men and women. Similarly, these theorists highlight the impact of opportunities, the organizational and resource balance among contending groups, and the authorities' social control powers on the ability of movements to mobilize and act.

In their desire to revise classical ideas, however, resource mobilization theorists have lost sight of the *matter* of movements, that is, the people. Collective action is more than the sum of its group parts. An analysis focused on the dynamics of groups ignores the intervening components that translate organization into action. The mobilization drama is played before an audience not only of organizations but of individuals, affiliated and unaffiliated. Within and outside associations, as members of family and informal work groups, in casual circles of friends, and alone, individuals make decisions about social movements. They listen to movement organizers, observe the reactions of government officials and establishment representatives, and choose to affiliate, oppose, or remain neutral. Authorities and contenders are acutely aware of this audience. It is this contest for public support, not only from groups but from the unaffiliated, that explains the importance that activists attach to their message and the intense struggle for control waged over a movement's image. It is people, in groups and singly, who contribute the resources—time, money, and energy—from which the movement draws life.

Thus, the resource mobilization approach is incomplete. We still must understand why a condition, long-standing or short-term, becomes intolerable. Or how people break the bonds of their traditional allegiances. Or why men and women join social movements. For answers to these questions we must graft a human component onto resource mobilization and return to the grass roots of America.

During a long-term change or a current crisis, many individual responses are possible. New circumstances may force some people to concentrate more intensely and imaginatively on securing the basic needs of food, shelter, and clothing. Others may turn to God, seeking answers to their problems in religious doctrine. Striking inward, some blame themselves and find consolation and escape in alcohol and drugs. A minority of any population will choose another path. Casting aside the deference, conformity, and apathy of daily routine, these men and women will protest. However, to touch more than an activist nucleus, a protest, organized or in the process of becoming, requires the transformation of people's perceptions of their world and themselves. According to political scientist Frances Fox Piven and professor of social work Richard Cloward, this shift in thought and behavior occurs in stages. Initially, the authorities lose "legitimacy" in the eyes of the people and are blamed for conditions. Rulers or institutions, previously accepted and followed, are redefined as unjust and immoral. Once people strip authorities of legitimacy, they are ready to move beyond apathy and fear to develop a "new sense of efficacy," which assures men and women that their efforts can make a difference, that they possess the ability to affect the conditions of life. "We are a new people," declared a Lawrence, Massachusetts, textile factory striker in 1913. "We have hope. We will never stand again what we stood before."[31] The shift in consciousness translates into behavior when individuals "become defiant," testing, ignoring, and opposing established leaders. Resistance enters a new phase when these sporadic acts of defiance are merged into a collective and sustained response under group leadership.[32]

Changes in legitimacy and efficacy and the emergence of a collective response require that people assign salience to the issue or condition. A problem or condition may never have existed before or it may always have been a feature of life, but until individuals perceive it as immediate and personal—salient—such a circumstance will rarely inspire conscious protest. Both personal history and present condition influence the issues men and women consider central and the degree of salience they ascribe to them. Thus, a sense of salience ignites protest for it prepares the detached bystander to take up the cause. Now, for the aggrieved, issues are no longer abstract or distant, but immediate, familiar, and vital.

THE SOCIAL MOVEMENT MOBILIZATION PROCESS

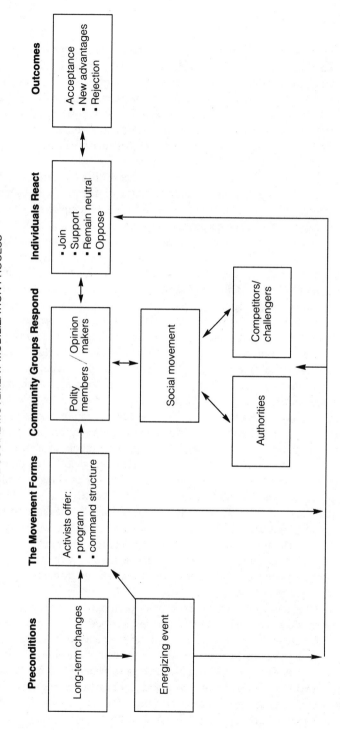

If salience is a factor related to location in space and time, then movement organizers must also be carefully attuned to the local environment. What is effective in organizing blacks in rural Mississippi, white students on northern college campuses, or workers in western mining camps depends upon the backgrounds and experiences of potential recruits and sympathizers. Movement activists must convey a message that lets men and women dream of a better world but that is rooted in their real lives. Salience is, thus, a measure not only of an issue but of a movement.

What is needed is a resource mobilization theory that takes account of the grass roots. The following model is one such attempt to include the factors of human motivation and response in the social movement equation.

Setting the stage for protest are long-term economic, political, and social changes. Industrialization, urbanization, migration, technological innovation, demographic change, political party transition, economic depression, and diplomatic events redefine the conflict equation. Such developments affect the positions of groups and alter the existing balance among them. As the terms of conflict change, opportunities to form or break alliances, attack opponents, deliver a persuasive message, make claims on government, or protest rise and fall. Resources may become scarce or plentiful, and they may be redistributed or available in different ways. Under new conditions, every group will be tested in its ability to make internal and external adjustments and innovations. Nor do authorities escape the demands of change. Government's efforts to exert control are similarly subject to its power to monitor, adjust, and take advantage of the new distribution of resources.

Within this environment may occur a more specific energizing event or a series of such events that are viewed as dramatic symbols of either the large-scale changes underway or of the past's refusal to yield to the future. Energizing events may even embody both messages. For the members of a given population, these events give shape to barely perceived forces. They substantiate the conditions of life in the present and signify the distance yet to travel for amelioration. A government or bureaucratic edict, an individual's public refusal to submit, an activist's speech, or the provocation of an opponent, any of these may prod a population to imbue an issue with salience. To energize men and women, such events focus attention and prime a sense of outrage at inequality, injustice, and treachery.

When such grievances go unaddressed or are prolonged by the connivance of authorities and established groups, the people's bonds to those groups are frayed. Unresponsive to claims for redress, governments risk losing their legitimacy in the eyes of the people. Acts of resistance encourage further defiance, both by individuals and groups, and heighten the confidence of men and women in their abilities to shape the world. The sparks igniting the tinder of resistance are the activists, who offer a program that is attuned to the culture and aspiration of the people and that identifies the sources and targets of discontent and proposes a remedy. Movement organizers seek to raise the consciousness of their followers, enabling them to reevaluate their lives and to realize their ability to effect change. Having already established a command structure, organizers promise adherents a viable means of action. This organizational power is an important inducement, especially in an environment inhabited by strong competitors and adversaries. In fact, activists are most effective in organizing when they create their protest movement from within existing groups. Using these organizations' membership lists, office space, communication networks, and reputations, a cadre of organizers can mobilize members, experience, and funds in blocs. While the support of organizations is critical in the initial stages of mobilization and is important throughout a movement's life, appeals to individuals to join, sympathize, or remain with the protest are vital components of resource gathering.

A movement is in constant interaction with its environment. Therefore, the stances of the authorities, polity members, and other challengers must be continuously analyzed and the movement's tactics and strategy kept flexible. As the power balance shifts, a movement must strengthen coalitions, guard against internal and external attack, generate and expend resources, and outmaneuver competitors.

A movement's organizational strength and leadership are important in explaining its capacity to survive in this arena of conflict. Also central to a movement's potential to succeed is its image. From a movement's initial appearance, activists attempt to cultivate an image of their protest as legitimate and necessary. Whether in the official literature or during informal recruiting pitches, activists portray the cause as a crusade to restore or establish justice in line with national traditions. But a movement's tactics, goals, and leadership style do not alone shape community attitudes. Public opinion makers, a breed of polity members, and government authorities are simultaneously seeking to mold the movement's image and thus its reception by individuals and groups. Respected community figures, religious leaders, newspaper editors, and television commentators act as interpreters for the wider society. Positioned as filters for information about movement events and personalities, they do much by way of sifting and managing news to influence community perceptions. Their acceptance, tolerance, or rejection of the protest affects the movement's ability to attract popular support and, in turn, gather resources. Like other contenders for power, they have their own agendas. Opinion makers, especially those in the media, are bound by codes of objectivity or fairness, but they are also influenced by their status in society and the demands of the job. Location in the power structure, political philosophy, and the search for "good copy," contend with movement actions under the constraints of air time and edition space. As a result, a protest may be portrayed as heroic, justified, illegitimate, violence-prone, or trivial. If deemed unnewsworthy, it may be screened out completely and never heard.[33]

Under the influence of changing times and energizing events, individuals and groups weigh a movement's words and deeds against the responses of government and polity. Do conditions justify working outside the established channels? Are the movement's actions and goals reasonable? Are media stories about protest leaders accurate? What action would the authorities take against protesters? Past experiences and current needs are analyzed in the family, at work, and in group settings. From these discussions, which calculate risks and rewards, individuals and groups make decisions to join the movement, to lend it support, to remain neutral, or to oppose it. As a movement grows, its presence becomes an even greater influence on such decisions.

The organization of protest is only a beginning. Since a collective protest may last for decades, continuous change is the norm of social conflict: The salience of issues shifts; community definitions and the role of authorities are adjusted; movement organization and strategy evolves; leadership fluctuates; or a potent opposition arises. With each revision, the movement's players must refigure the opportunities, the resistance, the availability of resources, and the organization's means of achieving acceptance and new advantages.

EIGHT MOVEMENTS

The following chapters will sketch the histories of eight twentieth century American social movements. With the mobilization model as our framework, we will investigate the Anti-Saloon League, the Industrial Workers of the World, the Ku Klux Klan, the Communist party, the John Birch Society, the Student Nonviolent Coordinating Committee, the Berkeley Free Speech Movement, and the National Organization for Women. These groups do not constitute a statistically drawn random sample. A variety of factors affected my choice of protest organizations. One primary concern was the existence of information; I selected organizations that scholars have repeatedly tracked rather than those barely visible. The nature of America in the twentieth century dictated that movements represent different time periods and regions to allow an analysis of shifts in protest methods and styles and the effect of the "climate of the times." The variables of race, class, and gender—key reference points in American history—helped to sort possibilities. I selected the largest protest organizations of the left and right wings as well as those illustrating diverse organizational structures and differing durations of activity. Finally, I made selections on the basis of the outcomes and results of the movements. The sample created from these criteria represents the diverse currents of protest and collective action in twentieth-century America. From the histories of these movements can be discerned the collective dreams and actions of men and women from all economic, political, and social strata.

My purpose in these historical case studies is to flesh out sociological conceptions of how movements mobilize and to enhance meaning and understanding by grounding the abstract and theoretical in human interactions. This historical approach, however, offers even more. By considering movements as much as possible from the local perspective, clearer answers may be unearthed to the following unresolved questions:

How have social movements changed over the course of the twentieth century?

Do present-day challengers differ tactically, organizationally, and demographically from those of the past?

Why do some movements succeed and others fail?

What is the impact of violence, the opinion-making public, the organizational structure, the size of the movement, and factionalism on the outcome of protest?

Does a single-issue movement fare better than one that proposes several changes?

What protest image is most conducive to success?

Does the timing of a challenge influence the reception a movement receives?

Who joins social movements?

Does organized protest draw disproportionately from particular elements in society or are men and women from diverse social and economic strata attracted to activism?

It is the task of this book to sift the historical evidence for clues and insights that will help answer these questions.

2

THE DEATH OF JOHN BARLEYCORN:

THE ANTI-SALOON LEAGUE

Good-bye John. You were
God's worst enemy. You
were Hell's best friend. I hate
you with a perfect hatred.
REVEREND BILLY SUNDAY

A company in every church;
a regiment in every city; an
army corps in every state;
a conquering army
in the nation.
A. J. KYNETT
ANTI-SALOON LEAGUE

In the late twentieth century, few dispute the legitimacy of alcohol in American society. In fact, liquor consumption has become so identified with the American way of life that it has attained the status of a national character trait. Celebrations of social and economic mobility and the observance of various rites of passage are incomplete without alcoholic refreshments. In thirty-second commercial spots, media celebrities and sports figures dramatize the macho allure of beer consumption. Television, film, radio, newspapers, and magazines urge us, again and again, to buy and imbibe.

Similarly, the bar or tavern occupies an important and respectable place in American life. Catering to diverse clienteles, bars enhance a sense of community based on neighborhood, class, race, sexual preference, or musical taste. They are an integral part of modern courtship ritual, as such phrases as singles' bar and bar-hopping attest. The image of the tavern as a haven for individuals seeking shelter from anonymity and loneliness is a familiar one. Thus the theme song from "Cheers," a popular television series set in a bar, invites patrons to take "a break from all your worries" and "get away" from daily stress. At the Cheers bar, "everybody knows your name. And they're always glad you came."

Compare the prevailing acceptance of alcohol and drinking today with the following images from the early twentieth century. In 1912, the editor of the Anti-Saloon League's *American Issue* declared: "The saloon is the resort of the underworld. There the inhabitants swarm like maggots and an awful cry goes up, 'Give us drink and you can have us body and soul.' The saloon with its unholy alliances is Hell on earth."[1] To the Reverend Mark Matthews of Washington state, "The liquor traffic is the most fiendish, corrupt, and hell-soaked institution that ever crawled out of the slime of the eternal pit. It is the open sore of this land."[2] These men were not representatives of an impotent fringe group, nor were their words lost in the wind. Rather, they helped organize and direct a movement that saw a part of its program enshrined in the Constitution of the United States.

Too often, the prohibitionists are dismissed as puritan killjoys, status-anxious members of the middle class, or religious fanatics. The repeal of the prohibition amendment, a little over a decade after its passage, satisfies observers that the movement was an aberration or a plot executed while the nation was distracted. Such characterizations mask the history of one of the most successful social movements in American history. The Anti-Saloon League and its allies, operating on local, state, and national levels, perfected an organization, gathered the resources, and planned the strategy necessary to effect change. ASL leaders not only converted their proposals into law but achieved polity-member status. To study the Anti-Saloon League and the prohibition impulse is to understand America as it came of age in the modern world.

NINETEENTH-CENTURY ROOTS

The history of American temperance and prohibition reform has followed a tidal pattern of ebb and flow. Agitation first emerged at the end of the eighteenth century in what has been described as "an alcohol-soaked culture."[3] Men, women, and children consumed prodigious amounts of rum, cider, whiskey, and beer to celebrate, to enhance strength and reduce fatigue, and to ward off disease. Births, barn raisings, election days, ministerial ordinations, and many other events called forth gallons of "the good creature of God."[4] By 1825, absolute alcohol consumption per capita was seven gallons. In contrast, the alcohol intake in 1980 was three gallons per capita.[5]

Local temperance efforts gained national direction in 1826 with the founding of the American Society for the Promotion of Temperance. By 1834, it counted five thousand local chapters and one million members. Aimed at personal reform, the society encouraged Americans to sign pledges of abstinence but did not agitate for legislation. In the late 1840s, activism entered a new phase when prohibitionists petitioned state legislators to act. By 1855, thirteen states had passed laws forbidding the manufacture and sale of "spirituous or intoxicating liquors" yet leaving personal use unregulated. Retreat soon followed these successes. Courts in eight states ruled the new laws unconstitutional while shifts in political climate and coalitions led to reversals elsewhere. As the issues of slavery and sectionalism consumed more and more attention, prohibitionist resources became scarce, and the movement lost salience.[6]

The prohibition drive was renewed after the Civil War. In 1869, activists established the Prohibition party to field candidates pledged to the reform of liquor laws. Five years later, the Women's Christian Temperance Union, the WCTU, began organizing educational and political campaigns against the menace of alcohol. In the second wave of agitation, Kansas, Iowa, Maine, Rhode Island, and North and South Dakota entered the ranks of "dry" states by outlawing the sale of alcohol. At the same time, prohibition efforts were blunted in fourteen other states. By the 1890s, the movement had been stopped far short of its goals. An economic depression brought new issues into focus and the rise of movements based upon economic distress. Prohibitionist party candidates bickered among themselves about tactics and program. Declining vote totals reminded them of their failure to break traditional party allegiances or broaden their appeal to disaffected voters. A party split only made the situation worse. Electoral setbacks also numbed members of the Women's Christian Temperance Union, generating dissension over the practicality of political partisanship and the future of the movement.[7]

The wave had receded. An activist core remained, but internal organizational stress and declining resources hobbled its work. Despite partial demobilization, sentiment favorable to liquor reform persisted. The years of legislative lobbying, church teaching, and electoral effort had conditioned the public to the issues of the debate. Antiliquor advocates had also looked toward the future. As a result of WCTU agitation, every state in the nation would pass legislation requiring temperance education programs in the public school curriculum. For those coming of age in the late nineteenth and early twentieth centuries, the message would be difficult to escape. If the prohibition movement was to revive then, the liquor issue had to be recharged and the organizational and resource vacuums filled. Before the turn of the new century, these conditions would be met and a new protest effort launched.

THE CHALLENGE OF THE SALOON

During the second half of the nineteenth century, the liquor and beer industries underwent dramatic change. Like many American corporations, brewing and distilling firms took advantage of technological innovations, expanded capital investment, increased production, and enlarged markets. Competition thinned the ranks, and ownership became concentrated in fewer corporate hands. Companies organized bureaucratically, creating different departments to handle procurement, distribution, sales, and personnel. As did steel and oil companies, brewers and distillers consolidated their operations vertically. That is, corporate officials controlled all of the processes necessary to convert a raw material into a finished product.[8]

Before the Civil War, breweries were small-scale operations and production was tied to local markets. The expansion of the transportation network and the growth of American cities opened possibilities to producers. Brewers such as Pabst, Schlitz, and Anheuser-Busch capitalized on these opportunities and incorporated the advantages of pasteurization and refrigerated railroad cars to expand their market shares. Beer production increased to meet a greater demand and a shift in consumers' taste away from hard liquor. In 1860 the output of the largest breweries in America ranged from 5,000 to 8,000 barrels of beer. By 1877 their output had grown to 100,000 barrels of beer and in 1895, to between 500,000 and 800,000 barrels. Even though production increased, economy of scale favored the larger concerns, and the number of breweries declined from 3,321 in 1870 to 1,644 in 1909.[9]

Competition for control of the market was intense between distillers and brewers. The struggle among brewers was even sharper. Despite the increase in American beer consumption from 3.5 gallons per capita in 1865 to over 20 gallons fifty years later, overproduction had forced prices down. To tap the market more effectively, beer producers expanded their operations to the retail level. This meant that the corporate battle for supremacy would be waged on the streets and corners of every American neighborhood and community. In the local saloon, the issue would be decided.[10]

The entrance of the brewing companies into the retail field had several effects. To stabilize markets and build profits, the brewer agreed to finance a saloon keeper's operations if he promised to market the company's product exclusively. Brewers paid licensing fees, assumed mortgages, and provided equipment and stock to insure a saloon keeper's loyalty. In another marketing strategy, a company would purchase land, build a saloon, and then contract its operation. As a result, the formerly independent saloon entrepreneur became economically dependent and responsive to the wishes of his superiors. Brewing companies exercised extensive control. By 1907, four-fifths of the saloons of New York City and Chicago were dominated by brewers. Eventually, brewers had a stake in 70 percent of the nation's saloons.[11]

Competition among brewers also led to a proliferation of retail outlets. Determined to give beer drinkers every opportunity to buy their product, rivals saturated communities with saloons, vying for the most popular and visible locations. Thus, in 1880 America had 150,000 saloons; by 1910, that number had almost doubled. In Chicago saloons were as numerous as grocery stores, meat markets, and dry-goods stores combined. More than 10,000 saloons operated in New York City. Houston residents counted one saloon for every 218 of its inhabitants. In 1909, sixteen saloons were available to Pasco, Washington's 2,000 residents. Walla Walla's forty-six saloons serviced a population of 16,000.[12]

The expansion in the number of saloons made competition fierce. Company demands for profits exacerbated the pressure on the financially dependent saloon keeper to increase business. To satisfy corporate officials and to eke out a living, operators did whatever they could to entice customers to their establishments. Saloons offered themselves as "poor man's clubs," providing a male refuge for amusement, relaxation, and fellowship. Unions, political groups, and ethnic societies were persuaded to meet in the saloon. Patrons found saloon keepers willing to cash checks, safeguard funds, and furnish loans. Saloons provided inexpensive lunches as well as shelter for the homeless. Such positive features, however, made little impact upon the saloon's detractors.[13]

Saloon keepers also used disreputable means to earn a profit. To expand their trade, saloon keepers ignored community closing laws and kept their businesses open twenty-four hours a day, seven days a week. Gamblers opened shop in the saloons, and a variety of games of chance tempted the clientele. Saloon keepers acted as pimps for prostitutes operating in back or upstairs rooms. Some served as fences for thieves seeking to turn stolen goods into cash. Looking to a new generation of patrons, managers opened their bars to children. Such operations could be kept running smoothly only when lubricated with bribes to policemen and politicians.[14]

The saloon's invasion of the community revitalized the salience of the liquor issue. The symbol of liquor's power, the saloon, had appeared and become entrenched in everyday life. For many Americans, the sight, smell, and sound of the saloon conjured up the antialcohol conditioning learned in church and school. The dangers of intemperance, immorality, and disorder were now imminent and threatening. Here was a menace whose very existence depended upon ensnaring the young, weak, and unsuspecting. Sons and daughters, relatives and friends demanded protection. Moreover, as a tentacle of a larger, nationally powerful corporate beast, the saloon was an especially ominous enemy. The peril became even more acute when territory once thought secure was lost. In 1894, "wets," those who favored the legal sale of alcohol, engineered the repeal of the dry law in Iowa. Two years later, South Dakota rescinded its prohibition statute. A problem existed, as well, in states that remained legally dry. For example, corruption and lax enforcement of the antiliquor law had enabled saloons to reopen in over one-half of the counties of Kansas. By 1897, one thousand saloons operated openly or secretly in the state. Energized by the enemy within, prohibitionists were ready to mobilize and extend a new challenge. With the passing of economic hard times, resources necessary to underwrite the effort became available. In the Anti-Saloon League, men and women, churches, and community organizations found a vehicle to gather these resources and lead the fight.[15]

THE PROHIBITIONIST RESPONSE

The Anti-Saloon League traced its roots to Oberlin College in Ohio and the work of Howard Russell. Russell came to Oberlin in 1884 to attend its theological seminary. A practicing attorney, he had experienced a religious conversion and decided to abandon his legal career to pursue a calling in the ministry. Russell soon became involved in local option campaigns aimed at passing laws allowing a town or county to adopt antiliquor ordinances. His temperance sentiment was of long standing. As a child, he had seen the early deaths from drink of "many near relatives and friends."[16] His brother was a reformed alcoholic. Through his temperance work in Oberlin, Russell became convinced that the defeat of the liquor interests necessitated a nonpartisan approach and an avoidance of political party labels—the badge of party divided temperance forces and weakened their power. He also determined that the liquor menace could not be routed by amateurs alone, working on the local level. A professional organization, composed of full-time activists with the financial and electoral support of a large membership, was crucial to the defeat of alcohol.[17]

Russell graduated in 1888 and assumed pulpits in Kansas City and Chicago. Experiences in these cities turned him from the ministry to full-time temperance work. It was God who showed Russell the path:

> At Kansas City I daily passed the Rochester Brewery located between my home and church. Always when I passed this devil's broth factory I prayed God to stay the tide of sin and shame flowing therefrom. During my ministry in those cities whenever I passed a saloon I sent up a prayer, "O, God, stop this!" At length God plainly said to me, "You know how to do it; go and help answer your own prayers!"[18]

Returning to Oberlin in 1893, Russell contacted friends in the Oberlin Temperance Alliance and gained their support for an expansion of the war against liquor. With funding from the Alliance, the Ohio Anti-Saloon League was formed, and Reverend Russell was named as its first superintendent. Since the saloon was the common target of antiliquor forces, and the symbol of alcohol's excesses, opponents of the saloon could fuse a coalition with a minimum of dissension. A headquarters was opened in Columbus, the state capital, and district units were established in Akron and Toledo. Within a year activists had taken advantage of preexisting sentiment and organization and built a network of four hundred local ASL committees.[19] Anti-saloon agitation occurred independently in Massachusetts and the District of Columbia. The Methodist church had also established a committee on temperance and looked to secular efforts to fill the organizational void in the movement. Presbyterian and Congregational church leaders were similarly open to a new challenge of liquor's power.

Gathering these pockets of strength, proponents summoned delegates from forty-nine temperance and religious organizations to a convention in Washington, D.C., in December 1895. The assembled groups voted to coordinate their efforts in a national Anti-Saloon League with Reverend Russell as its superintendent. The delegates of the constituent organizations pledged the funds to make their creation viable and to work until a prohibition amendment had been added to the Constitution of the United States. The second convention, in 1896, attracted 146 organizations, and two years later 190 groups were in attendance.[20]

The league's creators fashioned a movement in the likeness of their enemy. To match the new corporate giants, they devised an internal structure that was highly centralized, bureaucratic, and professionally managed. Officially, the league's constitution divided power among different governing boards. Such bodies, however, were designed more to insure group representation, grant status, and maintain the league's influence with constituent organizations than to yield control. Throughout the life of the ASL, a small group within the leadership cadre would hold power and determine organizational direction. Their chain of command ran virtually unchallenged from national headquarters to the precinct level of organization.[21]

The ASL divided its tasks into four parts. A department of agitation was charged with developing league branches and disseminating information. By building from scratch or enlisting temperance groups under the ASL banner, activists had, by 1902, organized thirty-nine states and territories for the cause. The league's American Issue Publishing Company was simultaneously inundating the nation with temperance and prohibitionist literature. In 1914 the company's eight presses printed ten tons of material every day. The league's mailing list eventually numbered more than one-half million names. A legislation department lobbied state and national lawmakers in favor of laws curbing liquor and the saloon. Its staff also testified before committee hearings, wrote legislation, and guided bills to passage. Members of the law enforcement department cooperated with police forces to maintain pressure and insure against corruption. The finance committee raised the funds to guarantee the league's effectiveness. With expenses always escalating and 90 percent of donations pledged in amounts of less than one hundred dollars, the task was formidable and complex. Financial shortages would plague the movement throughout its history.[22]

The national organization appointed and paid the salaries of its state superintendents. These men carried national policy to the lower tiers and, at the same time, served as conduits of information and local needs. ASL organization extended downward from the state level to the county, community, precinct, and church. Mobilization at the grass roots was in the hands of the "captain of ten." This individual was assigned to gather information about ten neighbors, including their voting behavior, church affiliation, and temperance attitudes. At petition signings, meetings, and elections, he pressed his charges to their prohibitionist duties. As in the national body, the loyalists and resources of affiliated groups were tied to the ASL by overlapping representation on committees at different levels of the institutional structure.[23]

The backbone of the movement was the local Protestant church. The ASL sought to establish a league organization in every congregation and to enlist every pastor, Sunday school superintendent, and prominent layman. Approximately fifteen thousand congregations eventually organized such branch units. This figure included 50 percent of the churches in New Jersey and Pennsylvania, 60 percent in Louisiana, and 98 percent in South Dakota. Under the direction of their religious leaders, churchgoing men and women attended rallies, distributed literature, campaigned, and voted for league-supported candidates and causes. Congregants were also the prime source of funds for the movement. Each year, cooperating Baptist, Methodist, Presbyterian, and Congregational churches, among others, set aside one regular Sunday service for ASL speakers. By 1915, almost forty thousand congregations participated in such activities. On these "field days" the league's representatives would distribute cards asking for pledges of from thirty-three cents to five hundred dollars per month to the cause's coffers. In addition, some church congregations made the ASL a line item in their budgets. Church ties were further enhanced when pastors and lay people represented their congregation's league on other ASL committees and boards. This interrelationship led one ASL spokesman to boast, "The Church is a machine and the League is a machine within a machine."[24]

Since the Protestant community was reluctant to pursue its temperance ends through direct action, the league eagerly offered to be "the Church in action against the saloon."[25] It would provide the means to navigate the unfamiliar political world. "The church folk," declared E. F. Jones of the Missouri ASL, "must wake up to the fact that the Lord doesn't vote. If we are to stamp out the saloons it must be by votes, not by prayers alone."[26] Unlike the church, the league could coordinate and manage a challenge to the "liquor power." Professional movement activists, not the clergy, had the knowledge and ability to field speakers, shepherd voters, and bargain with legislators. As the movement advanced, such credentials would be impossible to deny.[27]

The movement soon grew independent in the shelter of the religious community. The sponsorship of the churches, as national and local polity members, eased the ASL's reception and supplied the resources necessary for a successful challenge. The Protestant churches gave activists access to members, leaders, funds, organization, and facilities. A minister's endorsement made the movement the personal, religious, and patriotic duty of his congregation. To a lesser extent, Catholic priests and lay persons, as individuals rather than as members of their church, appeared under league auspices and prepared their coreligionists for mobilization. The ASL added to these tangible resources by cloaking itself in the prestige and respectability of the churches. Opinion makers such as newspaper editors, college presidents, public school administrators, and civic leaders perceived the movement not so much as a challenger than as a pillar of the community. This image also made business people and financiers more receptive to the movement's requests for contributions. At the same time, league leaders maintained tight control over their organization. The cadre welcomed ministers and church officials into the movement and appointed them to positions in the hierarchy. These appointments, however, restrained their power rather than released it. As figureheads, the clergy traded independence for acknowledgement and flattery.[28]

The men who held leadership positions in the league enhanced their movement's image of respectability. Howard Russell was a Methodist minister, as was Purley Baker, who replaced Russell as general superintendent in 1902. A collective biography of ASL and Prohibition party officials indicates that 80 percent belonged to Protestant evangelical denominations. Thirty-seven percent of the leaders were clergymen; one-fourth were the sons of clergymen. Middle class and politically conservative, they inspired the trust and respect of their followers.[29]

Competing in a crowded field   The ASL gained the acceptance of its competitors as well. Other challenging groups in the temperance-prohibition movement endorsed and supported the league. The Women's Christian Temperance Movement, the Good Templars, the Sons of Temperance, and the Catholic Abstinence League contributed money and members to the ASL. The Prohibition party, after initially opposing the league as undemocratic and greedy, cooperated with its members and aided its efforts.[30]

The antiliquor challenge did not occur in isolation. The first decades of the twentieth century, called the Progressive Era, witnessed a diversity of movements acting to effect change in the United States. Groups mobilized in reaction to the social, economic, and political transformations that took place in the wake of industrialization, urbanization, and immigration. Men and women determined to preserve and protect their vision of America proposed to regulate business, assimilate minorities, ease the working conditions of labor, and achieve electoral and governmental reform. A wide range of remedies was proposed, including women's suffrage, antitrust regulation, conservation measures, minimum wage and maximum hours legislation, and consumer protection laws. The urge to reform, perhaps enhanced by the perception that the new century had ushered in a new age, was heightened by exposés and investigative reports in newspapers and muckraking journals. Politicians, too, found it expedient to use the rhetoric of reform. The American public was thus prepared and receptive to challenges of the status quo. Still, in the public mind, the seeming urgency and inevitability of change legitimized only those solutions that left the fundamental distribution of wealth and power intact.

Although competing for attention and resources, challengers found their opportunities for success enhanced. Alliances against common enemies could bolster the means to influence. Thus, when the league moved against the saloon, it added the resources of its allies in the purity crusade and the antitrust and women's rights movements. This diversity of challengers presented many targets for the government and polity members to take aim at, straining their coercive power. Anti-Saloon League activists realized this and continually probed the enemy on different fronts while maintaining pressure with all the means at their disposal.[31]

The ASL prepared for a long campaign. It had the support of important and influential groups and opinion makers. League leaders were capable men, at home in both the religious and the political mainstream. They had built an organization that was based on the local church congregation and was firmly grounded in the grass roots. Competitors in the temperance-prohibition movement acknowledged the league's prominence and encouraged its progress. The ASL was, moreover, perceived in the wider context of Progressive Era reform. The reform's many voices had keyed public perceptions to the need for change and thus facilitated reception of the ASL. Government at the local, state, and national levels was tolerant, if not receptive, and did not move to hinder the ASL's mobilization. Success, however, would not be achieved until the Anti-Saloon League had expanded beyond its church support base, modified its evangelical image, and generated a momentum that convinced politicians that opposing the league meant their defeat.

BUILDING A CONSENSUS

The ASL spent considerable time, money, and energy attempting to convince Americans to abstain from drink, fight the saloon, and vote for prohibitionist candidates. Through a spectrum of arguments, the movement cadre touched Americans personally by relating the liquor danger to real community problems and experiences. They expertly weaved traditional condemnations of alcohol with police reports, government investigations, and new scientific discoveries. The league called upon men and women prominent in business, society, the arts, and sports to add their voices to the antiliquor outcry. Magazines and newspapers outside the prohibitionist fold legitimized ASL claims with articles attacking the liquor industry and proclaiming an antidrink message. Tuned to the changing environment, league speakers exploited the national and international events that increased the salience of their cause. In the end, the ASL cast the image of a movement that had successfully broadened its religious base into a national consensus favoring liquor reform.

Not surprisingly, the religious rationale for temperance and prohibition was an important mainstay of ASL educational efforts. The league argued that liquor dulled religious consciousness and sapped enthusiasm. Under the influence of drink, men and women ignored God's commandments and acted immorally, making personal salvation unattainable. The presence of the saloon, the ASL contended, exacerbated the problem by encouraging the breaking of moral and religious law and tempting Christians even on the Lord's day. Finally, many believed that alcohol and the saloon prevented Christ's return. Only if Americans washed away the sins of intemperance would the millennium's approach be hastened. The league was a crucial part of the divine plan. Few of the faithful doubted Reverend Russell's words: "The Anti-Saloon League movement was begun by Almighty God."[32]

ASL speakers confronted other Americans with liquor's impact on the secular world. Alcohol gutted reason, character, discipline, and self-respect. Weakening inhibitions, drink provoked men to crime, personal violence, and racial and religious rioting. Liquor and the saloon's retinue of gamblers, pimps, and prostitutes corrupted men and women and exposed the family to poverty, adultery, incest, spousal abuse, and divorce. Movement claims that liquor weakened the body's immune system and made it highly susceptible to venereal disease fed into the syphilis hysteria that gripped America at the time. In fact, such fears were given credence when the United States Army released evidence during World War I that Wassermann tests were positive for 10 percent of its inductees.[33]

Statistical support for ASL assertions was distributed widely. According to a league poster, "Liquor is responsible for 19 percent of the divorces, 25 percent of the poverty, . . . 37 percent of the pauperism, 45 percent of child desertion, and 50 percent of the crime in this country. And this is a very conservative estimate."[34] The league never hesitated to revise these figures upward. It was difficult to argue with statistics that seemed to prove the league's contention that "the saloon is the storm center of crime; the devil's headquarters on earth; the schoolmaster of a broken decalogue; the defiler of youth; ... the beast of sensuality; ... the vagabond of poverty; the social vulture; ... a ponderous second edition of hell, revised, enlarged and illuminated."[35]

Medical and scientific evidence bolstered the ASL's propaganda. Physicians published studies concluding that alcohol was a depressant that inhibited memory, judgment, and physical and mental agility. They linked drinking to a variety of diseases of the heart, stomach, liver, and kidneys. Alcohol was also said to trigger brain disorders. Doctors confidently attributed one-fourth of all cases of insanity to drinking and similarly linked the occurrence of epilepsy and retardation. Drinking parents were repeatedly warned that their children would suffer genetic damage unless they abandoned the "racial poison."[36] In light of the evidence, the house of delegates of the American Medical Association unanimously resolved that it was "opposed to the use of alcohol as a beverage."[37] Insurance companies supported health findings. Actuarial statistics indicated that consumption of even minimal quantities of beer shortened life expectancy. As a result, insurance companies rewarded abstainers with bonuses and lower premiums. In light of all of these claims, prudence dictated an obvious course.[38]

Drink took an economic toll as well, declared league speakers. Men who squandered wages in the saloon left their families destitute and without hope of social mobility. Children were forced from school and wives from the home to replace the money lost to alcohol. Prohibition, the ASL told employers, would increase profits by reducing liquor-related accidents and making workers more efficient. Ending liquor-generated crime, disease, and poverty would cut taxes. In an alcohol-free America, money previously spent on intoxicating beverages would be freed for savings, investment, and the purchase of socially beneficial consumer goods. A few unions of the American Federation of Labor also condemned liquor for hampering organizing activities and diluting workers' solidarity.[39]

Politics was another arena of conflict with the "liquor power." The beer and liquor manufacturers, in corporate behavior typical of the time, exercised an arrogant control over their industries; without compunction, they fixed prices, bribed elected officials and judges, and influenced elections. On the local level, the saloon was the prime lever of this power. As the headquarters of the urban political machine's precinct and ward captains, the saloon served as the nexus for business, politics, and vice. Here, in "the rendezvous of demagogues,"[40] votes, influence, and protection could be traded as the different parties bargained for advantage. This situation was made possible and even more dangerous, anti-saloon advocates argued, because of the large immigrant populations inhabiting American cities. Manipulated and controlled by the liquor-fed political machine, they allowed their votes to "go to the ballot box via the rum hole."[41] The concentration of power in hands so

irresponsible and self-interested threatened the American system of government and demanded confrontation.[42]

Disguised but apparent in this campaign was a bias against immigrants.
The league maintained that large-scale immigration had increased the drinking "hordes" and bolstered the antiprohibition forces. League concern about
the foreign menace meshed with a larger nativist enthusiasm to curb immigration, tighten citizenship requirements, and speed Americanization. The
liquor issue thus had ethnic and cultural dimensions. For both natives and
immigrants, alcohol was another issue in the struggle for power in the
American homeland.

Thus, in its fight against liquor and the saloon, the ASL called forth a
broad coalition. Ministers, churchgoers, social workers, police officers, physicians, employers, labor union officials, antivice activists, civic and business
reformers, women's rights proponents, nativists, and parents enlisted, each
group for its own reasons, as the shock troops of the prohibition movement.
Magazines such as the *Outlook*, the *Independent, Collier's Weekly, McClure's*,
the *World's Work, Harper's Monthly*, and the *Atlantic Monthly* published
articles in support of temperance and prohibition. In fact, more than one-half
of the nation's daily and weekly newspapers were friendly to the cause in
this war to protect the innocents of American society. To preserve the home,
prevent social disruption, restore economic and political democracy, and save
those more easily seduced, the cancer had to be destroyed. It was time to cut
from the community the symbol and source of immorality, crime, and alien
influence.[43]

THE MOMENTUM OF PROTEST

The Anti-Saloon League was determined to avoid the mistakes that it believed had plagued the Prohibition party and the Women's Christian Temperance Union. Unlike these two groups, the ASL would focus only on the liquor
enemy and evade such potentially divisive issues as women's suffrage, business regulation, and governmental reform. It would also assume a nonpartisan stance, neither creating a new political party nor identifying with
Republican or Democratic organizations. The league's key to every election
was to hold the balance of power between the candidates. Office seekers,
regardless of their personal drinking habits or political affiliation, could
obtain ASL endorsement in exchange for their pledge to fight the saloon. In
tightly contested elections where a small bloc of voters decided outcomes,
the ASL nod meant the difference between victory and defeat.[44]

The characterization of the league as a single-issue movement, however,
disguises the complexity of its program. The ASL had two long-range objectives—prohibition and abstinence. An amendment to the constitution ban-

ning the manufacture and sale of intoxicating beverages would be a major step in the transformation of American attitudes and drinking habits. But an America without breweries, distilleries, and saloons would not free people from alcohol's grip. A war against liquor meant its absolute defeat and abolition. While rhetorically true to these goals, the ASL pragmatically masked them at the tactical level of operations. "Let Us Emphasize," advised the leadership, "Points On Which We Agree and Avoid Subjects as to Which We Differ."[45] Pursuing a course of least resistance, the league concentrated its guns on the liquor traffic and not on private consumption. The liquor industry and the saloon were simpler issues to grapple with than was personal freedom.[46]

To fix means to ends, league cadre assessed local opportunities and resources. As early as 1900 leaders had cautioned followers, "Do not strive after the impossible. Study local conditions and reach after the attainable."[47] A variety of weapons was available to corner the enemy. ASL forces petitioned city and county governments to approve regulations cutting saloons' hours of operation, establishing saloon-free zones around churches and schools, enforcing Sunday closing laws, and tightening the licensing of liquor dealers. Working from these bases, activists pressured officials for local option laws that called elections to decide on the banning of saloons from city and county. Meanwhile, the ASL weighed the positions of local and state candidates for political office before making its endorsements. Once the word was given, the men and women of the ASL went into action. The scene on election day in 1919 in a North Carolina town, described below, was a common one:

> Hundreds of women and children were stationed along the sidewalks of the streets upon which the polling places were located. . . . When a voter came within range he was immediately surrounded by the ministers and the women and children. The clergymen employed words of advice and confined their activities to the proprieties. But the women and children were less tactful. They clutched at the coats of the voter. They importuned him to vote the dry ticket. A phrase constantly employed was "Mister, for God's sake don't vote for whiskey," repeated with parrot-like accuracy that results from thorough coaching. . . . A few of the wets ran the gauntlet of the women and children . . . but the greater majority of the voters viewed the conflict from afar and returned to their offices and homes. The drys won the day.[48]

Moving to a higher level, antiliquor advocates were able to strike at the bastions of wet control power. State laws proscribing saloons and proclaiming prohibition did from without what the ASL legions could not do from within.

As dry territory expanded and momentum accelerated, a sense of inevitability mesmerized politicians and enhanced ASL influence. Congressional candidates prepared position papers on the liquor question. Their futures had come to depend upon the ASL's exercise of power in the balance. When league cadre calculated that the time was right and the votes at hand, they laid seige to Washington, D.C. The passage of the Eighteenth Amendment to the Constitution signaled the end of one crusade and the beginning of another. The United States would now carry the dry message to the rest of the world.

In its drive to expand the antiliquor consensus, the ASL further enhanced its positive image through its process of mobilization. It pursued change electorally, in a nonviolent and orderly fashion, with established vehicles. The league made no challenge to the legitimacy of American government or capitalism; it sought only to displace an interest that it had successfully identified as predatory. As anti-saloon and liquor laws entered the statute books, local, state, and national governments joined the crusade in word and deed.

The dynamic of ASL mobilization unfolded over two decades. From its initial base of temperance groups in Ohio, Massachusetts, and the District of Columbia, the league dispatched field workers to organize the United States against the saloon. They carried the cause to the Midwest, the Northeast, the Southwest, and the Pacific Coast, convincing existing temperance bodies to affiliate and building movements from church foundations. Piecemeal, in the aftermath of countless agitation meetings, lobbying efforts, and election campaigns, the borders of wet territory were pushed back. By 1906 more than one-half of the counties and over 60 percent of the incorporated communities in the United States had voted themselves dry by local option. Two years later, the ASL counted over 37 million Americans, or 48 percent, living under dry laws, an increase of almost 20 million people since 1900. Although the league was organizationally weak in the South, local prohibition efforts carried almost two-thirds of the population into the dry camp. Georgia, Alabama, Mississippi, North Carolina, and Tennessee had, by 1909, augmented these local option measures with statewide antiliquor laws.[49]

The wet counterattack   But the Anti-Saloon League advance did not go unchecked. In the fourteen state referendums held between 1900 and 1912, wet voters rallied to defeat nine prohibition initiatives. Catholics, Jews, Lutherans, immigrants, and industrial workers required little prompting to oppose the actions of the Anti-Saloon League. These groups considered prohibition an assault on their values and their way of life. They voted consistently and in large numbers to preserve the saloon and their ability to choose. The heavy concentration of immigrant and working-class populations in the large urban area made the cities wet citadels. Still, prohibition sentiment was not simply a rural and small-town phenomenon. Local option by 1908, for example, had cleared saloons from Birmingham, Alabama; Worcester, Massachusetts; and one-half of the precincts of Chicago.[50]

Liquor and brewing interests raised the large sums necessary to combat the anti-saloon movement by assessing producers and distributors bottle and barrel taxes. Contractors doing business with beer and liquor companies were expected to kick back a percentage of their profits to aid the fight against the saloon. The industry also blacklisted those individuals and firms refusing to cooperate or having any dealings with the ASL. Proponents budgeted their funds to convince the public that prohibition efforts endangered personal freedom and the rights of business people. Supplementing legitimate expenditures for image building were allocations to bribe newspaper editors, lubricate lobbying activities, and buy votes. Meanwhile, the industry's allies in the urban political machine exploited their control of election procedures to insure the desired result.[51]

The image of a monolithic "liquor power," however, was more a product of ASL propaganda than a representation of reality. Rather than a cohesive and organized trust, the league faced a fractionalized foe. Business rivalries between brewers and distillers and among the companies in each industry carried over to inhibit an effective opposition. Distillers, recognizing the rallying power of the ASL, attempted to deflect the movement by prodding beer makers to saloon reforms. Brewers spurned these advances. Misjudging the antiliquor agitation, the beer companies advertised their product as "the temperance drink," hoping to sacrifice distillers and save themselves. In California wine growers distanced their business from both producer groups and invoked the state's cultural heritage and ambience to quiet opposition. Industrywide trade associations, while offering the promise of proliquor unity, lacked the experience, authority, and corporate cooperation to be successful.[52]

Divided within, the makers of intoxicating beverages found themselves challenged on thousands of fronts throughout the United States. To the very end, they defended themselves and used resources with plans that were ad hoc and always tuned to the stimulus of an antiliquor campaign. In retreat, their image problems worsened. Authorities uncovered attempts to bribe legislators in Maryland and Florida. In 1916 Texas fined and stripped seven state brewing companies of their charters for violating election law. The federal government, in the same year, convicted the United States Brewing Association and approximately one hundred corporations of conspiracy to commit election fraud. Outmaneuvered in the contest for image, suffering from self-inflicted wounds, and demoralized by the rising prohibition tide, the liquor interests could find few supporters in government and among polity members.[53]

ON TO WASHINGTON

The leaders of the ASL reassessed their efforts in late 1913. They were proud of their local and state victories that had rolled back wet power. They also congratulated themselves on the buildup of dry influence in both houses of Congress. The "liquor power," while still a dangerous adversary, had been made vulnerable. A successful advance, however, did not ordain a victorious future. The large cities of America remained in wet hands. Continued immigration from Europe promised to strengthen the saloon's grip. Reapportionment scheduled for 1920 threatened to add congressional votes to urban areas and to advance liquor's cause. It was critical, the league believed, to strike for a Constitutional amendment and not wait for liquor interests to rally and their power to grow. With an amendment, the league would secure its work from public, legislative, and judicial backsliding. Only through national action would places impervious to dry campaigns be freed of the liquor traffic.[54]

League leaders focused their attention on Washington, D.C., as they prepared for the final stages of the crusade. Hard campaigning in the 1914 elections brought the dry movement simple majorities in the House of Representatives and the Senate. In 1916, the ASL built on this base, rewarding friends and punishing enemies. As a result, the dry movement commanded the two-thirds majorities in both houses necessary to pass an amendment. The ASL also continued its pressure on local levels to maintain momentum and prepare for the ratification process by the state legislatures. By April 1917, twenty-six states had passed prohibition laws, 80 percent of America's counties were dry, and 60 percent of the population lived in communities with no saloons.[55]

America's entrance into World War I hastened the coming of national prohibition. ASL speakers took advantage of the new circumstances and easily shaped the crisis to the contours of the arguments they had used for decades. They argued that prohibition would cut waste, increase efficiency, free workers for essential war production, and conserve vital foodstuff lost in the manufacture of useless and harmful alcoholic goods. Real Americans stood for "bread, not beer"; "Lager über Alles" was the cry of the enemy. The ASL refused to allow the brewers to escape the onus of their German roots. In the face of anti-German hysteria, accusations of disloyalty were made with telling effect and were difficult to combat. Thus, changing times had cut even further the number of potential coalition partners, business or otherwise, available to proliquor groups.[56]

With strong popular support, legislators closed the circle quickly. In December 1917 Congress passed the Eighteenth Amendment to the Constitution, prohibiting "the manufacture, sale, or transportation of intoxicating liquors."[57] By January 1919 thirty-six states had ratified the amendment; it became the law of the land in January 1920. In fact, the Wartime Prohibition Act had already made America dry six months earlier.

Congress authorized the enforcement of the amendment with the Volstead Act. Written under the auspices of the ASL, this measure defined as intoxicating any beverage with more than one-half of 1 percent alcoholic content. As originally drafted, the bill had also outlawed possession. But the league's pragmatic focus on the saloon had failed to prepare legislators for abstinence. Compromise, despite ASL objections, would leave the personal use of alcohol unregulated.[58]

The Anti-Saloon League had gained entrance into the polity and achieved national prohibition, one of its two primary goals. But the seeds of the movement's defeat were planted. The ASL had misled itself and the nation in two important ways. Tactically, the leadership blurred ends and means. By screening its long-range goal and making the saloon the focus of its attack, the ASL gathered support but lost control of the purpose of its reform. What did prohibition mean to the American people? Did the effort spell an end to the saloon, personal consumption, or both? Who was the enemy? Strategically, the ASL had waged a two-pronged assault on drink. It directed a political thrust at the saloon and an educational campaign at personal attitudes and behavior. While interrelated, the two efforts were separate and did not evolve in tandem: The ASL would find laws easier to change than attitudes and behavior. When the sinner became a criminal, the disparity between the two goals was painfully apparent. The result was a victory lost in a decade of disillusionment, cynicism, and confrontation.

VICTORY AND DEFEAT

The sponsors of the *noble experiment*, as prohibition was described, predicted the transformation of American society. In a nation that had chosen to be the dry beacon to the rest of the world, longstanding social, political, economic, and health problems would be solved. Evidence of reduced consumption and significant declines in alcoholism and liquor-related diseases cheered sponsors and convinced them of their course. So, too, did the disappearance of the saloon from the main streets of the community.

Jubilation, however, was short-lived. The prohibition statute provoked the first period in American history of massive disobedience to a law affecting personal habits. Americans craved the now-forbidden alcoholic fruit and demanded the means to quench their thirst. Smugglers and bootleggers weighed risk against reward and responded to the call. The profits generated in breaking the law attracted many entrepreneurs and proved an important stimulus to the activities of organized crime in America. In the 1920s the nation's borders became sieves, with Miami, Detroit, El Paso, and Seattle serving as important liquor distribution centers. Stills and bathtubs were pressed into service to meet the demand from the tenement flat to the Oval Office in the White House. Drinking was faddish and exciting, the fashionable thing to do in the right social circles. From its ashes, the saloon arose again, phoenix-like, and assumed the guise of the speakeasy. Operating under the protection of the authorities, the speakeasy opened its doors to both men and women, who went drinking together for the first time in significant numbers. Arrests did little to stem the flow of booze. Congested court calendars and jails forced judges to declare "bargain days" during which they reduced prison terms to fines and released violators. Congressional appropriations were sufficient to hire only 1,150 federal prohibition agents to patrol the entire country. In an atmosphere of corruption and temptation, the low salaries paid local, state, and federal liquor agents merely enticed them from their responsibilities.[59]

The breakdown in law and authority caught the leaders of the ASL by surprise. Some disobedience to the new law had been expected, but not massive resistance. Geared to winning political campaigns and propagandizing, the organization was ill-prepared to cope with the attack on their legislative creation. The cadre split on a response. One faction called for an iron fist and demanded that the crisis be met with increased government expenditures of men and money and harsher punishments. The escalation of coercion and pain, they argued for years, would bring the situation under control. For those who bemoaned the emphasis on prohibition over abstinence, such measures were counterproductive. Their answer was education. The law could never be enforced unless wets were persuaded of the pernicious impact of alcohol and the liquor traffic. Although the law enforcement group initially gained the advantage, the debate, aggravated by personal ambitions and animosities, divided the ASL for seven years. Dissension not only consumed time, energy, and trust, it weakened the ASL's ability to bargain and exert influence. When leaders proposing abstinence and an educational solution captured control in 1927, they found that the opportunity to act had disappeared. Circumstances, both internal and external, had left the ASL more a victim than an initiator of change.[60]

Infighting had distracted leaders from shifts caused by the new realities of the 1920s. Once the liquor traffic had been outlawed, the ties that bound the ASL coalition began to unravel. Many league supporters interpreted the ratification of the Eighteenth Amendment as the end of the struggle and sharply reduced their donations. With the saloon routed and authorities supposedly assuming the burden of defense, the ASL was forced to defend its legitimacy. Those opposed to restrictions on the personal use of intoxicating beverages spurned league leaders when they turned to the cause of abstinence. The pragmatism of mobilization, which had obscured ends, now thinned the ranks of those who had taken the ASL's message literally. The rise of the Ku Klux Klan, fueled by religious conflict and the prohibition-generated crime wave, repelled others who rejected identification with a hooded ally. Also, the Anti-Saloon League's intimacy during the 1920s with the Republican party and the administrations in Washington, D.C., shattered its nonpartisan image for Democrats and Independents. Added to these setbacks was an Internal Revenue Service ruling that donations to the ASL were no longer tax-exempt.[61]

These desertions, when added to the fallout suffered because of the widespread assault on the prohibition law, seriously reduced the league's resource base. Declining budgets and rising debts curtailed new initiatives. A scarcity of resources also handicapped the defensive measures the ASL was required to continue: lobbying for prohibition enforcement and education appropriations, holding politicians accountable, and defeating wet referendums. Money troubles afflicted the state leagues as well, with over one-half of these organizations in difficulty as early as 1921. A change in leadership, through death and retirement, accentuated the sense of instability and uncertainty produced by organizational drift and financial crisis. Charges of corruption and misuse of funds together with erosion from personal conflict and jealousy further robbed the leadership of its respectability.[62]

The ASL suffered declining support from within the polity as well. Religious organizations and churches turned away from the league for the same reasons their members did. There were, moreover, new foes to battle in the 1920s. Religious groups now directed their resources against the theory of evolution, promiscuous dancing, provocative motion pictures, and adolescent immorality. The decade also witnessed the transition of the Democratic party. Catholics, Jews, and immigrants entered the fold and wrestled for control with the Protestant dry wing. In the end, the party was weaned from prohibition, and the bipartisan foundation of the dry cause collapsed. Republicans in Washington, D.C., aware that their party was the prohibitionists' only haven, could afford to deflect ASL pleas for increased appropriations and make budget cutting their highest priority.[63]

Some polity members mounted a direct challenge to the Anti-Saloon League. Corporate America's leaders such as Pierre, Lammont, and Irenee Dupont; John Raskob of the automobile industry; Wall Street's Charles Sabin; and Edward Harkness from oil enlisted friends and business associates to power an antiprohibition drive with their energy and funds. Incorporated in 1920, the Association Against the Prohibition Amendment contended that the Eighteenth Amendment was an unprecedented expansion of government power at the expense of community rights and personal freedoms. In attacking the liquor and beer interests the law struck at all Americans, for it unjustly regulated personal behavior and threatened the sanctity of private property.

The AAPA, with a well-known and prestigious group of supporters, would make a far more difficult target than had the so-called liquor trust.[64]

Mirroring the ASL's professionalism and centralization, the AAPA organized in twenty-five states and claimed over 700,000 members by 1926. Its speakers pummeled prohibition for generating crime, corruption, and disrespect for authority. Repeal would cut taxes, government expenditures, and federal control. In 1929, socially and economically prominent women founded the Women's Organization for National Prohibition Reform. It proclaimed a membership of over one million women in 1932. The ASL's image of defender of home and family had been effectively challenged.[65]

Despite a mounting attack, the 1928 elections convinced drys of the security of their hold. President Herbert Hoover was committed to prohibition, as were large majorities in both houses of Congress. The dry reign, however, would not last another five years. The Depression of the 1930s invigorated the wet cause, for it changed the public's frame of reference on the prohibition issue. Attuned to shifts in salience, the AAPA promoted repeal as a means of creating jobs and increasing government revenue. More important, the ASL had unwittingly helped redefine prohibition by deserting nonpartisanship. Identification throughout the 1920s with the Republicans had left the league and prohibition in the embrace of a party tarred with economic failure. The Democratic party, already in the hands of antiprohibitionists, nominated Franklin Roosevelt on a pledge of relief, recovery, and repeal. Thus discredited by events and their Republican ties, the drys were overwhelmed in the Democratic landslide of 1932. Congress quickly passed the Twenty-first Amendment to the Constitution, repealing the prohibition law. To avoid confrontation with prohibitionists in the state legislatures, the amendment called for ratification in conventions. The entire process was completed in 288 days. Prohibition died on December 5, 1933.[66]

In victory, then, the ASL suffered internal dissension, a depletion of resources, organizational decay, and the loss of its aura of invincibility and necessity. A shift in the power balance resulting from both long-term change and immediate events further undermined the ASL in the late 1920s and early 1930s. The meaning of dry reform and the image of its principal crusader had changed in the atmosphere of economic depression. With weaknesses exposed and its bases of support in the polity, the opinion-making public, and the wider society eroding, the ASL fell prey to its enemies within the establishment. The wet forces, capturing what the ASL had abandoned, rode the Democratic party to victory. The league's fate was to lose not only the privileges of membership in the polity, but the prohibition amendment for which it had fought so hard and for so long.

AFTERMATH

The Anti-Saloon League was demoralized, unable to remove the stigmata of prohibition's failure and its association with the Republican party. Moreover, temperance and prohibition seemed irrelevant to a nation consumed with the crises of depression and international aggression. Drys did promise to fight on and return the dry amendment to the Constitution by 1945. Looking to the past, they revived their successful local-option, grass-roots strategy. But the anticipated momentum to carry the movement from town to county and from state to nation never materialized. By the end of the decade, the ASL had ceased campaigning and evolved into the Alcohol Problems Association, a public interest group engaged in education and research. Demobilization occurred despite the existence of extensive support for the dry cause. Gallup Polls revealed in 1936 and 1945 that one-third of the American people were in favor of a return to prohibition. As late as 1966, 20 percent of those polled favored a dry America.[67]

The Anti-Saloon League's rise to power was neither unusual nor accidental. Fastening itself to the resources of polity members, it created a machine-like organization capable of harnessing widespread antiliquor sentiment. The ASL spoke to men and women about real threats to family and community and promised to expunge the dangers from American life. Opinion makers seconded the league's pronouncements and added intensity to a favorable image already heightened through association with church and religious groups. Professional and successful, the league convinced politicians of its clout. Having broadened its power and support base in preparation for the final drive, the league was perfectly positioned to take advantage of the opportunities presented in wartime. Yet, in the everyday struggle for influence, the ASL lost sight of the future. It ignored the centrality of abstinence to prohibition and traded the role of reformer for warden. Nor could it adapt to its new place in a changing America. Tactical errors compounded internal dissension and organizational difficulties, and the league failed to generate new approaches against continued resistance to liquor laws. With its defenses crumbling, opponents went on the offensive. The Depression, a seemingly unrelated event, exacted so powerful a toll because prohibition had lost its Democratic anchor and had become a partisan issue.

The echoes of the antiliquor crusade may still be heard today. Two national news magazines in the late 1980s ran cover stories detailing alcohol's impact on health, the family, and the community. According to *Time*, alcohol has been implicated in one-fourth to one-half of the cases of violence between spouses, one-third of the incidents of child molestation and one-half of automobile fatalities. The Department of Justice estimated that nearly one-third of the nation's state prison inmates drank heavily before committing their crimes. Prohibition also appears relevant as Americans move through the second period of massive disobedience to laws affecting personal habits. The parallels between the wars on drugs and liquor are easily drawn. Similarly, restrictions on cigarette smoking and the tobacco industry conjure up memories of the early decades of the twentieth century. These campaigns against drugs and smoking, like the antiliquor drive, promise a better America once the threats to life and society have been removed. Perhaps, in light of current events, the image of the Anti-Saloon League may become more sympathetic and realistic.[68]

3

ONE BIG UNION: THE INDUSTRIAL

WORKERS OF THE WORLD

There is but one bargain that the IWW will make with the employing class—complete surrender of the means of production.
VINCENT ST. JOHN

Tell the boys I died for my class.
WESLEY EVEREST

On 27 June 1905 William D. Haywood of the Western Federation of Miners opened the founding convention of the Industrial Workers of the World. "This is," Haywood declared to the delegates, "the Continental Congress of the working class. We are here to confederate the workers of this country into a working class movement that shall have for its purpose the emancipation of the working class from the slave bondage of capitalism."[1]

Haywood's message that June morning in Chicago had been heard before in American history. His vision reached back to the American Revolution and before, when men and women had confronted a distribution of wealth and power that allowed the few to dominate the many. They, too, had beckoned their neighbors to a cooperative society that

promised an opportunity for all individuals to realize their full potential. The Industrial Workers of the World and its fellow left-wing challenger, the Socialist Party, would carry forward the radical tradition in the early decades of the twentieth century. Activists protested the disparity between reality and the American dream and pointed to a road not taken. They hoped to guide America through a fundamental social and economic reorganization along collectivist lines. Their voices, however, were barely heard and, if acknowledged, heeded only from a defensive posture. Authorities and polity members, with strong popular support, devised legal and extralegal means to discredit and rout the forces of radicalism. In the devastation of radical protest may be seen not only the strength of traditional patterns of thought and behavior in America but the intense fear of different drummers.

"CONDITIONS THEY ARE BAD"[2]

In the second half of the nineteenth and the early decades of the twentieth centuries, America laid the foundation for an economy of mass production, distribution, and consumption. Railroad building linked the growing urban centers, providing businesses with expanding markets for their products. Corporate officers, in their quest for efficiency and profit, extended the factory system to meet demand. Economic growth, drawing upon technological innovation, natural and human resources, government aid, and abundant capital stores, propelled America into the front ranks of the world's powers.

The impact of industrialization was felt strongly at the grass roots. The factories attracted jobseekers from the countryside and from abroad and vitally stimulated urban expansion. City growth fed upon itself and generated further economic development. The quality of life, if measured in terms of commodities, improved as more and more products were available for purchase. On the whole, real wages for American workers between 1860 and 1890 increased by 50 percent. From 1890 to 1919 wages climbed an additional 37 percent. Upward mobility, whether on the job or in the acquisition of goods and security, was a fact of many workers' lives. Thus, their hopes for their children's success were quite realistic. While such social and economic advancement usually meant only incremental movement within and between classes, it was sufficient to bolster faith in the American economic and political system.[3]

Yet the fruits of industrialization were not evenly distributed. Across America, a sizable minority of workers bore the burdens and became the victims of change. In the West, the demand for ore combined with the high costs of extraction and processing to transform mining boom camps into corporate-managed industrial oases. As surface ore deposits became scarce and placer mining unprofitable, eastern businesses began to take advantage of the vast mineral wealth still locked in the earth. Metal mining went underground and employed the new industrial technologies. The entrepreneur-prospector gave way to the absentee owner and traded his independence for a wage or left for other sites and occupations.[4]

Displaced miners worried about more than lost status. As they burrowed deeper in the ground with the more sophisticated machinery of mining, risks to health and life increased. Mine shafts lacked ventilation and light, and men worked in slime and offal. In Bisbee, Arizona, copper miners labored in temperatures over one hundred degrees while pools of water covered their shoe tops. Production quotas and schedules meant fewer experienced workers, less timbering, more blasting, and greater carelessness. Accidents were common, and cave-ins and explosions exacted a heavy toll. Poorly designed equipment injured and killed others. Death was not always sudden. Drills biting the rock in Butte, Montana, mines produced a fine silica dust that filled workers' lungs. Between 1907 and 1913, some 675 Butte miners succumbed to respiratory diseases.[5]

Working conditions in the lumber camps of the Pacific Northwest and the timber belt of Louisiana and east Texas were no better. Loggers worked long hours, exposed to the elements, for low pay. Company food was procured at the cheapest cost and was of poor quality. Overcrowded bunkhouses lacked adequate bedding and washing facilities. The only things the camps offered in abundance were lice, fleas, and rodents. Frequent layoffs and seasonal employment added to the grim labor picture. Life at the subsistence level, with even the basic refinements of the time absent, tore at the humanity of the men. It is not surprising that they called themselves timber beasts.[6]

Migratory farm workers had similar experiences. Men, women, and children labored from daybreak to sunset under the hot summer sun gathering the products of America's "factories in the field." Following the harvests through the Midwest, Southwest, and California, they led a makeshift life void of the most rudimentary comforts. Employers felt no obligation to provide their workers with shelter, food, medical care, or even water. Once the crop was in, field hands became expendable, and authorities drove off any undesirables who remained in their jurisdiction.[7]

In the Midwest and East, factories demanded semiskilled men and women who were paid a wage for tending a machine. These workers bore the brunt of corporate competition and their employers' drive for profits. Businesses lowered production costs by pressing the unskilled and semiskilled to work as long as possible for the least return. In the sweatshops and factories of the textile industry, nine- and ten-hour days in weeks that included Saturdays and sometimes Sundays were common. Pay scales failed to match the cost of living, and families maintained a precarious existence by opening their homes to boarders and sending children to work. Seasonal industries, moreover, offered no job security; slack time meant reduced hours, pay cuts, and layoffs. Aggravating this instability were the periodic depressions that plagued the American economy. Hard times during the periods 1873–1878, 1883–1885, 1893–1897, 1907–1909, and 1913–1915 inflicted the most pain on the men, women, and children who lived on the economic margins of the society.[8]

Deplorable working conditions accompanied the long hours and low wages. Workers' health suffered in the noisy and overcrowded workplaces. Heat, ventilation, and light were inadequate to workers' needs. Safety, too, was a casualty of the urge for profits. Unsafe equipment, lax standards, long hours, and the pressure of production combined to kill 35,000 workers each year between 1880 and 1900. As late as 1914, 25,000 men and women still died in industrial accidents with 700,000 more injured and maimed.[9]

Worker resistance to industrial conditions met a strong reaction from management. Employers organized to undermine protest with spies and informers, company unions, blacklists, layoffs, strikebreakers, and plant closings. Private detective agencies offered their assistance and stationed armed men on the industrial battlefield. At other times, state and federal authorities responded to corporate polity members and stood with capital against labor. These violent and negative countermeasures were employed in tandem with pay raises, improvements in the work environment, and other benefits to continue production, weaken solidarity, and maintain control.[10]

Thus, while the majority of American working men and women advanced in their occupations and realized material gains, a significant minority remained mired in misery. A government commission reported in 1915 that many "of the families of wage earners employed in manufacturing and mining [are] living in conditions of actual poverty."[11] With neither the ability to bridge their isolation nor the skills with which to bargain, these workers were little more than numbers in the cost-of-production equation.

"Outcast and starving"   However, grievance alone is not a sufficient cause for mobilization. Many workers, convinced that life would improve, assured themselves that present conditions were only temporary. They vowed to work harder and raise themselves and their families to a better life. Others performed the cog-like routine while praying daily for salvation in the world to come. Drink or moving from place to place provided a brief respite as well. For discontent to be stirred, workers had to recognize their collective power in the production process and question the legitimacy of the machine's masters. Also, once ignited, a protest needs an organization to achieve its ends. There were few vehicles in turn-of-the-century America, however, prepared or even willing to assume such a role.

The only viable national labor union in existence at the time was the American Federation of Labor. Organized in 1886 as a coalition of craft unions, it promoted the interests of carpenters, masons, painters, cigar makers, and other skilled workers. The AFL recognized the permanence of capitalism and fought to carve a more secure place in the wage system for its members. It thus promised to enhance the worker's autonomy in the production process while making immediate bread-and-butter demands for higher wages, shorter hours, job stability, and better working conditions. By 1897 the AFL had enrolled only 447,000 members, fewer than 5 percent of the American wage-earning population.[12]

The AFL's concentration on skilled workers led critics to fault its leaders for taking the path of least resistance and deserting the mass of semiskilled and unskilled workers. To the radicals, the AFL was a collaborator of the ruling class because it fostered elitism among skilled workers and struck at labor solidarity. In the labor wars of the early twentieth century, the organizers of the industrial workers would array themselves for battle not only against the corporate bosses but against skilled workers in their own ranks.

The Socialist party was eager to lead America in an anticapitalist crusade. Its answers to the rise of corporate power and the tragedies of industrialization were the redistribution of wealth and collective ownership of the means of production and distribution. Founded in 1901, the party was a coalition of diverse regional, ethnic, and ideological groups. Its chief means were political; through the electoral process and legislative action, the party hoped to nationalize industry and transportation and phase out the profit motive from the economy. Socialists nominated candidates for office and campaigned for their election on the local, state, and federal levels. In 1912 Eugene Debs, the Socialist party candidate for president, polled 900,000 votes or 6 percent of the total cast. Nearly twelve hundred Socialists were elected to office that year in over 340 cities and towns. While the words of Socialist speakers might raise the consciousness of laboring men and women, the party was not designed to mobilize industrial workers to combat working conditions. Conceived as the political arm of the working class, it had little to offer women and blacks who could not vote, immigrants who had not yet become citizens, men too mobile to maintain voter residency, or laborers too isolated and scattered to exert political power. Socialists were aware of these weaknesses, and they invested much time and energy to find an economic arm to organize working people and broaden the anticapitalist front.[13]

The problems confronting industrial workers were obvious. So, too, were the difficulties inherent in organizing them to effect change. The men and women who labored in the mines, fields, forests, and factories had not developed a sense of common class or even shared workplace grievances. They held no lever of skills with which to move employers. Moreover, race, gender, and ethnicity separated workers, fostering divisions that employers creatively exploited. Yet, if the mobilization of the miners, factory operatives, bindle stiffs,[14] and timber beasts was risky, it also offered great opportunities. As the twentieth century began, radicals saw a world in flux. A challenge to capitalism was viable, they believed, for the corporate grip on power was still not secure. If the unskilled and semiskilled workers could be forged into a united force, victory could be achieved. The birth of a better world demanded the action of the industrial class.

"WORKINGFOLK UNITE"

The mobilization of industrial workers, culminating in the formation of the Industrial Workers of the World, began in the mountains of Colorado, Montana, and Idaho under the direction of the Western Federation of Miners. The WFM had been created in 1893 to unite all men, without regard to craft or skill level, who worked in and around the mines. The WFM's leaders believed, initially, in "pure and simple unionism." That is, they accepted the legitimacy of capitalism and fought for higher wages, shorter hours, and union recognition. The union's demands for improved conditions met a determined resistance. Beginning in 1894, and lasting for a decade, a state of war existed as corporations and their allies within state and local government attempted to destroy the union. Sensing that the problems of mine workers were not unique and seeking to expand its base of support, the executive board of the WFM in 1896 invited all western unions to unite in a common effort. This appeal produced the Western Labor Union, which evolved later into the American Labor Union. An industrial brotherhood, the ALU promised to organize all American workers in direct action against corporate power. Heavily dependent upon the resources of the WFM, the fortunes of the ALU waxed and waned with those of its benefactor.[15]

This unceasing onslaught of private and public power turned the WFM to radicalism. Union leaders called for a general strike against capitalism, seizure of corporate property, and the abolition of the wage system. The ALU followed suit and echoed these demands in the shops and factories. Events in the mining camps of Colorado during 1903–1904, however, sharply reduced the thrusts of both the WFM and the ALU. The mining companies, with the support of state militia units and local vigilante groups, forced the WFM into retreat, stripped of members and funds. The ALU could not exist without infusions of WFM resources, and its challenge lost effect.[16]

The leaders of the Western Federation of Miners refused to surrender their plan to arouse industrial unionism beyond the western mines. Acknowledging its own weaknesses, as well as those of its ALU subsidiary, the WFM approached others in the labor movement, testing sentiment for the creation of a new industrial organization that would embrace all workers. As a result of these contacts, a secret meeting was convened in Chicago in January 1905 "to discuss ways and means of uniting the working people of America on correct revolutionary principles."[17]

The conference brought together representatives of nine organizations and included Charles Moyer and William Haywood of the WFM, Daniel McDonald and Clarence Smith of the ALU, W. L. Hall of the United Brotherhood of Railway Employees, Charles Sherman of the United Metal Workers, and prominent Socialists Eugene Debs, A. M. Simons, and Frank Bohn, and charismatic labor organizer Mother Jones. After three days, the delegates had shaped a Manifesto setting forth their aims. The Manifesto condemned capitalism for forging a "mass of wage slaves" who suffered not only "common servitude . . . to the machines which they tend" but conditions in which "wages constantly grow less as . . . hours grow longer and monopolized prices grow higher." Meanwhile, the Manifesto continued, craft unionism undermined from within the workers' defenses against the united front of business, the courts, and the state. "Union men scab on union men; hatred of worker for worker is engendered, and the workers are delivered helpless and disintegrated into the hands of the capitalists. . . . This worn-out and corrupt system," declared the Manifesto, "offers no promise of improvement and adaption. There is no silver lining to the clouds of darkness and despair settling down upon the world of labor." The situation demanded the creation of "one great industrial union embracing all industries." All committed to this end were invited to assemble in June to formalize such an organization.[18]

The promise of industrial unionism drew many of the prominent members of the American left wing to the convention in June 1905. The presence of these men and women, however, did not guarantee a transfer to the new movement of the resources essential for building an organization. Of the 203 delegates attending, 72 belonged to, but did not officially represent, a union; 70 acted in the name of unions having a combined membership of just over 50,000; and 61 had no allegiance beyond themselves. Sixteen unions affiliated with the American Federation of Labor registered, yet all were small and carried little weight in their parent organization. The resulting power disparities allowed five groups to dominate the proceedings. The Western Federation of Miners, with a membership of 27,000, dwarfed all other organizations and played the central role in deliberations. It, alone, could back policy positions with members and funds. The American Labor Union claimed 16,750 members and enhanced WFM power. Also active were the United Metal Workers, the United Brotherhood of Railway Employees, and Daniel DeLeon's Socialist Trade and Labor Alliance.[19]

An uncompromising declaration inaugurated the challenge of the Industrial Workers of the World: "The working class and the employing class have nothing in common. There can be no peace so long as hunger and want are found among millions of working people and the few, who make up the employing class, have all the good things in life."[20] Thus, the IWW was organized to the sound of labor solidarity and devised to transcend divisions of craft, skill, race, ethnicity, gender, and politics. On paper, the movement's internal structure was bureaucratic and centralized. At the base was the local union, which every man, woman, and child working in a factory was encouraged to join. All locals in an industry then affiliated to form an industrial union. Framers designated industrial councils to coordinate the activities of two or more of these unions in a given geographic area. When ten allied industrial unions with not less than three thousand members had formed, an industrial division was created. Organizers assigned all American wage earners to thirteen such divisions, including mining, transportation, agricultural, public service, and building.[21]

The national headquarters was composed of a president, a secretary-treasurer, and an executive board on which the leader of each industrial division sat. The executive board theoretically commanded great power. It managed the affairs of the IWW between conventions, issued charters to locals and industrial unions, called out unions to support striking locals, approved all agreements between unions and employers, and had the "power to control the industrial unions in matters concerning the interests of the general welfare."[22] Revenues to support the IWW and its activities came from union chartering and initiation fees and members' dues.[23]

Despite the convention's show of radical unity and the erection of an imposing internal structure, there were serious underlying weaknesses in the new movement. The support base of the IWW was neither strong nor broad. Conflict had damaged the WFM, the prime mover behind the early IWW. Its membership figures were inflated, and its power was eroded in the western mining camps. The ALU was little more than a scattering of union locals. Accurate assessments of its strength place membership at eleven hundred rather than the more than sixteen thousand claimed. Similarly, the United Metal Workers numbered seven hundred and not three thousand members.

The IWW, then, was supported on a few weakened pillars and commanded no more than fourteen thousand men and women. Six months after the convention, membership stood at less than eight thousand. As a result, leaders were able initially to organize just the transportation, metal, and mining industrial divisions. Of the three, only the mining division (the WFM) was viable. IWW inroads into the American Federation of Labor were also virtually nonexistent. The most effective labor contender for power, the AFL exerted considerable power to eliminate the IWW foothold and any drain of members or funds. The Socialist groups of DeLeon and Debs offered encouragement, but few resources. They were less interested in the IWW as an independent force than in the movement's role in furthering the fortunes of their respective Socialist factions. Radical contenders backing the Wobbly*

---

*The origin of the term "Wobbly" is not clear. The most popular story recalls a Chinese restaurant owner who fed workers during a strike in Vancouver. Because he could not pronounce "W" correctly, his rendering of IWW sounded like "I Wobble Wobble."

challenge, moreover, suffered their own image problems and were unable to facilitate the IWW's reception by the wider community. Finally, the nature of the IWW challenge denied the movement the sponsorship of polity members. Facing displacement in the event of Wobbly success, elite groups were relentless in attacking their opponent.[24]

"COMMONWEALTH OF TOIL"

The IWW ideology magnified its organizational weaknesses. An antielitist philosophy exalting the working class animated the movement and infused every effort. All officers were elected annually, and limits were placed on the number of successive terms a position might be held. All leaders were subject to recall, and a referendum of the membership could overrule decisions of the leadership. These mechanisms of popular control rarely had to be invoked, for both activists and rank and file believed in the leadership of the worker. A low-dues policy, consistent with this philosophy, insured that no worker would be deprived of the benefits of membership.

Such an ideology undercut the ability of the leadership to manage and direct the movement. Activists found that their exercise of authority came less from position and more from the power of personality or the scars earned in wars against the workers' enemies. Chains of command easily rusted as individuals assumed the mantle of leadership and shed the burdens of accountability. A scarcity of resources hindered daily operations, expansion plans, the building of adequate strike funds, and an effective defense. The IWW usually lacked the funds to coordinate activists or support them in concerted organizing drives. Unable to finance such efforts, the IWW had to be opportunistic and take advantage of situations not necessarily of the movement's making. On these battlegrounds, the Wobblies faced foes better prepared and armed for combat.[25]

The IWW plan of attack was straightforward. To complete the unfinished American Revolution and bring industrial democracy to the working class, the movement vowed to capture the means of production, abolish the wage system, and redistribute the wealth. This demanded the mobilization of all workers into factory-based unions. In these grass-roots locals, workers would raise their consciousness of capitalist oppression and realize the strength of class solidarity. It was an education of words and deeds. Workers were encouraged to learn movement songs written to "fan the flames of discontent." Singing built morale, heightened unity, and told of the world to come. On the job, conflict with the bosses over wages, hours, and conditions eroded the legitimacy of the prevailing system and heightened the workers' sense of efficacy. Wobblies did not lose sight of the future in the pursuit of the short-term goals. Rather, each blow against the capitalist fortress brought the worker-controlled world closer. "Strikes," declared Wobbly Andre Tridon, "are mere incidents in the class war; they are tests of strength, periodic drills in the course of which the workers train themselves for concerted action."[26] "We are forming," they said again and again, "the structure of the new society within the shell of the old."[27]

The Wobblies believed that revolution would come through evolution. Gradually, as the unions expanded and industrial divisions formed, the power to break the shell would grow. Worker control at the point of production would be the force of change. Noncooperation, not violence, was the means to power: In a national general strike, men and women had simply to lay down their tools and halt the production process. According to Joseph Ettor, "If the workers want to win, all they have to do is recognize their own solidarity. They have nothing to do but fold their arms and the world will stop."[28] Only the complete surrender of corporate America could bring this economic standstill to an end. In the aftermath of this complete evolution, corporations would have no role, and a new society based upon the Wobbly organization would arise. Workers, not private interests, would own the means of production, and democratic elections would determine the best-qualified foremen and managers. Factory locals, industrial unions, and district and regional councils would replace city, county, and state governments in this new industrial republic. America was to be the Commonwealth of Toil, and the new age would be free of war, depression, injustice, and bigotry. "The Industrial Union shall be the human race."[29]

There were, however, several unanswered questions in Wobbly strategy and tactics. For example, what role did the election process play in the overthrow of capitalism? The IWW stressed action at the point of production as the most important route to industrial democracy. Many agreed with Thomas Hagerty, who argued, "Dropping pieces of paper into a hole in a box never did achieve emancipation for the working class and . . . it never will achieve it."[30] While believing that political action might forestall antilabor legislation and bring reforms, Wobblies considered the vote a relatively insignificant weapon in their arsenal. This was a realistic assessment of the movement's resources, for many potential recruits could not or did not possess the franchise. Yet many Socialists, inside and outside the IWW, charted their path to power through the ballot box. They believed that with IWW support, elections would be won and legislation enacted to end the capitalist reign and usher in the new era. Wobbly resistance to Socialist direction would provoke dissension and help divide the radical challenge to corporate control. The Wobblies rejection of the electoral route to power would also curry no favor with the wider American public.[31]

Also unresolved was the question of whether the labor union was a means to industrial democracy or an end in itself. In organizing unions, IWW activists rejected methods designed to enhance stability. They refused to sign written contracts with employers, give notice of strikes, create checkoff systems for dues, or accumulate strike funds. As a result, unions seemed like expendable way stations on the road to the new society. In contrast, the eyes of the rank and file were not as steadily fixed on the coming revolution. Their union was an important objective in itself, vital to securing immediate gains. The debate over the role of the union, then, created another source of tension within the IWW. Without continuous and intensive efforts at union mainte-nance, ideological education, and consciousness-raising, the ties that bound the present to the future could unravel. The vehicle of revolution was always in danger of becoming a bulwark of the reformed status quo.[32]

Finally, did the IWW preach peaceful revolution? The Wobblies con-tended that workers would overwhelm capitalism with their arms folded and their hands in their pockets. By simply refusing to cooperate with employers, the chains of exploitation could be broken. Yet the American public heard a different message. The goals of the movement alone seemed to portend violent upheaval. Misunderstanding also resulted from the Wobblies' use of the word *sabotage*. Ignoring prevailing perceptions, Wobblies carelessly talked sabotage without confining its meaning to passive resistance, malin-gering, or poor service. Bill Haywood, for example, ambiguously declared: "Sabotage means to push back, pull out or break off the fangs of capitalism."[33] IWW newspapers and pamphlets even flaunted the symbols of sabotage, and some of its speakers deliberately cultivated confusion in the public mind. Many Americans, with the guidance of opinion makers, took the movement's message literally and believed their worst fears. The movement's image of violence, which was in part self-generated, thus helped legitimize the actions of those who, opposing the movement, would brook no challenge to their interests.[34]

"ARE YOU A WOBBLY?"

The IWW opened the crusade for industrial democracy on several fronts in 1905. Initially, Wobbly activists organized most aggressively among workers already holding union cards. Capturing blocs of supporters disenchanted with their leaders in the American Federation of Labor, or under fire from employ-ers, promised vital and quick transfusions of members and funds. The AFL responded to these "union smashers" and vigorously blunted Wobbly raiding parties. AFL president Samuel Gompers denounced the IWW as "fanciful and chimerical and absolutely impossible" and directed union members to refuse Wobblies all aid and comfort.[35] Thus, the AFL cooperated with employers and denied IWW members jobs, crossed their picket lines, and helped break their strikes. This alliance of labor and corporate power, combined with the Wobblies' inadequate planning, defused the first wave of IWW protest. All strikes called by Wobblies failed, and many locals died shortly after their birth. In its wake, the effort left a dispersed network of locals connected only through the national body. Failure in the field intensified criticism of the administratively inept central office. Officials were deficient in organizational skills with membership records and financial accounts continually in arrears. Accusations of incompetence, extravagance, and even corruption turned the headquarters against itself. Personal and ideological differences fueled further the process of factionalization.[36]

The new movement suffered another setback in early 1906. The murder of Frank Steunenberg, former governor of Idaho and ardent foe of the Western Federation of Miners, led to the arrests of WFM and IWW leaders Charles Moyer and Bill Haywood. The men spent eighteen months in prison before a jury acquitted them of the crime. The long incarceration and subsequent trial robbed the IWW of two of its most experienced union men and drained it of scarce funds. Despite the not-guilty verdicts, the IWW's first appearance before the public left an impression of lawlessness and violence. Even more important, the actions of the authorities intimidated Moyer and the conservatives in the WFM. Impressed by what these men believed to be a deliberate effort of repression, they reconsidered the meaning of radicalism and the WFM's ties to the IWW.[37]

By the time the delegates to the second IWW convention had assembled in September 1906, the lines of confrontation were well marked. The crisis in national leadership provided the focus for disputes over ideology and strategy. The power struggle within the WFM between its conservative and radical wings carried onto the convention floor, where adversaries backed opposing candidates for leadership positions. Socialists, already severely criticized for allegiance to the IWW rather than the AFL, balked at Wobbly disinterest in political change and its rejection of the party program. Socialist suspicion of DeLeon and his rival organization remained unabated and laced internal politics. In the face of IWW organizing failures, Socialists had little reason to justify a continued commitment.[38]

The victory of the radicals in the election of new officers fragmented the IWW. WFM conservatives bolted from the convention. Within a few months, however, they would wrestle control of their union from the radicals, and by the summer of 1907 the WFM would end its affiliation with the IWW. Debs, Simons, and other Socialists, realizing that their influence within Wobbly circles had been eclipsed, retreated. DeLeon's place in the movement, however, was hardly secure. In 1908 those who placed their faith in change through direct economic action refused DeLeon a convention seat and deleted the Socialists' call for electoral politics from the IWW program.[39]

Internal dissension had cost the IWW dearly. The desertion of the WFM meant the loss of the Wobbly base in the West. The mining department became a paper organization devoid of members and revenues. Socialist resources, which included prestige in the left-wing community, leadership experience, and funds, were similarly drained. The IWW suffered additional blows during the financial panic of 1907–08. Hard times brought unemployment and slowed union building. IWW income fell by half, locals dissolved, and newspapers suspended publication. In early 1908 the IWW organizing staff consisted of only five men for the entire United States.[40]

"All hell can't stop us"   The birth pains that racked the national organization certainly affected its grass-roots momentum. Internal dissension drove away supporters and wasted precious resources. Yet the nature of the movement was such that its adherents could continue grass-roots organizing. Wobblies functioned like soldiers in a guerilla war. Often cut off from logistical support and leadership, they acted with relative autonomy while obtaining sustenance from the local population. The IWW's anti-elitist mentality fed such initiative, and few bureaucratic restraints existed to harness grass-roots activism. These localized efforts became the cutting edge of the movement, and the national organization moved in response to these stimuli. "They really had no center," remarked an observer, "no national office, no leadership. It ran on the voluntary instincts of people sticking together."[41]

Thus, neither organizational position nor administrative skills conferred authority in the Industrial Workers of the World: Influence was won in organizing. Yet it was more than the power of organizers' oratory that evoked intense loyalty and respect. Wobbly activists had led lives familiar to their supporters. They, too, had come from the bottom and could speak knowingly of the experiences of laboring men and women. To their audiences they became the symbols of a common grievance. Big Bill Haywood, six feet tall, broad shouldered, and missing his right eye, went into the mines at the age of fifteen. "He was not elegant," wrote fellow activist Carlo Tesca. "He had not much culture. He was just one of the mass."[42] Vincent St. John was a Kentucky-born miner with a crippled left hand who had been blacklisted for union activities. Said a fellow Wobbly, "The air was clean in his presence."[43] Elizabeth Gurley Flynn, "a very pleasant Irish housewife," brought her blend of feminism and socialism from the tenements of New York City.[44] Joseph Ettor, son of immigrant parents, had by his twenty-first birthday worked as a water boy on the railroad, a saw filer, and a cigar maker. With Arturo Giovannitti, Tesca, Frank Little, Matilda Rabinowitz, and hundreds of others, these individuals reached to the outsiders of American society. They found many of these outsiders—the homeless, the poor, the uneducated, people of color, immigrants, and the unskilled—ready to build within themselves a strength that would power a resistance.[45]

Between June 1905 and September 1907, the IWW had chartered more than nine hundred local unions. Wobblies recruited tailors in Seattle and smelter men in Tacoma, Washington; textile workers in Paterson, New Jersey;

miners in Illinois, Colorado, Kansas, and Pennsylvania; and electrical workers in Schenectady, New York. The most impressive gains were made in Gold-field, Nevada. Following a successful strike for higher wages and better working conditions in the mines, the IWW expanded from its WFM affiliate to organize town workers. To the miners, it joined clerks, waiters, dishwash-ers, and newsboys. By March 1907 the three thousand members of the One Big Union exerted enough power to order an eight-hour day and demand control over hiring.[46]

Wobbly pressure, however, could not be sustained. Lost strikes, employer sanctions, economic recession, and internal problems had broken three of every four locals. By the fall of 1907, the IWW could count only six thousand members in approximately two hundred unions. In Goldfield, mine owners and businessmen had capitalized on the IWW-WFM split to breech labor solidarity and regain leverage. With conservative unionists' cooperation, they purged radical workers from the WFM and broke the town organization. The intervention of federal and state militia sealed the defeat not only of the IWW, but of Goldfield unionism. The following year brought the IWW no relief. The downturn in the national economy tightened the job market, freeing few resources for union activities. In 1909 the number of Wobbly locals had been cut in half, and no national convention was held.[47]

A renewed IWW organizing drive accompanied the return of more pros-perous times in mid-1909. Activists continued their scatter-gun efforts in California, Oregon, Washington, Montana, Arizona, Nebraska, Indiana, New York, and Vermont. In McKees Rock, Pennsylvania, striking steel workers called for Wobbly leadership after a spontaneous walkout against low pay and poor safety conditions. Six thousand workers enrolled in the IWW and compelled employers to grant wage increases. But this Wobbly success was temporary. Skill and ethnic differences divided a union lacking management skills and financial resources. In three years, the local dwindled to twenty dues-paying members. Organizers also went South and recruited black and white timber workers in Texas and Louisiana. Demands for an eight-hour day and higher pay led employers to blacklist workers, employ scabs, close down mills, assault strikers, and deport union members. After a two-year war, the Brotherhood of Timber Workers had been gutted.[48]

The IWW supplemented these on-the-job organizing efforts with free speech campaigns waged between 1909 and 1912 in twenty-six cities. Re-stricted from company property and recognizing the itinerant nature of harvest, lumber, and construction labor, activists followed workers to key transportation and hiring centers. In such cities as Missoula, Denver, Spo-kane, and San Diego, Wobblies mounted soapboxes to educate workers and build unions. Employers prodded city officials, who responded with ordi-nances restricting public speech and assembly. Wobblies countered with civil disobedience tactics, choosing to confront police nonviolently in the exercise of their rights. Crowding the jails and clogging court calendars, they hoped to attack the legitimacy of capitalist government, provide workers with role models of resistance, and bring repeal of the laws curtailing free speech. Authorities demonstrated little restraint in their determination to crush the protest. They gave arrested Wobblies bread-and-water rations and subjected them to intolerable unsanitary conditions. Police beat their prisoners and opened the jails to vigilante terrorist squads. As a result of such determined opposition, few new labor organizations were built, and victories proved costly—many were broken in spirit and health. "Organize the wage slave," said critics, "not the bourgeois, the street moocher and the saloon soak."[49] Yet, by exposing the uninitiated to the message of industrial unionism and the determination of IWW members, the campaign may have prepared the ground for future mobilization.[50]

"They go wild . . . over me"   The Wobbly campaign to protect free speech and the right of assembly was, for many Americans, their first encounter with the Industrial Workers of the World. The Wobblies had issued their challenge publicly and dramatically, inviting the scrutiny of the wider community. Few opinion makers, themselves targeted by the IWW for destruction, came to its defense. "Hanging is none too good for them," declared the editor of the *San Diego Tribune*, "they would be much better dead, for they are absolutely useless in the human economy; they are the waste material of creation and should be drained off into the sewer of oblivion there to rot in cold obstruction like any other excrement."[51] The *Fresno Herald* (California) was similarly vituperative: "For men to come here with the express purpose of creating trouble, a whipping post and a cat-o-nine tails well seasoned by being soaked in salt water is none too harsh a treatment."[52] The observation of *New York Evening Post* reporter Robert Bruere, about the situation in Arizona in 1916, can be generalized to that of the rest of the nation: "Very few people had any accurate knowledge of the tenets or tactics of the I.W.W. The three letters had come to stand in the popular mind as a symbol of something bordering on black magic."[53]

Anti-IWW sentiment was partly a reaction to the IWW's civil disobedience tactics. In the early twentieth century, few considered nonviolent confrontation a legitimate act of protest. Breaking the law, regardless of reason or method, was a disruption of community standards and an invitation to anarchy. Wobbly songs and speeches made under the radical banner heightened such fears. Speakers attacked basic American values of self-help, thrift, and industry. They questioned the sacredness of property, the necessity of marriage, and the existence of God. Calls for direct action, class war, and revolution pushed Wobblies outside the pale of acceptable thought, behavior, and speech. Nor were political and social conservatives and moderates alone in rejecting the IWW. In 1912 the Socialist Party of America called for the expulsion of any member who opposed political action in favor of sabotage and violence, resulting in the purging of Wobblies like Bill Haywood. This quest for ideological purity proved compatible with the party's desire to deflect anti-IWW hostility.[54]

To the settled community, not only was the Wobbly message dangerous but it was carried by social outcasts. The Wobblies were proud to identify themselves and appear as hobos, bums, and bindle stiffs, outsiders America has never been comfortable with. Senator W. H. King of Utah scorned the Wobblies as "nomadic, houseless, and homeless. They have no family ties; no habits of thrift or sobriety, and in every sense of the word, are utterly at war with our institutions and form of society and our industrial and governmental life."[55] Wobblies were everything 100 percent Americans were not. This dehumanization and de-Americanization of the Wobblies would deny them not only the protection of the Constitution, but even the right to exist.[56]

This negative image of the IWW facilitated countermeasures by polity members and government. Also, at a time when membership in any union was potentially dangerous, it markedly tempered workers' enthusiasm for joining. Nevertheless, those who defied the public will found within the movement countervailing factors that justified participation. IWW halls were havens where workers created friendships and community. Leaders worked to instill in members a sense of dignity, self-worth, and purpose. The charismatic Haywoods, Flynns, and St. Johns of the IWW strengthened resolve, prodding men and women to believe in themselves and their united power. "I could see a future," remembered Jack Miller, "that I could be part of creating. . . . I saw what love was in the finest sense."[57] Henry Pfaff concurred: "The IWW gave me a vision of how we could change America—from a profit motivated society to a cooperative society where no man needs to work for another for his livelihood, but all cooperate together."[58]

Joining the IWW, however, did not necessarily translate into commitment. Even for the membership, Wobbly organizers cast a radical image, and the IWW failed to effect a rigorous and systematic program of ideological indoctrination. It could not bridge the gap between the activists' dreams of the Commonwealth of Toil and the rank and file's concentration on bread-and-butter demands. Wobblies might rage against the myth of the self-made man, yet the appearance of mobility and American opportunity could not be blurred for immigrants and natives yearning for advancement. If workers tolerated Wobbly rhetoric during a crisis, they were too practical to dedicate themselves to a dream so radical and rebuked. Workers' allegiance, then, owed less to the IWW program and long-range goals than to a lack of alternatives and to the personal magnetism and skills of individual Wobbly leaders.[59]

The negative perception of the public, the opposition of polity members and government, and the limits of loyalty shackled the IWW's ability to influence decision making. So, too, did the movement's failure to build internal strength. The movement's organizational structure had little meaning beyond the union local; coordinating links remained in the planning stage. Wobblies could win strikes but could not manage gains. As a result, the IWW could exert power only briefly, in scattered grass-roots locations, in the name of and at the forbearance of its members. Starved for resources, internally weak, and operating in a hostile environment, its impact on the nation's economic direction was negligible. Yet, the movement's impotence at least insured its survival. However, when the union accelerated the tempo of its protest, the growing IWW "menace" provoked authorities and elite groups to marshall resources for a more methodical counterattack.

"DUMP THE BOSSES OFF YOUR BACK"

The dawn of 1912 revealed little change in the status of the Industrial Workers of the World. The movement numbered approximately ten thousand dues-paying members in locals dispersed across America. Growth remained slow, with advances offset by continuing erosion. But this situation changed quickly. In the early days of the new year, Wobbly leaders exploited fresh opportunities and adroitly managed events to bring their organization its first significant successes.[60]

When Massachusetts law reduced the work week from fifty-six to fifty-four hours, the American Woolen Company of Lawrence cut the already low wages of its employees accordingly. In response, ten thousand men, women, and children left their looms and marched out in protest. A day after the walkout, IWW activist Joseph Ettor arrived to offer his assistance to the strikers. Speaking five languages and operating from a small IWW local, he helped organized workers into strike and relief committees with representation on each assigned by ethnic group. As the strike spread, twenty three thousand workers eventually joined the stoppage. Meanwhile, Haywood, Flynn, Giovannitti, and other Wobbly activists converged on Lawrence to direct the effort.[61]

Workers paraded, picketed, and attended mass meetings to gain their demands of a wage increase and protection for strikers against company reprisals. Employers rejected negotiations, secure in the support of local business associations, city government, and the Catholic Church. State militia units supported the Lawrence police force in harassing, intimidating, and arresting strikers and their Wobbly leaders. To secure needed funds for food, clothing, and fuel, workers downplayed IWW support and voiced an appeal beyond Lawrence. With the help of sympathetic journalists like Lincoln Steffens, Walter Weyl, and Ray Stannard Baker, they informed America of their plight. Reports of company arrogance and police brutality brought money, sympathy, and a congressional investigation. After ten weeks, employers capitulated and granted the workers' demands.[62]

The IWW reaped sixteen thousand members for its rejuvenated textile union. It also sensed a new momentum. Two weeks after the settlement at Lawrence, the *Industrial Worker* announced: "The revolutionary pot seems to be boiling in all quarters. The day of transformation is now at hand."[63] Activists followed up their Lawrence victory by organizing the mills of Lowell and New Bedford, Massachusetts, and winning strikes of eighteen thousand and fifteen thousand workers, respectively.[64]

The IWW approached its next major target with confidence. Employers in Paterson, New Jersey's silk industry attempted to speed up production without increasing wages by having workers tend four looms instead of two. Walkouts began in January 1913 and spread to include twenty five thousand workers. Sensing a replay of Lawrence, Bill Haywood, Elizabeth Flynn, and Carlo Tesca offered the IWW's support to the strikers. Employers and city government officials moved to end the strike by confiscating literature, closing the city to public gatherings, and arresting over eighteen hundred workers. The strike continued through the winter and spring of 1913, with neither side willing to compromise. As strike funds ran low and morale declined, activists decided to stage a pageant in New York City to dramatize the events of the strike. Organizers spent a considerable amount of time, money, and energy on a production they believed would raise spirits, generate publicity and sympathy, and restore financial health to the strike. The pageant's failure to raise money plundered the movement of its resources, both material and spiritual. In July workers began to return to the mills, their demands for an eight-hour day, an end to the four-loom system, and pay increases rejected. During the strike the Paterson IWW had numbered ten thousand members; six months later, only fifteen hundred workers remained.[65]

Autopsies of the strike suggest several causes for the IWW's failure. The Paterson silk industry was declining and becoming less competitive. Many companies faced bankruptcy if the strike succeeded. With the Lawrence strike fresh in their minds, government authorities and business leaders resolved to avoid the actions that had rebounded in the workers' favor and generated sympathy. Daring the rising revolutionary tide, they portrayed themselves as unyielding bulwarks defending industrial peace and American capitalism. As the days of deadlock lengthened with no significant infusion of support, the resource-depleted IWW could not save members from destitution and hunger.[66]

Paterson was not the only Wobbly defeat in 1913. The Lawrence local, too, faded, reduced to seven hundred members. Employing spies, capitalizing upon ethnic divisions within the work force, and manipulating the job market to create a labor surplus, textile companies sowed dissension among their employees and weeded radicals from their factories. Wobblies were ineffective in countering these measures. Attempts to organize the automobile and rubber industries were also turned aside. The recession of 1913–1915 further deepened the defeats that corporate America had inflicted on the movement. Again, economic crisis stifled worker protest and facilitated employers' management of labor. In the East, only the seamen and longshoremen of the Maritime Transport Workers Union remained of the Wobbly surge.[67]

In this setting of failure, the movement drained of prestige, spirit, and funds, activists searched inward for answers. Perhaps 200,000 workers had joined the IWW since 1905. Why did only a fraction remain? Why was the IWW's strength only one one-hundredth of the membership of the American Federation of Labor? How could the movement overcome its powerlessness? Some saw salvation in sabotage. The IWW would excite the working class by employing more radical means in its confrontation with capitalism. A few suggested that the IWW abandon its independent unions and bore from within AFL locals. Others demanded an end to the sensational word and deed and a concentration upon the more mundane tasks of union building. In addition to tactical issues, issues of organization were raised. Could the IWW increase its effectiveness by becoming more centralized and exerting stricter control over field operations? Or should the executive board be abolished and freer rein given to local activists? This soul-searching became highly personal and degenerated into exercises of blame fixing and character assassination. An emerging consensus for centralization and quiet union building produced further casualties. Flynn, Ettor, Tesca, and other experienced organizers resigned or let their memberships lapse.[68]

If the IWW was moribund in the East, it found new life in the West. Organizing opportunities emerged there as European war orders spurred production, expanded the job market, and lifted America from recession. Wobblies were especially effective in recruiting harvest workers, who were now in great demand to meet the food needs of Europe. Headquartered in Minneapolis, the Agricultural Workers Organization lowered the volume of revolutionary rhetoric to urge union building and secure a bread-and-butter program of a ten-hour day, minimum wage, and decent room and board. To recruit mobile workers who were scattered from the Mexican to the Canadian borders, the IWW dispatched "job delegates" who organized as they worked. These unpaid activists agitated, initiated, collected dues, and kept records at the point of production. In control of the railroad boxcars, the main means of migrant worker transportation, Wobblies instituted a "1,000 mile picket line." No one could ride the rails to work without producing a red Wobbly card. By harvest time in 1916, twenty thousand men and women had joined the Agricultural Workers Organization. Dues from these workers financed organizing drives in the Mesabi Iron Range of Minnesota, the copper mines of Montana and Arizona, the lumber camps of the Pacific Northwest, and the oil fields of California, Oklahoma, and Kansas. The IWW boasted sixty thousand members in 1917 assigned to functioning unions of agricultural workers, lumbermen, railway workers, metal and machinery workers, maritime workers, and mining industrial workers.[69]

Reports of increased Wobbly activity alerted government officials. In October 1915 the governors of California, Oregon, Washington, and Utah expressed concern about "abnormal disorder and incendiarism" and jointly urged President Woodrow Wilson to investigate the IWW.[70] Federal officers in the Northwest had already deemed membership in the movement sufficient to deny immigrants American citizenship. In lieu of more decisive federal action, states acted individually to curb the Wobbly threat. Idaho, in March 1917, became the first state to pass a criminal syndicalism law. Under this statute, those advocating or belonging to organizations that preached violence and sabotage to bring change were guilty of a felony punishable by up to ten years in prison. However, these official acts of repression would pale before the anti-IWW crusade of World War I.[71]

"HOLD THE FORT"

The American declaration of war against Germany in April 1917 drastically altered the context of the IWW challenge. Since its founding convention, the movement had unequivocally condemned militarism and war as destructive of international working-class solidarity. Now, patriotic fever to make the world "safe for democracy" ignited public hysteria and official repression against any instance of suspected pro-German or pacifist disloyalty. Vigilante groups and government agencies ignored civil liberties in their determination to eliminate slackers, spies, and saboteurs. Seeking to continue its successful organizing campaigns in the fields, mines, and forests, the IWW attempted to shift direction and temper word and action. The IWW silenced its antiwar speakers, toned down its rhetoric of sabotage and class struggle, and ruled that registration for the draft was an individual decision. But the movement could not so easily shed its antiwar and "un-American" images. In fact, the war raised the salience of the IWW as a threat. IWW organizing and its refusal to pledge a no-strike policy gave credence to detractors and enhanced its identity as sinister and alien. To many Americans, the disruption of essential food, lumber, and copper industries in the face of war spelled treason. In a time of external danger, the presence of internal enemies could not be tolerated.[72]

Taking their cue from a government-orchestrated propaganda campaign, public opinion makers, in concert, added disloyalty to the charges against the IWW. They accused Wobblies of accepting German gold, poisoning foodstuffs, spreading hoof-and-mouth disease, breaking factory machinery, flooding mines, and burning wheat fields. Newspapers and magazines throughout the United States demanded quick and decisive government action to curb "Imperial Wilhelm's Warriors." The *Independent* announced, "It is time for the American public to take them in hand, put them behind bars and break their organization."[73] "Why wait," asked the *Wall Street Journal*, "until grain or elevators be burned, . . . factories dismantled, or even these utilities temporarily held up? The nation is at war, and treason must be met with preventive as well as punitive measures. . . . The price of delay must be paid on the field of France."[74] The Tulsa *Daily World* favored direct action: "If the IWW . . . gets busy in your neighborhood, kindly take the occasion to increase your supply of hemp."[75]

Thus, the war crisis energized the Wobbly issue and solidified opposition forces. With the support of corporate leaders, journalists, and other opinion makers, the federal government confronted the IWW. The Department of Justice initiated nationwide raids of IWW centers in September 1917. Operating under the recently passed Espionage Act, which promised imprisonment of up to twenty years for those interfering with the war effort, agents seized Wobbly records, ledgers, and even spittoons. The Justice Department later indicted Wobblies for entering into a conspiracy to disrupt the war effort through sabotage and antidraft agitation. Against the great majority the only evidence of treason was membership in the Industrial Workers of the World. In Chicago, 101 Wobbly leaders, including Bill Haywood and Vincent St. John, were charged with over 17,500 offenses and tried. The jury deliberated for fifty-five minutes before returning guilty verdicts that sent thirty-five Wobblies to Leavenworth Penitentiary for five years, thirty-three for ten years, and fifteen for twenty years. Trials in Sacramento, California, and Wichita, Kansas, resulted in an additional seventy-three convictions. By the end of 1919, the IWW had been decapitated. Leaders were either in jail, about to be tried, free on bail, or fugitive. The IWW, wrote Bill Haywood, had been shaken "as the bull dog shakes an empty sack."[76] In all, over two thousand Wobblies, Socialists, and pacifists became trapped in the World War I witch-hunt that transformed dissent into subversion.[77]

Action at the community level supplemented legal sanctions. Army troops and vigilante groups raided IWW halls, detaining and deporting Wobblies in Idaho, Oregon, Montana, and Washington. In the lumber camps, federal officials combated IWW disruption by organizing a government labor union. With government-sponsored proposals of an eight-hour day and a minimum wage, the Loyal Legion of Loggers and Lumbermen broke the IWW. Near Tulsa, Oklahoma, the Knights of Liberty whipped, tarred, and feathered seventeen Wobblies. In Butte, Montana, vigilantes lynched IWW organizer Frank Little. Wobblies were beaten, kidnapped, and deported from towns in New Mexico, South Dakota, Michigan, Nebraska, and Minnesota. In Arizona, during the summer of 1917, ten communities witnessed systematic deportations of IWW members. The largest of these actions occurred in the copper town of Bisbee. In coordination with the sheriff's office, El Paso and Southwestern Railroad, and local vigilantes, the Phelps-Dodge corporation defeated an alleged "pro-German" strike for higher wages and better safety conditions by deporting "every suspicious looking individual" to New Mexico.[78] Of the 1,186 people forced from their homes, 426 were Wobblies, 520 owned property in Bisbee, 472 had registered for the draft, and sixty-two were veterans.[79]

The pressure did not ease during the Red Scare that followed World War I. On the first Memorial Day after the war, four members of the newly formed American Legion lost their lives in an attack on the IWW hall in Centralia, Washington. In revenge, a mob castrated and lynched war veteran and Wobbly Wesley Everest. Eight other Wobblies were sentenced to the penitentiary for terms of twenty-five to fifty years. Wobbly strikes in the California citrus fields were broken with arrests and deportations. By the end of 1919, sixty Wobblies were awaiting trial under that state's criminal syndicalism statutes. By 1922, nineteen states had outlawed membership in the Industrial Workers of the World.[80]

During the war, opponents had completed the process of staining the IWW as illegitimate and intolerable. Marked as deviant, the movement fell victim to a concerted offensive waged by government and polity members. Reeling under the blows, the IWW could no longer claim the right to challenge, let alone exert influence, even on a limited scale. Its most experienced and dynamic leaders were jailed. Others were on the run mentally and physically, impotent under the barrage. The terror consumed more than the leadership. Rank-and-file Wobblies were hunted down, beaten, discarded, and dispersed. IWW records and membership lists were in the hands of federal prosecutors, and Wobbly literature and newspapers were banned from the mails. Never strong internally, resources were exhausted in the safeguarding of the accused and the support of their families. Lost ground could not be reclaimed as revenues from dues and union-chartering fees declined. The IWW had become less a labor union or revolutionary movement than "a committee for the defense" of the persecuted.[81]

"Now the final battle rages"   As the IWW weakened, dissension gnawed from within. Critics condemned Wobbly prisoners who accepted commutation of their sentences as traitors to the cause. Fear of spies and agent provocateurs also heightened instability. The leadership's inexperience and continuing repression prevented the organization from regaining its balance and reopening the strike front. Meanwhile, centralizers and decentralizers revived their feud and struggled for control. In 1924 they divided the remains of the movement.[82]

Also clouding the movement's future was the rise of a new challenging group. In October 1917 the Bolsheviks under Nicolai Lenin and Leon Trotsky had effected the world's first "people's democracy" in Russia. The Red dawn had appeared in the East and beckoned to workers to throw off their chains and unite. In January 1920 the Communist International formally invited the IWW to come under its banner of world revolution and fight for the overthrow of capitalism. Many prepared to abandon the IWW for the new radical wave. Bill Haywood welcomed the Russian Revolution as "the greatest event in our lives."[83] "Here is what we have been dreaming about; here is the I.W.W. all feathered out."[84] For Wobbly Harold Varney, "Bolshevism was but the Russian name for IWW."[85] The Communist party promised success through a disciplined movement combining political activity with direct action. Haywood joined the party in 1921 and fled the United States for the Soviet Union. In all, between 10 and 20 percent of the IWW membership entered the party, including Elizabeth Gurley Flynn, Len DeCaux, William Foster, and Earl Browder. Most Wobblies, in dismissing the Communist party, scorned its members as politicians and cited their opposition to armed insurrection and the seizure of power by force. They also denounced the foreign control of the movement, its stress on bureaucracy, and an authoritarianism that subjugated individualism to the party line. Its rejection of the Communist party, America's most powerful left-wing challenger for the next forty years, would further isolate the IWW from the radical mainstream.[86]

IWW losses were especially dramatic after 1924. From 35,000 members in 1923, rolls dropped to 7,350 in 1926 and 2,310 in 1930. In 1932, the movement claimed 1,450 members in thirty-two locals and a treasury fund of twenty-nine dollars. Those who continued to carry a red card were "flat-broke members of a flat-broke union."[87]

Since the 1930s the IWW has been more a memory than a movement. The Congress of Industrial Organizations assumed the task of unionizing the semiskilled and unskilled workers during and after the Depression. Working within the capitalist system and with government support, the CIO succeeded in establishing permanent and powerful unions. During the second Red Scare, in the 1940s and 1950s, the federal government placed the IWW on its list of subversive organizations and prohibited it from acting as a collective bargaining agent. By 1961, the movement counted 115 dues-paying members, nearly all elderly and retired. While the left-wing movements of the 1960s passed the IWW by, an infusion of radical students and workers not only kept the organization alive but allowed it to grow. In the late 1980s the IWW claimed one thousand members in twenty states and three foreign countries. Wobblies have recently added environmental concerns and antinuclear protest to their program, yet the One Big Union and direct action to end the wage system remain the reasons for its existence. Publishing books, selling tracts, and continuing to organize, they are a cadre-in-waiting prepared to fan the sparks of working-class dissent.[88]

"STILL AIN'T SATISFIED"

The Industrial Workers of the World proclaimed a vision of a better world. To alleviate the misery of laboring men and women, it proposed a redistribution of American wealth and power. Change would come at the point of production when workers realized their collective identity and power. In the Commonwealth of Toil, the bosses would be banished, suffering dispelled, and the public good triumphant. But calls for the complete transformation of America's social, economic, and political structure faced determined opposition. Polity members, aware that defeat meant displacement, mobilized to confront Wobbly activists and confine their advance. Local, state, and federal authorities vigorously sustained their constituents in protecting the status quo from disruption.

The radical nature of the IWW's goals, its rejection of political reform, and its rhetoric of violence narrowed the movement's appeal and its bases of outside support. The great majority of middle- and working-class Americans accepted the verdict of opinion makers and perceived the IWW in a negative light. Even those who joined the movement viewed their membership as a means to a more comfortable place in American society rather than revolution. Organizational weaknesses confirmed their judgment. With few resources and tuned to direction from the bottom up, activists had difficulty coordinating activities and exerting influence on a national level. Opportunism, not careful planning and astute management, guided the movement's course. In addition, the IWW was unable to safeguard members from retaliation by employers. Nor could it develop within the rank and file a unifying sense of class consciousness that would place incremental gains in the context of a coming revolution. Thus, a constant turnover of members plagued the IWW in the face of opposition from employers, the hostility of the community, poorly maintained unions, occupational and property mobility, and reforms that humanized capitalism. The risks of membership were too great, improvements too real, and the future too distant and vague to fix loyalty. When hostility to the IWW became a measure of allegiance to country, no gains, even if small and briefly held, could be tolerated. In defeat, the movement could not maintain its grip on the radical mantle. Thus, the IWW flare was extinguished, its light dimmed by repression and invisible from the mainstream.

4

INVISIBLE EMPIRE:
THE KNIGHTS OF THE
KU KLUX KLAN

Our organization is more than a secret order; it is a movement; in a sense, it is a Crusade.

PAUL S. ETHERIDGE
IMPERIAL KLONSEL, KKK

Well, this might not be as funny as it looks. There is something big starting in this country, and we've just joined it.

DENVER KLANSMAN

When most Americans hear the words Ku Klux Klan* their minds conjure up an image of southern rednecks sadistically terrorizing blacks. The hooded and robed night riders of the Klan are perceived as fanatical, violent, and dedicated to the preservation of white supremacy. This image stems from the Klan movements that have received the greatest publicity or are of the most recent origin. The first Klan arose in the South during the Reconstruction Period following the Civil War. In response to the emancipation of slaves and

---

*In 1866, the first Klansmen manipulated the Greek word for circle—*kuklos*—to derive Ku Klux. Ku Klux Klan was their final alliterative creation. Alliteration also explains Klan terms like Kludd, Klaliff, and Klexter.

Republican party rule, Klansmen threatened, flogged, and killed those who sought racial equality and a more just distribution of wealth and power. The third Klan resistance appeared in the South after World War II and grew in reaction to black assaults upon the racial status quo. In the 1970s a fourth Klan movement emerged from a southern base to penetrate the North and West in alliance with other racist groups.

Interest in these Klans has hidden from view the second Klan, the Invisible Empire of the 1920s, which was the most powerful social movement of the decade and probably the most significant challenger from the American right wing. Unlike its predecessor of the Reconstruction Era or its descendant of today, this Klan was not primarily southern, white supremacist, or terrorist. Preaching a multifaceted program based upon "100 Per Cent Americanism" and militant Protestantism, the Invisible Empire of the Knights of the Ku Klux Klan enlisted recruits in every section of the nation. Perhaps as many as six million Americans had by 1925 heeded its call to resist Catholics, Jews, lawbreakers, blacks, and immigrants.

The notoriety of the Ku Klux Klan should not deflect attention from its identity as a social movement. Klansmen and women, like other movement activists, seized opportunities to give meaning to their program, shaped perceptions, and offered a vehicle to those who sought change. In constant interaction with authorities, opinion makers, polity members, and other contenders, they mobilized people, money, and votes to gain advantages and entrance into the inner circle. Condemning the Klan's challenge as deviant inhibits an understanding of its rise to power and provides false comfort to its enemies.

THE KLUXING OF AMERICA

The second Klan's beginnings were humble. On Thanksgiving night in 1915 William Joseph Simmons, a former Methodist circuit rider, history instructor, and fraternal organizer, persuaded fifteen men to follow him to the summit of Stone Mountain in Georgia. There they knelt before an American flag and a burning cross and dedicated themselves to the revival of the Invisible Empire of the Knights of the Ku Klux Klan. Simmons traced his inspiration to a vision he experienced upon his return from the Spanish-American War. One summer evening he stood transfixed as the clouds in the sky were molded into charging white-robed horsemen. When the images faded, Simmons fell to his knees and promised to convert this divine sign into reality.[1]

The resurrected Ku Klux Klan was not an immediate success; by 1920 the Invisible Empire consisted of only four or five thousand knights in scattered Klans throughout Georgia and Alabama. To revitalize his dream, Simmons enlisted the aid of two shrewd promoters, Edward Clarke and Elizabeth Tyler of the Atlanta-based Southern Publicity Association. On 7 June, 1920 they signed a contract stipulating that the association, henceforth the Propagation Department of the Invisible Empire, would promote and enlarge the Klan in exchange for eight dollars of every ten-dollar membership fee, or klectoken. Clarke and Tyler hired an initial sales force of more than two hundred *kleagles*, or recruiters, and directed them to exploit any issue or prejudice that would lure men to the movement. Since the kleagles worked on a commission basis, they sought to attract as many new members as they possibly could. The sharp rise in the secret order's membership reflected their success, for between June 1920 and October 1921, eighty-five thousand men joined the Klan. Simmons later said of Clarke: "He put an army of 1,100 paid organizers in the field; hundreds of smart men working for him. They made things hum all over America."[2]

Three events enhanced the kleagles' industriousness. In 1915 the motion picture *Birth of a Nation* opened in theaters across America. Pioneering a variety of filmmaking techniques the nearly three-hour extravaganza, with a cast of thousands, revolutionized the infant movie industry. Millions eagerly paid the two-dollar admission price, more than ten times the customary fee, to see depicted, in broad expanse, the history of America. The film climaxed with the rise of the Reconstruction Klan and its salvation of the South from black rule. It was the first film to be shown in the White House, and President Woodrow Wilson declared that it was "like writing history with lightning."[3] Klan organizers basked in the glow of adulation and used the movie to launch recruiting drives.[4]

The Klan gained, too, when the New York *World* published in September 1921 a series of articles about its activities. Syndicated over a three-week period in twenty newspapers around the United States, the exposé focused upon Klan secrecy and violence. If the editors of the *World* had hoped to smother the Klan movement, their series had the opposite effect. The articles served to introduce the Klan to curious Americans and to facilitate recruitment. Many in the hinterland, hostile to anything with a New York City imprint, even clipped facsimile membership application forms appearing in the exposé and sent them to Atlanta for processing.[5]

A congressional investigation of the Ku Klux Klan in the wake of the New York *World* series also generated increased momentum. Imperial Wizard Simmons ably defended the Klan, representing his movement as nonviolent, fraternal, and patriotic. The Klan emerged from the glare with the apparent endorsement of congressional leaders and national opinion makers. According to Simmons, "It wasn't until the newspapers began to attack the Klan that it really grew. Certain newspapers also aided us by inducing Congress to investigate. . . . The result was that Congress gave us the best advertising we ever got. Congress made us."[6]

Selling the Klan   Kleagles lectured Americans about all aspects of the Klan creed. They portrayed the Klan as a patriotic organization dedicated to the preservation of the nation's institutions and ideals. The white-robed "guardians of liberty" stood for fair elections, honest leaders, efficient government; they were against unresponsive and corrupt politicians. Disclaiming partisanship, the Klan infiltrated both major political parties and elected hundreds of candidates pledged to its version of "100 Per Cent Americanism." For those demanding political reform, the Klan provided a convenient vehicle for mobilization.

Clothed in the symbols of Protestantism, the Klan posed as the savior of the "old time religion" and promised to unite Protestants in a crusade that would combat the teachings of evolution and restore faith in God, the Bible, and the Christian fundamentals. Vigorous recruitment of ministers and generous donations to Protestant churches enhanced the organization's aura of religiosity.

Law and order was another Klan rallying cry. In the immediate postwar years, a sharp upsurge in crime jolted Americans. "Murder, theft, robbery, and hold-ups," declared Texas Governor Pat Morris Neff, "are hourly occurrences that fill the daily press. The spirit of lawlessness has become alarming. Our loose method of dealing with violators of the law is in a large degree responsible for the conditions that today confront us."[7] Although crimes of all types increased, most attention was focused upon the breakdown of the prohibition laws. Moonshiners and bootleggers infested the nation, pursuing their trade with impunity as local authorities seemed unwilling or unable to stamp them out. Men and women in cities, suburbs, and towns, frustrated by inadequate law enforcement, demanded action. Speaking for many of its readers, the Tulsa *Tribune* declared in 1920: "Lawlessness in Tulsa MUST STOP. If you have not enough police Mr. Mayor make a loud noise that sounds like HELP and demand that the citizens give you help."[8] Four years later, the *Denver Post* echoed the *Tribune*: "When the law is not enforced, when it is disregarded spurned and trampled upon . . . when its lack of enforcement and its delay fail to protect the citizen and taxpayer, he has but one immediate recourse, and that is to enforce the laws himself. . . . The zero point is just about reached in this community."[9]

The Klan also saw the traditional code of morality under attack. Challenges to the moral status quo had appeared before World War I and rapidly multiplied in the 1920s. Evidence of moral laxity was everywhere; new styles of clothing, "suggestive" dances, and "titillating" motion pictures were symbols of the decay sapping America's strength. Klansmen vowed not only to banish loose women, roadhouses, and "joyriding neckers and petters" but to restore decency and decorum to their communities.

The Klan's message of Americanism and law enforcement was not aimed at all Americans; only white, native-born Protestant males, eighteen years or older, were accepted for membership. Later, Klansmen encouraged their wives, mothers, and sisters to form an auxiliary. Foreign-born Protestants were allowed to enroll in the Klan-sponsored Royal Riders of the Red Robe and the American Crusaders. Klansmen even organized their children. Completely excluded from "100 Per Cent Americanism" and depicted as threats to the nation's ideals and values were Catholics, Jews, immigrants, and blacks.

Catholics, constituting 36 percent of the nation's population in 1920, bore the brunt of Klan hatred. Preying upon long-time suspicions and prejudices, the Klan excoriated Catholics for their devotion to a false church and "pagan" worship. More important, kleagles accused Catholics of placing their allegiance to the pope above their loyalty to the United States. They maintained that the pope, ever ready to expand his power, had long coveted Protestant America. With Catholic votes he would elect men to do his bidding. Once the Catholic hierarchy had gained control of the government, it would end the separation of church and state, ban the Bible, and destroy the freedoms of press, speech, and religion. Klan leaders warned Protestants that this conspiracy was in reach of victory, for 85 percent of federal government employees, 60 percent of elected and appointed office holders, and the entire secret service were Catholic. The time for talk had passed. The Klan was the spearhead of the Protestant offensive against this conspiracy.

Anti-Semitism also drew recruits. In the Klan litany the Jews were "Jonah[s] on the Ship of State," incapable of assimilation because of their conceited religious and social exclusiveness. Scornful of American traditions, the Jews planned to undermine Protestant hegemony. Well-organized "Hebrew syndicates," kleagles told listeners, forced Protestants from positions of economic power. The motion picture industry, an early victim of the Jews, produced debauching films, commercialized the Sabbath, and lured Protestants from their churches. Further, the Klan accused Jews of leading the movement to brand the Bible a sectarian book and exclude it from the public schools. Some kleagles even charged that Jewish financiers were aiding the pope in his scheme to disinherit Protestant Americans.

Immigrants presented another challenge to pure Americanism, a Trojan horse filled with inferior and disloyal men and women. The Klan maintained that the newcomers from southern and eastern Europe cared little for justice and liberty; they wanted only to siphon America's wealth and return to lives of ease in their homelands. Clustered in urban foreign quarters, immune to the forces of Americanization, the immigrants were accused of perpetuating their alien lifestyles and retaining allegiance to the Old World. Underlying much of the Klan's animosity were the religious affiliations of the immigrants. Because they were predominantly Catholics and Jews, immigrants were merely pawns in the anti-Protestant conspiracy.

White supremacy had always been a tenet in the Klan's creed. In the wake of black migration to the North, kleagles exploited white fears of a "new Negro" emerging from World War I demanding political, economic, and social equality. They even spread rumors that black leaders advocated intermarriage with whites. Citing the Bible and "scientific evidence" of black mental inferiority inherited from "savage ancestors, of jungle environment," Klansmen stood ready to battle for the purity of the white race. "WE MUST KEEP THIS A WHITE MAN'S COUNTRY," proclaimed a Klan recruiting ad. "Every effort to wrest from the White Man the control of this country must be resisted. No person of the White Race can submit . . . without shame."

Klansmen, lamented Dr. John Galen Locke, the Grand Dragon of the Colorado Ku Klux Klan, were "now outlaws in the land of their forefathers, forced to conceal their activities and identity with a mask of secrecy." Their birthright was imperiled by the Jew, "his eye . . . on the prosperity, wealth and resources of America"; the Roman Catholic, who would "have us bow down our heads in worship to his foreign pope"; and the Negro, "the untaught would fain be teacher." "Should they gain sway," he continued, "no more would America be a land of liberty, justice and equality, a land of resources and opportunity, the land of virgin hope, the land of the ideals and aspirations of our forefathers. All this would these people sacrifice on the altar of self." Called to defend God, country, race, community, and family, white Protestant Americans donned the hood and robe and pledged their allegiance to the Invisible Empire of the Knights of the Ku Klux Klan.

During the first half of the 1920s, the Klan made dramatic gains. In Texas, the Invisible Empire's first self-governing realm, 200,000 men joined, and a Klansman was elected to the United States Senate. Oregon furnished the cause with 50,000 of its citizens, and Klan-endorsed candidates won the governor's chair and a Senate seat. In neighboring Washington state, forty-two klaverns housed 35,000 to 40,000 Klansmen. The Klan enrolled 50,000 Protestants in California and helped capture the statehouse for its approved candidate. The Midwest proved quite fertile to Klanism. Kansas Klan leaders boasted a realm population of 100,000. Kleagles organized twenty local chapters for Chicago's 50,000 Klansmen, while 35,000 wore the hood and robe in Detroit. The Klan citadel of Indiana sheltered 240,000 knights who succeeded in electing two governors and two U.S. senators. In neighboring Ohio 400,000 men paid their klectokens for the privilege of entering the Invisible Empire. New York added 200,000 more Klansmen, and Pennsylvania 225,000. The Klan found receptive Protestants even in New England: Connecticut provided 20,000 men, and Maine 15,000.[10]

Imperial rule, klavern power   According to its constitution, the Ku Klux Klan of the 1920s was a centralized and bureaucratic organization. Power resided in the Atlanta, Georgia, headquarters and emanated from the Imperial Wizard and his advisors. These included, all with an Imperial prefix: the Klaliff (vice-president), Kludd (chaplain), Kligrapp (secretary), and Klabee (treasurer), among others. (Such offices were duplicated on both the state and local levels.) The Imperial Palace planned national policy, chartered state chapters and local units or klaverns, and held a veto over all activities of lesser Klan organizations. The Grand Dragon, appointed by the Imperial Wizard, commanded the state body or realm. He, in turn, named Grand Titans to supervise the affairs of provinces or groups of counties. At the local level, the Exalted Cyclops and his assistants directed the affairs of the klavern.[11]

Centralization and bureaucratization did not insulate the Klan from dissension. Edward Clarke and Elizabeth Tyler came under fire in 1922 when critics accused them of sexual immorality and financial misconduct. Tyler relinquished her Klan ties, but Clarke, with Imperial Wizard Simmons's support, clung to power. Simmons's refusal to confront charges of his friend's corruption made him, in turn, vulnerable. So, too, did the Imperial Wizard's administrative incompetence and drinking problem. In November, David Stephenson, H.C. McCall, and James Comer, the Grand Dragons of Indiana, Texas, and Arkansas, respectively, engineered an Imperial Palace coup. They convinced a gullible Simmons to resign temporarily as Imperial Wizard for the good of the movement and accept the ceremonial post of Emperor. Hiram Wesley Evans, a former dentist, Exalted Cyclops of the Dallas klavern, and Grand Titan of Texas Province No. 2, was elected Imperial Wizard, a post he would hold for seventeen years. Evans quickly consolidated his power. Taking advantage of Clarke's indictment for violation two years before of the Volstead and Mann acts, Evans cancelled the Southern Publicity Association's contract with the Klan in March 1923. Simmons eventually awakened to the situation and turned to the courts for relief, initiating a two-year legal battle. The resulting out-of-court settlement placated Simmons financially and severed his relationship with the Invisible Empire. Although some klaverns in Georgia splintered as a result of the infighting, and newspapers highlighted the Klan scandal, Evans retained the confidence of his legions.[12]

Its constitutional mandates for strict control and coordination also belied the reality of life in the Invisible Empire. Imperial officers were well aware that diversity within the Klan world and inadequate communications defied national dictation on issues and activities. Members accepted the advice of Imperial Wizard Evans, who insisted, "You cannot put into effect any set program for there are different needs in the various localities. Your program must embrace the needs of the people it must serve." Moreover, conflict within the Imperial Palace, distance, underdeveloped coordinating channels, and the rise of Grand Dragons with strong personalities and their own power bases made realm affairs relatively immune from national meddling. As a Klansman from Grand Junction, Colorado, recalls: "We knew that the Klan came out of Georgia, but we never thought of them being at the head of it. We knew that they probably got a dollar out of our ten dollars to join . . . and we knew our bed sheets came from there. As far as we were concerned Denver was the head of it." Only in time of crisis, and with sufficient support from within the state organization, would imperial intervention be tolerated. For similar reasons, local leaders, while amenable to realm direction, had great autonomy to develop their klaverns and programs with a minimum of interference.

Local control did not mean democratic decision making. The central organization bestowed authority on klavern leaders, who exercised power according to Klan principles and procedures. All Klansman, on entering the Invisible Empire, knelt before an altar and a burning cross and publicly swore an oath to "faithfully obey our constitution and laws, and conform willingly to all our usages and regulations."13 "Mortal men," proclaimed a Klan officer, "cannot assume a more binding oath. . . . Always remember that to keep this oath means to you honor, happiness, and life, but to violate it means disgrace, dishonor, and death." In small communities or in those with strong Klans, banishment from the Invisible Empire was an effective sanction against disobedience.

Because Klan realms were autonomous and communities were isolated from each other, the Invisible Empire is best analyzed through case studies. To explore in detail the meaning of the KKK for the participants of the drama, for those who joined or were affected by its actions, it is essential to descend to the local community. Local leaders and needs shaped an already flexible program to fit a particular time and place. In the community, then, may be discerned the stances of authorities and opinion makers and the reasons for Klan success or failure.

An investigation of the Denver klavern of the Colorado realm offers an excellent opportunity to probe fully the hooded society on both the community and state levels. The Klan arrived in Colorado in 1921 and in less than three years converted the state into one of the Invisible Empire's strongest bastions. The Colorado realm and the Denver Klan were entwined, for the secret society drew its leadership from and headquartered in the city. Moreover, Denver accounted for nearly half of the state's thirty-five thousand Ku Klux Klansmen. No other city in the Rocky Mountain West compared in membership or clout. Only in Indiana did the Klan's political influence rival that attained in the Centennial State. From Denver and Colorado emerges a history that counters commonly held generalizations and stereotypes and mirrors the Klan experience across the United States.

DENVER: QUEEN CITY OF THE COLORADO REALM

During the 1920s Denver was the financial and commercial center of the Rocky Mountain West, unchallenged in a wide trade area extending for hundreds of miles in all directions. Denver was also Colorado's capital and largest city, inhabited by slightly more than one-fourth of the state's total population. The city's 256,000 residents were predominantly white and Protestant. Only 6,175 blacks, 37,748 Catholics, and 17,000 Jews made their homes in the community. Aside from a few immigrant neighborhoods, the city was ethnically and culturally homogeneous.

In the spring of 1921, Imperial Wizard Simmons, at the behest of a fellow member of the Masonic Lodge, came to Denver to organize a klavern. With the fervor of a revivalist, Simmons extolled the virtues and principles of his new secret society to a select group of prominent Denverites. The men were persuaded to join, and Simmons promptly initiated them. From this base, the Ku Klux Klan would penetrate every county in the state.

The leader of the Denver organization was John Galen Locke, a local physician. Born in New York City in 1873, he came to Denver twenty years later to complete his medical education. In appearance, Locke was hardly awesome or inspiring. He was a short man, weighing 250 pounds, who wore a Vandyke beard and carefully trimmed moustache. Yet despite his unprepossessing exterior, Locke was a charismatic leader. His genius for organization and eloquence, along with his ability to inspire fanatical loyalty, made him one of the most important factors in the growth of the Colorado Klan. Under his astute direction as Exalted Cyclops and later Grand Dragon, the Klan came to dominate not only Denver but the state.

Denver's inspired Klan initiates wasted no time in spreading the message to friends and relatives. They used their church, lodge, business, and professional connections to secretly gather those native-born, white, Protestant males ripe for the cause. Particularly fertile ground was tilled in such fraternal orders as the Masons and Knight Templars. Thirty churches in Denver, almost 20 percent of the Protestant total, would eventually support Klan efforts. One-third of the Methodist, one-fourth of the Baptist, and five of seven Disciples of Christ churches had Klan links. These inroads not only enhanced the Klan's respectability but augmented its resource base. The organization also worked hard in other ways to build a favorable public image. The Klan proclaimed itself ready to defend law and order and promised to place members at the disposal of the police department in the fight against crime. In addition, the hooded order made donations to local charities, aided widows and orphans, and contributed to church coffers.

Anti-Klan sentiment surfaced. In 1921, Denver's mayor condemned the Klan as a threat to lawful government and ordered an investigation. The city tax collector launched a probe into the local Klan's alleged failure to pay federal taxes. A 1922 grand jury report on Klan activities returned no indictments but recommended continued scrutiny. Meanwhile, the district attorney ordered five of his men to infiltrate the secret society and spy on its activities. Leaders of the Catholic and Jewish communities and Denver liberals joined those who hammered the Klan as a menace to the liberties of all Americans.

This resistance only temporarily slowed the Klan's momentum. After an early demonstration of opposition, Denverites acquiesced to the Klan's presence. The mayor's determination to fight the Klan turned out to be a political ploy to deflect attention from an administration linked to organized crime. When the district attorney confined his anti-Klan efforts to filing weekly spy reports, he removed the government as an effective obstacle to the Klan's ambitions. The city's major newspapers kept silent about the Klan issue or swiped at Klansmen not so much because they were members of the secret order but because they were political opponents.

During the Klan's formative years, Denver's inability to generate a determined counterforce of attitudes, government or polity-member action, or an opposition organization, facilitated the movement's expansion. City officials underestimated their adversary and failed to pursue a policy of continuous harassment and confrontation. Opinion makers—Protestant ministers, editors, and other leading community figures—emitted ambiguous signals; most were unable or perhaps unwilling to define the Klan as illegitimate. Rather than intimidating and exhausting the Klan, their silence created the atmosphere that allowed the secret society to gather resources with only minor interference. The Klan easily defended itself against a confused and sporadic opposition composed mainly of minority group members. It is not surprising, then, that within a year after its creation the Denver Klan boasted two thousand members.

The Klan program   The Klan's most effective draw was its pledge to clean up Denver and rid the city of its criminal element. Police statistics revealed a significant rise in the crime rate during the early 1920s. Prohibition law violators accounted for much of the increase. Liquor was cheap and easily obtainable, and police raids failed to dam the city's supply. Prostitution also flourished in the city. Although Denver police had officially closed the red-light district, lax regulation after World War I had enabled sixty brothels to reopen and scores of prostitutes to work the streets. Denver's drug problem was less publicized, but equally alarming. To stimulate business, organizers of the drug traffic were reported to be visiting high schools and distributing free samples. In addition to bootlegging, prostitution, and narcotics, the city reeled under frequent and intense epidemics of burglaries, holdups, and sometimes murders. Unsolved crimes proliferated and further compromised police who already were indicted for inefficiency and corruption. Distrustful of their police force and impatient with the court system, many Denverites turned to the Klan as the only organization capable of driving crime and vice from the city.

The Klan also raised the Catholic specter to garner members, pointing to local manifestations of the papal conspiracy. In 1921 a Colorado chapter of the National Council of Catholic Men was organized in Denver. Its vague objective was to unite Catholic men all over the United States for "general welfare work." In 1921 Catholics also established the Colorado Apostolate to attract converts and to aid Protestant ministers in their "leap toward the light." Klansmen even spread rumors of a Knights of Columbus plot to arm the city's Catholics. For those alert to Catholic activities, the news was ominous. Denver needed the Klan, said one early joiner, because, "the Catholics and the Jews were taking over and we had to do something. So we went down to the Masonic Lodge and organized." The long-dreaded Catholic revolution, given credence by local, tangible evidence and Klan speakers, had begun. Protestant rule was being challenged. Denver and Colorado had to be defeated.

The kleagles did not create Denver's anti-Semitism; they merely exploited it. Denver's Jews, many of them recent immigrants, were primarily concentrated in an area derisively referred to as "Jew Town." Culturally, ethnically, and religiously distinct, this community generated distrust and disgust among many Protestants. The inhabitants of the section, contended a Klansman, were "cagey and aggressive, with Jew-stuff oozing out of every pore." Denverites were suspicious for reasons other than the community's alien nature. The public linked the Jews to bootlegging and illicit gambling operations.

The Italians of North Denver also incited Klan hostility. Little Italy was an enclave of Old World culture where Italian was spoken as often as English. The Klan's indictment, however, went beyond ethnicity and religion; the colony was tagged as the source of Denver's supply of bootleg whiskey and wine and the center of the city's drug traffic. The Italians, like the Jews, concentrated in a small but highly visible ethnic pocket, were an obvious fulcrum upon which to raise the Klan.

The number of blacks in Denver was small, but this community was in rebellion against its second-class status. In the 1920s, blacks attempted to integrate downtown movie theaters, school social events, and municipal recreational activities. Meanwhile, blacks were escaping their ghetto and buying homes in white neighborhoods. They received a hostile reception. Whites reacted with mob violence, bombings, and covenants prohibiting the sale of homes to blacks. Thus, black efforts to achieve equality posed an immediate threat to white control. It is not difficult to understand why some

Denverites looked to the Ku Klux Klan to preserve neighborhood purity and restrain contentious blacks.

The Klan appeal involved more than its issue-oriented campaign. The Invisible Empire offered an exotic fraternal life featuring ghostly costumes and eerie burning crosses. Regular lodge nights were supplemented with parades, outings, concerts, and picnics. Somewhat akin to the lodge men were those seeking fun, adventure, and a share of the secret. Membership became for a time faddish: "everybody wanted in the Ku Klux Klan because it was the thing to do." As the Klan grew, it also wielded an economic club that convinced businessmen and their employees to join or risk reprisals.

Thus, the multifaceted image and platform of the Ku Klux Klan offered something for every white Protestant. The result was a loose coalition of diffuse, unorganized camps distinguished by their particular needs and fears. Distinct groups are discernible although the pattern is blurred, for few took out membership on the basis of a single feature of the Klan program. Aside from the opportunists, the coerced, and the faddists whose influence was minimal, several salient groupings can be identified. The Klan contained a small hard core of true believers eager to save the community from marauding Catholics, Jews, and blacks. An allied bloc, less steeped in the rhetoric of prejudice, reacted to immediate threats to their homes and neighborhoods. The lodge men found the mysteries of Klan ritual more satisfying than baiting minorities. Yet none of these groups, alone or combined, was sufficient to propel the movement to power. Success came only when the Klan merged their grievances with demands to restore law and order to Denver. Many of those concerned about the spreading lawlessness were not particularly bigoted. They tolerated the rabid passions of fellow Klansmen primarily because of the white Protestant heritage of distrust and the minority connection to crime. The Denver Klan's emphasis on law and order reflected its drawing strength and the needs of its membership. Klan leaders representing the different interests guaranteed, however, that no issue was neglected.

The Denver environment proved congenial to the Klan's mobilization success. City government could not solve a stressful crime problem or suppress what appeared to be a coordinated minority uprising against Protestantism. Denverites who believed that local authorities had abandoned them could look to the Ku Klux Klan alone for their salvation. They sought an outlet, too, for unfulfilled fellowship and spiritual needs. John Locke, assisted by capable and energetic lieutenants, centralized control and effected a clear chain of command capable of molding the Klan to the community. In addition, the Klan met no substantial counterattack. A man did not fear his minister's censure or his neighbor's scorn when he enlisted in the secret society. The risks were few, the rewards unlimited. With all variables tilted in the Klan's favor, it is not surprising that seventeen thousand Denver men passed through the portals of the Invisible Empire by 1925.

Still, the Klan had one other hurdle to clear on the road to power. It had to attract the support of men and women who did not feel strongly enough the need to join the Klan but were nevertheless sympathetic to its aims. Crucial to gaining the support of this population, too, was the interplay of Klan leadership and organization, local tensions, community perceptions, and the actions of government and established groups.

Reaching for influence   The Denver Klan's program and growing strength dictated political action, and the first opportunity came in the Denver mayoral election of 1923. The Klan's candidate pledged a war on crime and vice, lower taxes, and efficient government. A close friend of Exalted Cyclops Locke and an early joiner, he kept his invisible connections secret and publicly condemned the hooded order to appease Jewish and Catholic supporters. On election day, a coalition of Klan and anti-Klan forces swept him into office over an incumbent tainted with corruption.

The newly elected mayor quickly implemented many of his campaign promises. His administration stressed economy, weeded out corrupt members of the police department, and intensified anticrime efforts. Despite statements to the contrary, the Klan's mark was very much in evidence. The mayor named Klansmen to important posts in his administration. A Klansman was appointed chief of police, and the department was heavily infiltrated. The Klan was so sure of its control that it even requisitioned men and vehicles from the department. Secret influence upon the court system was readily apparent, for Kluxers served as justices of the peace and district court judges. The threat of Klan justice emanated not only from the bench but from juries drawn from Klan membership lists.

Klan control encouraged militancy. Klansmen burned crosses at will throughout the city. Businessmen advertising in anti-Klan or minority newspapers were threatened with boycotts. Routing their kavalkades past synagogues, Klan members mocked worshippers. Catholic priests and Jewish activists were subjected to physical harassment and death threats. At least two Klan opponents were kidnapped and pistol-whipped.

While such acts were reprehensible and condemnable, it is also necessary to consider them as tactics in a struggle for power. Protected from government retaliation, Klansmen were attempting to strengthen their position in the community. These incidents demonstrated to members and nonmembers alike that the Klan intended to carry out its pledges to shackle minorities. Moreover, the public distinguished such violence from other acts of lawlessness. Cross burnings, harassment, and terror to effect Protestant ends were perceived as legitimate and provoked no outcry. Finally, violence served to heighten the movement's unity and to hamper the mobilization of anti-Klansmen. Bigotry is thus only a partial answer. The quest for power plays a vital explanatory role.

The Klan's stand for law and order was well received in Pueblo, Trinidad, Walsenberg, and other southern Colorado towns. As in Denver, white Protestants blamed immigrants for the crime epidemic. In south-central Fremont County, for example, Klan leaders tailored a program that combined anti-Catholicism with a drive for civic improvement and reform. Beyond the Rocky Mountains, on the Western Slope, Klansmen in Grand Junction announced no platform of change or plan of action. Local leaders spoke to another need. The Ku Klux Klan offered Protestants an opportunity to enter an exciting fraternal lodge, to share in the secret, the fun, and the fellowship. Thus did the Klan adapt to each local environment, finding the conditions that would make its vague solutions relevant and concrete. Each Klan, attuned to its community's concerns, became a differentiated cell in a larger organism.

Outside of Colorado, community tensions and unresponsive government authorities nurtured the Klan's growth. Klansmen throughout the United States seemed to share the belief that public officials had left them defenseless or had actually betrayed them to a conspiracy of criminals, Catholics, Jews, and immigrants. Men entered the Klan in Madison, Wisconsin, because the police force appeared to have capitulated in the war against crime. The department, pockmarked by inefficiency and corruption, could offer the community no respite from bootleggers, murderers, and prostitutes. In El Dorado, Arkansas, residents accused the city government of collaborating with lawbreakers and ignoring rampant vice. Disgusted with the situation, Protestants accepted the Ku Klux Klan as the only means of cleansing their town. In the face of government lethargy, Klansmen in Chattanooga, Tennessee, compiled a list of one hundred suspected bootleggers and demanded their apprehension. All Klansmen knew the reason for the government's failure to act: Two Catholics, a Jew, and a renegade Presbyterian, who hired "papists" to teach in the public schools, sat on the Chattanooga city commission. The openly run and apparently protected "nigger whorehouse opposite the schoolhouse" prodded men to join the McKees Rock, Pennsylvania, Klan.[14] El Paso, Texas, Klansmen condemned neighboring Ciudad Juarez as a haven for drug dealers, bootleggers, thieves, murderers, and prostitutes. They were determined to seal the border and save their community from the infection of immorality and lawlessness. In Anaheim, California, Klansmen were instrumental in forcing an incompetent city official from office and later helped replace an administration branded as ineffective and fiscally irresponsible.[15]

BENEATH THE HOOD AND ROBE

Who joined the Ku Klux Klan of the 1920s? Were these Klansmen the stereotypic marginal men of American society seeking shelter from failure in a mass organization? Was the Klan a movement of a particular social and economic class? Although the Klan was a secret society and guarded its membership rosters well, a few lists have survived to allow a peek under the white mask.

A statistical investigation of the Denver Klan's seventeen thousand members offers key insights into the Invisible Empire. To reflect changing organizing methods—from selective recruitment to open enrollment—I divided the Klan roster into early and late joiners and drew random samples from each. There were few differences between these two groups in age, marital status, place of birth, and military service. The Denver Klan was a movement of mature men, not an uprising of callow, thrill-seeking young people. The overwhelming majority of members were thirty years of age or older when they entered the Invisible Empire. Teenage Klansmen represented just 1 percent of the recruits. Stability and maturity are also reflected in the fact that more than three-quarters of the men were married, and only 1 percent divorced. Most Klansmen were born on farms or in the small towns of Colorado and the Midwest. In the ranks, recently discharged veterans were noticeable by their absence. All but a fraction of the Klansmen had escaped service in any of America's wars. Missing past crusades to save American freedom and democracy, perhaps many saw the Klan as a means to compensate for lost opportunities to serve.

Despite these similarities, occupational differences between the two Klan groups were considerable (see Table 1).[16] Early joiners in high and middle nonmanual occupations accounted for over 50 percent of their group, while just 21 percent of the late joiners worked in these occupations. At the same time, 43 percent of the late joiners labored in occupations below low nonmanual, compared to a little over 16 percent of the early joiners. Only in the low nonmanual category do the groups contain similar proportions of men.

The occupational distribution of late joiners reflects a cross section of the wider Denver structure in all but the unskilled category. Conversely, high and middle nonmanual jobholders among the early joiners are heavily overrepresented relative to the Denver population. When the two groups are united, the early joiners, skewed as a result of recruiting bias, disrupt the representative nature of the later joiners. In the combined Klan membership, the high and middle nonmanual categories are overrepresented, the low nonmanual bloc equivalent, and all blue-collar divisions underrepresented. Thus, a larger proportion of men in upper occupational groups appeared in the Klan than did in the community at large. It seems that semiskilled and unskilled workers were the least likely to share the secrets of the Invisible Empire.

Fremont County's Klansmen were older than their Denver counterparts, having entered their organization at a mean age of 47.5 years. Forty-two percent of the members were 50 years of age or older, and only 9 percent of the men were between 20 and 29. Not surprisingly, 86 percent of the

TABLE 1

OCCUPATIONAL DISTRIBUTION OF SELECTED KLAVERNS

Occupation Group	Denver			Fremont County (200)	Aurora (73)	Knox County (399)	Winchester (180)
	Early (375)	Late (583)	Total (958)				
High nonmanual	15.5%	3%	7.6%	11.0%	19%	8.5%	12%
Middle nonmanual	36.0	18	25.0	39.5	30	12.0	46
Low nonmanual	20.3	24	22.6	7.0	25	15.1	9
Skilled	8.5	19	15.0	8.5	5	26.6	8
Semiskilled and service	7.5	17	13.6	8.0	14	30.0	7
Unskilled	.5	7	4.4	1.5	7	7.8	18
Retired	—	—	—	1.5	—	—	—
Unknown	11.7	12	11.8	23.0	—	—	—

SOURCES: Robert A. Goldberg, *Hooded Empire: The Ku Klux Klan in Colorado* (Urbana: University of Illinois Press, 1981), 46, 135; Kenneth T. Jackson, *The Ku Klux Klan in the City, 1915–1930* (New York: Oxford University Press, 1967), 62, 119, 120.

Klansmen were married. The majority came to Colorado from the Midwest, where they were born and lived on farms or in communities of twenty-five hundred or fewer people. Small businessmen and farmers, representing 75 percent of the middle nonmanual group, dominated the occupational structure of the rural Fremont County Klan. When combined with members holding other nonmanual occupations, they dwarf the 18 percent laboring in blue-collar jobs.

The table also summarizes the available occupational information for Klansmen in three klaverns outside of Colorado. To facilitate comparisons, data for Aurora, Illinois (1920 population 36,400), Knox County, Tennessee (113,000), and Winchester, Illinois (1,540) were re-sorted into the occupational categories used for Denver (256,000) and Fremont County (17,880). Farmers and small businessmen combined with the professional class to control numerically the smaller Fremont County, Aurora, and Winchester Klans. Similarly, Klansmen in the high and middle nonmanual status groups ruled the occupational structure of the Denver early joiner sample. Conversely, lower-middle and working-class membership in the Denver late joiner group and in the Knox County Klan stood at 67 percent and 79.5 percent respectively. When the Denver blocs are joined, one-third of the Klansmen held occupations in the high and middle range while just over 55 percent were employed in jobs below the line. In no Klan other than Winchester did the unskilled comprise more than 8 percent of the membership. On another level, every Klan but Knox County's contained a white-collar population of 45 percent or more.[17]

Simple counting substantiates the notion of the Klan as a lower-middle-class and working-class movement. Of the eighteen hundred men represented in the table, two-thirds labored in occupations below middle nonmanual. The Denver Klan, however, suggests significant qualifications. Here, the lower-status groups had an advantage because Denver's economy generated more clerical and blue-collar jobs and not because organizers made special appeals to the occupationally marginal or because workers are more likely to join a social movement. There were simply more Denverites in occupations below the middle nonmanual line than above it, and the Klan reflected this distribution. Hence, what at first glance seems to have been a movement of the lower-middle and working classes was actually a wider-based organization, a somewhat distorted mirror image of the population encompassing all but the most wealthy and the unskilled. Distortions of this pattern were probably the product of defections, recruiting bias, a socioeconomically skewed Klan leadership or opposition, and unrepresentative samples.

As Table 1 illustrates, diversity is as much the key to understanding Klan membership as it is to interpreting the Klan's appeal. Prominent men led and held together a heterogenous membership attracted from almost every stratum of the society. The Klan was not an economic movement or a mouthpiece for society's failures. The Denver Klan demonstrated that, excluding the elite and unskilled laborers, the Klan rank and file was an occupational cross section of the local community. Common generational experiences and backgrounds acted to lessen disharmony provoked by class differences. The young, the elite, and the proletariat were the only groups that could not be accommodated under the invisible panoply.

TRIUMPH AT THE POLLS

In 1924 Colorado Grand Dragon Locke outlined a plan of political organization designed to win the state's two United States Senate seats, the governorship, control of the state legislature, and scores of county offices. Reminiscent of the Anti-Saloon League's tactics, every county was assigned a Klan major who appointed a captain to each bloc of six precincts. For each precinct, captains designated a sergeant who in turn chose corporals if more than six Klansmen or Klanswomen resided in his area of responsibility. To the sergeants and corporals was handed the primary mission of corralling voters, registering them, and inducing them to vote. The organization demanded strict discipline and a regular flow of information up the chain of command. Locke later boasted that Klan methods were modeled "on those of the United States army, . . . {with} the added advantage of secrecy maintained by the uniform worn by the members. In secrecy resides the element of mystery; mystery shrouds strength and members and fear as well."

The Klan's political strategy eschewed violence and acceded to the accepted rules of acquiring power. Rather than forming a new political vehicle, Klansmen organized thoroughly at the grass-roots level and captured one of Colorado's major political parties. Absorbing new resources, continuing its intensive efforts, exerting strong discipline, and exploiting opportunities, the secret society triumphed where more conventional players had failed. The minority had begun by outmaneuvering the majority and finished by commanding it.

When the state Democratic party fielded anti-Klan candidates for governor and the Senate, the hooded order moved to infiltrate and capture the Republican party. The Klan selected as its candidate for governor a member of the Denver klavern. Vowing to "clean up the statehouse and place only Americans on guard," he entered a three-man race that saw the anti-Klan vote split between his opponents. For one of the Senate seats Locke chose another Denver Klansman. He, too, faced a divided opposition. For the second Senate seat, the Klan endorsed Colorado's incumbent senator, who was unchallenged in his bid for renomination. Given little chance of reelection because of a lackluster voting record, the senator allegedly contributed a major share of the Klan's campaign funds to obtain its endorsement.

Flooding precinct meetings and county conventions, Klan members placed their slates of candidates on the primary ballot for county offices and elected a sizable bloc of delegates to the Colorado Republican gathering. Although controlling a minority of state convention votes, the Klan commanded sufficient strength to place its candidates' names on the primary ballot. In some communities the Klan was so powerful that it could split its forces and still dominate the local organizations of both political parties.

During the campaign the Klan built momentum for its candidates with continuous rallies, parades, and political meetings. Klan politicians, meanwhile, gathered support outside the hooded ranks with promises of government efficiency, spending cuts, and stricter enforcement of the prohibition laws. Other candidates, unsure of the Klan's political clout and unwilling to take a risk, avoided the Invisible Empire issue. On primary day the Klan took advantage of the Colorado law that permitted voters to choose ballots regardless of party affiliation and concentrated its attention on the Republican contests. As the Grand Dragon reminded his followers: "We are not Democrats or Republicans but Klansmen." Bloc voting by the Klan, combined with a split in the opposition, produced a sweep for the secret society.

The Klan takeover of the Republican party fixed the course of the fall campaign. Although Colorado Democrats campaigned vigorously for farm relief and the rights of labor, they leveled their heaviest guns at the Ku Klux Klan. This assault on the Klan rallied their party and appealed to disaffected Republicans. In Denver, Colorado Springs, and Boulder, Republican newspapers turned away from the nominees of their party. However, more important than these defections were the new resources available to the Klan. Klan candidates, as the party's official representatives, laid legitimate claim to the organization's vote-getting machinery and to its respectability. The Klansmen had also obtained the Republican birthright, the allegiance of dedicated party-line voters. This tie was so firm that many men and women voted for Klan Republicans against their personal principles.

Ignoring the Invisible Government issue, the Klan's candidates benefitted from a well-financed, grass-roots organization and rode to victory on the "Keep Cool With Coolidge" wave that engulfed Democrats throughout the United States in 1924. Klan supporters were elected to both Senate seats and to the offices of governor, lieutenant governor, and attorney general, among others. Only two Democratic candidates for state office survived the Republican landslide, and both had the endorsement of the Ku Klux Klan. Returns from races for county offices and state legislative seats also cheered the knights.

As Colorado and other Klansmen mobilized on the state and county levels, imperial officers intervened in national politics. Since 1924 was a presidential election year, Democrats and Republicans had assembled during the summer to nominate candidates and write party platforms. Imperial Wizard Hiram Wesley Evans was assured of bases in both parties, for Klansmen in the North and West registered as Republicans, and those in the South registered as Democrats. Seeking to avoid schism and return Calvin Coolidge to the White House, Republicans were receptive to the lobbying efforts of the secret society and kept an anti-Klan plank out of their platform. The Democratic party, in transition as its Protestant, native-born, and prohibitionist wing battled for control with emerging Catholics, Jews, wets, and immigrants, was more volatile. Anti-Klan forces backing Governor Al Smith of New York, a Catholic and wet, demanded a resolution condemning the hooded order by name. The issue split the convention. Exerting strong influence in southern, southwestern, and midwestern delegations, the Klan was able to defeat the effort by a single vote. Although the Klan did not have sufficient strength to nominate its own choice for president, it did stall Smith's bid for nine days and 103 ballots until a compromise candidate was selected. In just four years the Klan had emerged as a significant force in American politics.[18]

A week after the November 1924 elections Imperial Wizard Evans and the Grand Dragons of Georgia, Indiana, and Kansas arrived in Denver to bask in the Klan victories. They lauded the knights for the successes of Klansmen and Klan-endorsed candidates in Senate and governorship contests in Alabama, California, Colorado, Georgia, Illinois, Indiana, Iowa, Kansas, Kentucky, Oklahoma, and Oregon. In addition, Klan support had been crucial in scores of races for House of Representatives seats, and thousands of city and county officials and state legislators were indebted to the Klan for their election. In the winter of 1924–25, the Ku Klux Klan in Colorado and the nation had reached the height of its power.[19]

The Klan's solution to community problems and unresponsive government was usually political. Klan members retained a basic faith in the prevailing system and used their movement to mobilize the discontented and reassert the influence of the Protestant majority. In electing trusted officials they would be assured that crime would be suppressed, minorities regulated, and community improvements initiated. The lash, the tar bucket, the gun, and other means of terrorism were never official Klan policy; violence was mainly perpetrated by independent bands of radicals. Only in the Southwest did Klansmen believe that conditions had deteriorated too rapidly to await election day. They had reacted systematically to government failure with direct action. However, after 1923 the Klansmen of Texas, Oklahoma, and Arkansas discarded their night-riding tactics and joined the rest of the Invisible Empire in pursuing their goals through the ballot box.

FALL OF THE INVISIBLE EMPIRE

The Colorado Klan's entrance into the polity had been swift. In the state's major population centers, the Klan organization routinely influenced its members who sat in the seats of governmental decision making. The Colorado statehouse sheltered a Klan governor eager to effect a program making "Every Man under the Capitol Dome a Klansman." The Klan's grip, however, was more tenuous than it realized, and its descent from the polity would be even more abrupt than its rapid climb. A chain reaction of events in the first half of 1925 reversed the factors that had been crucial to Klan growth. Internal dissension weakened the Klan's organizational power as program failures discredited its leaders and altered community perceptions about its value. But failure was not the only cause of decline—success, too, devastated the hooded society and drained it of resources and influence.

The Colorado Klan's first defeat was suffered in state government. To make government more responsive to the Protestant majority, the Klan governor attempted to remove "disloyal" civil servants and minority group members by abolishing all government agencies. He then proposed to recreate the same bureaucratic boards under new names, this time with Klan staffs. In the state senate an opposition formed, composed of Democrats and anti-Klan Republican holdovers elected before the emergence of the KKK, to thwart the administration's intentions. Pursuing a strategy of delay and smothering Klan bills under the weight of procedure and debate, opponents stalemated the legislative process. These setbacks in state government drained the Klan's credibility, leading members and nonmembers to reevaluate the movement's promise.

As the Klan faltered in the legislature, events brought new opportunities to curb hooded influence. John Locke's dictation of the Klan's course had alienated several of its leading members, including Denver's mayor and Colorado's recently elected junior United States senator. Chafing under Locke's commands, they used their influence to exert independence. In striking at Locke, the symbol of the Colorado Klan, they not only strengthened their own power bases but shattered the foundation upon which the Invisible Empire had been built.

In April 1925, to reassert his authority over the police force and to embarrass the Klan, Denver's mayor launched a series of vice raids. Bypassing the chief of police, a Klansman, and the hooded vice squad, the mayor deputized over one hundred private citizens to execute the operation. The raiders arrested over two hundred bootleggers, gamblers, and prostitutes and exposed a complex network of tipoffs, graft, and protection at the center of which were the men of the Klan vice squad. These revelations seriously damaged the Klan's prestige and its image as the community's protector. This was hardly the responsive government the Klan had promised discontented citizens. As authorities uncovered other scandals implicating prominent Klansmen, in and out of government service, the sheets of the Invisible Empire were further stained.

Soon after the police raids Klansmen learned that Grand Dragon Locke was under federal investigation for failure to file income tax returns for over a decade. Perhaps instigated by Colorado's Klan senator, this exertion of federal power through the Internal Revenue Service overruled the Klan's influence in state and local government. When Locke failed to cooperate with tax examiners, he was imprisoned for ten days and fined. Jail buffered Locke from the dissension that was tearing his organization apart. Upon release he attempted to rally his shaken followers, holding private conferences with leading Klansmen and calling a mass meeting of the seventeen thousand members in the Denver klavern to protest his innocence. Many Klansmen, numbed by the spectacle of their leader behind bars, remained unconvinced. According to one Klansman, Locke had betrayed their trust and "took out a good part of the money."[20]

The income tax investigation was the decisive incident the insurgents had long awaited. Meeting with Imperial Wizard Evans, Colorado's junior senator argued the case for Locke's removal. The police department scandal, the debacle in the state legislature, and now the imprisonment of the Grand Dragon had demoralized the knights and caused mass defections. Evans was receptive to these pleadings because he had for some time been suspicious of Locke's ambitions. On 30 June 1925 the Imperial Wizard asked for Locke's resignation, and he later froze all Colorado Klan assets.

Locke relinquished command but then moved to challenge the Klan for the allegiance of its members by setting in motion the Minute Men of America, a new secret society. Nearly five thousand of Denver's seventeen thousand Klansmen followed Locke into this organization. Less than 1,000 men reaffirmed their loyalty to the Invisible Empire. For the majority, the revolt provided an opportunity to sever all ties to "100 Per Cent Americanism." Many who joined the cause to save Denver from lawlessness and to restore government responsiveness felt deceived. The police scandals and the behavior of the Grand Dragon had corrupted the organization's law-and-order reputation and discredited every member. Further, as the crime issue gradually waned, men questioned their obligations to a now superfluous body. Similarly, the Catholic and Jewish conspiracies to seize Protestant rights never materialized, and blacks, after their initial challenges to the racial status quo, settled back into their prescribed positions. Thus, the question of governmental responsiveness could act in both a positive and negative manner upon the movement's fortunes. Those who perceived Klan authorities as responsible for the decline in crime and minority challenges could leave the order assured that the crisis had passed. On the other hand, it was the Klan's governmental failures that convinced many others to withdraw their allegiance. Dramatic Klan growth had created other problems. Men entering the Invisible Empire in search of fellowship and fraternity instead found meetings to be random affairs attended by hundreds and sometimes thousands of anonymous men. Interest and commitment vanished and with them money, votes, skills, and the various resource tokens necessary to influence community decision making.

By the end of 1926 the Minute Men had faded from the scene, never really having expanded beyond its Denver base. Infrequent press notices marked the final years of the Denver klavern. In 1928 two hundred Klansmen ignited a cross on the lawn of a woman convicted of child abuse. In 1933 Klansmen announced that they had infiltrated the Denver Communist party and were aware of the Red menace's every move. Having influenced neither opinion nor events for years, the Denver Klan's demise shortly thereafter went unnoticed.

Beyond Denver   The Klan's fall was precipitous throughout the United States for reasons similar to those discerned in Denver. In each community, shifts in the salience of issues, the stances of authorities, polity-member support, the Klan's leadership and organization, and its image interacted to diminish resources and force the secret society into retreat. In nearby Colorado Springs, demoralized Klansmen abandoned their movement following repeated losses in city and school board elections. The arrest of three local Klansmen in 1925 and 1926 for child molestation or statutory rape confirmed the decision. Pueblo, Colorado, Kluxers dispersed when strict law enforcement eased the crime problem and the movement could not develop new goals. Anti-Klan laws barring public meetings of masked men hamstrung Phoenix, Arizona, knights, and the threatened publication of membership lists forced retreat. Infighting among ambitious leaders generated charges and countercharges of corruption and riddled the fifteen-thousand member Portland, Oregon, klavern. Reports of Klan lawlessness and misconduct shocked the men of the Madison, Wisconsin, chapter who had sworn to uphold law and order. The behavior of Klan leaders added to their disillusionment. Especially stunning to Klansmen throughout the United States was the fall of David Stephenson, the Grand Dragon of Indiana. In the spring of 1925 police arrested him for rape and murder. Men who believed that the Klan stood for law and order, the sanctity of the home, and the defense of American womanhood left the order in disgust.[21]

By the mid-1920s the dangers that had sparked Klan mobilization had passed or had never materialized. Crime waves and minority "offensives" no longer provoked widespread concern. The National Origins Act of 1924 had set a limit of 150,000 immigrants per year and severely restricted Catholic and Jewish migration from southern and eastern Europe. With northern and western European countries allotted 85 percent of the immigration total, America's nineteenth-century ethnic composition had received official sanction. Motion pictures, radio, and the automobile, meanwhile, had distracted men from lodge activities. The hooded vehicle had outlived its usefulness or betrayed its trust. Besides, there were far more interesting topics in the "ballyhoo years" of the 1920s: Would Lindbergh arrive safely in Paris? How high would hemlines go? What was the price of a common share of American Can?

Klan leaders could not stop their organization's slide. They were unable to refocus the Klan program, and it lagged behind events. Arrogance and corruption infected Klan leaders and tarnished the organization's reputation and image. No longer could the movement count on the support or even silence of opinion makers who had smoothed its path to power. Ministers, editors, and government officials found their voices as the risks of opposition declined. Their needs either met or unsatisfied, members withdrew their loyalty and resources, and the Klan coalition crumbled.

Even as the walls of the Invisible Empire collapsed, imperial officers refused to surrender. In August 1925 they organized an impressive parade down Washington, D.C.'s Pennsylvania Avenue. In military formation, forty thousand Klansmen and women marched sixteen abreast in an impressive celebration of Klan power. A parade the following summer, however, drew only half as many participants. During the fall of 1925 Imperial Wizard Evans moved the order's offices to the nation's capital, promising to promote a "100 Per Cent American" legislative agenda. Klan leaders also hoped to stir interest in the organization by introducing new fraternal degrees and levels. But such efforts had little effect on the movement's decline. By the end of the 1920s, the Ku Klux Klan was so discredited that even the Democratic party's nomination of Al Smith for president could not spark a resurgence. The Invisible Empire vacated its offices in Washington, D.C., and returned to Atlanta in 1929. It could now count only 82,000 subjects. In the Depression decade Klan ranks continued to thin, with few responding to its anti–New Deal message. A flirtation with the pro-Nazi American Bund just before World War II backfired with the country's declaration of war against Germany. In 1944 the Internal Revenue Service demanded $685 thousand in back taxes from the Klan, effectively forcing out of business the movement Colonel Simmons had founded twenty-nine years before on Stone Mountain in Georgia.[22]

Although it was a national organization, the thrust of the Ku Klux Klan was toward local change and not presidential action or congressional legislation. This chameleon of a movement fashioned itself to each community's needs and drew a heterogeneous membership with a cafeteria of appeals. In the hands of well-known local figures who capitalized upon their connections and positions of trust and respect, the Klan was able to elicit support from clergymen, newspaper editors, fraternal group leaders, and other shapers of community attitudes. Such support inhibited repression against the Klan and isolated its opponents, keeping Klansmen free of government harassment and public reproach. Klan leaders built a coalition of factions with a program salient to white Protestants and exercised a tight internal rein as they guided their followers into power.

Mastering the means to power, however, proved far simpler than exercising it. Politicians, bureaucrats, and Klansmen with their own agendas challenged the secret order and stalled its drive to influence policy. When the Klan could not deliver on its promises, when its leaders became infected with corruption or hubris, or when it lost relevance as a result of either success or failure, it could no longer resist internal disruption and external attack. Declining resources and a damaged image prevented the movement from surviving the tests of membership in the polity, and it began its free-floating descent from power.

EVOLVING REINCARNATIONS

The Ku Klux Klan did not stay dead very long. Burning crosses reappeared in 1946 and by 1949 over two hundred klaverns housing twenty thousand Klansmen had been organized. Unlike the 1920s movement, this was a southern campaign focused upon the blacks' quest for racial and economic equality. Splintering early into more than a dozen separate Klan bodies, the hooded resistance resorted to bombing, arson, and murder to stop the black challenge. The Klans competed unsuccessfully with the more respectable White Citizens Councils for members and funds and remained a secondary impulse in the 1950s and 1960s. Only in the rural communities of Mississippi, Alabama, and Georgia was it unrestrained in the use of terror and violence. Nevertheless, it became again the center of national attention. In 1961 Klansmen assaulted Freedom Riders testing segregation laws in Anniston and Birmingham, Alabama. In 1963 Klansmen bombed a Birmingham church, killing four black children. The following year Klansmen murdered three civil rights workers in Mississippi. Klansmen were also charged in 1965 with killing Viola Liuzzo following the civil rights march from Selma to Birmingham.[23]

With public opinion polled at 76 percent unfavorable to the Klan and fears of terrorism escalating, the Federal Bureau of Investigation launched its Counter-Intelligence Program against seventeen Klan groups in 1964. Agents infiltrated klaverns and paid Klansmen to disrupt Klan activities by sowing discord among fellow Kluxers, between leaders and members, and even between husbands and wives. Using stolen membership lists, the FBI mailed postcards reading "We Know Who You Are," indicating to Klansmen that their secret lives had been compromised. Agents identified Klansmen to their employers and suggested that the men be fired. The FBI even provided dissident Klansmen with funds to build rival organizations. By the early 1970s one of every six Klansmen was on the FBI payroll. Repression was effective: Klan membership, which had inflated to fifty thousand men in the mid-1960s, declined to sixty-five hundred by 1975.[24]

Later in the 1970s the Klans evolved and assumed a new guise. College-educated leaders, proficient in their use of the media, offered a "modern" movement that denied terrorism as a means to its ends. Welcoming Catholics for the first time and women as equal partners, the Klans thundered against busing to reduce school segregation, affirmative action programs, and illegal immigration from Mexico. When the more acceptable groups of the New Right and Moral Majority shunned their advances, Klansmen sought alliance with neo-Nazi organizations like Aryan Nations in a United Racist Front. Growth inside and outside the South again multiplied Klan groups, and several of the organizations preached and engaged in violence.[25]

By the late 1980s the Klan was once more in retreat. Although still claiming the allegiance of approximately five thousand men and women, the Invisible Empire lost over half of its members in this decade when public sentiment remained hostile and the Klan faced attack from several sources. Federal and state prosecutors brought Klansmen and their leaders to trial for violent acts, sedition, and conspiracy to overthrow the government. Groups like the National Association for the Advancement of Colored People, the Anti-Defamation League, and the Southern Poverty Law Center monitored hooded activities, compiled information on individual members, and filed civil lawsuits on behalf of Klan victims to collect damages and drain the movement of funds and energy. One such suit against the three-thousand-member United Klans of America resulted in a jury award of $7 million and forced the organization to relinquish the deed to its national headquarters. This recent anti-Klan offensive waged by government authorities, polity members, opinion makers, and other contenders for power has proven effective in denigrating the movement's image and reducing its organizational resources. The tenacity of prejudice in America, however, suggests that the struggle against the Ku Klux Klan is far from over.[26]

5

THROW OFF YOUR CHAINS:
THE COMMUNIST PARTY

As the Industrial Workers of the World and the Socialist party stars dimmed, the radical world awoke to a new sun in the eastern skies. The victory of the Bolsheviks in Russia signaled the emergence of a vigorous challenge to the capitalist status quo. The first manifesto of the Communist Party of America announced in 1919: "The World is on the verge of a new era. Europe is in revolt. The masses of Asia are stirring uneasily. Capitalism is in collapse.... Out of the night of war is coming a new day."[1]

For those seeking radical change in the American environment, the Communist movement offered not only the evidence of recent success but a carefully reasoned program and a centralized and battle-ready organization. Here was a movement that could fill America's left-

When the locomotive of history takes a sharp turn only the steadfast cling to the train.
LENIN

wing void and deliver on promises of victory. There was more to membership than direct action in building the workers' utopia; the movement offered a world apart where individuals meshed into a network of personal, social, economic, and even residential relationships with the like-minded.

The shelter of ideology, party discipline, and interpersonal ties was necessary to protect members and absorb shocks from the outside. From the beginning, communism repelled the overwhelming majority of Americans, who perceived it as an extreme solution and an alien growth: The "Reds" were disloyal revolutionaries and godless conspirators eager to betray America's birthright. Even when events heightened Communists' expectations only selected populations were receptive to the message. Government authorities and polity members preyed upon the party, often fueling public fears for their own ends. With communism defined as illegitimate and beyond the bounds of reasonable dissent, repression required little justification.

The party's structure and authority, often sources of strength in a hostile setting, also acted to undercut the organization's influence. The movement's dynamism was rooted in the self-sacrifice of members who braved abuse to mold the party's program to local concerns and audiences. Robbed neither of mind nor will, these men and women dedicated themselves to the achievement of racial equality, the rights of labor, and a classless society based upon the often-quoted ideal, "from each according to ability, to each according to need." Yet their freedom to shape a movement to the contours of American life was restricted. The American Communist party was an appendage of an international movement with an agenda of its own. On issues of war and peace, labor policy, and political strategy, American Communists deferred to their mentors in Moscow. Dissonance between the party line and the conditions of local organizing required agility in word and deed and forced members to weigh immediate goals against larger loyalties. The party's subordination to foreign authority did more than bolster negative images and create opportunities for enemies. Deference undercut the movement's efforts to chart an American road to socialism, thus short-circuiting its potential for growth and power.

"ACUTE REVOLUTIONARY CRISIS"[2]

A wave of revolution appeared ready to inundate Europe and North America in the aftermath of World War I. From Russia the assault on the ruling class had spread to Hungary, Austria, and Bulgaria. In 1919 revolutionary momentum seemed to quicken. Workers' councils exercised power in Finland and Germany's Bavaria. Numerous and widespread labor strikes unsettled Italy, France, Great Britain, and Canada. The United States did not escape the unrest. As soaring inflation ate into paychecks, workers struck for higher wages and shorter hours. The number of strikes escalated from 175 in March, 1919 to more than twice that number in May. By the end of the year, more than four million American workers had participated in over thirty-six hundred work stoppages. During the same period, but unrelated to the strikes, authorities foiled a bomb plot against American business and government leaders. In June bombs did explode simultaneously in eight cities across the country. For Americans who had long tied radicalism to violence, the connections between Bolshevism, labor unrest, and terrorism were easily drawn.[3]

Events in Russia, the subsequent anticapitalist advance, and the rise of labor militancy energized the unmobilized left-wing faction of the American Socialist party. The Russian model of revolution cheered radicals who railed against the gradual reform of capitalism along socialist lines, political action, and their party's middle-class orientation. Posed, they believed, on the brink of revolution, activists advocated direct action and mass struggle to hasten the overthrow of the system and the erection of a dictatorship of the working class. "The proletarian world revolution has begun," announced radical leader Charles Ruthenberg. "In a few years—two, three, perhaps five—the workers of the United States would be marching step by step with the revolutionary workers of Europe."[4]

Slowly, the left-wing faction defined itself and organized in Chicago, New York City, Boston, and ten other cities. Strong support for the radical program came from the language federations, affiliated with the Socialist party, that housed groups of immigrants with the same language and similar ethnic backgrounds. In particular, members of the Russian, Lithuanian, Polish, and Hungarian federations, for ideological and nationalistic reasons, joined the insurgency. By May 1919 the radicals claimed the allegiance of seventy thousand Socialist party members and moved to challenge more conservative leaders for control. Conservatives responded by revoking language federation and branch charters and expelling opponents, thus driving two-thirds of their organization's membership into political exile.[5]

Dissension, however, soon splintered the radicals. Members of the foreign language federations, composing 90 percent of the dissident group, decided to form a communist party while the minority led by John Reed continued efforts to capture the Socialist party. Infighting peaked in September 1919. Gathering in Chicago, members of the language federations under the direction of Ruthenberg, Jay Lovestone, and Benjamin Gitlow organized the Communist Party of America. Just 7 percent of the membership could read, speak, or write English. A few days later, after failing to gain seats at the Socialist party convention also meeting in Chicago, Reed and his followers created the Communist Labor party. Together, the two groups totaled not more than forty thousand members, with the Communist party of America commanding the allegiance of a membership three times that of its rival.[6]

The energizing events of the Russian Revolution and American labor unrest had aroused salience and fired a sense of efficacy. From the Socialist party and the language federations American Communists gathered the means to begin their challenge. They took advantage of longtime political and personal relationships, already established communications channels, and existing organizational structures to stockpile funds and members for their anticapitalist efforts. As vanguards of the working class, Communists were now ready to spearhead a mass struggle for immediate gains that would evolve into a campaign for the complete transformation of America.

The American masses rejected not only the Communist message but its bearers. Communism meant atheism, free love, and the abolition of private property; it meant, in short, the destruction of the American Republic's cornerstones. Moreover, World War I had tagged radicals as disloyal and dangerous, images that had facilitated the repression of the Industrial Workers of the World. The impression of Lenin as an agent of the Kaiser, an impression bolstered by the Communists' withdrawal of Russia from the crusade against Germany, gave even greater credence to the perspective that bolshevism was anti-American. No wonder that Americans cheered President Woodrow Wilson's commitment of seven thousand troops to an allied invasion of Vladivostok and Archangel in late 1918.[7]

In the context of these world events, domestic labor unrest signaled to many Americans that the enemy had breached the home barricades. This fear of a Communist invasion fed into the needs of polity members, government officials, and opinion makers who fanned the hysteria that was America's first Red Scare. The crisis began in January 1919 when shipyard employees in Seattle, Washington, went on strike for higher wages, supported by the threat of a general strike by local unions. Newspapers across the nation sounded the alert, quoting Seattle Mayor Ole Hanson's contention that the workers "want to take possession of our American Government and try and duplicate the anarchy of Russia."[8] Americans, many still in military uniform, assaulted May Day paraders in Boston, New York City, and Cleveland. Opinion makers escalated rhetoric to match the violence. Not unusual was the exhortation of the *United Presbyterian*, which demanded that every Communist be forced to "change his course or swing at the end of a rope."[9] Scores of magazines and newspapers, the American Legion, the American Federation of Labor, the Ku Klux Klan, and major business organizations like the National Association of Manufacturers and the National Founders' Association added their voices to the uproar.[10]

Attorney General A. Mitchell Palmer, sharing these fears and with presidential ambitions in mind, prepared to confront the "Red Menace." He created within the Department of Justice a Bureau of Investigation charged with gathering information on all domestic radicals. Under J. Edgar Hoover's direction, a file index of sixty thousand radicals was compiled. The bureau also leaked news stories linking strikes and summer race riots to Communist provocateurs. In November and December 1919 agents without arrest warrants organized coast-to-coast raids and jailed alleged radicals. On 2 January 1920 more than four thousand suspected Communists were seized in coordinated raids in thirty-three cities. Those arrested, if citizens, were tried in state courts under antisyndicalist laws; if immigrants, they were held for deportation hearings. Attorney General Palmer stressed their deviancy: "Out of the sly and crafty eyes of many of them leaps cupidity, cruelty, insanity, and crime; from their lopsided faces, sloping brows, and misshapen features may be recognized the unmistakable criminal type."[11] Although the red-baiting hysteria faded in 1920, an antiradical mentality pervaded the decade. Throughout the 1920s, when corporate leaders were praised as the high priests of prosperity and the business of America was business, the public perceived Communists as not only abnormal but irrelevant.[12]

THE LIMITS OF AUTHORITY

Fear of continued repression convinced Communists to retreat underground, where they assumed aliases and met secretly to avoid detection. This tactic probably heightened the public's suspicions and further blackened the movement's image. It also failed to shield Communists from their enemies. Authorities infiltrated the movement and even installed an informer in a leadership position. Aware of Communist plans, Justice Department agents raided the secretly convened 1922 national convention, arrested thirty-two delegates, and later indicted forty more for violation of criminal syndicalism statutes. The move underground decimated the membership; at the end of 1922 only six thousand to eight thousand men and women held party cards.[13]

During the underground period the Communist International, or Comintern, began to exert control over the American movement. Founded in 1919 and headquartered in Moscow, the Comintern offered "to fight by all means available, including armed struggle, for the overthrow of the international bourgeoisie and for the creation of an international Soviet republic."[14] In the war against capitalism, the Comintern was the command post; national parties were subordinate to its directives. Linked to the hierarchy of the Communist party of the Soviet Union, it offered members throughout the world the status associated with the first and only successful revolution of the working class. What it gave could also be withdrawn, for the Comintern had the ultimate authority to expel individuals and parties from the movement. Comintern subsidies to constituent parties financing agitation and propaganda work enhanced its dominant position. So, too, did its creation of schools for educating promising leaders in Communist ideology, history, and methods. It was this juxtaposition of Comintern prestige and power with American communism's factionalism, defensive position, and submissiveness to the revolutionary icons that gave instructions from Moscow so much weight. "I am convinced," said party leader William Foster, "that the Communist International, even though they were five thousand miles away from here . . . understood the American situation far better than we did."[15]

In their subordination to the Comintern, Americans bypassed the necessary development of an independent and self-confident leadership. American Communists appealed to Moscow tribunals for intervention in decision making and leadership disputes. Comintern officials complied with these requests, overriding national party conventions and dictating the internal distribution of power. Submission did more than infect the American movement with the maladies that wracked the Soviet leadership. It also conveyed to outsiders the appearance of an organization that had assumed the guise of a fifth column without loyalty to the American homeland.

From abroad, then, could be imposed the unity and direction that had so far eluded American Communists. Under orders from Moscow, personal, cultural, language, and ideological differences were reconciled, and the two rival parties united in 1921. The Russians also encouraged the Americans to end their underground operations at the end of 1922. Assured by their Russian mentors that capitalism had stabilized and that the revolution had been postponed, American Communists emerged from hiding and re-formed in the Workers' party under the banner "To the Masses." This vehicle would compete above ground according to established rules for the allegiance of the American people.

However, the Communists realistically gauged the difficulties of mobilization in a hostile environment. To overcome their isolation, they developed united front organizations as the stepping-stones to power. In these alliances with progressive groups Communists sought short-term goals in race relations, civil liberties, and working conditions. Despite their small number, hard work and concentration of power would allow Communists inordinate influence. Moreover, this tactic would familiarize Americans with the Communist cadre, methods, and program, thus bringing within the party's orbit potential recruits and supporters with resources to devote to the cause. In the mid-1920s Communists had some united front success with the Farmer-Labor party, which campaigned for an eight-hour day, unemployment insurance, and the abolition of child labor. Communists also dropped attempts at dual unionism, or the maintenance of competing labor organizations, deciding instead to extend influence by boring from within existing locals.[16]

Workers' party membership rolls during this period reflected tactical gains, for between 1922 and mid-1925 twenty thousand Americans joined the party. Membership proved unstable, however, for only six thousand maintained commitment. This was particularly true for English-speaking joiners; 12,742 entered the party but just one thousand remained in the ranks.[17]

Communists hoped to use the united front to springboard into the political mainstream. They planned to make overtures to Wisconsin Senator Robert LaFollette, who was mounting a third-party challenge in the 1924 election for president. Word from the Comintern abruptly halted these efforts. Shockwaves from tests of strength and ideological purity among Lenin's lieutenants in Moscow forced a course reversal in America and disoriented leaders who searched for a new champion or an indication of future direction. Correct policy now meant organizing a Workers' party campaign, which in November captured thirty-three thousand of the nearly twenty-nine million votes cast for president. The shift in party line was also felt in union organizing. Communist leaders directed cadre to bypass the American Federation of Labor and build locals under the party's aegis.[18]

Bolshevizing the American party   While effecting these changes, American Communists focused inward to complete the organizational restructuring, or *bolshevization,* of their party. American Communism, growing from the Socialist movement, had incorporated a network of party groups based on neighborhood and electoral districts and had absorbed language federations en bloc. As early as 1920 the Kremlin had ruled this structure out of step with the centralized Russian model based on the factory unit. Without regard to American circumstances and context, party leaders intensified their efforts to cut the Socialist roots of the American party. All Communists were organized into *shop nuclei,* composed of Communists working in the same factory, or *street nuclei,* composed of neighbors who were unemployed or in an establishment without a sufficient number of party members to form the preferred shop unit. From these nuclei the structure rose through *branches* (groups of ten units), *sections* (divisions of large cities), *subdistricts* (encompassing several cities), and *districts* (usually several states). At the pinnacle was the *national convention,* representing all party members, which was slated to meet annually to elect the party's Central Committee. This committee convened three times during the year and guided the movement between conventions. The smaller political bureau, or Politburo, determined policy when the Central Committee was not in session. The leadership core was the Secretariat, composed of four or five officials and headed by the general secretary. It was this body that exerted daily control. Assisting the Secretariat within the national office were departments concerned with organization, research, trade union, agrarian, and "Negro" issues. In addition to united fronts, Communists were encouraged to create bridges to nonmembers through *fractions.* These cohesive groups of party members in outside organizations furthered Communist influence and facilitated the mobilization of resources.[19]

The result was a highly centralized, bureaucratically structured, and easily mobilized challenger eager to contend for power. The party planned rigorous indoctrination courses and offered a plethora of activities for members. It presented an image of a disciplined movement in which members accepted command without hesitation and sacrificed personal interests for organizational goals. It was an image which both Communist and anti-Communist shared. Yet government and polity members' opposition and a negative image offset the enhanced control over resources brought by centralization and bureaucratization. In fact, the party's organizational apparatus and the perception of the Communists' discipline may have heightened public fears and intensified repression.

In this combat-ready organization there was no place assigned to the members of the foreign language federations. They were advised to forego the ties of language and forge allegiances based on work. Party leaders thus hoped to reduce the number of the ideologically suspect whose membership was an artifact of place of birth. Dispatching the immigrants would also lower the language and cultural barriers that had minimized the party's impact and separated it from the majority. As the immigrants withdrew, the party intensified efforts to Americanize itself by recruiting natives and even encouraging its members to anglicize their names.[20]

Bolshevization was costly. Immigrants resisted, some holding to their language branch memberships as late as 1930. Most of the disaffected, including those who rejected the increased emphasis on regimentation, abandoned the cause, and the party lost approximately one-third of its rank and file. Party membership, which had climbed to over fourteen thousand in 1925, declined to ninety-five hundred in 1927. Native-born Americans remained resistant. Information concerning party members in Pittsburgh, Philadelphia, Cleveland, Minneapolis, and Kansas City indicates that 88 percent were foreign-born in 1929.[21]

Independence and self-reliance continued to elude the American movement at the end of the 1920s. The death of Ruthenberg prodded the emergence of Jay Lovestone, a Lithuanian-born Jew who had attended City College in New York. Lovestone's grip on the organization, however, loosened when he miscalculated ideologically and backed the loser in a Kremlin power struggle. After Joseph Stalin had successfully isolated then purged his Russian competitors, he withdrew the Comintern's support from the Lovestone faction, even though it commanded a majority in the American party. American Communists followed Stalin's lead. Lovestone's base evaporated and he was expelled from the party. The limits of authority had been made clear.[22]

Meanwhile, Communist party impotence continued. Shifting back and forth between the dual unionism and the "bore from within" strategies handicapped labor work. In the 1928 elections William Foster, running for president on the Communist party ticket, polled forty-eight thousand of thirty-six million votes. The party's self-anointed vanguard role was also threatened when Socialist Norman Thomas gathered more than five times as many votes as his Communist competitor. After ten years, the Communist party had not broken from isolation. Events, however, would soon give Communists opportunities to transcend their powerlessness.[23]

THE CRISIS OF CAPITALISM

A chain of events beginning in the 1920s drastically altered the context of contention. Industrial overproduction, the saturation of consumer credit, the stock market crash, the collapse of the banking system, international trade wars, and the restriction of credit thrust the nation into a downward economic spiral. Factory closings and layoffs riddled the work force. Jobless men and women totaled 4.2 million or nearly 9 percent of all workers in 1930, increasing to over 13 million or just over one-fourth of the work force by 1933. Even these statistics disguise the enormity of the crisis. Millions more could find only part-time employment, suffered wage cuts, or were paid in script.

The Depression overwhelmed public and private relief agencies. Across America the homeless gathered in "Hoovervilles," hastily built shanty towns of tar-paper shacks, packing crates, and abandoned automobiles. Conditions were no better in the countryside. Already depressed prices for wheat, corn, and cotton plummeted in declining markets. Drought created the Dust Bowl and intensified misery. Foreclosure and flight were common throughout the American heartland. Hard times were blamed for postponing marriages, lowering the birth rate, raising suicide risk, and increasing spousal and child abuse. Like a stone thrown into a pond, the Depression's effects rippled to all areas of American life.[24]

Many Americans personalized the economic collapse, blaming themselves for losing a job or being unable to support a family. Those who looked beyond their immediate situation condemned President Herbert Hoover and placed faith in the election process to right the economic wrongs. Some, while retaining faith in the system, could not wait for relief. In 1930, eleven hundred men in Manhattan broke ranks on a breadline and attacked trucks carrying food. In 1931 police dispersed food rioters in Oklahoma City, Minneapolis, and St. Paul. A hunger march on the Ford Motor plant in Dearborn, Michigan, left four dead and fifty injured. To obtain bonus payments for World War I service, fifteen thousand veterans and their families bivouacked in Washington until driven out with tanks and tear gas. On the Great Plains farmers armed to resist foreclosure actions, tax sales, and eviction orders.[25]

The Depression heightened the importance of economic issues for all Americans. It also initiated a questioning across the political spectrum of the

)f government and business leadership. Declining revenues and protest on the farm and in the city strained the ability of state and polity members to repress or control challenging groups. Now was the time, as never before, to expand Communist influence.

The party positioned itself to serve as the vehicle for men and women whose discontent was immediate and situational as well as those receptive to a more thorough critique of American capitalism. In championing the cause of the homeless and unemployed, the movement could reshape its image and enhance its prestige. Defense of the weak would begin the process of building revolutionary consciousness and make the party a mass movement. On shop floors and in breadlines, soup kitchens, and relief offices, party activists convinced men and women of the power in solidarity. Fueling a sense of efficacy in the local context would, party leader Earl Browder assured the cadre, "at the same time strengthen the working class for the bigger battles and finally for the overthrow of Capitalism."[26]

Under Communist leadership, men and women sat down in relief offices, staged hunger marches, and resisted eviction. By 1932, the Communists had helped establish unemployment councils in one hundred cities across the United States. These fronts focused the power of the jobless on demands for relief, unemployment insurance, and moratoriums on evictions. Communists coordinated nationwide demonstrations in nearly every major city on 6 March 1930 to mark International Unemployment Day. For those with jobs, the Communist party offered the Trade Union Unity League under the slogan, "Class Against Class." Organizers competed with the American Federation of Labor and created industrial unions among textile, marine, automobile, and steel workers.[27]

Campaigning again for president in the 1932 elections, William Foster proposed an unemployment insurance plan, an end to wage cuts, and equal rights and self-determination for black Americans. Pledges of support for Foster and his black running mate James Ford from intellectuals Sidney Hook, Sherwood Anderson, John Dos Passos, Theodore Dreiser, Granville Hicks, Lincoln Steffens, and Langston Hughes, among other opinion makers, encouraged Americans to vote Communist. According to Dos Passos, "Becoming a socialist right now would have just about the same effect on anybody as drinking a bottle of near-beer."[28] Foster collected 103,000 votes, more than double his 1928 total. Still, Socialist Norman Thomas polled 918,000 votes, nine times that of his radical rival. Capitalist candidates Franklin Roosevelt and Herbert Hoover had together gathered 38 million votes. Even in the depth of the Depression, the American people's faith in the system, while shaken, was not destroyed.[29]

After five years of Depression the Communist party in 1934 was forced to lower its expectations. Despite its most severe test American capitalism had not succumbed to the revolutionary wave. In fact, Franklin Roosevelt's

New Deal had restored a significant measure of public confidence in the government and economy. While sixty thousand people had joined the movement between 1930 and 1934, the party could not hold on to recruits, and membership had only increased from 7,500 to 24,500 persons. The movement remained outside the mainstream: 70 percent of the rank and file were foreign-born, and more than two-thirds were unemployed. The perception continued that the Communist solution was too radical, un-American, and illegitimate to solicit widespread support. Further, although claiming a membership of 125,000 workers, the party recognized the failure of the Trade Union Unity League and directed organizers to dissolve their unions and work within the AFL. While the party's path to power remained blocked, distant events dictated a new strategy that would bring the movement to the height of its influence.[30]

THE POPULAR FRONT

The rise of Adolf Hitler and the growing threat of Germany forced Kremlin leaders to revise their priorities. Nazism posed an immediate danger, not only to the world communist movement but to the Soviet homeland itself. Hitler's destruction of the German Communist party, his creation of a fascist state, his rearmament policy, and his signing with Japan and Italy of the Anti-Comintern Pact convinced Stalin to retreat from confrontation toward a policy of cooperation with socialists, liberals, and even conservatives. Communists in France, Spain, Great Britain, the United States, and elsewhere heeded the call to fashion alliances with domestic antifascist groups, galvanizing opinion and power to isolate Germany and bolster the Soviet Union.[31]

The American party's acceptance of Moscow's new line was more than an empty parroting of official doctrine. Meeting Moscow's vital needs also addressed the weaknesses of the American movement. Long outside the mainstream, Communists eagerly grasped the opportunity to reshape American perceptions of the party, increase membership, reach sympathizers, and sway decision makers as partners in larger, broad-based coalitions. The means were now at hand to develop the legitimacy and influence of the movement. Discarding radicalism to pursue power, the party Americanized its image by boasting of its deep roots in the nation's past. Claiming that Communists were the true heirs of the American Revolution, the party joined Washington, Jefferson, and Lincoln to Marx, Lenin, and Stalin in the movement's pantheon. The watchwords of the American party became: "Communism is Twentieth Century Americanism."[32] The shift in party line also touched the individual. The popular front enabled members not only to put their visions of economic democracy and social justice into action but to shed their sense of isolation and realize meaning and place within the

American community. At the same time, the American movement remained tightly tethered to the Comintern. Change in the European situation would present Americans with choices demanding sacrifices that were both political and personal.[33]

To Americanize communism the Comintern relied upon the party's general secretary, Earl Browder. Born in Kansas in 1891, Browder had been a member of the AFL and the Socialist party before World War I. During the war he was arrested for conspiracy to violate the draft laws and refusal to register for the draft and, along with two brothers, was imprisoned. On release in 1921 he joined the Communist party. By 1933, with Comintern backing, Browder triumphed over rival William Foster, who suffered a heart attack during his campaign for president, and assumed the party's helm. Schooled in party discipline and the lessons of the Lovestone affair, Browder described himself as "a pupil of Stalin."[34] "If one is not interested in directives from Moscow," announced Browder, "that only means that he is not interested in building socialism at all."[35]

The shift from "Class Against Class" to the popular front was a gradual one. As late as spring 1936 Communist speakers condemned President Franklin Roosevelt as a "social fascist." Comintern directives, fortified by a lack of domestic enthusiasm, encouraged the party to change direction. Internally, the Communists revised the bolshevization process to adjust movement units to electoral boundaries. Yet unable to endorse Roosevelt, the party nominated a Browder-Ford ticket, which supported the president by attacking the Republican challenger and drawing conservative fire. The resulting Roosevelt landslide cheered party activists, who were hardly dismayed by the fact that Browder had collected only eighty thousand votes.[36]

Communists continued their move toward Roosevelt and away from radicalism after the election. They supported New Deal efforts at reform and congratulated Roosevelt on his "Quarantine the Aggressors" speech in 1937 in which he called for a collective response to stop the international fascist advance. The party's tenth convention, carried live on the CBS radio network, proclaimed a liberal platform of "Jobs, Peace, Democracy, and Security" as Communist goals.[37] By 1938 the Communist movement was embracing the Democratic party and was eager to participate as a respected and legitimate member of the New Deal coalition. But the party's endorsement still did not translate into significant influence among Roosevelt's decision makers. On the local level, however, Communists traded hard work and organizational skills for positions of prominence and responsibility in the Democratic party and its affiliated groups. In New York, California, Minnesota, and Washington, Communists entered political organizations; some held elected office on the community and state levels, and others sat on policy-setting councils. Lacking numbers and accepting popular goals, however, these men and women exercised influence as individuals and not to the benefit of the Communist party.[38]

Complementing these efforts were Communist gains in the labor movement. The New Deal's endorsement of the American worker's right to organize and bargain collectively sharply stimulated union building during the 1930s. American Federation of Labor leaders differed, however, on the means to exploit their advantage. This conflict produced division and led to the expulsion of those favoring unions that embraced all workers regardless of craft or skill level. Led by John L. Lewis of the United Mine Workers, dissidents created the Committee of Industrial Organizations (CIO) in 1936 and prepared to unionize the unorganized under its banner. Communists eagerly answered Lewis's call for organizers. In light of their failure at dual unionism, their central focus on the working class as the instrument of social change, and the purpose of the popular front, party cadre promised the CIO their organizational skills, determination, and discipline.[39]

Communist organizers proved critical to the growth and success of the CIO. They earned respect and influence for their union work and were rewarded with leadership positions from the national office to the local. By 1938, Communists or party sympathizers led from one-fourth to one-third of the CIO's forty international unions. Communist control was particularly strong in the United Electrical, Radio and Machine Workers Union, the International Longshoremen's and Warehousemen's Union, the National Maritime Union, and the Transport Workers Union. Still, the Communists' penetration was limited. Leadership and bureaucratic position did not translate into a mass following. Of the more than one million members of the textile union just 206 were Communists; only 1,500 of the 400,000 Auto Workers carried party cards. In all, the Communists could count 27,000 trade unionists in the United States at a time when the CIO alone claimed three million members.[40]

The Communists' adherence to the popular front tactic actually worked against its broader influence. Activists worked for conventional trade union demands of higher wages, shorter hours, and employee benefits and were unwilling to jeopardize the coalition or their own positions by mouthing party propaganda. Eventually, union-derived prestige and potential conflicts of loyalty weakened the party's hold on these leaders. Moreover, in hiding their Communist affiliations from the union rank and file, party members, or *submarines*, reinforced the movement's image as dangerous and deceptive while opening themselves to charges of conspiracy. The union experience, then, did not legitimize the Communist solution, expand radical consciousness, or create a mass base. Power, if it existed, was personal and not amenable to the party's use.[41]

Under the popular front arch the Communists formed and led a network of organizations that addressed the varied concerns of the American people.

Antifascism, civil rights, intellectual freedom, and peace were causes around which targeted groups could be mobilized for their own ends as well as those of the Communists. The American Student Union, which grew to twenty thousand men and women in 1939, organized on campuses, against war. The National Negro Congress championed expanded educational opportunities and higher wages while fighting against lynching and police brutality. Other important fronts were the American Veterans Committee, the League of American Writers, the International Workers Order, and the American League for Peace and Democracy. In addition to these creations, Communists built fractions within established groups like the National Association for the Advancement of Colored People and the Urban League in an attempt to bring those outside under the party's influence.[42]

Allegiance to the party Moderation and Americanization brought the Communist party its greatest recruiting success. As the party became more conventional, fears of repression subsided and the onus of membership decreased. Between 1936 and 1938 recruiting drives doubled the rolls to 82,000 men and women, with another 500,000 organized in affiliated groups. After signing their own party cards, parents enrolled their sons and daughters in the Young Pioneers and, later, the Young Communist League. With recruits came funds. Initiation fees and monthly dues supplemented donations, the sale of literature, and Comintern subsidies to maintain the organization and facilitate its growth.[43]

As the party grew, its complexion changed. The movement's foreign-born, working-class character gave way as native-born, middle-class Americans entered the ranks. Immigrants, a 70 percent majority in 1933, became a minority by 1936. In 1941 Communists in professional, business, and white-collar occupations accounted for 44 percent of the membership. During the popular front period the Communist population became more heavily concentrated in New York City, where 40 percent of the members resided. At the same time, the movement dispersed geographically, with the most populous of the thirty-five state organizations, in California and Illinois, each claiming six thousand members. Still, with only three thousand southern members and insignificant units between the Mississippi River and the Pacific Coast, the party's territorial base was quite limited.[44]

Turnover, although cut to a 46 percent rate, continued to plague the party. In the face of this membership instability, the movement cadre braced the organization and provided continuity and permanence. This vanguard of the party, having served apprenticeships in the Young Communist League and in movement training schools, made and administered policy, organized unions, and participated in front work. Full-time revolutionaries on salary, the cadre constituted the party's core and exhibited a far greater commitment and discipline than did the rank and file.[45]

The relevance of the party's message depended upon the interaction of personal and community frames of reference. Breadlines, evictions, layoffs, strikes, and the specter of nazism were the salient concerns of the 1930s. For some Americans the situation demanded more than a reform of capitalism or a foreign policy of isolation and noninterference. They believed that a radical solution was necessary to alleviate suffering, bring relief to working people, and quicken the pace of social justice. Men and women unschooled in Marxist ideology embraced the movement in reaction to problems at the grass roots. "I joined the party," said one member, "when it moved a widow's evicted furniture back into her house. I thought it was right."[46] Another asked, "Will this party help to improve the lot of mankind? Will they keep a cop from smashing some poor working man's brains out, who is fighting for a cheaper loaf of bread? Will it feed a family? Bring a cheaper rent? . . . Those are the essential things."[47] Activists assured audiences of the party's power to effect change and pointed to their working model of the great society. Before the Soviet Union's planned economy, full employment, and victory over prejudice and discrimination, America dulled. Even in coalition with the New Deal, which facilitated recruitment, the Communist party retained for its members the image of an organization on the cutting edge of change, an initiator of action.[48]

Yet an individual's desire for change is not sufficient to explain his or her membership in the Communist party. Throughout the United States people confronted the same events and selected more traditional routes to power. The Communist alternative primarily gained sustenance from communities and subcultures that defined a radical solution as acceptable. That is, the community mediated between its members and left-wing activists, familiarizing and legitimizing the rhetoric of revolution. What was impossible in Dallas or Des Moines became viable in Philadelphia and New York, where men and women had been conditioned to the radical approach and where organizational networks and channels of communication were available to facilitate party mobilization.[49]

Membership in the Communist party can thus be explained as a result of the personal reaction to national and international events in a context of community acceptance. This community or subculture support of radicalism is central to understanding the Communist party's attraction to Jews. While a very small minority of American Jews joined, Jewish Communists may have accounted for as much as 50 percent of the movement. Radicalism was one Jewish response to the suffering experienced in the ghettos of Eastern Europe and the Tsar-imposed Pale of Settlement. Officially restricted in space and goals, Jewish men and women lived in poverty, faced economic and religious discrimination, and were brutalized by mobs. On emigrating to America, radicals found new enemies in sweatshops and slums. In response, they, like many of their coreligionists, erected an infrastructure of groups to cushion the transition. Left-wing organizations proliferated, and a network of cultural, educational, mutual benefit, fraternal, youth, and leisure associations was created. This network provided the base for radical political parties and newspapers. Daily contact in a compact environment familiarized the wider Jewish population with radicals and their approaches. There were few who did not know a person significant to their lives who was in the left-wing community. In this tolerant atmosphere, radicalism gained legitimacy.[50]

Socialization marked a clear path into the party. "Red-diaper" babies raised in left-wing households, students influenced by radical teachers, and relatives and friends introduced to front and party functions found membership an act of conformity. Said a Los Angeles member: "It's like drinking milk. It was simply in the family and in all the friends."[51] While condemning anti-Semitism, the party did little to encourage Jewish membership. In fact, it scorned Judaism and opposed Zionism and the creation of a Jewish state. The secular Jews who joined were Communists first and were expected to relegate any ethnic and religious loyalties to the party line.[52]

At the urging of both Lenin and Stalin, who wondered about the absence of America's most exploited group from the movement, the party made every effort to recruit blacks. Officials followed the Russian-imposed model, which decreed a territorial base for each nationality and advocated black self-determination and the creation of a "Negro Soviet Republic" in the South. When blacks rejected this as segregation, or "Red Crow," Communist activists muted self-determination and agitated for social and civil equality and an end to bias in employment, housing, and unions. In black ghettos, Communists led marches of the unemployed, stopped evictions, and reconnected gas and electric services to those unable to pay. They also gained entrance into black organizations and churches with antilynching appeals and defense campaigns for the victims of southern injustice. Proclaiming itself color-blind, the movement rapidly advanced blacks to leadership positions. While blacks never joined in significant numbers, they did constitute 7 percent of the movement in the late 1930s and occupied nearly one-fifth of the seats on the party's Central Committee.[53]

The Communist cocoon   To transform a commitment based on issues into loyalty to the movement, leaders sought to envelop recruits in party work and activities. Weekly meetings, often lasting three and four hours, were only a part of the regimen. Communists were also expected to attend lectures and rallies, participate in petition drives, recruit new members, and sell movement literature and newspapers. The complaint of one member was common: "Directives, directives, directives. . . . Hell, I could not do one tenth of it. I am just as much a Communist as ever, but I am not 10 Communists."[54]

Communist membership also meant absorption in a network of social relationships. After meetings, members attended movies together, went dancing, or met at one another's homes. Weekends brought picnics, hikes, and retreats. Members found their closest friends, even marriage partners, within the movement. "It was a total world," remembers a Philadelphia Communist, "from the schools to which I sent my children to family mores to social life to the quality of our friendships to the doctor, the dentist, and the cleaner. We had community."[55] In such a world, a loss of commitment meant more than a shearing of political ties. Ostracism was "worst tyranny than jail ... far worse than anything in the world. It's your mother and father, it's your social base, it's your raison d'etat [sic]. ... You've got to be willing to wander alone in the night."[56] Such sanctions were particularly powerful in regulating the cadre, for, if they left the movement, they sacrificed not only friends but career.[57]

This enclosure in the Communist cocoon, which required so much more than attendance at a few meetings, soon overwhelmed many. At the same time, bureaucratic mishaps, incompetent leaders, and inaction caused others to defect. Indoctrination efforts, meanwhile, could not keep up with demand, and over two-thirds of the membership never received formal training. Some members remained outsiders unable to match haughty comrades who were better steeped in party jargon and nuances. For less-dedicated members, changing levels of repression, reversals of the party line, and personal needs led to spotty attendance at first and then desertion.[58]

Overall, the achievements of the popular front period were clouded with irony. The Communist party had attained a measure of influence, moderated its image, and avoided government repression while strengthening its base with members and resources. It achieved these gains, however, by departing from its purpose, by relinquishing the role of revolutionary agent and clutching the banner of New Deal liberalism. While the course of moderation had been conducive to the personal and political needs of party members, its continuance was beyond American control. The Kremlin's hand alone was on the rudder.

CHANGES IN THE PARTY LINE

The signing of the Nazi-Soviet nonaggression pact on 23 August 1939 temporarily ended the popular front period. Within a month, coded radio messages from Moscow directed the American party to withdraw its support from President Roosevelt and cease agitation for rearmament and collective security. Communist leaders announced a campaign to "Keep America Out of the Imperialist War," proclaiming both sides in the new conflict equally guilty.[59]

The fallout was immediate. Front organizations such as the American League for Peace and Democracy, the League of American Writers, and the American Student Union disbanded. Many liberal organizations and unions expelled party activists. Public opinion polls indicated that 25 percent of the American people believed that American Communists took orders directly from Moscow and only 10 percent that the party was independent of foreign dictation. Communist-led strikes in defense plants in 1940 and 1941 further eroded the small measures of tolerance remaining from the popular front years. Meanwhile, government authorities increased pressure on the movement. The Federal Bureau of Investigation, which had begun collecting information about party members in 1936, intensified telephone and mail surveillance. Earl Browder and other Communist leaders were jailed for violating passport regulations on their trips to Moscow. With the support of the American Legion, the Veterans of Foreign Wars, the Chamber of Commerce, and more than one hundred other organizations, Congress passed the Smith Act in 1940. This measure prohibited any group from advocating or teaching the violent overthrow of the government of the United States or anyone from belonging to such an organization. Anti-Communist repression on the state level was even more vigorous. Mobs attacked meetings of "Communazis" in San Antonio, Texas; Detroit, Michigan; Aberdeen, Washington; and Chicago, Rockford, and Peoria, Illinois. During the 1940 election campaign, 350 party members were arrested in thirteen states on charges ranging from disturbing the peace to voter fraud and conspiracy.[60]

Lenin's locomotive of history again tested the party faithful. How did members cope with Stalin's abrupt policy reversal? Most accepted the assurances of their leaders that the pact with Nazi Germany bought time for an unprepared Soviet Union to rearm for the coming conflict. Others believed that Stalin acted to protect millions of Eastern European Jews from the Nazi threat. For these individuals, faith in the Kremlin's infallible wisdom, akin to a religious belief, resolved any dissonance. Doubters unwilling to abandon their dreams of a collective future and ties to friends and relatives bowed to party discipline and remained silent. Many took a pragmatic approach and convinced themselves that their local activities were more important and ignored pronouncements on international affairs. The 1939 pact, they reasoned, had no bearing on union organizing, the problems of the poor, or the advancement of rights for blacks. Only 15 percent of the membership found Stalin's deed unacceptable and renounced the party.[61]

The Nazi invasion of the Soviet Union in spring 1941 shocked the party into another reversal. The new line meant a crusade combining antifascism, the defense of Soviet Russia, and Americanism, stands that were compatible to American party members and dissipated the tensions created by the Nazi-Soviet pact. American members subordinated all activities to the defense of the Allies and later to the opening of a second front to relieve German pressure on Russia. They doused union militancy, pledging a no-strike policy, and promoted work speedups despite resistance from workers. The party's calls for minority rights were sounded less urgently with Japanese-Americans and black advance sacrificed to the war effort.[62]

The return to Americanism and moderation reinvigorated the Communist advance. So, too, did the transformation of the Soviet Union into an ally of the United States. Bearing the brunt of the German offensive, the Russians gained new prestige and American respect. In books, motion pictures, and magazines, American opinion makers convinced themselves and their countrymen of the common interests of the two peoples. *Life* magazine, for example, effusively praised the Russians as "one hell of a people . . . [who] to a remarkable degree . . . look like Americans, dress like Americans, and think like Americans."[63] As a sign of solidarity, the federal government released Earl Browder from prison in 1942 and desisted from additional repressive measures. Freed from government attack, in harmony with the national mood, and with the Russian connection now a benefit, the party expanded to nearly seventy thousand members. The movement also demonstrated power at the polls, electing two Communists to the New York City council.[64]

Party head Browder, for political as well as personal reasons, pressed for an American revision of the popular front. Browder believed that a national unity coalition was essential to continued international cooperation in the postwar world. To gain liberal as well as conservative support, he attempted to dispel fears of an internal revolutionary challenge. On 20 May 1944 Browder replaced the Communist party with the Communist Political Association, a nonpartisan, Marxist pressure group that would be a "small, if important sector of the great patriotic coalition."[65] But the American Communist leader had misread Soviet cues and changing times. The world Communist movement rebuked Browderism as a "notorious revision of Marxism." On Kremlin command Browder was replaced with William Foster, whose predictions of capitalist crisis and rising class consciousness were more acceptable. The expulsion of Browder and several thousand of his followers in 1946 ended another chance for the American party to walk a path independent of Soviet dictation.[66]

Postwar fallout   The defeat of the Axis powers in 1945 exposed the brittleness of the American-Soviet alliance. Once the common foe had been eliminated, divergent ideological, economic, and political interests revived longtime suspicion and mistrust. A spiral of escalating disagreements evolved into cold war—a confrontation short of war and far from peace. Despite a massive industrial base untouched by war and a monopoly of atomic bombs, the United States felt on the defensive. To Americans, events assumed a devious rationality and direction: Setbacks in Eastern Europe, the Middle East, and Asia appeared the work of an international Communist conspiracy, the purpose of which was world conquest.

Searching inward, Americans believed that the Communist party was the cause of their country's impotence. It was the enemy within, the agent of the world revolution at home. Party members, disciplined to obedience, had infiltrated the government, defense industry, and media to spread defeatism, engage in sabotage, and prepare America for a Communist dictatorship. Several sources fed this anti-Communist hysteria, which later became known as McCarthyism after Wisconsin Senator Joseph McCarthy joined the crusade in 1950. The 1946 Congressional elections brought Republican party majorities in both houses of Congress for the first time since 1928. Eager to tighten their legislative grip and advance to the presidency, Republicans made the anti-Communist issue a priority and accused those in the highest circles of disloyalty. The House Committee on Un-American Activities grabbed headlines with accusations of "Red" influence in the State Department, Hollywood's motion picture industry, and the nation's universities. Revelations of espionage in Canada, Great Britain, and the United States, culminating in the arrest, trial, and conviction as spies of Julius and Ethel Rosenberg, gave credence to Republican charges.[67]

The actions of the Democratic administration also enhanced the legitimacy of the attack on domestic radicalism. Stung by accusations that he was "soft on Communism," President Harry Truman attempted to shore up his credentials. He elicited congressional and public support for military assistance to Greece in 1947 by rhetorically transforming the world into monolithic blocs of free and slave nations. "Scaring hell out of the American people," the president announced the Truman Doctrine, a crusade for freedom and justice and against atheism and communist dictatorship. Logically, the war on communism had to be waged at home as well as abroad. Thus, nine days after the Truman Doctrine speech, the president instituted a government loyalty program to investigate federal employees and dismiss those for whom "reasonable grounds" existed for suspicion of disloyalty. State governments, universities, and corporations soon enacted similar programs to weed out "security risks." Dissent had become synonymous with treason and guilt by association a proper measure of subversion.[68]

Against the background of world events, politicians, government officials, business leaders, and media personalities sincerely and cynically focused the public into a patriotic rage. Anti-Communist riots occurred in Columbus, Ohio, and Rochester and Peekskill, New York. In 1948 pollsters recorded that over two-thirds of the population believed that American Communists' first loyalty was to the Soviet Union. The following year 68 percent favored outlawing the American Communist party. In this atmosphere it was politically prudent to step up the anti-Communist effort.[69]

Harry Truman, facing an uphill battle for reelection in 1948, appeased the public will by moving against what he privately believed to be a negligible threat. Without evidence of an actual plot or any incidents of violence, the

Justice Department arrested the twelve members of the Communist party's national board for conspiring to organize a movement teaching and advocating the violent overthrow of the United States government. The mere existence of the party, prosecutors argued, was sufficient evidence of wrongdoing. Eleven of the leaders were convicted and served a minimum of four years in prison. The decision, later sustained by the Supreme Court, garnered widespread support; the *New York Times, Chicago Tribune, San Francisco Chronicle, Los Angeles Times,* and *Washington Post* registered editorial approval. In 1951 federal authorities targeted the party's second echelon, arresting more than fifty Communist officials. The Eisenhower administration carried forward Smith Act prosecutions until 1956. In all, 126 high-level cadre were arrested, 105 were tried, and 93 convicted. Although only 29 Communists were ever imprisoned, the government's attack was particularly damaging to a movement that measured its leaders' tenure in decades and operated according to a strict chain of command.[70]

Beginning in 1946, officials in the Justice and Defense departments formulated plans for the arrest of Communist party members in event of war. Hoping to arouse panic among the membership, the Federal Bureau of Investigation leaked information to the press that it was prepared to detain more than twenty-six thousand people. These contingency plans, while modified, received formal authorization in 1950 from the McCarran Internal Security Act. To protect the country during an emergency, the law mandated the arrest of Communist subversives and their confinement in detention centers. Congress closed the legal circle in 1954 with the passage of the Communist Control Act, which outlawed the Communist party in the United States.[71]

The American labor movement, fearing exposure on the Communist issue, dared not deviate from the national trend. The Taft-Hartley Act, passed in 1947, had already reduced labor's power and attempted to punish unions under Communist leadership. Labor's disassociation from the Communists would secure its alliance with the Democratic party and reaffirm its establishment ties. Motivated by personal ambitions and rivalries, in addition to considerations of power and ideology, labor severed its ties to the Communist party. In November 1949 the Congress of Industrial Organizations expelled the United Electrical, Radio and Machine Workers Union, the body's largest Communist-led group. Within nine months ten more unions had been forced out and Communists in four others ousted. To destroy their power the CIO charted rival unions and directed its affiliates to raid the exiles for members. Business cooperated in the purge. Corporations withdrew their recognition of the banished unions, cancelled labor contracts, and refused to participate in their dues checkoff systems. Lacking a sense of class-consciousness, touched by the anti-Communist agitation, and feeling isolated, the unions' rank and file had little reason to support men accused of divided loyalty. Few of the exiled unions had the resources to survive the onslaught.[72]

Communist party miscalculations aggravated the impact of events. During the late 1940s, Communists predicted the imminence of World War III and a depression worse than that of the 1930s. Infiltrating the Progressive party of former Vice President Henry Wallace, they attempted to create an alliance of workers, the poor, blacks, the middle class, and veterans "to pull the teeth of American reaction" and continue the struggle for reform.[73] The Progressives, the Communist cadre believed, would split the Democratic party and replace it, legitimizing American communism and hastening the world revolution. Party resources were pumped into the Wallace campaign in 1948, and members subordinated all activities to election work. Communists in unions were reminded of their duty to obey and directed to break labor's ties to the Democrats. Ordered to choose between loyalty to the Communist party or the union, many balked, realizing that such a choice played into the hands of anti-Communists and jeopardized their power bases within the labor movement. This ill-conceived and poorly executed intrusion accelerated the decline of Communist union leaders and alienated the party from its natural constituency. When Wallace earned just 2 percent of the vote, demoralized party members had numerical proof of their isolation.[74]

Retreat and ruin   In an atmosphere of electoral defeat, witch hunts, and trials, the party turned against itself. Party leaders, consumed with fears of informants and FBI agents, instituted an internal security probe to remove the "unreliable" from the ranks. The ideologically unsophisticated, homosexuals, and suspected infiltrators were banished. A campaign against white chauvinism forced demotions and expulsions for real and imaginary offenses. Defensively postured, the party did little recruiting to counteract the drain on its resources.[75]

The purge was only a prelude to more drastic Communist restructuring. Party leaders announced the "five minutes to midnight" line, convinced that the "fascist danger" had reached the stage of mass arrests. To insure the party's survival, several thousand cadre members were sent underground into a world of secret hiding places, passwords, telephone codes, and aliases. They would resurface, the trusted and tested core of a revived party, once repression had receded. But American Communists paid dearly for the move underground. With its leaders in hiding or prison, the movement suffered organizational and communication breakdown. Scarce funds, whose sources were shrinking, were consumed in preservation, not challenge. Removed from their families and Communist support groups, many activists found their ideological commitment small comfort against emotional stress and declining morale.[76]

The "objective situation" had profoundly changed when these men and women emerged from the underground in the mid-1950s. Neither depression nor war had occurred, McCarthyism had ebbed, and the courts had reined in prosecutors. The 1950s ushered in rapid industrial growth, a baby boom, suburbanization, and consumerism. Ethnic and working-class urban pockets, which had reinforced radicalism, had given way to geographic and social mobility. Raising a family and paying bills commanded more attention than anti-Communist or anticapitalist crusades. The party seemed directionless, out of touch with current events. The stirring of a civil rights movement for integration and equality made Communist plans for a black homeland anachronistic. Anti-Zionism in the wake of the destruction of European Jewry and the creation of the state of Israel robbed the party of legitimacy and respect in Jewish communities. In the aftermath of Stalin's death and the Korean War cease-fire in 1953, the cold war had begun to thaw.[77]

Repression, blunders, purges, drift, and a loss of salience had eroded membership in the Communist party and shut off its flow of resources. The seventy-three thousand names on party books in 1946 had declined to fifty-four thousand in 1949, forty-three thousand in 1951, and just under twenty-three thousand at the end of 1955. The losses were staggering, but the party had survived. Party discipline and faith in Soviet Russia, on a base of Communist social networks, had allowed the movement to weather adverse conditions and continue, albeit in a weakened state.[78]

However, in 1956 Communists would find neither respite nor recovery. In April, for the first time in five years, Central Committee members met to evaluate their party's position. Cadre criticized William Foster's leadership, scoring his predictions of war and depression and policies on labor and race. Dissenters urged the movement toward decentralization and greater emphasis on democratic decision making. Communism, they argued, had to adapt to the American environment or remain wedded to failure.

Reports of Nikita Krushchev's secret speech on the Stalin era abruptly halted the American Communists' self-criticism. Khrushchev attacked Stalin for creating a cult of personality, torturing and executing opponents, and destroying Jewish culture. Even the most devoted and longstanding Communists were shaken. "I could see," said one member, "people, old Party leaders crying in the audience."[79] For party official George Charney, "Our whole world was falling apart."[80] "Piece by piece," wrote Junius Scales, "the whole once-trusted structure began to disintegrate, leaving me desolate and lost."[81] The crimes documented, American Communists knew, could neither be denied nor attributed to one man. They reflected upon the entire Soviet system. Gone was the faith that had kept the commitment of both members and leadership strong; the keepers of the flame had betrayed the revolution and denied them their god. In November another shock followed: American Communists watched on their televisions as Russian tanks crushed an uprising of Hungarian workers.[82]

When reformers attempted to capture the party and promote the Americanization of communism, William Foster and the old guard spoke in the

Kremlin's name and reasserted their control. A mass exodus followed. By 1958 the party counted three thousand men and women; it had lost 85 percent of its members.[83]

PASSING OF THE OLD LEFT

Federal prosecutors continued to pursue the Communists into the 1960s. Assistant Attorney General J. Walter Yeagley, heading a team of forty lawyers in the Kennedy administration's Justice Department, was blunt: "Our objectives are to keep the party off balance, to know what they're up to, to keep their membership low through harassment, to expose their leaders."[84] The courtroom consumed the movement's resources until 1967, by which time the Supreme Court had vitiated the Smith and McCarran acts. The FBI was more persistent. In 1956 J. Edgar Hoover initiated the bureau's first counter-intelligence program, COINTELPRO, which continued its previous disruption efforts—operating listening devices, planting false information to damage reputations, and provoking internal dissension. It is estimated that in 1962 the FBI had fifteen hundred of the party's eighty-five hundred members on its payroll. In addition, the Internal Revenue Service investigated 262 movement leaders for possible tax evasion and sued the party to collect past taxes.[85]

The Communist line after the 1956 debacle resembled latter-day Browderism. Party Secretary Gus Hall, the son of Wobblies, called for the Americanization of communism and a peaceful transition to collectivism. The party held its first national convention in seven years in 1966 and offered to lead a united front of antiwar and civil rights groups against racism, imperialism, and monopoly. Few even acknowledged the call of the discredited movement.[86]

The party had little impact on the emergence of the New Left in the 1960s. Campus radicals who rejected bureaucracy for ad hoc organization and ideology for an issue orientation studied the Communist movement to avoid its mistakes. Officially, the party was contemptuous of the New Leftists. Gus Hall condemned their "petty bourgeois radicalism" and dismissed them as "crazies."[87] More receptive members felt isolated and removed. "Now I was the outsider," wrote Al Richmond, "the sympathetic observer, received with tolerance and regarded, in the jargon of the day, as irrelevant."[88]

During the 1970s the party echoed Soviet policy, opposing American rapprochement with China and condemning Israeli aggression. As repression efforts decreased and the New Left disintegrated, the party registered membership gains. Despite its expulsion of pro-Maoists and "revisionists" who condemned the leadership as too conservative, the movement grew from twelve thousand members in 1966 to twenty thousand in 1980. Today, the party remains peripheral to the American experience; it inspires neither hope nor fear. "Our socialism will be stamped 'Made in the USA'," declared Hall on a daytime television talk show in 1988.[89] Few who heard him understood the historical irony of his words nor their relevance to the American present and future.[90]

The Communist party was the largest and strongest of America's left-wing challengers from the 1930s to the mid-1950s. Perhaps as many as 350,000 men and women joined the movement, and it attracted twice as many sympathizers in united front organizations. Through the party they grasped for the ring of revolution and a transformation in the meaning of class, race, and nationality. Yet, their vehicle was fatally flawed, for the Communist party in America was subject to a will beyond its own. It could never summon the power that comes of a large resource base or ideological self-confidence to prevent its sacrifice to Soviet needs. Its allegiance to foreign powers, reinforced by a large number of immigrant members and an almost puppet-like obedience to changing lines, troubled Americans always suspicious of movements they perceived as radical. The party could achieve its greatest successes only when it moderated its program and draped itself in the American flag.

Public disapproval, which rose and fell with domestic and foreign pressure, cleared the path for repression by polity members and the government. The harassment and disruption that intensified during the cold war and the Red Scare turned the party into a shadow organization, forced to the defensive and deprived of its ability to challenge. Self-mutilation decimated both internal resources and external support, leaving a hard core of cadre and members. A strong internal structure, while important in sustaining survival and continuity, was nevertheless insufficient to bring influence. When internal revelations stripped the movement of sinew and bone, it lost viability not only as a promise but as a threat.

6

BRIDGING McCARTHYISM
AND REAGANISM:
THE JOHN BIRCH SOCIETY

Communism [is] . . . a gigantic conspiracy to enslave mankind, an increasingly successful conspiracy, controlled by determined, cunning, and utterly ruthless gangsters, willing to use any means to achieve its ends.
ROBERT H. W. WELCH, JR.
THE BLUE BOOK

A lot of people in my home town have been attracted to the Society and I am impressed by the type of people in it. They are the kind we need in politics. They are the finest people in my community.
BARRY GOLDWATER

The 1950s was a decade of transition. The quieting of the Communist party challenge had created a vacuum on the left-wing conducive to the appearance of new ideas, activists, and constituencies. At the same time, change was occurring on the American right wing. In the 1920s and 1930s, anti-Catholicism, anti-Semitism, and racism had tainted challengers from the Right. The Ku Klux Klan, the Black Legion, and the American Bund had preached a restricted version of conservatism and invited opposition and repression. Other groups like the Liberty League promoted programs of economic conservatism while railing at New Deal "collectivism." Such messages went unheeded in a decade of economic depression. Conservatives could not shed an image of privilege nor gather the resources vital to influence.

The second American Red Scare, or McCarthyism, revised the equation for conservative challenge. The campaign against communists in American government and society appealed across religious, racial, and social spectrums. Speaking to the fears of the American people in a language blunt and colorful, conservatives shed their elitist image. But McCarthyism was more a political tactic than a social movement. Devoid of both economic and social content, it also failed to create the organizational structure needed to mobilize potential recruits.

The evolution of American conservatism was not halted when McCarthyism waned. In the aftermath of the Red Scare emerged the John Birch Society, which attracted those who feared the communist conspiracy long after the majority of Americans had lost interest. Making belief rather than race or religion prerequisite to membership, the Birchers sought to build a grass-roots organization under centralized control with chapters across the United States. Society members helped broaden the conservative platform of anticommunism, free enterprise, and individual freedom. Working in the local community, they focused attention on issues of immediate concern while condemning an unresponsive federal bureaucracy for high taxes and welfare programs. Birchers pragmatically entered politics in the 1960s, contributing to the Goldwater wave that was engulfing the Republican party.

The John Birch Society's influence, however, would not be felt in that decade. Nor would its power be measured in the number of laws passed or candidates elected to office. The society's uncompromising message of conspiracy, perceived as too radical, lacked salience. While concurring with the Birchers' opinion of the symptoms of America's social and economic disease, most conservatives could not accept their diagnosis of its etiology. Polity members similarly distanced themselves from and rejected the movement's embrace. Yet, the society's impact on the future was profound. In its message the John Birch Society set the agenda for the New Right of the 1970s and Reaganism of the 1980s. Through word and deed it taught conservatives how to use the media and build an organization. Many Birchers would become activists in New Right causes. Like a link in a chain, the society gave American conservatism continuity while drawing meaning from that which came before and that which followed.

McCARTHYISM

On 9 February 1950 Wisconsin senator Joseph R. McCarthy climbed into the center ring of American politics. His intentions were clear. His lackluster record of service in the United States Senate threatened his bid for reelection. Taking the nation's pulse, McCarthy prepared to claim the anticommunist mantle and the publicity that would accompany it. His monotone belying the intensity of his message, McCarthy warned the members of the Wheeling, West Virginia, Women's Republican Club with these words: "Today we are engaged in a final, all-out battle between communistic atheism and Christianity." America was losing this struggle, McCarthy contended, "not because our only powerful potential enemy has sent men to invade our shores, but rather because of the traitorous actions of those who have been treated so well by this Nation." In his hand McCarthy claimed to hold a list of names "that were made known to the Secretary of State as being members of the Communist party and who nevertheless are still working and shaping policy in the State Department."[1]

Neither a lack of evidence nor detailed rebuttal slowed McCarthy's campaign against internal subversion. Repeatedly, he cast the net of accusations wider. President Harry Truman, General George C. Marshall, and Secretary of State Dean Acheson, McCarthy charged, had organized "a conspiracy on a scale so immense as to dwarf any previous venture in the history of man."[2] Those who denounced McCarthy were "Commiecrats," "dupes of the Kremlin," or "egg-sucking phony liberals."[3] Attacking men, not ideas, McCarthy grabbed the headlines with hyperbole; he personified the abstract, simplified the complex.[4]

While commentators have given McCarthy's name to the 1950s Red Scare, conservatives had volleyed accusations of communist infiltration at the American government since the 1930s. World War II and America's alliance with the Soviet Union smothered these early witch hunts and silenced Red baiters. But in the postwar world, the anticommunist clamor was energized and received heightened attention. Russians balked at American needs, and frustration soon replaced the sense of omnipotence that had mushroomed dramatically in the clouds over Hiroshima and Nagasaki. Americans now saw themselves in retreat before a well-organized conspiracy bent upon world domination. A Red tide of barbarism, atheism, and collectivism was rapidly rising and threatening to engulf France, Italy, Greece, Turkey, the Middle East, and Asia. Containing the threat meant drawing a military, economic, and moral line dividing the free world from the slave world, friend from foe, and patriot from traitor.[5]

Despite American resistance, the Communists became stronger and bolder. In 1948 Russian troops blockaded road and rail approaches to Berlin. In 1949 the Soviet Union ended America's atomic monopoly by exploding its own bomb, and China was "lost" to the Communists. The following year, North Korean infantry crossed the thirty-eighth parallel and invaded South Korea. By early 1951, 850,000 Chinese "volunteers" confronted American and United Nation troops in bloody and indecisive combat.[6]

To many Americans the cause of their country's decline soon became obvious: The United States had been betrayed, its secrets exposed to the enemy. Testimony before congressional committees and arrests both at home and abroad revealed the existence of communist spies in the State and Defense departments. Accusations touched those at the highest levels of the American government. Hiss, Fuchs, and Rosenberg became household names, living symbols of the threat to the American way of life.[7]

Republicans preyed on the issue of "communists in the government." Sensing the salience of the cause and determined to return to power after their New Deal exile, Republican candidates hammered at Democrats for being soft on communism. They traced the growing Red stain to Franklin Roosevelt's New Deal. In the guise of reformers, communist infiltrators had subverted individualism and initiative, weakening America's will. Government regulations, welfare, and other forms of "creeping socialism," had propelled the nation far along the road to collectivism and dictatorship. As Republicans asked voters in 1946, "Got enough inflation? . . . got enough debt? . . . got enough strikes? . . . got enough communism?"[8] This identification of undesirable social changes with treason brought the conservative critique out of the political wilderness where it had been consigned as radical and the property of the privileged. Harnessing domestic liberalism to diplomatic setbacks and internal subversion diverted the mainstream and offered conservatives enhanced respectability and legitimacy.[9]

Joseph McCarthy was hardly alone in linking cold war tensions and domestic issues. Ohio's Republican senator Robert Taft described Democratic legislative requests as "bordering on Communism."[10] Congressional candidate Richard Nixon attacked his Democratic opponent as a "lip service American" who "fronted for un-American elements . . . by advocating increased federal control over the lives of people."[11] William Jenner, a senator from Indiana, named Secretary of Defense George Marshall "an unsuspecting stooge or an actual co-conspirator with the most treasonable array of political cutthroats ever turned loose in the Executive Branch of Government."[12] Meanwhile, President Truman's federal loyalty program and his attack on the American Communist party gave credence to Republican charges.

McCarthyism's appeal was inclusive rather than exclusive. Anticommunists erected no racial, religious, or ethnic barriers that would limit the acceptance of their message. In the wake of revelations of espionage, of cold war setbacks, and of the conflict in Korea, they addressed issues of vital concern to all Americans. Even in their choice of word and phrase, McCarthyites reached beyond traditionally conservative constituencies. Opinion polls registered strong support for Senator McCarthy among Catholics, a reflection not only of his message but his religious background. Blue-collar workers similarly gave McCarthy high marks. But the most important factor in McCarthy's popularity was political party affiliation. Men and women supported McCarthy's crusade because they were Republicans and he was an officially endorsed party spokesman. In January 1954 polls measured 50 percent of the American public in support of McCarthy and 29 percent opposed. Nearly two-thirds of Republicans approved McCarthy's work.[13]

Despite such public approval, McCarthyism was a fragile campaign that lacked an organizational base and was heavily dependent upon polity-member support. The election to the presidency of Republican Dwight Eisenhower in 1952 and the decimation of the American Communist party rapidly diminished McCarthy's opportunity to shape policy. With the White House now in their grasp, Republican strategists found the subversion issue expendable and McCarthy an embarrassment. In addition, the death of Joseph Stalin and a truce in Korea led to a thaw in the cold war. As tensions eased and Americans relaxed, the anticommunist message lost urgency.[14]

McCarthy's personality exacerbated his precarious position. Never an anticommunist ideologue, he had sought the spotlight in a personal quest for power and publicity. Undeterred by his failure to uncover a single communist or spy, McCarthy pressed his crusade forward during the Eisenhower administration. In 1954 he launched an investigation of the United States Army for "coddling communists." Televised hearings exposed McCarthy to viewers, who were repelled by his abusive and arrogant behavior. President Eisenhower denounced the witch hunt, and both the Republican party and the press deserted him. Now that he was vulnerable, others were encouraged to attack. The Senate's censure of McCarthy for activities unrelated to his anticommunist campaign further isolated him from power and attention. Ignored and without influence, McCarthy succumbed to the effects of alcoholism in 1957.[15]

While Americans had become more receptive to a conservative message during the Red Scare, subsequent events dispelled their fears that communists were infiltrating the government and society. For some, however, the danger had not vanished but had become even more insidious and menacing. The rise of Eisenhower and the fall of McCarthy only confirmed in their minds the power of the conspiracy and the facts of betrayal. With the investigations ended and the threat of exposure diminished, the subversives could carry on their work of destroying America from within. According to these conservatives, complacency had replaced vigilance, and the nation had been lulled to sleep. Time was running out.

ROBERT WELCH'S CREATION

On 8 December 1958 eleven men took seats before a lectern set up in the living room of a three-story, brick house in a residential section of Indianapolis, Indiana. The group included President Eisenhower's first commissioner of internal revenue, the former personal aide of General Douglas MacArthur, two past presidents of the National Association of Manufacturers, a banker, and a University of Illinois professor. The rest were well-to-do businessmen who managed family companies that were independent of the major national corporations. Most were Protestants, but a few Catholics were present. The men were not strangers to each other. All were prominent in various conservative and anticommunist causes and had cooperated in the past. Now they were answering the summons of their friend Robert Welch to attend a meeting of critical importance to the future of the nation.[16]

For two days the men listened to a Welch monologue.[17] Nothing they heard was unfamiliar. We are engaged, declared Welch, in "a *world-wide* battle, the first in history, between light and darkness; between freedom and slavery; between the spirit of Christianity and the spirit of the anti-Christ for the souls and bodies of men."[18] According to Welch, Lenin and the Bolsheviks had drawn a blueprint for world conquest. The conspirators planned to encircle America, first targeting Russia and Eastern Europe, then Asia, and finally Central America, South America, and Africa. It was not invasion from without that would bring America down, but subversion from within. Increasing government control, high taxes, and unbalanced budgets meant the gradual death of capitalism and the economic power to resist. Infiltrating schools, the media, and the churches, the communist fifth column would brainwash Americans to accept a hedonistic and immoral creed. Meanwhile, Welch continued, conspirators plotted to exploit prejudices and foment conflict to divide and then conquer. Permissiveness, disrespect for law and order, and government's "socialist controls" would mutilate the Constitution, religion, and the family. Once plunged into moral and social chaos, the United States would be the last domino to fall to the godless, communist dictators. Thus, Welch concluded, patriots had to act quickly, for the traitors within already controlled 25 percent of the nation and their timetable was ahead of schedule.[19]

Welch's message blended traditional fears of government power, economic orthodoxy, militant anticommunism, and concerns about the loss of America's moral fiber. What set Welch apart from fellow conservatives was his insistence, long after the Red Scare, on the existence of a plot. Where others attributed diplomatic setbacks, government action, and domestic controversy to the natural course of human events, Welch detected purpose and direction. Nothing was a random occurrence or the product of error. All circumstances gained meaning when woven into a fabric of conspiracy.

Unlike many anticommunists, Welch painted the conspiracy without religious and racial tones. A Unitarian, Welch rejected anti-Catholicism and anti-Semitism as communist ploys to create dissension and discord. He forbade membership to Ku Klux Klansmen and paramilitary Minutemen. Welch later boasted that 40 percent of the John Birch Society was Catholic and "many of our finest Chapter leaders are Jewish."[20] Blacks were also encouraged to join, and Welch was proud "of our small but growing number of Negro members."[21]

Welch planned to defeat the conspiracy with an organization modeled on his nemesis—the American Communist party. To withstand factionalism and crisis, Welch envisioned a "monolithic body" that was "under completely authoritative control at all levels," for the movement could build morale and secure loyalty only if members felt a personal commitment to its leader. Such allegiance would "offer something that people are willing to die for." As leader, Welch demanded the absolute power to determine policy, allocate funds, appoint and remove officers, and expel members. Welch proposed an advisory council limited to thirty men that would meet four times a year, select a successor if he were murdered by communists, and reflect the stature of the membership. From this council he would choose a smaller executive council to meet monthly. A paid, professional staff divided into public relations, speakers, and publishing departments would enhance command control.[22]

Welch reached to the grass roots through a series of bureaucratic layers. Directives were to pass from the central office to major coordinators, each of whom supervised four or more field coordinators entrusted with regional, state, or substate areas. Coordinators managed volunteer section leaders who, in turn, directed eight to ten chapter heads. Between ten and twenty "dedicated patriots" would form each chapter and meet monthly in a member's home. Annual dues of twenty-four dollars for men and twelve dollars for women were to be paid in monthly installments. (These dues would account for one-third of the movement's funds; publication sales and donations eliminated any budgetary shortfall.)[23]

Chapter members were the shock troops in the war against communism. As twentieth-century Paul Reveres tuned to local manifestations of the conspiracy, they would sound the alarm to awaken their fellow Americans. Welch believed that education was the principal weapon to turn the communist advance. He called on members to establish bookstores stocked with approved literature, to circulate conservative periodicals, and to bring anti-communist speakers to their communities. Coordinated letterwriting campaigns, petition drives, exposés of community communists, and local political action would supplement these activities. In addition, Welch championed the creation of front organizations to bring members and nonmembers together, spur action, and expand movement rolls. By the end of 1959, Welch hoped to recruit thirty thousand men and women; his long-range membership goal was one million patriots.[24]

All but one of the men who heard Welch's presentation answered the call to enlist against the communist conspiracy. Robert Welch named the new organization for John Birch, a Baptist missionary killed by Chinese communists just ten days after the victory over Japan. The first casualty of the cold war, Birch was a martyr to American freedom. In his name, men and women would alert their country to the growing cancer within and thus insure the survival of the republic.[25]

Portrait of an anticommunist The founder of the John Birch Society was born on a North Carolina farm in 1899. Robert H. W. Welch, Jr., was a precocious child: He could read at the age of two, and he mastered multiplication tables by four. He entered the University of North Carolina in 1911 when he was twelve years old and graduated four years later. After college, his steps were more uncertain. Welch enrolled at the United States Naval Academy but left after two years. Similarly, he left Harvard Law School before completing his course of study. Academic wandering ceased when a brother offered Welch a position in his Massachusetts-based candy company. Welch found success as the company's vice president for advertising and sales. His rounds of the company's sales offices in Atlanta, Pittsburgh, Chicago, Los Angeles, and Seattle not only enhanced business but generated personal contacts that became essential for Welch's future organizing. Welch also built a network of business and personal contacts during his seven-year term on the board of directors of the National Association of Manufacturers. Serving as a regional vice president for three years, he espoused NAM's conservative line in favor of business interests and against labor unions and government regulation.[26]

In the 1930s Robert Welch began to suspect that communists exercised an inordinate influence in American government. During the Red Scare he campaigned for increased aid to anticommunist forces in China and supported Senator McCarthy's activities against subversion. Meanwhile, Welch maintained his network of conservative friends and business associates and kept them abreast of his interpretation of current events through extensive correspondence. In one important letter, which eventually reached a manuscript length of nearly three hundred pages, Welch traced the path of the communist conspirators to the White House.[27] Both Franklin Roosevelt and Harry Truman, he argued, were under the control of communists. In Dwight Eisenhower "the Communists have one of their own actually in the presidency. . . . There is only one possible word to describe his purposes and his actions. That word is treason."[28] Critics would continuously cite Welch's provocative manuscript, eventually printed as *The Politician*, to prove the society's irresponsibility and discourage membership.[29]

Robert Welch—sincere, intelligent, and seemingly well-read— appealed to his followers as a man who had penetrated the conspiracy and revealed its secrets. His flat, emotionless rhetoric, punctuated with facts and statistics, conjured up the absent-minded professor sure of his message and unmindful of gain or glory. Sixty years old in 1959, bald, of medium height, and paunchy, he was an elder statesman willing to risk all for his country. This was a leader men and women would describe as "charismatic." Their loyalty, combined with his organizational and fund-raising expertise, gave Robert Welch the tools to lead. And many were ready to follow.[30]

RETURN OF THE RIGHT

Robert Welch personally organized the first John Birch Society chapters in early 1959. After initial success in the Boston area around his Belmont base, he repeated his two-day presentations for small, select groups in Los Angeles, San Francisco, and Seattle. Again, Welch culled audiences from his network of friends, business acquaintances, and contacts in such conservative organizations as the Americans for Constitutional Action, the Cardinal Mindszenty Foundation, and the American Coalition of Patriotic Societies. Those recruited in Indianapolis supplemented Welch's work by spreading the Birch message in their communities.[31]

Anticommunist "schools" also provided fertile recruiting grounds for the new movement. In 1958 the Department of Defense's National Security Council directed "the use of military personnel and facilities to arouse the public to the menace of Communism."[32] This order helped spawn an anti-communism education industry dedicated to teaching reserve officers, businessmen, and the wider community about the Red danger and the threats of subversion. Under the legitimizing auspices of "Project Alert," right wingers reached large audiences. Graduates of these anticommunist seminars were prime Birch Society recruits. Meanwhile, anticommunist Christian evangelists and conservative radio broadcasters were issuing similar calls, which Birch activists were prepared to channel.[33]

By the end of 1959 the John Birch Society had planted chapters in sixteen states, including California, Massachusetts, New York, Illinois, Florida, and Texas. It also counted scattered membership cores in nine other states. In Belmont, Massachusetts, Welch had assembled a professional staff to publish the movement's *American Opinion* and to oversee the society's five field coordinators. The society accelerated its efforts in 1960, organizing active chapters in thirty-four states and doubling membership every four months. Dues from the estimated eighteen thousand members increased the society's budget from $129,000 in 1959 to $198,000 in 1960 to over $.5 million in 1961. The Birch bureaucracy grew to match the financial infusion, with twenty-eight persons manning movement headquarters and thirty coordinators and one hundred section leaders supervising regional and community activities. The California organization outpaced all others. Split into two districts to accommodate recruiting successes, the society's golden state demanded two full-time major coordinators and six field coordinators. Elected officials, including two of California's congressmen, were among the new recruits. By the end of 1962 California communities housed three hundred Birch Society chapters.[34]

The apparent renewal of the communist world offensive in the late 1950s and early 1960s increased interest among conservatives in the Birch Society. Revolution in Cuba and Fidel Castro's embrace of Marxism alerted Americans to a communist incursion in the Western Hemisphere and a danger on their doorstep. When coupled with Russian space feats and boasts of hydrogen bomb megatonnage, the threat became even more terrifying and immediate. American leaders, at the same time, seemed unwilling or unable to counter communist thrusts in Vietnam and Laos and impotent before the building of the Berlin Wall. At home, John Kennedy's election to the presidency promised increased government spending and additional regulation and controls. In the civil rights movement, with its sit-ins and freedom rides, conservatives detected the danger of domestic turmoil and federal intervention to the detriment of states' rights. Those schooled in anticommunist ideology could not miss the relationship between internal and external events.[35]

Movement recruiters also benefited from the general revival of American conservatism. The Eisenhower administration's failure to roll back New Deal social programs or international communism's advances spurred conservatives to mobilize their resources and contest for control of the Republican party. Kennedy's defeat of Richard Nixon in 1960 opened the door wider for a conservative challenge, which crystallized in the emergence of Senator Barry Goldwater of Arizona.

In tone and target, the more established conservatives echoed Welch and his Birchers. Barry Goldwater, in *The Conscience of a Conservative*, warned: "Our defenses against the accumulation of unlimited power in Washington are in poorer shape, I fear, than our defenses against the aggressive designs of Moscow. Like so many other nations before us, we may succumb through internal weakness rather than before a foreign foe."[36] In *Why Not Victory,* Goldwater asked Americans to "realize once and for all that our enemy is not a nation but a political movement made up of ideologically possessed people who have organized themselves as an armed force and secured control over entire countries. They have cadre in every country and use Moscow as their command post."[37] According to J. Edgar Hoover, director of the FBI, the communists "infiltrated every conceivable sphere of activity: youth groups, radio, television and motion picture industries; church, school and education groups; the press, nationality minority groups and political units."[38] Ezra Taft Benson, Eisenhower's secretary of agriculture and a Mormon church leader, called the anticommunist crusade "a fight against slavery, immorality, atheism, cruelty, barbarism, deceit, and the destruction of human life."[39] Clearly, it was Robert Welch that Ronald Reagan had in mind when he declared in 1961: "One of the foremost authorities in the world today has said we have ten years. Not ten years to make up our minds, but ten years to win or lose—by 1970 the world will be all slave or all free."[40]

Conservatives, however, could not grant Robert Welch his central assumptions: They rejected Welch's equation of liberalism with treason and his indictment of Eisenhower as a communist agent. Still, conservatives did not initially repudiate Birch Society support nor distance themselves from Welch's accusations. Conservatives would count on the movement's resources as long as Welch's controversial theories remained outside the national media spotlight. In the rush to power, Birchers and their conservative allies became entwined in a "semialliance" to advance each other's cause, and their own. Exposure would force a reappraisal of this coalition.[41]

Not surprisingly, Robert Welch spoke at a Goldwater-for-president rally in Chicago before the 1960 Republican convention. Welch placed *The Conscience of a Conservative* on the approved Birch Society reading list and had it stocked in the organization's local bookstores and libraries. Barry Goldwater credited Dean Clarence Manion, a member of the Birch Society's national council, with the responsibility "for the writing of the book *The Conscience of a Conservative*."[42] Birchers, like many other conservatives, looked to Goldwater as their champion. Their commitment of time, money, and energy to his campaign translated into a personal and direct confrontation with the communist conspiracy. At the same time, conservatives recognized that Bircher enthusiasm and grass-roots organization were essential if the Republican party was to be wrested from the moderates. As Goldwater told reporters, "[Birchers] are the finest people in my community."[43]

CONFRONTING THE CONSPIRACY

Birchers aggressively initiated anticommunist wars in their communities. They waged educational campaigns by opening bookstores and buying radio time to broadcast their concerns. To keep the movement's message constantly before the public, chapters erected large billboards festooned with slogans like "Cuba Free in '63," "Get the US out of the UN," "Support Your Local Police," "Impeach Chief Justice Earl Warren," and "No to Gun Control." Society speakers also promoted Americanism before such community groups as the chamber of commerce, the American Legion, the Lions Club, and others. Investigations of schools, churches, and libraries to detect communist influence were high priorities for society members. Similarly, they questioned local opinion makers about their communist sympathies. To underscore their position as a powerful movement that could not be ignored, they followed up their investigations and interviews with letter-writing campaigns and petition drives directed at community officials and institutions. Meanwhile,

Birchers activated plans to capture the Republican party from the precinct level up.[44]

Supplementing these efforts, the John Birch Society launched a variety of single-issue, ad hoc front organizations to reach and educate sympathiers. With MOTOREDE, or the Movement to Restore Decency, Birchers campaigned against pornography and sex education in the public schools. The Committee to Warn of the Arrival of Communist Merchandise on the Local Business Scene encompassed fifty cities in ten states and organized boycotts and picket lines to warn shoppers of Red-tinted stores. Like Communist party affiliates, these fronts exposed nonmembers to the Birch Society's program and proved important recruiting conduits.[45]

The John Birch Society expected every member to immerse himself in a rigorous self-education program. Leaders advised the rank and file to read one hundred books—"One Hundred Steps to the Truth"—to understand fully the danger confronted. Only when members were completely convinced of the seriousness of the communist threat could the society be assured of their loyalty and thirst for offensive action. Approved reading lists and the organization's *American Opinion* and *Review of the News* not only fashioned the proper perspective but shielded members from a publishing industry and news media assumed to be communist-infiltrated.[46]

A centralized bureaucracy insured unity of purpose among the many local branches. In addition, the Belmont headquarters supplied each member with a monthly *Bulletin* suggesting projects and assignments to defeat the communist conspiracy. At chapter meetings members would read and discuss this newsletter and plan activities suitable to their community. Welch established an even more direct line of communication between the membership and himself. Birchers individually informed Welch in "member's monthly messages" of their contribution to the cause, including books read, actions taken, and tasks completed. The memos, whether read in Belmont or not, were personal oaths of monthly allegiance and served to heighten participation and morale.[47]

However, the movement never resembled the single-minded anti-communist machine of Robert Welch's dreams. Despite his claim of absolute authority, Welch continually reminded members that they were not bound to accept his pronouncements nor participate in activities with which they disagreed. Section and chapter leaders also intervened, modifying instructions to fit the local environment and adjusting to feedback from the rank and file. Individualistic and assertive with many having attained high social and economic status, Birchers did not follow Welch blindly. Large numbers had never accepted Welch's contention that Eisenhower was a communist, nor were they fully convinced of his description of the extent of the conspiracy. Specific goals of impeaching Earl Warren, withdrawing from the United

Nations, and exposing the "civil rights fraud" were of less significance than a personal and amorphous stand in defense of America and against communism. Still, they turned to Welch for direction and inspiration. It was he who personified the movement, not only to outsiders but to those dedicated to the cause. As volunteers, however, they would withdraw if the movement failed to meet their needs.[48]

For conservative men and women, the John Birch Society filled a vacuum. They were no other groups as professionally organized with so prominent a leadership engaged in direct action against communism. As retired Marine Major General Robert Blake explained: "I saw in it the first opinion group to come to my attention which possessed the potentialities for organizing the scattered voices of conservatism into an effective influence on the political environment of our country."[49]

Opinion makers' response The John Birch Society first attracted media attention in the early months of 1961. Thomas Storke, editor and publisher of a Santa Barbara, California, newspaper exposed the Birch Society as the source of a rash of attacks on local school officials and ministers. These revelations prompted California's United States Senator Thomas Kuchel to call for a congressional investigation of the "ultra conservative, semisecret" movement. Senators from Montana, Connecticut, and Ohio supported Kuchel's request for hearings.[50]

A flurry of articles in national newspapers and magazines followed these events. Most focused on what *Time* called Robert Welch's *"Mein Kampf"*—*The Politician*—and its labeling of President Eisenhower as a communist. The Birch Society, *Time* concluded, was "a goose step away from the formation of goon squads."[51] The *Los Angeles Times* criticized the organization as authoritarian and irresponsible and warned that it posed "a peril to conservatives."[52] Responding to reports of a large Catholic membership, Catholic newspapers and journals joined the anti-Welch chorus. *America* editorialized about the "pseudo-hysteria of the society's leadership."[53] *The Pilot*, the official newspaper of the Boston archdiocese, and *New World*, its counterpart in Chicago, likewise rejected the movement's patriotic claims. The *New York Times Magazine, Life, Newsweek, Look,* and *Saturday Evening Post* ran similar articles about "extremism." In response to a reporter's question, Attorney General Robert Kennedy dismissed the movement: "I think that they are ridiculous, and I don't think that anybody should pay much attention to them."[54] A spokesman for the Justice Department, however, targeted the John Birch Society as "a matter of concern."[55] FBI agents would soon open files on the organization and begin surveillance of its activities.[56]

The nation's leading conservative journal, the *National Review*, attempted to steer a middle course through the media storm. Seeking no break in conservative ranks, William F. Buckley, Jr., characterized the society as "An organization of men and women devoted to militant political activity." Few members, he was certain, fully subscribed to Robert Welch's sensational charges of communist influence in the White House. Although disagreeing with him on many issues, Buckley said of his friend Robert Welch: "I have always admired his personal courage and devotion to causes." "I hope it thrives," he concluded, "provided it resists such false assumptions as that a man's subjective motives can automatically be deduced from the objective consequences of his acts."[57]

A year later, perhaps in the face of 1962 Gallup Polls showing that 43 percent of the American people looked at the society unfavorably and only 8 percent registered approval, the editors of *National Review* lashed Welch for "damaging the cause of anti-Communism." They concurred with fellow-conservative Russell Kirk's admonition: "Cry wolf often enough and everyone takes you for an imbecile or a knave, when after all there *are* wolves in this world."[58] In a letter to the *National Review*, Barry Goldwater accused Welch of being "far removed from reality and common sense" and called for the resignation of the society's founder.[59] Senator John Tower, Richard Nixon, and retired Admiral Arthur Radford similarly bypassed the membership to assail Robert Welch.[60]

The John Birch Society brushed off the "smear campaign" as part of a coordinated offensive launched "on directives issued from Moscow."[61] But the broad and united counterattack by opinion makers was effective and forced the movement off balance. Their portrayal of the society as extremist sharply limited its ability openly to marshall support while energizing victims and opponents to withstand the society's strikes. The recruiting pace slackened and chapters adopted low profiles to limit the loss of resources.[62]

These setbacks, however, proved short-lived. The agitation by opinion makers had come in two short bursts in 1961 and 1962. It was not sustained in 1963 and 1964, when only scattered anti–Birch Society articles appeared in national magazines and journals. The media had, as well, delivered a mixed message by condemning Welch, but not the rank and file. Insulated and already distrustful of opinion makers, members maintained their allegiance. Moreover, government repression had been kept to a minimum and required few resources to counter. The Republican party, a key polity member, remained open to influence. The society could even point to an investigative report of the California state senate, which concluded that members were not "mentally unstable, crackpots, or hysterical about the threat of Communist subversion."[63]

When the seige lifted, Birchers again took advantage of the growing conservative momentum aroused by the draft-Goldwater movement and by concerns about black activism and Russian power. Commitment was facilitated even in a hostile environment, for nearly half of the movement's recruits joined relatives or personal friends already belonging to local chapters. In the spring of 1962 Birch Society leaders reported renewed interest and, within a year, a rapid expansion of membership to sixty thousand men and women. With an estimated budget of 1 million dollars, the organization entered all of the forty-eight continental states and employed forty coordinators. By the beginning of 1964 the movement claimed the allegiance of seventy-five thousand members. Thus, while the majority of Americans had accepted the opinion-making public's portrayal of the movement as radical, the Birchers still had room to maneuver.[64]

A CHOICE NOT AN ECHO

The draft-Goldwater movement within the Republican party furnished the Birch Society the opportunity to end its isolation. Birchers rushed to Barry Goldwater with an army of political operatives and volunteers prepared to donate funds, answer telephones, ring doorbells, and shepherd voters to the polls. Successfully performing the unrecognized but essential grass-roots work brought them influence within the campaign. Birchers honeycombed the Goldwater organization; some rising to decision-making levels. Through such efforts, the John Birch Society gained new legitimacy and respectability as well as a broader base of outside contacts.[65]

The Goldwaterites could scarcely refuse the Birchers' assistance. They faced a well-financed, multicandidate opposition through a long primary season. Moreover, the assassination of President John Kennedy had dramatically altered the contours of American politics. Lyndon Johnson had made himself heir to the martyred president's legacy and commanded enormous popular support. In a time when war appeared far-off and the economy sound, Johnson's position seemed impregnable.

Barry Goldwater, on capturing the nomination of his party, confirmed in Birchers' minds the correctness of their choice. In his acceptance speech Goldwater solemnly declared: "I would remind you that extremism in the defense of liberty is no vice! And let me remind you also that moderation in the pursuit of justice is no virtue!"[66] Robert Welch's John Birch Society had taken its place as a partner in the Republican party coalition.

To spur recruitment, and to counter 1964 opinion polls, which continued to indicate that only 8 percent of Americans were favorable to the movement, the John Birch Society attempted to refashion its image. An important part of its public relations campaign was a sixteen-page supplement placed in the Sunday editions of ten major newspapers, including the *Los Angeles Times*, the *Chicago Tribune*, the *Boston Herald*, and the *Dallas Morning News*. In it, the Birchers downplayed their movement's emphasis on conspiracy and focused on big government, riots, and faith in God. The supplement also rewrote *The Politician*, presenting President Eisenhower as a victim, like all

Americans, not an agent of communism. Pictures of Robert Welch, the national council, and a chapter meeting in a member's home revealed a movement less secret than the Elks or Moose Club. Catholic and black members testified to the inclusive nature of an organization free of religious and racial prejudice. The insert even carried an endorsement from President Eisenhower: "The John Birch Society is a good, patriotic society. I don't agree with what its founder said about me but that does not detract from the fact that its membership is comprised of many fine Americans." Readers were encouraged to attend a chapter meeting and join the "men and women of integrity and purpose building rededication to God, to family, to country, and to strong moral principles."[67]

Despite a determined campaign, Lyndon Johnson was easily victorious over Barry Goldwater at the polls. The Republican candidate captured just 39 percent of the vote and five states. The American people had rejected a conservative critique that seemed out of touch with current realities and even frightening. Militant anticommunism, growing government power, and concerns about public morality lacked salience for Americans. If established conservatives had appeared neither reasonable nor relevant, the Birchers were surely extremists. The movement, however, remained organizationally viable and retained influence within the Republican party. Although far from power it was still capable of growth within the conservative minority.[68]

Birch Society membership continued to grow in the wake of the conservative debacle. Without any other vehicle, Goldwater partisans followed their Birch contacts and friends into the movement. Affiliation was a simple matter. Four thousand chapters, in all major metropolitan and suburban areas, blanketed the nation. Activists had established strong society chapters in the Northeast cities of Boston, Philadelphia, and greater New York City. One-fourth of the members resided in the South. Fifty chapters operated in Atlanta and one-half of the Florida membership concentrated in Miami and Dade County. Texas alone consumed the energy of six full-time coordinators, with significant movement populations in Dallas, Houston, and San Antonio. Midwestern Birchers, accounting for 20 percent of the membership, mobilized in Milwaukee, Chicago and its suburbs, Kansas City, St. Louis, and Omaha. With 40 percent of all members, the West was the movement's most successful recruiting field. The map hanging in the Belmont headquarters decorated Denver, Salt Lake City, Phoenix, Seattle, and Spokane with numerous chapter pins. But the center of Birchism remained in California. Seventeen coordinators worked the state with influential chapters throughout the Los Angeles Basin and Orange County. A staff of nine operated the regional office in San Marino and tended the needs of Birchers in the fourteen western states.[69]

Profile of the membership   As Robert Welch had planned, the high social and economic standing of the national leadership enhanced the attraction of the John Birch Society for those seeking an anticommunist instrument. The national council, during the 1960s, counted among its members a former assistant secretary of state, the dean of the Notre Dame Law School, retired military officers, several Catholic priests, and past state and federal government officials. Throughout the movement's history, nearly two-thirds of those in leadership positions were wealthy entrepreneurs who operated their own businesses. All council members were white and only one, Marian Welch, was a woman. Protestants and Catholics shared power, and at least one Jew sat on Welch's governing board. Turnover in the leadership often meant the replacement of fathers with sons in a continuing family tradition of conservatism. Interestingly, Frank Cullen Brophy, a council member from Phoenix, was the son of William Brophy, who had helped organize the deportation of Wobblies from Bisbee in 1917. Council members, exploiting business and personal networks and allowing their names to be used to build the society's reputation, partially counteracted negative publicity and the opposition of other opinion makers.[70]

The John Birch Society drew its members primarily from the middle and upper middle classes. Three-quarters of the Birchers wore white collars, and over half of these men and women had professional and managerial careers. Members commanded significantly larger incomes than their fellow Americans. Over one-fifth of the members, compared to just 4 percent of all Americans, had an annual income of $15,000 or more. Not surprising, Birchers claimed more years of formal education. Thirty-one percent of the movement's members had graduated from college as opposed to 7 percent of the wider population. Reflecting their education and economic standing, these Birchers were active in more national and community organizations than their neighbors. Two-thirds of the society's members but only one-third of all Americans had ties to two or more groups. For the vast majority of Birchers, membership outside the movement meant identification with the Republican party. Well educated, financially secure, with families and children, Birchers were vitally interested in community life and were accustomed to voicing their concerns. At the same time, the movement attracted lower-middle-class and working-class Americans. Approximately one-fourth of the members collected less than $7,000 in wages annually. Twelve percent had not earned a high school diploma.[71]

The movement appealed to Protestants of all denominations. Evangelical Protestants, as well as Episcopalians, Congregationalists, and Presbyterians, were at home in chapter meetings. Large numbers of Catholics also joined. The society's attack on communism as an atheistic force and its intent to roll back the conspiracy from Catholic Eastern Europe brought many into the ranks. "Fighting Communism," said Gerald Schomp, "seemed to be a useful and exciting way to practice my religion."[72] Catholic opinion makers also encouraged membership. Richard Cardinal Cushing of Boston praised Robert

Welch as a dedicated anticommunist and called on Catholics to support his efforts. Pro-Birch Catholic journals like *Tidings* of Los Angeles and *Tablet* of New York similarly trumpeted the cause. Jews also entered the movement, creating their own Jewish Society of Americanists. Their numbers, however, remained quite small.[73]

Approximately one thousand blacks joined the John Birch Society and were assigned to integrated chapters in the North and segregated units in the South. Welch condemned Jim Crow discrimination but believed in gradual change effected at the community level without federal intervention. He opposed the civil rights movement as a creation of the conspiracy and characterized Martin Luther King as a "troublemaker" and "favorite of the communists." This position was publicized through the front group, Truth About Civil Turmoil, and effectively short-circuited black enthusiasm for the movement.[74]

For these Americans, joining the John Birch Society meant taking a stand against those who threatened family, community, religion, and country. They saw themselves as members of an action organization, alert while others slept, fighting when many had retreated. In accepting or tolerating an explanation of manipulated events they separated themselves and incurred public disfavor. Yet in affluent suburbs and working-class neighborhoods, the Birchers drew strength from their personal economic and social achievements, the support of family and friends, and the words of religious and community leaders. Their affiliation with the society, however, never meant a relinquishing of will. If the society lost touch with its members, the same strengths that had produced allegiance would fuel dissent.

VEERING FARTHER RIGHT

At the crest of the movement's surge in 1964 and 1965 80,000 to 100,000 Americans were card-carrying Birchers. The society's growth necessitated the establishment of regional offices in California, Illinois, New York, Texas, and Washington, D.C., and the fielding of seventy-eight coordinators. The 1965 budget called for the expenditure of $5 million to maintain the society. Seeking to strengthen and expand Bircher footholds in the Republican party, leaders announced plans to organize one hundred chapters in each of the 435 congressional districts. From these bases would emerge society activists prepared to gain control of party machinery and insure the nomination of suitable candidates. Members also continued to preach the watchwords of their faith: "to promote less government, more responsibility, and a better world."[75] Now was the time for Americans to rededicate themselves to God, family, and country. Against a rising tide of black power, college campus disruption, urban violence, and crime, Bircher appeals became more fervent.[76]

However, the Birch Society was soon forced to abandon its advanced positions. An important reason for this retreat was a change in the movement's ideology. The revision, first broached in 1964 and fully elaborated during the next two years, shifted the society's focus, isolated it from conservative sympathizers, and generated dissension in the ranks. Robert Welch, after additional study, had decided that the communist offensive was only a subplot in a more encompassing and dangerous intrigue. According to Welch, history revealed a master conspiracy hatched in Bavaria, Germany, on 1 May 1776 by a group of men known as the Illuminati. Their aim was world domination and the creation of police states subordinate to a single international government. To undermine established government, law, religion, and the family, they provoked war, revolution, depression, and famine. Welch traced the plot through the French Revolution, the Revolutions of 1848, World War I and II, and into the cold war. Communism, socialism, and liberalism were merely their tools of conquest. Marx, Lenin, Stalin, Roosevelt, Eisenhower, and Johnson served higher masters. Concealed behind their puppets, the identities of these "INSIDERS" were unknown even to Welch.[77]

The Birchers judged America as "60 to 80 percent" lost to the Insiders' conspiracy in 1965. The income tax, federal aid to education, and Medicare demonstrated the power of the plotters over decision making. Pornography, drugs, tolerance of homosexuality, and lawlessness were evidence of the intrigue. Opposition forces were eroding. With government, media, both political parties, and the churches in their grasp, the Insiders had reached their end game in America.[78]

Welch patched the Vietnam conflict, too, into the guilt of conspiracy. It was, he wrote, "a completely phony foreign war"[79] because the conspirators operated on both sides of the struggle. The Insiders had precipitated the war to expand the borders of their dominion and to siphon away American resources. Their minions within the government of the United States were preparing to prolong the conflict to justify increased censorship, the imposition of wage and price controls, and the rationing of food supplies. Thus, America's anticommunist stand in Southeast Asia was merely a screen to further the regimentation of society and hasten the coming of the world dictatorship.[80]

Opponents within the Republican party reacted quickly to the John Birch Society's political inroads and increased ideological vulnerability. Linking the society to the Ku Klux Klan, Thruston Morton, Kentucky senator and chairman of the Senate Campaign Committee, denied: "room in the Republican Party for a clandestine organization engaged in character assassination."[81] National chair Ray Bliss, with the support of the party's coordinating committee, denounced the society for using the Republican organization "for its own ends."[82] The conservative wing of the party concurred. Ronald Reagan, preparing for the California governor's race, disavowed Birch Society assistance and suggested it had recently been infiltrated by a "kind of lunatic fringe."[83] Barry Goldwater, Everett Dirksen, Gerald Ford, and other members of the party hierarchy also went on record against Welch and his organization. These opinion-maker assaults and the attendant negative publicity were effective. The Birchers' position in the party became precarious. In late 1965, moreover, the number of Americans polled as favorable to the society had been cut by more than half.[84]

The shock waves of this repudiation rumbled through the movement. Forced to choose between the John Birch Society and their party, many returned to the Republican fold. Ideological revisions facilitated this decision. Men and women who had joined the society to fight the communist menace were bewildered when asked to refocus their efforts against a new enemy. While anticommunism was a legitimized tradition in America, a campaign against Insiders raised doubts about Welch's judgment. Recruits had misperceived the nature of the organization and drew back from its radicalism. Others grew weary of unending requests to read, write, and circulate petitions. When balanced against the alleged power of the conspirators, such measures seemed ineffective and inappropriate.

Internal dissension and leadership instability intensified the crisis. In 1965 and 1966 some Birchers detected Jews in the nucleus of the conspiracy. Welch's confrontation with these anti-Semitic "neutralizers" was costly. He disbanded at least three chapters and forced the resignations of several leaders, including a member of the national council. Two other council members, one deriding the movement as a "bookselling operation," also departed. In addition, the former California congressman and head of the western regional office, John Rousselet, and the public relations chiefs of the midwestern and eastern divisions resigned for personal reasons.[85]

The Birch Society attempted to staunch its resource drain by resuming the offensive. Robert Welch organized a new front—TRIM (Tax Reform Immediately)—to rally support. Jeremiads appeared in the *American Opinion* to ignite a backlash against the New Left, feminist assaults on the family, the civil rights movement, and countercultural experiments in drugs and sexual behavior. At the same time, Welch became more specific in targeting the Insiders. The conspiracy, he maintained, operated through the Council on Foreign Relations and he condemned recently elected President Richard Nixon for appointing fellow members Henry Kissinger, William Rogers, and Melvin Laird to positions in the new administration. Despite reversals, Welch assured his followers that they would "expose and rout" the conspiracy within ten years.[86]

Brave words and renewed effort did not halt the movement's decline. Perhaps as many as thirty thousand men and women, or one-third of the membership, deserted in 1966 and 1967. Still more became inactive without formally severing ties. Bookstores closed and chapters dropped from organizational charts. Membership continued to fall precipitously in the late 1960s and early 1970s as conservative competitors, unhampered by a negative and radical image, attracted support. The movement's drive for influence had been turned aside within the Republican party. A "curtain of silence" descended as the media no longer found the society newsworthy. Discredited, unable to jettison Robert Welch or his controversial theories, the John Birch Society could only watch the rise of the New Right from a position of isolation.[87]

TOWARD REAGANISM

To many Americans, the events of the 1960s and 1970s proved the bank-ruptcy of liberalism. They blamed federal bureaucrats for sponsoring a war on poverty that raised already heavy tax burdens and elevated welfare over work and minority over majority. Paternalistic and out of touch, the "social engineers" had forced busing and affirmative action programs without regard to the will of those affected. The liberal Supreme Court had sanctioned these abuses while coddling criminals, eliminating prayer from the public schools, easing restrictions on pornography, and legalizing abortion. The result was a countercultural plague of violence, sexual promiscuity, teenage pregnancy, illegitimate births, and drug abuse.[88]

The Nixon administration appeared to mount only a feeble defense. In fact, in the early 1970s feminists had prodded congressional passage and presidential approval of the Equal Rights Amendment, which conservatives feared would undermine the family, obscure sex roles, and encourage homo-sexuality. America's moral reserves were further depleted during the Waterg-ate scandals. Deceit and improper conduct at the political pinnacle numbed those already concerned about the nation's moral future. An energy crisis, shortages, recurring recessions, and double-digit inflation signaled a decline that was economic as well as spiritual.

Conservatives could derive little solace from international events. They denounced detente with the Soviet Union and rapprochement with the Peoples' Republic of China as appeasement and policies of retreat. Relaxation of cold war tensions, arms limitation agreements, and domestic budgetary restraints surely meant the loss of American military superiority. Meanwhile, few would claim victory in the withdrawal of American troops and the Vietnamization of the war in Southeast Asia. News footage of the hurried helicopter evacuation from the roof of the embassy in Saigon stunned a nation sobered by the heavy losses in blood and materiel after a decade of war.

The dominoes did not stop falling with the "loss" of Vietnam, Cambodia, and Laos. Communist gains were also recorded in Africa, the Middle East, and Central America. As the 1970s ended, the failure of American policy in Iran placed in bold relief a decade of malaise and drift. The seizure of the

American embassy revealed the limits of power and provoked a grass-roots concern unseen for three decades.

Conservative activists diagnosed the sickness in familiar terms. "Godless liberal philosophies," wrote the Reverend Jerry Falwell, had corrupted basic values and sapped the strength of the American people. "The godless minority of treacherous individuals who have been permitted to formulate national policy must now realize they do not represent the majority."[89] Their medium of mobilization was a phalanx of single-issue movements, multipurpose political organizations, think tanks, and religious federations united in support of conservative candidates and issues. These New Rightists initiated direct-mail fund raising, a communication tool enabling them to reach targeted, single-issue constituencies. When this technique was fused to the political action committee, a response to legal restrictions on personal campaign contributions, the conservatives could gather scattered grass-roots interests into a focused and national force.

The broad conservative umbrella sheltered a variety of groups and individuals. Dramatic growth in conservative and fundamentalist religious churches like the Southern Baptist, Assembly of God, and Church of Christ made resources available to activist ministers preaching a right-wing social agenda. Like those who brought their congregations into the Anti-Saloon League at the beginning of the century, these ministers galvanized support for the Moral Majority, America for Jesus, and the National Christian Action Coalition. Meanwhile, Americans donated heavily to the nearly sixteen hundred televangelists who were broadcasting a conservative socioreligious message. Catholics and Jews, as well, accepted the conservative social program and joined with Protestants in Right to Life, the Eagle Forum, Pro-Decency, and Stop-ERA. To restore prosperity, conservatives advocated a "supply-side" agenda. Tax cuts would revive the American economy and pay for themselves by generating increased production and government revenue. Deregulation of business, government budget cuts, and reduction of the federal bureaucracy were also prescribed for recovery. Militant anticommunists enlisted with social and economic conservatives in such groups as the American Freedom Coalition, the Conservative Caucus, and the Committee for the Survival of a Free Congress. Allied but separate, neoconservative academics and journalists condemned the assault on traditional institutions and values by government and left-wingers. The leaders of the New Right had built an alliance reaching across the religious, class, ethnic, and regional divisions of American life. Within this coalition, Birchers past and present were welcomed and prized for their experience and zeal.

These New Right activists moved against diverse targets in the 1970s. They boycotted television programs and their sponsors to protest the exploitation of violence and sex. Anti-abortionists marched, picketed, gathered petitions, and wrote legislators to show support for a constitutional amendment banning abortion. Some invaded clinics, destroying property and intimidating patients and staff. Conservatives mobilized to defeat gay-rights referenda in Florida, Minnesota, Kansas, and Oregon. Men and women in Stop-ERA and the Eagle Forum confronted feminists and prevented passage of the Equal Rights Amendment. Tax opponents achieved their greatest victory in California with the Proposition 13 rollback of property levies. Conservatives were also successful in defeating liberal Democrats running for state and national office. With enhanced respectability, strong organizational and communication tools, and a quickening resource-gathering momentum, New Rightists bolstered further their position in the Republican party.

The John Birch Society was ambivalent about the rise of conservative activism in the 1970s. On the local level, individual Birchers participated in campaigns against abortion, gun control, and the ERA. They also joined with conservatives to defeat the election bids of liberal candidates. Yet the society was critical of the New Rightists. It believed that, without benefit of a comprehensive theory to interpret events, the New Right was handicapped and could only be a "passing fancy." The inner secrets of history could be learned only in a movement that was, as well, a "university without walls." Officially, then, the society continued to act in isolation to advocate tax reform, limited government, and opposition to the Insiders. The society's aloofness also reflected its impotence. Bypassed, no longer a significant contender for power, the movement had turned inward.[90]

New Rightists claimed victory for the landslide election of Ronald Reagan in 1980. The new administration recruited from conservative ranks and incorporated New Right leaders into the decision-making process. The president's verbal anticommunism and jibes at the "evil empire" played well before conservative audiences. So, too, did his acceleration of defense spending. By reducing taxes, borrowing, and cutting Great Society programs like job training, food stamps, and aid for dependent children, the Reagan administration generated revenues for a massive military buildup. Although Congress balked at Reagan proposals on abortion, school prayer, and busing, it did mandate work requirements for welfare recipients. As part of the Reagan Revolution, presidential appointees became less vigilant in the defense of civil rights and affirmative action and more restrictive in applying birth control and abortion guidelines. Perhaps most significant was President Reagan's appointment of almost one-half of the nation's federal judges, which assured a conservative court system into the next century.

Reagan's advocacy of much of the movement's agenda did not shield him from the censure of the John Birch Society. Robert Welch accused the president of being a "lackey" of the conspirators, acceding to their demands that he choose his appointees from the Council on Foreign Relations pool. George Bush, William Casey, and Alexander Haig, among others, bore the mark of the conspiracy. Deficit spending, moreover, was an Insiders' tool to precipitate America's internal decay. Birchers also decried the administration's cooptation of conservative activists and its preemption of issues. They believed that conservatives faced their greatest danger under Reagan, for his rhetoric deceived the American people and reduced support for right-wing causes. The Reagan presidency, said Birch Society official John McManus, "has been devastating. Everybody went to sleep."[91]

After Welch   Insiders' advances in the 1980s accompanied crisis within the movement. Robert Welch, at the society's helm since its birth, suffered a stroke in 1983 and was forced to step down. The National Council appointed Georgia congressman Larry MacDonald as his successor. MacDonald, active in such organizations as the Conservative Caucus, the Committee for the Survival of a Free Congress, Young Americans for Freedom, and the American Security Council, gave promise of ending the society's isolation and increasing influence within the New Right mainstream. Such hopes were snuffed out later in 1983 when a Soviet jet fighter downed a South Korean commercial airliner killing MacDonald and 268 other persons.[92]

Welch's death in 1985 further demoralized Birchers while, at the same time, reducing contributions from those loyal to the founder but not the movement. MacDonald's replacement was unable to halt the society's decline. In 1986 an emergency transfusion of $1.5 million raised from donations and property sales "prevented literally the shutting down of our operation" and forestalled creditors owed over $9 million. Under the direction of Charles Armour, the society balanced itself by sharply reducing costs while generating sufficient funds to insure continued operation. Restructuring also included a purge from the rolls of twenty thousand to thirty thousand inactive Birchers and the replacement of *American Opinion* and *Review of the News* with the biweekly *New American*.[93]

At the end of the 1980s, the movement claimed fifteen hundred chapters, primarily concentrated in the Rocky Mountain states, with fifteen thousand members. Aware of the movement's weaknesses, leaders have announced plans to spur recruiting, build resources, and remedy "an image problem." Education remains the movement's primary weapon, and the dream of rallying America against the conspiracy its goal. Through monthly chapter meetings, summer camps for teenagers, a research center, and a speakers bureau, the movement continues to agitate. "When the time comes," says McManus, "if the society's base is strong enough and there is enough residual morality left in the American people then we could very easily triumph. So where do we go? We continue to build the base."[94]

The John Birch Society, in program and overlapping membership, served as the bridge connecting McCarthyism to the New Right and Reaganism. From a narrow anticommunism, the movement assisted in broadening the conservative agenda to moral and social issues of growing importance to grassroots

America. In the 1960s, it stood as the only conservative organization capable of mobilizing tens of thousands of men and women in every region of the country against liberal inroads. Membership in the cause was unrestricted; Catholics, Jews, and blue-collar ethnics were encouraged to join traditional conservative constituencies. For a time the Birchers touched the mainstream and exerted power within the Republican party.

If the movement helped direct conservatives to influence, it would not be their vehicle to membership in the polity. With opinion makers' guidance, Americans defined the movement as radical and irresponsible. Robert Welch's firm control of the movement's ideology and bureaucracy meant that little could be done to alter these negative perceptions. When the 1970s brought new opportunities, the Birch Society was in no position to exploit them. Having been branded as illegitimate and suffering from the Republican party's recent rejection, the movement could not attract new recruits or hold on to old members. The nucleus remained intact only because of the society's bureaucratic strength, the discipline of the loyal, and an absence of repression by government and polity members. Whether the movement can continue for very long to afford the luxury of survival in isolation is unclear.

7

"WE SHALL NOT BE MOVED": THE STUDENT NONVIOLENT COORDINATING COMMITTEE

The black struggle for civil rights is one of the few social movements of the twentieth century to be incorporated in the celebration of the American pageant. This attack on racial prejudice and discrimination is judged as the inevitable and legitimate fulfillment of the American promise. The movement's geographic milestones—Montgomery, Little Rock, Greensboro, Birmingham, and Selma—have become part of America's collective memory. In a cause defined as just, America is perceived to have moved beyond racial reaction and toward the color-blind society.

Celebration, however, obscures. In triumph, the past's tenacity is underestimated. It

Grass roots people
will enter history.
BOB MOSES

also neglects the social movement dynamic easily attributing change to charismatic leaders and overlooking the decisive interplay of chal-

141

lengers, elite groups, and authorities. The civil rights movement of the 1950s and 1960s, taking advantage of shifting political and economic opportunities, pressed a campaign against caste and class discrimination. Activists in several organizations mobilized tens of thousands of men and women against prohibitions based upon skin color in public accommodations and voting and injustices rooted in economic disparities in housing and employment. The realities of southern power dictated that organizers had to do more than promote salience and efficacy at the grass roots. Change necessitated intervention from the North. Movement activists promoted disruption and prodded northern opinion makers and polity members to reconsider the claims of southern authorities and to support the protest agenda.

Diverse tasks promoted a multipronged offensive. Manning one of the movement fronts was the Student Nonviolent Coordinating Committee (SNCC). SNCC (pronounced "Snick") drew its breath from Martin Luther King, Jr.'s Southern Christian Leadership Conference (SCLC) in the wake of the sit-in demonstrations that swept across the upper South in 1960. Choosing to mobilize in the "iceberg" of the Deep South, SNCC attempted to transform conditions from the bottom up. Lasting change would come only through an indigenous leadership in local "pockets of power" that were strong in spiritual and material resources.

Nonviolent and integrationist at its inception, SNCC confronted the intransigence of the southern system. Its members' faith in established northern elites buckled as pleas for protection went unheeded and demands for justice were compromised. In their time of disillusionment, SNCC activists became the protest vanguard. Nonviolence gave way to militancy, integration to cultural and racial nationalism, and middle-class values to calls for the redistribution of wealth and power. As SNCC redefined itself, established groups and opinion makers adjusted their images of the movement. Cries of black power and identification with Third World peoples of color frightened whites, who cut support. A lack of consensus over class issues and the growing importance of Vietnam split further the civil rights coalition. The federal government, once a vital sponsor, became repressive. Without a strong organizational foundation, SNCC shattered from within. In its victory and defeat may be understood the contradictions of race and the limits of reform in America.

"FREEDOM'S COMIN' AND IT WON'T BE LONG"[1]

For the white South at midcentury, race was an issue resolved long ago. Debate had ceased in 1896 when the United States Supreme Court's *Plessy* v. *Ferguson* decision had decreed white southern autonomy in matters of race. Law and custom transformed this "separate but equal" judgment into an

American system of apartheid. Beginning at the cradle and ending at the grave, the South drew a color line segregating whites from blacks, superiors from inferiors. Underfunding of black institutions cemented inferiority in place, resulting in substandard education, health care, and living comditions. For the 75 percent of American blacks who lived in the South, existence was a daily confrontation with humiliation, with few opportunities available for redress. Having successfully relegated blacks to the bottom social and economic tier of southern society, whites saw no need to grapple with the dilemma of race.[2]

Grievances alone, however, could not power a sustained challenge. Effective resistance presupposed rising salience and efficacy, development of a resource base, and shifts in the allegiance of polity members. Yet the racial status quo would prove more fragile than white authorities realized. Large-scale demographic, economic, and political changes were gradually unfolding that would alter the possibilities for protest and facilitate the mobilization of the movement.

Resuming a migration begun during World War I, black Americans left the farms and towns of the rural South in the 1930s and continued to leave in increasingly greater numbers in the decades that followed. By 1960, three million men and women had migrated to the North and West and one-half of all blacks lived outside the South. Push and pull factors primed this movement. Under New Deal programs limiting agricultural production, southern owners forced black sharecroppers and tenant farmers from the land, triggering a mass exodus. The subsequent mechanization of farm production further reduced agricultural labor needs. At the same time, defense industries, the military draft, and business expansion guided blacks to southern and northern urban centers. In 1960 three-quarters of black Americans resided in metropolitan areas. The southern black presence in both urban and rural worlds would require activists to devise creative strategies and tactics to accommodate the different environments.[3]

An occupational upgrading accompanied the black movement from farm to city. In 1940 90 percent of blacks worked in agriculture or held jobs as semiskilled and unskilled workers. Fewer than 8 percent were employed in occupations classified as middle-class. During the next two decades, there was a more than twofold increase in the black middle class, with 20 percent of men and women holding professional, clerical, and skilled positions. This occupational advance brought economic improvement, and the black family's median income doubled. Nevertheless, the black family in 1960 still earned just over one-half of the income of its white counterpart. Rising socioeconomic status also stimulated educational gains and black colleges experienced dramatic enrollment spurts in the 1940s and 1950s.[4]

Income was not the only resource blacks gained in departing the southern countryside. Northern residence opened the voting booth. During the Depression, blacks joined the Democratic coalition and, in 1940, cast 97 percent of their ballots for Franklin Roosevelt. Yet it was more than sheer numbers that made the black community essential to Democratic success. Black migration patterns led southern immigrants to New York, New Jersey, Pennsylvania, Michigan, Ohio, Illinois, and California. With four-fifths of the electoral votes needed to win the White House, these seven states were the stepping-stones to victory.[5]

After World War II, politicians became increasingly sensitive to the position of the black community in the balance of power. In 1948 a southern Dixiecrat revolt and a left-wing Progressive party challenge put President Harry Truman's reelection bid in jeopardy. To set his course and bolster his chances, Truman merged idealism and pragmatism: He courted northern blacks with executive orders prohibiting discrimination in federal employment and desegregating the armed forces. Blacks gave Truman 80 percent of their votes and were an important group in the Democratic coalition. Dwight Eisenhower's victories in 1952 and 1956 bolstered Democratic appraisals of black political power. Securing enough white votes to win Virginia, Florida, Texas, and Louisiana, the Republican party broke the Democratic hold on the "solid South." Eisenhower, at the same time, beckoned to blacks by pressing integration of the armed forces and public facilities in the District of Columbia. Blacks responded, delivering 40 percent of their votes to the president in 1956, a gain of 20 percent over 1952. With their eyes on the 1960 presidential election, both parties backed passage of civil rights legislation in 1957 and 1960.[6]

The Supreme Court went beyond the other branches of the federal government in conferring legitimacy on the cause of racial equality. As early as the 1930s the Court began to chip away the legal foundations of caste discrimination. Supreme Court decisions opened graduate and professional schools to black students, integrated interstate railroads, and outlawed the whites-only primary. In 1954 the Court issued its landmark *Brown* v. *Board of Education of Topeka, Kansas* decision, which overturned *Plessy* v. *Ferguson* in the area of public education. Blacks cheered the ruling, not only for its commitment to equal educational opportunities but as the lever to uproot Jim Crow completely from their lives. Yet the Supreme Court intended no revolution in race relations. It proposed gradual change and assigned local southern authorities the responsibility for drawing desegregation plans and federal judges the power to determine the pace of progress.[7]

"Get on board"   Such piecemeal reforms handed down by white authorities may frame dreams of protest with justice, but they were insufficient to create a movement. In fact, progress achieved in such a manner may even inhibit mobilization by crippling efficacy. White decision makers could alter the racial environment, but blacks would remain observers and not participants in the circumstances of their lives. Without grounding in a grass-roots organization, the strength of energizing events would be abbreviated and untapped.

Yet these government reforms were critical because local organizations existed to amplify their impact. The urban ghetto, despite overcrowding, poverty, and difficult living conditions, became the crucible of protest. In the segregated community, blacks drew strength from their numbers and a sense of common grievance. The ghetto also provided security and freedom from constant police intimidation and white terrorism. Shielded from disruption by whites and aided by economic mobility, blacks developed organizational power. Churches, lodges, clubs, and civic organizations united the community through a variety of communication channels and interlocking networks of personnel and funds. A relatively more independent black leadership of clergy, professionals, editors, and entrepreneurs emerged from within this organizational core. Immune from white coercion, they built upon institutional affiliations and personal ability to fill roles as opinion makers and activists.8

The significance of the black church in the mobilization of protest cannot be underestimated. Ministers trained as organizational managers and public speakers were critical to the movement's growth and success. Leading congregations, clergy had direct and privileged access to church resources and the black masses. The shared ideology, language, and symbols of Christianity infused the movement and legitimized the act of rebellion. As superior Christians, blacks preached a message of love, peace, justice, and forgiveness. Their stance of nonviolence reflected not only a clear perception of the social control situation, but an assertion of the power of the oppressed to turn the other cheek. Civil rights activists were well attuned to the traditional beliefs and values of their communities. Meeting in churches, singing civil rights songs to familiar hymns, and adapting speeches to the rhythm of the sermon, they were able to legitimize their cause and activate common people.[9]

In dozens of southern towns and cities, activists built protest organizations upon a base of the black church, college, and civic group. These diverse movement centers prepared the local ground by breaking Jim Crow conditioning and convincing men and women of their own power to bring change. Stockpiling resources, raising new leaders, and training cadre, grass-roots movements positioned themselves to act.[10]

The need for regionwide coordination was obvious, and several organizations offered themselves as protest vehicles. The National Association for the Advancement of Colored People, founded in 1910, pursued equality primarily through the courts and was instrumental in pressing the Supreme Court to reverse legal support of caste discrimination. With branches in many southern communities, the NAACP had already built a substantial organizational base by 1950. Still, its middle-class complexion and legalistic approach kept the movement from gaining mass support. In 1957 Martin Luther King, Jr., formed the Southern Christian Leadership Conference to help focus the rights struggle. The SCLC, rooted in the black churches, was a federation of organizations rather than a membership body. Through King's charismatic direction, the SCLC encouraged local groups to reach those outside the protest community. The smaller, northern-based Congress of Racial Equality had only recently extended its work to the South.[11]

If Supreme Court decisions and grass-roots mobilization had stimulated the salience of civil rights for blacks, it had a similar effect on white southerners. Southern resistance in the wake of the *Brown* decision was widespread and multifaceted. With the encouragement of regional political and religious elites, local authorities balked at school desegregation and adopted tactics of delay, tokenism, and outright rejection. By the end of the 1961 academic year, only 7 percent of black children were enrolled in integrated schools, with the largest gains registered in the border states.[12]

Whites simultaneously squeezed an economic vice. Black "troublemakers" were evicted from their homes, denied credit, and fired from jobs. Organizationally, southerners countermobilized in the White Citizens Council. Formed in 1954, this movement claimed 250,000 members within two years. The Ku Klux Klan also resurfaced and with it a rising wave of bombings, cross burnings, and assaults.[13]

Before this white counterattack, black protest receded. Reprisals raised the personal risks of activism while forcing the expenditure of scarce resources in defensive reaction. Internal weaknesses further compromised activism. Competition between the SCLC and the NAACP for resources and prestige inhibited cooperation. Both groups had difficulty in securing the allegiance of existing grass-roots organizations jealous of their own prerogatives. At the close of the 1950s, civil rights activists had failed to generate the enthusiasm or regionwide networking necessary to support a massive direct-action insurgency.

Yet as white resistance flared, civil rights advocates perceived their strengths. Through confrontation, blacks had forced a reluctant federal government to take a more activist stance in defense of the Constitution. Cold war competition increased this pressure. Embarrassed before Third World peoples by Soviet propaganda, American decision makers found new impetus to end racial discrimination. Republicans and Democrats sensitive to partisan considerations were also tuned to southern events. The media had awakened, as well, to the good copy of the civil rights "story." Trickles of aid had already begun to flow south to black activists from northern religious groups and labor unions.[14]

In the South, new leaders emerged; they proclaimed pride, dignity, and nonviolent action. Couched in the themes and symbols of black Christianity, their words translated as simple justice and gained acceptance. Demands for an end to second-class citizenship moved a people because they spread through an established organizational base preparing for struggle. Energizing events, as well, had punctuated the lives of black Americans and enhanced the significance of the civil rights campaign. The *Brown* decision, the Montgomery bus boycott, and the violence at Little Rock High School had convinced many that they had a personal stake in defying segregation. The next decade would bring new incidents that not only touched black men, women, and children at the grass roots but fired them with the belief that they had the power to create the future.[15]

"FIGHTING FOR MY RIGHTS"

On 1 February 1960 four black college students sat down at a segregated lunch counter in Greensboro, North Carolina, and refused to leave when denied service. Their action was not impulsive. As members of the local NAACP youth council, the four were already within the protest network. News of this simple act of defiance passed quickly to movement centers throughout the South. Activists from the SCLC, the NAACP, CORE, and local movements prodded their communities into a chain reaction of insurgency. By 1 April blacks had adopted the sit-in tactic in seventy cities stretching across the upper South from North Carolina and Virginia to Texas. Television captured the protest for northern audiences. For many Americans, events became a twentieth-century morality play with the forces of good and evil, right and wrong personified before them.[16]

The sit-in demonstrations provoked an immediate reaction among young blacks. The protest confronted them with a personal opportunity, in their own community, to stand up and reject submission. Greensboro, wrote high school student Cleveland Sellers, "hit me like a shot of adrenaline." [17] Sellers joined demonstrations already in progress and began a decade-long commitment. Spellman College sophomore Ruby Doris Smith "began to think right away about it happening in Atlanta. . . . And when two hundred students were selected for the first demonstrations, I was among them."[18] After viewing newsreel footage of the sit-ins, Harlem mathematics teacher Bob Moses experienced the opening of "a whole new world. Before that I knew nothing about the South. . . . My image of the Southern Negro was fearful, cringing. But the faces on those kids were sullen, determined, and I knew that was relevant to my life."[19] For John Lewis, a seminary student and Nashville activist, participation brought a heightened sense of efficacy: "Being involved tended to free you. . . . you saw yourself as the free man, as the free agent, able to act."[20] Many, in the aftermath of personal involvement, would share Lewis's rejection of apathy and move to take control of events.

Students occupied the front ranks of the sit-in offensive. They perceived the demonstrations as their cause and prided themselves in hastening the pace of change. Students, moreover, were at less risk than others in the black community. Unlike their mothers and fathers, they had fewer family and financial responsibilities and more time to devote to protest activities. Students were also prepared for action, having been trained in nonviolence tactics under the auspices of movement centers. With local activists coordinating resource support and encouraging protest, students put their bodies on the line knowing they sacrificed for community goals.[21]

The sit-in campaign forced a dramatic shift in the civil rights movement. Confrontation replaced legalistic solutions and quiet negotiations. The large numbers of men and women engaged in direct action had a rippling effect upon local black populations, raising issue salience and efficacy. The sight and sound of protest could not be ignored in the North, either. Nevertheless, the effects of the demonstrations were limited. Lunch counters were only a single rampart of the segregation fortress. Disproportionately, the sit-ins had breached segregation along the southern periphery while the Deep South remained unyielding. It was clear that coordination and direction had to be centralized and given organizational form to focus more effectively the student resistance.

"We'll never turn back"   A few looked beyond the immediacy of the sit-in wave and attempted to fashion the means to harness the momentum of insurgency. A month after the sit-ins began, Ella Baker, the executive secretary of the Southern Christian Leadership Conference, built a consensus within her organization to sponsor a conference of student activists. With $800 from the SCLC treasury and the support of Martin Luther King, Jr., she convinced Shaw University in Raleigh, North Carolina, to provide facilities for the meeting. The gathering would enable activists to meet, share experiences, build trust, and answer the question "where do we go from here?"[22]

Three hundred men and women attended the Student Leadership Conference on Nonviolent Resistance to Segregation from Good Friday to Easter Sunday 1960. A diversity of groups had answered Baker's call. Fifty-six black high schools and colleges in twelve southern states and the District of Columbia, nineteen northern schools, and organizations like the National Student Association and the Students for a Democratic Society sent representatives and observers. Approximately one dozen southern white students were also present. Baker was a central moving force during the conference. She encouraged students to create a vehicle independent of existing civil rights organizations. Her plan for the new movement went beyond the coordination of student activism. Believing that dependence upon a few leaders would not bring meaningful restructuring at the community level, she argued for the development of an indigenous black leadership mounted on a strong local resource base. For Baker, students were the movers of change, for they could encourage common people to find the power of resistance within themselves.[23]

Although he had the prestige and charisma to bring the students under the SCLC's wing, Martin Luther King, Jr. supported Baker's call for an independent organization. Students, he agreed, could infiltrate the base of southern society and compel a break with the past. Such suggestions conformed with student activists' needs and beliefs. Nonviolent, yet committed to confrontation, they were prepared to expand off-campus and work for community change. To effect the dream, participants voted to create a temporary Student Nonviolent Coordinating Committee and elected Marion Barry its first chair. In a founding statement the group announced:

> We affirm the philosophical or religious ideal of nonviolence as the foundation of our purpose, the presupposition of our faith, and the manner of our action. . . . Through nonviolence, courage displaces fear; love transforms hate. Acceptance dissipates prejudice; hope ends despair. . . . Mutual regard cancels enmity. Justice for all overthrows injustice. The redemptive community supersedes systems of gross social immorality.[24]

SNCC struggled to survive its first year. Launched when the sit-in tide had already crested, SNCC seemed to have missed its moment. Local activists guarded their autonomy and were reluctant to accept direction from an unknown organization without protest credentials. Nor was SNCC inclined to exert influence. From the beginning, SNCC officers deferred to activists in the field and were reluctant to stifle innovation or grass-roots decision making with centralized direction or bureaucratic controls. The new movement lacked even the means to maintain contact with community protest. The SNCC Atlanta headquarters consisted of a single desk in the corner of the SCLC office. Much of the movement's $5,000 budget came through SCLC funding channels. "SNCC," said Jane Stembridge, "was not coordinating the movement. . . . I would say the main thing done was to let people know we existed."[25]

Although lacking a clear identity and direction, SNCC ended its provisional status in October 1960. Student delegates from forty-six southern protest centers meeting with observers representing northern colleges and activist groups agreed to create a permanent organization. A coordinating committee consisting of one representative from each southern state and the District of Columbia would gather monthly to consider movement action. When Marion Barry returned to graduate school, Charles McDew became SNCC's new chair. McDew, who would occupy the position into 1963, was a northern black and convert to Judaism who was attending college in South

Carolina. At year's end, SNCC remained a collection of scattered, autonomous groups composed of activists dividing their time between protest demonstrations and college studies.[26]

It was through the actions of another challenging group that SNCC found the means to increase its visibility and stake out a place within the civil rights struggle. To test the enforcement of Supreme Court decisions desegregating interstate travel, the Congress of Racial Equality chartered two buses to travel from the District of Columbia through the Carolinas and the Deep South to New Orleans. The Freedom Riders, who left Washington on 4 May 1961, hoped that their arrests would prod the federal government into action against segregation. But they were unprepared for the violence that engulfed them. In Anniston, Alabama, mobs firebombed one of the buses. Klansmen met the second bus in Birmingham and, with police conveniently absent, so brutally beat the Freedom Riders that CORE called off the effort.[27]

But SNCC activists refused to relinquish the offensive, believing that confrontation in the glare of the media could force federal intervention, stir black communities, and touch the northern public. On 20 May they continued the rides, leaving Birmingham for Montgomery. Despite assurances from Alabama authorities, men and women were again beaten and later besieged in a black Montgomery church by white mobs. Attorney General Robert Kennedy intervened personally; he sent federal marshals to the scene and convinced the governor of Alabama to mobilize state national guard units. Under protective escort, the Freedom Riders left Montgomery for Jackson, Mississippi where twenty-seven civil rights demonstrators were arrested for attempting to use whites-only rest rooms and for breaching the peace. Opting for jail rather than bail, the SNCC activists were confined. As the Freedom Rides continued throughout the summer, three hundred more men and women joined their fellow protesters in jail.[28]

The Freedom Rides accelerated SNCC's evolution. The movement had placed itself in the struggle's front line and gained new visibility. Donations and fund raising nearly tripled the organization's budget to $14,000 for 1961. Members had proven to themselves the leverage of confrontation. Confinement, meanwhile, acted as an initiation rite. It strengthened the activist core by heightening mutual respect and bolstering a personal sense of power to overcome hard times. The rides also focused SNCC attention on the Deep South and the fierceness of its resistance. If SNCC activists hoped to establish politically and economically independent black communities, they realized that they could not do this through hit-and-run attacks by part-time students.[29]

"I'm gonna sit at the welcome table"   As SNCC weighed alternatives, the Kennedy administration intervened in the movement's affairs. During the summer of 1961 Robert Kennedy met with Charles McDew of SNCC and representatives of the SCLC, CORE, and the NAACP. Kennedy offered to arrange private funding through the philanthropic Taconic, Field, and Stern Family Foundations for a coordinated drive to register blacks to vote. Kennedy also gave black leaders the impression that the Justice Department and FBI field agents would protect civil rights workers and enforce the law. In 1962 President John Kennedy bolstered this belief: "I commend those who are making the effort to register every citizen. They deserve the protection of the U.S. government, the protection of the states, the protection of the local communities. And if it requires extra legislation and extra force, we shall do that."[30] Tax exemptions for movement organizations and draft deferments for activists were added inducements to accept the government's proposal.[31]

Support of a voter registration drive offered the Kennedy administration escape from a difficult position and the means to build reserves for future use. John and Robert Kennedy, looking back to the rise of the Irish to power in Boston and Massachusetts, saw the vote as the key to full citizenship for black Americans. With large numbers voting as a bloc, blacks could elect their own while forcing southern white politicians to bow before a new electoral reality. Quiet voter registration drives, moreover, would not spawn the confrontations with whites that fed Russian propaganda. Devoid of social and sexual overtones, the integration of the voting booth meant less resistance than had greeted efforts to achieve equality of access to schools and public accommodations. The Kennedys were also aware of the power of the southern members of the national polity. Successful registration would dampen the demand for new civil rights legislation that might provoke a southern filibuster and endanger other New Frontier requests. At the same time, the growing black electorate, aware of its benefactors, would reward Kennedy and the Democratic party. The registration drive, then, promised gradual, directed change. Low-profile Justice Department litigation in support of voting rights would complement this strategy and arouse little controversy.[32]

SNCC activists, however, were suspicious of the administration's plan, for the Kennedy record on civil rights left much to be desired. During the 1950s according to aide Theodore Sorensen, Senator Kennedy "simply did not give much thought to this subject." Kennedy's votes for civil rights legislation in 1957 and 1960 came "more as a matter of course than of deep concern."[33] Blacks had welcomed presidential candidate Kennedy's rhetoric of equality and his intervention to secure the release of Martin Luther King, Jr., from a Georgia prison. In office, Kennedy accelerated the federal government's hiring of blacks and directed the Justice Department to press litigation for school desegregation and voting rights. In the wake of the Freedom Rides, the Interstate Commerce Commission banned segregation of all facilities for interstate and intrastate passengers. At the same time, Kennedy appeased the South with appointments of avowed segregationists to the federal bench in Mississippi, Georgia, Alabama, and Louisiana. Disappointing to blacks also was his reluctance to sponsor new civil rights legislation. If civil rights was an urgent moral issue to black activists, for John Kennedy it remained a political question assigned a low priority.[34]

While the Kennedy approach smacked of paternalism, it still offered SNCC an important opportunity. Through debate, activists weighed the options. Some derided Kennedy's inducements and called for a stepped-up, direct-action campaign to expose segregation and force federal intervention. Others believed the means were in their grasp to expand beyond the Atlanta headquarters and recruit a professional, full-time staff to ignite electoral rebellion at the grass roots. Events already in motion bolstered the advocates of voter registration. Bob Moses and Charles Sherrod had reconnoitered Mississippi and southwest Georgia, respectively, establishing contacts and laying preliminary plans for registration drives. With the help of Ella Baker, SNCC members crafted a compromise by creating separate wings devoted to direct action and voter registration. The distinction, however, would soon become moot. Voter registration and direct action efforts became entwined at the community level, two paths toward the same destination. White southerners, meanwhile, found any civil rights action provocative and would not fine-tune their responses. With the support of the federal government, then, SNCC workers assumed a commitment to long-term struggle and moved deeper south to challenge local authority and raise black power.[35]

"BEEN DOWN IN THE SOUTH"

Civil rights activists targeted the counties of the South's black belt for intensive organization. Known for its black, fertile soil and large concentrations of black Americans, the area was seen as the central foundation upon which to build a New South. The vote would give black majorities political influence and precipitate a drive to local economic and social independence. The black belt promised large rewards, but it also had strong barriers to effective mobilization. Blacks in these counties were mired in poverty dependent as sharecroppers, agricultural wage workers, and domestics upon white employers. Large black populations steeled white minority resistance and tightened the reins of legal and extralegal social control agencies. Agitation, while locally rooted, could survive only upon outside resources and the decisions of authorities outside the county and state polities. Under such circumstances, gains, if they could be achieved, would come only at a high cost.[36]

The first inroad was made during the summer of 1961 in McComb, Mississippi, in the southwest corner of the state. Bob Moses organized a school to help blacks interpret the Mississippi constitution, a test prerequisite to voter registration. Soon, blacks in neighboring Amite and Walthall counties asked Moses, now assisted by SNCC-affiliated student volunteers, to expand his work to their communities. Whites reacted swiftly. Mobs assaulted and then police arrested the SNCC workers and black applicants. FBI agents on the scene refused to intervene; instead, they fulfilled their obligation to defend the exercise of constitutional rights by taking notes and pictures. Night riders later shot to death an Amite County black who had worked with Moses.[37]

While voter registration efforts continued, Marion Barry, Charles McDew, and Bob Zellner of SNCC's direct-action wing organized nonviolence workshops to prepare for sit-in demonstrations in McComb. They, too, were beaten and arrested. Unable to fund bail, SNCC members remained in jail for several months. To undermine the protest further, police passed the names of SNCC's local supporters to employers who threatened them with the loss of job and home. Violence, arrests, and economic coercion brought the movement to a standstill. With few blacks registered to vote, the McComb project came to a temporary halt.[38]

In the spring of 1962 SNCC, CORE, the SCLC, and the NAACP, under the auspices of the Council of Federated Organizations, began the Kennedy-prompted voter registration drive in eight Mississippi towns. SNCC's main thrust was Laflore County, an obvious objective since blacks comprised two-thirds of the population but only 2 percent of registered voters. With the infusion of northern funds, SNCC fielded an enlarged staff of professional activists and volunteers. They inspired hope and trust by going door to door, traveling on mule and foot, wearing field-hand overalls, picking cotton, and adopting the diet of the underprivileged. Obvious targets, their assumption of risk on behalf of the powerless further enhanced their acceptance. As role models, SNCC activists motivated through example. Believing that the resistance movement would not grow by command, they did not impose authority on the black population. They knew that change would not endure unless common men and women took responsibility for their lives. These activists tried to live SNCC's watchwords: "We are all leaders."[39]

Again, local whites refused to yield ground. Mobs ransacked SNCC's Greenwood headquarters and snipers riddled the organization's cars and offices. Arrests followed clubbings and strained financial and personal reserves. Economic terror accompanied the violence. In October 1962 Laflore County supervisors voted to withdraw from a federal program that supplied surplus food to thousands of poor blacks. Only a massive food drive through SNCC's northern affiliates forestalled serious privation. Repression intensified in 1963. Arsonists fired SNCC's voter registration office and burned and bombed black supporters' homes and businesses.[40]

By the summer of 1963 SNCC was stalemated. Only 5 percent of Mississippi's voting-age black population was counted as registered after a year of determined effort. Workers had also failed to draw federal authorities into a defense of black rights. The Kennedy administration had misjudged the strength of white resistance to change. Citing the limits imposed by federalism, the White House reneged on its pledges of protection and avoided confrontation. While SNCC members were distrustful and angry, they still realized that success depended upon the funding raised by the Kennedys and upon a federal confrontation with local authorities.[41]

Events had transformed the frames of reference of SNCC workers. Close daily contact with those at the bottom of American society radicalized SNCC workers. The right to eat at a lunch counter or to sit at the front of a bus paled before the more fundamental issues of inequality in wealth and power. Southern resistance and federal inaction caused some to rethink the importance of nonviolence to their movement. This growing radicalism and militancy, however, remained unfocused. Such questioning had not yet broken the activists' basic faith in the justice of the American system.[42]

The white counterattack also strengthened SNCC's resolve and sense of fellowship. In the storm, activists cleaved to one another, willing to accept risk and sacrifice in a cause they knew was morally right. For many the movement became their career, even their life. To Casey Hayden, "it was everything: home and family, food and work, love and a reason to live. . . . The movement in its early days was a grandeur that feared no rebuke and assumed no false attitudes. It was a holy time."[43]

Mississippi was not the only SNCC offensive in the Deep South. While Bob Moses organized in McComb, former Freedom Riders Charles Sherrod and Cordell Reagon opened a second front in southwest Georgia during the fall of 1961. Their objective was to create a protest center in Albany that would launch a "people's movement" against all forms of community segregation and win the ballot for blacks. Working with black organizations and churches and recruiting high school and college students for workshops on nonviolence, Sherrod and Reagon sparked the creation of a contending group primed for challenge. "We offered before the people our minds and our bodies. That was all we had. Three months later, nearly a thousand bodies and minds were being offered before us."[44]

In November 1961 the black community began sit-in demonstrations, marches, and boycotts to protest segregation in restaurants, libraries, and swimming pools. SNCC activists also gathered the names of blacks willing to confront voter registrars. By mid-December, police had arrested and jailed five hundred black demonstrators. Albany's authorities made every effort to avoid "newsworthy" incident. Protesters were seized with minimal force, thus reducing media attention, public outcry, and the likelihood of federal intervention. Demonstrators crammed city jails, and officials in adjoining jurisdictions prepared their facilities for future mass arrests.[45]

SNCC had provided the spark, but without white miscalculation did not have the means to sustain morale or activity. To maintain momentum, local black leaders bypassed SNCC and appealed to Martin Luther King, Jr., and the SCLC to join the campaign. King came to Albany, demonstrated, and was arrested. This boosted protest enthusiasm and within days seven hundred more blacks were taken into custody. To remove the charismatic King from the scene and defuse the movement, Albany city officials agreed to a truce. They promised to appoint an interracial commission to investigate discrimination and to release those jailed in return for a demonstration moratorium. As they had planned, with King's departure, the movement stalled. By the time it was obvious that whites would frustrate any progress on desegregation, SNCC could not revive resistance activity. Setbacks in voter registration matched defeats in direct action. Although SNCC remained in Albany, its words had lost their urgency for black residents.[46]

Albany was an important way station for the civil rights movement. There, King learned a valuable lesson about the necessity of choosing targets wisely. In 1963, he pinpointed Birmingham, a community capable of the unprovoked violence conducive to favorable protest outcomes. Chief of Police Bull Connor took the bait, and his use of fire hoses, clubs, and dogs against unarmed men, women, and children became imprinted on the American mind. Backed by northern public opinion, President Kennedy awakened to the morality of civil rights and pressed for legislation to end discrimination in public accommodations.[47]

Albany was pivotal for SNCC. Again, Washington had ignored black suffering and given the lie to liberal promises. Events there also confirmed SNCC's conviction that only local leadership could forge effective protest. Activists denounced King as "De Lawd" and condemned a cult of personality that created a flash of popular commitment but not long-term dedication. The SCLC, in turn, had begun to voice concerns about its protege's militancy and radicalism. Philosophical differences widened a breech already opened in their competition for resources. In the contest for a finite store of headlines, funds, and supporters, the SCLC, CORE, the NAACP, and SNCC were all rivals. While these organizations often acted to complement one another's efforts and advance the civil rights campaign, growing differences in tactics and strategies eventually brought dissension and a drain of resources.[48]

"I've got a hammer"   In 1962 and 1963 SNCC converted from a campus-based, student-activist coalition to a movement of full-time, professional cadre distributed throughout the South. Its initial staff of field secretaries increased from sixteen in 1961 to forty in 1962 and seventy in 1963. More than one hundred volunteers assisted these organizers in projects in Mississippi, Georgia, North and South Carolina, Arkansas, Alabama, Maryland, and Tennessee. The majority of SNCC men and women were black, young, southern-born, former college students. Of the white workers, most were northerners and one-fourth were Jewish. The Atlanta headquarters had grown to accommodate SNCC's expanded needs. Under the direction of executive secretary James Forman, SNCC's twelve office personnel coordinated field efforts and established links to the media. SNCC also organized an effective fund-raising network with branches in major northern cities. Between 1962 and 1964 the movement gathered over $1 million to finance its operations. Still, funds were always tight, and staff members were limited to a weekly salary of $10.[49]

In theory, a coordinating committee of student group representatives governed SNCC, while an executive committee assisted the chairman and executive secretary in day-to-day activities. In reality, these bodies played supporting rather than command roles. Ambivalent about authority and bureaucracy, SNCC headquarters deferred to initiatives from the field staff. In championing a weak chain of command, it traded off the bureaucracy and strong organization that would better insure long-term survival.[50]

As the chair of one of the movement's principal organizations, John Lewis, who had replaced McDew, was invited to speak at the March on Washington demonstration in late August 1963. Lewis prepared to vent his organization's frustrations after two years in the Deep South. In his draft of the speech, he wrote that SNCC could not support Kennedy-sponsored civil rights legislation because it was "too little, and too late." The administration had appointed racist judges and refused to intervene in the defense of constitutional rights. "I want to know," he wrote in the draft, "which side is the federal government on?" The Kennedy administration found the draft unacceptable and demanded revision. Civil rights leaders prevailed upon Lewis to moderate his remarks for the sake of unity. He did so, but he still condemned the great disparities in wealth and power in America and asked blacks and whites to "stay in the streets . . . until the unfinished revolution of 1776 is complete."[51]

For John Kennedy, SNCC had become dangerous. "SNCC has got an investment in violence," he said. "They're sons of bitches."[52] In late November of 1963, *Life* magazine carried the first media piece that was negative of SNCC. Theodore White warned in the article that the organization had been radicalized and rejected nonviolence.[53]

"AIN'T GONNA LET NOBODY TURN ME ROUND"

The Mississippi stalemate prodded SNCC in the fall of 1963 to improvise. To outmaneuver white resistance, SNCC organized a "freedom vote" campaign that encouraged blacks to select candidates for office in a mock election outside regular political channels. Activists believed that this symbolic act of participation would heighten salience and efficacy. They also hoped it would convince northern polity members and opinion makers that blacks were not content with their lot and questioned the legitimacy of Mississippi's accepted representatives. Under the guidance of SNCC staffers and one hundred volunteers from Stanford and Yale Universities, eighty thousand blacks registered and cast "freedom ballots" in the statewide effort.[54]

The freedom vote success outlined SNCC'S future direction. Sure that the means to influence were finally within their grasp, field secretaries called for an expanded drive in the summer of 1964. They envisioned a four-pronged assault on inequality to expose the nation to the grievances of blacks and to provoke a confrontation between federal and state authorities. The struggle would, as well, invigorate the grass roots and fashion a determined people united by strong local institutions and an independent leadership. The keystone of "freedom summer" would be a registration drive that would bypass the traditional political machinery to develop support for a Mississippi Freedom Democratic party (MFDP). This alternative to the regular state Democratic organization promised to take the black challenge before the 1964 National Convention and stand as the rightful representative of the people of Mississippi. In addition, SNCC refused to abandon the recognized path to power and continued attempts to register voters on the official rolls of the state. To build leadership for the future, SNCC proposed "freedom schools," alternative educational institutions to cultivate black pride and racial consciousness in children. Finally, a direct action thrust was planned to keep the pressure on government and business to integrate.[55]

Vital to the outcome of the project was the recruitment of hundreds of northern, white college students. The speaking and writing skills of college students had helped make the fall campaign a success. Philosophically, they were central to a movement that envisioned a biracial drive to realize a color-blind future. More cynically, many black staffers were convinced that only the sons and daughters of white middle-class America could spark the nation's interest in racial change. By raising the stakes and putting white bodies on the line, the movement would be assured of the federal protection and media coverage that had eluded it when black people alone faced danger. The massive participation of whites fired debate within the organization. Some, citing the fact that SNCC's staff was one-fifth white, argued that this minority already exercised too much power; it was paradoxical for a movement attempting to build black institutions and leadership to allow such significant white inroads. With their hopes fixed on a potential breakthrough effort, SNCC members overrode these concerns without fully coming to grips with their implications.[56]

During the winter and spring of 1964, SNCC worked in preparation for the summer struggle. It mobilized liberal, northern supporters and raised volunteers and almost $100,000. New resources enabled SNCC to increase its staff to 160 members and incorporate more than 700 student volunteers from

Harvard, Yale, Stanford, the University of California at Berkeley, and Columbia. As SNCC broadened, some veterans experienced a heightened racial
consciousness. They looked to Africa for cultural and intellectual support and
embraced its music and literature. Verbal attacks on whites, friend and foe,
also grew in number.[57]

SNCC spearheaded the Mississippi summer campaign by directing operations in four of the state's five congressional districts. Civil rights workers
registered tens of thousands of people for the Mississippi Freedom Democratic party, giving substance to its claim as the only broad-based, democratic,
and nonracist political entity in the state. Although more than seventeen
thousand blacks attempted to register under state guidelines, only sixteen
hundred were allowed to exercise the official franchise. Meanwhile, forty-one
freedom schools, attended by over two thousand children, were in session
during the summer.[58]

Great sacrifice brought these gains, as, almost immediately, tragedy
darkened the summer campaign. On 22 June civil rights activists James
Chaney, Andrew Goodman, and Michael Schwerner were reported missing.
Few were surprised when their mutilated bodies were uncovered from shal-
low graves in August. Nor were they surprised that among those arrested
were a county sheriff and his deputy. Official and extralegal violence scored
the whole campaign. "Violence," said a volunteer in Ruleville, "hangs over-
head like the dead air—it hangs there and maybe it'll fall and maybe it
won't."[59] During that summer in Mississippi, remembered Cleve Sellers, "I
had never experienced such tension and near-paralyzing fear."[60] The white
counterattack produced six known murders, thirty bombed homes, thirty-
five burned churches, and one thousand arrests. Despite the terrorism and
white student influx, the federal government had failed to protect civil rights
workers or those seeking to exercise their rights.[61]

SNCC bled from internal wounds as well. Tension between blacks and
whites, present at the beginning of the summer, intensified in the Mississippi
hothouse. Conflict tore in several directions. The black staff rejected white
volunteers as "fly-by-night freedom fighters," on summer vacation, who were
less committed to the cause than blacks were. Cultural and social wedges
further divided SNCC. Blacks accused whites of assuming leadership roles by
virtue of their education and organizational skills. Resentful whites asked:
"How much energy and resources can we exert in helping people like this
who have personality problems."[62] Often, infused with guilt, whites overcom-
pensated and believed the blacks' indictment of their protest credentials or
their "patronizing" ways. Some volunteers sought to overcome barriers and
gain acceptance through sexual activity, which generated additional stress.
Real or imagined, conscious or unconscious, such provocations proved more
difficult to surmount than blows from the outside. Still, many white volunteers would later regard freedom summer as a "personal crucible" that had

vitally shaped their lives.[63] Radicalized and experienced in the running of an organization, they returned from Mississippi to shape emerging campus, antiwar, and women's movements.[64]

"Eyes on the prize"   Despite these setbacks, in building the MFDP SNCC had attained an important goal. It now looked to the 1964 National Democratic Convention for affirmation of its sacrifices and acceptance of its challenge. President Lyndon Johnson, however, had other plans for his convention. Johnson was concerned about a northern white backlash against civil rights, which had materialized as strong support during the primaries for segregationist George Wallace's candidacy. Holding the vice presidential nomination as a lure to liberals, Johnson pressured them to frame a compromise amenable to the majority of southern delegates. Meanwhile, he ordered the FBI to put SNCC and MFDP headquarters under surveillance. Liberals acceded to the president's will and deserted the MFDP. Martin Luther King and CORE's James Farmer joined in pressing SNCC to accept a compromise that alloted the MFDP two seats at large and left the Mississippi regulars in control of the state banner. SNCC and MFDP members bitterly rejected the plan as tokenism and left the convention. The press, unable to see the issue as anything but political, condemned SNCC activists as ungrateful, moral zealots unschooled in the art of politics. With Barry Goldwater the Republican candidate for president and a law ending discrimination in public accommodations enacted, Lyndon Johnson had little fear that black voters would turn away from the Democratic party. In November, blacks cast 95 percent of their ballots for the president.[65]

The convention "sellout" staggered SNCC members. "We had reached the point," wrote Mary King, "where everything we tried, no matter how creative, ran aground on the obduracy of America's political institutions."[66] Cleve Sellers was incensed: "Never again were we lulled into believing that our task was exposing injustices so that the 'good' people of America could eliminate them."[67] The federal authorities, the Democratic party, and civil rights allies had deserted the cause. With its endorsement of the Democratic ticket, even the MFDP turned away from SNCC. This loss of faith was even more destabilizing because it drew on the reserves of men and women already suffering from "battle fatigue." Anxious, exhausted, depressed, and suspicious after a summer in Mississippi, activists had difficulty mustering the will to return to organizing.[68]

In response to defeat and disillusionment, SNCC turned inward to reassess its past and calculate the future. In a fall 1964 conference, members confronted the most basic questions: "Where ... How ... Why do we organize?"[69] How relevant was direct action after the Civil Rights Act of 1964? Did integration efforts detract from the more significant goal of building black institutions to confront inequalities in wealth and power? In a contest where

opponents acted with few holds barred, was nonviolence viable either tactically or ideologically? Some looked to black nationalist Malcolm X for guidance: "Be peaceful, be courteous, obey the law, respect everyone; but if
someone puts his hand on you, send him to the cemetery."[70]

After the summer campaign, eighty-five volunteers asked to join the
SNCC staff. Middle-class, northern, and mostly white, their inclusion reig-
nited debate over the white minority's role in a black movement. It also
provoked questions about organization. Should SNCC remain an organization
of full-time activists or become a mass movement of poor people? Some
proposed that the movement became more disciplined and centralized. They
berated those "philosophers, existentialists, anarchists, floaters and freedom-
high niggers" lost in the romance of activism.[71] Finally, a few women members confronted men with the problem of sexism. Wasn't male superiority as
immoral as white supremacy? The issues were raised, but not resolved. Like
open wounds, disillusionment and purposelessness drained the morale and
resources of the movement, with no remedy prescribed.[72]

SNCC continued its drift in 1965. Field work was neglected, established
projects lost their thrust, and few new programs were initiated. Influential
members such as Charles Sherrod and Bernard Lafayette became inactive. Bob
Moses, concerned that his influence stifled others, grew silent and gradually
withdrew. To Unita Blackwell, "We just sort of fragmented out. Different
people went their different ways to do different things. . . . I was worn out in
body and mind. I was burned out. It was a war zone."[73]

SNCC responded now to the initiatives of other civil rights vehicles. In
Selma, Alabama, despite a SNCC presence since 1963, Martin Luther King, Jr.,
and the SCLC controlled the tempo of events. Using the formula he learned
from the Albany experience, King created the moral confrontation that
elicited northern outrage and federal action. The result was the passage that
summer of legislation authorizing federal examiners to suspend literacy tests
and register black voters. Gains were rapid and dramatic. By 1968 57 percent
and 59 percent of the blacks of Alabama and Mississippi, respectively, had
registered to vote. Between 1964 and 1968, the number of the South's black
voters had increased from one million to over three million.[74]

SNCC could claim little credit for the victory in Selma. Its activists had
participated in the campaign individually, but the organization was content
to remain in the background. Nor did other efforts in 1965 enable SNCC to
steady itself. Organizing in Lowndes County, Alabama, had produced a Black
Panther party, but until the passage of the Voting Rights Act only 250 blacks
had secured the vote. A second Mississippi freedom summer project im-
ploded from sexual, class, and racial pressures and made few gains before
federal action. Meanwhile, SNCC's Atlanta headquarters had initiated a review of the field staff, and purged "floaters" from the ranks.[75]

Interaction with a rapidly changing environment shaped SNCC's evolution. The civil rights movement's attack on caste restriction in public accommodations and voting rights discrimination had won new legislation. Direct action had lost relevance while the southern struggle was rechanneled into traditional political activity. The Democratic party, although concerned about a northern white backlash, felt it had a lock on a mushrooming black vote. The War on Poverty appeared to address black grievances in housing, jobs, and health care. These poverty programs, along with now-receptive business, industry, and educational institutions, offered blacks improved career opportunities and funneled activists from the movement into established groups and government offices. With equality in the process of becoming a reality, authorities and elite groups assigned civil rights a lower priority. Increasingly, events in Southeast Asia began to absorb their attention.[76]

Public opinion makers and the American people also assigned less salience to a resolving civil rights issue. Meanwhile, by 1965 the black problem had assumed a new meaning. Less than a week after the passage of the Voting Rights Act, the black ghetto of Watts, outside of Los Angeles, erupted, leaving thirty-four dead, nine hundred injured, and $30 million in property damage. Watts was only a beginning. Joblessness, crowded and substandard housing, inadequate services, and police brutality were common problems in black ghettos throughout the country. Violence spread, and by the end of 1968, three hundred race riots and disturbances had scared American communities with their toll of eight thousand casualties and fifty thousand arrests. A 1967 opinion poll found that 45 percent of white Americans attributed the violence to "outside agitators," "minority radicals," or "Communists." In the riots' wake, some would remember reading a nationally syndicated column by Rowland Evans and Robert Novak that described SNCC as "substantially infiltrated by beatniks, left-wing revolutionaries, and—worst of all—by Communists."[77] With the escalation of the war in Vietnam after 1964, the public would become even less sensitive to civil rights issues. Both support for and opposition to the war spelled declining interest in the black struggle and a diversion of white resources from movement organizations.[78]

The evolution of the black movement also restricted opportunities for further progress. Victory fragmented a campaign already frayed by philosophical disagreements, tactical disputes, and competition for resources. For the northern public, issues of class discrimination lacked urgency and even legitimacy. Agitation against housing and employment discrimination appeared radical and could summon few Bull Connors to suggest a moral confrontation. Even less appealing was the fact that these concerns signaled a shift of the movement to the northern community. Public indifference or hostility, black opposition to the Vietnam War, and growing movement militancy, led government officials to intensify repressive measures. Thus,

the civil rights coalition had begun to unravel. Success, the desertion of elite
supporters, public distraction, and internal shifts meant that activists had to
adjust to new mobilization realities.[79]

"HARD TRAVELIN' "

In reaction to change and in a manner consistent with SNCC philosophy and
style, activists attempted to revive the mobilization impulse. With little
central direction, SNCC members expanded their operations to the North and
began the work of building independent black institutions and community
power. They turned their attention to real problems of police brutality,
joblessness, white control of business and housing, institutional racism, and
low voter turnout. By the fall of 1965, thirty-five SNCC field secretaries were
organizing in Newark, Philadelphia, Chicago, Los Angeles, New York City,
and the District of Columbia.[80]

Increasingly, the thrust of SNCC community work in the North and South
was toward black self-determination and separatism and away from integration and biracial cooperation. Grounding the organization in racial consciousness and pride, activists identified their effort as part of an international
struggle of the peoples of color against racism and oppression. Consistent
with this ideological change was SNCC's public stand in early 1966 against
the war in Southeast Asia. Also reflecting a shift in direction was the
replacement of John Lewis and James Forman and the election in May 1966
of Stokely Carmichael as chair. Carmichael, a Freedom Rider, Mississippi
Summer coordinator, and Lowndes County organizer, was described as "a
man who didn't have fear in him."[81] He would become in the eyes of many
Americans the symbol of black nationalism and the new militancy.[82]

A few weeks after his election, Carmichael returned SNCC to the forefront
of the civil rights movement. On 6 June, during a walk through Mississippi
against fear, James Meredith was gunned down. When Martin Luther King,
Jr., Floyd McKissick of CORE, and Carmichael vowed to continue the march,
the media spotlight refocused on the black struggle. Carmichael, following an
arrest for trespassing, announced:

> This is the twenty-seventh time I have been arrested—and I ain't
> going to jail no more! The only way we gonna stop them white
> men from whippin' us is to take over. We have been saying free-
> dom for six years and we ain't got nothin'. What we gonna start
> saying now is Black Power.[83]

SNCC activists took up the black power cry. As King supporters chanted "We
Shall Overcome," they answered with "We Shall Overrun" and "Seize
Power."[84]

In newspapers, magazines, and a book, Stokely Carmichael explained the meaning of black power. "It is a call," he wrote, "for black people to begin to define their goals, to lead their own organizations, and to support those organizations. It is a call to reject the racist institutions and values of this society."[85] Blacks had to close ranks and bargain from strength. Like the Irish and Jews before them, blacks could only look to themselves to secure equal participation in the social, economic, and political decisions that affected their lives.[86]

"We've been 'buked and we've been scorned"   The black power slogan challenged the integrationist ideal and frightened whites with its militancy. The positive media image SNCC enjoyed quickly changed. As recently as early 1965, journalists had attempted to allay fears of SNCC radicalism. They had reassured the public that its inflammatory rhetoric was actually "long-aggrieved underdoggism."[87] In the aftermath of black power, the media rejected the former "rebels with a cause." *Time* condemned black power as "the new racism."[88] The *Saturday Evening Post* predicted that SNCC's "paranoid self-segregation" had doomed it to failure.[89] *Newsweek* quoted Ralph McGill of the *Atlanta Constitution:* "SNCC is no longer a . . . civil-rights organization. It is openly, officially committed to a destruction of existing society. It can not expect society to remain passive under attack."[90] Already removed, the black power campaign further distanced SNCC from white sympathizers. Financial support evaporated quickly, and the movement's 1966 budget was only one-half of its 1964 total. Black power further fractured black unity. King condemned SNCC's approach as counterproductive and believed future cooperation impossible. Roy Wilkins of the NAACP and Whitney Young of the Urban League rejected black power and separatism outright. Carmichael had succeeded in verbalizing black aspirations and frustrations, but, more isolated than before, SNCC was less able to reify its slogan.[91]

Authorities responded to the cues of press and public. The Internal Revenue Service launched a probe of SNCC finances. Congressmen called for an investigation of the organization. Police in Philadelphia, Chicago, and Atlanta raided SNCC offices, arrested staffers, and disrupted operations. In 1967 the FBI's counterintelligence program targeted SNCC to "expose, disrupt, misdirect, [and] discredit."[92]

As outside pressure mounted, SNCC strove for greater internal purity. In December 1966 the organization's seven remaining white staffers became pawns in a struggle for power. Those championing "racial loyalty" succeeded in expelling the white members and placing blacks with white friends and even those with light skin on the defensive. The Arab-Israeli War in June of 1967 led SNCC to bolster its Third World ties by condemning "Zionist terror gangs."[93] Anti-Zionism, when added to tirades against Jewish businessmen and landlords, spelled anti-Semitism to American Jews. They curtailed further their contributions to SNCC coffers. Two years later, SNCC resolved the final contradiction by dropping *Nonviolence* from its name and becoming the Student National Coordinating Committee under the direction of a Revolutionary Political Council.[94]

In the spring of 1967 H. Rap Brown, who had organized in Mississippi and Alabama, replaced Stokely Carmichael as chair. Compared to Brown, Carmichael appeared a moderate. "Violence," said Brown, "is as American as cherry pie. If America don't come around, we'll tear her down."[95] A few weeks after assuming office, Brown was charged with inciting to riot, the beginning of a series of arrests that ended in 1973 when he was sentenced to a five-to-fifteen-year prison term for armed robbery. When such rhetoric was set against the backdrop of racial rioting and violence, the American public drew a cause-and-effect relationship. Federal and local authorities, acting with opinion makers and popular support, waged war on SNCC and other black militant groups. Charges of inciting to riot, possession of weapons and drugs, and draft evasion consumed the time, energy, and funds of activists. Planted informants, meanwhile, stirred dissension and induced paranoia in the movement.[96]

Rhetoric without a concrete program, repression, and dwindling resources made SNCC impotent. Resignations and purges closed down projects and left SNCC by the end of 1967 less a national movement than a few uncoordinated and underfunded community outposts. Their survival soon became precarious. In 1968 an attempt to restore the organization's energy through an alliance with the Black Panthers was stillborn. SNCC retreated as the decade ended to a room in the rectory of New York City's St. Peter's Episcopal Church, becoming a mail drop without telephone or full-time personnel. On 11 December 1973, having discerned no activity for months, the FBI wrote SNCC's obituary and announced it was "closing the case."[97]

The dispersion and deterioration of SNCC was part of the fragmentation and localization of the larger civil rights movement. National groups had lost their thrust. The SCLC had factionalized after the assassination of Martin Luther King, Jr. Internal strife also afflicted CORE. The NAACP lacked the dynamism and inclination to provide leadership. By the end of the 1960s, civil rights activists were pursuing private lives, engaged in community groups, absorbed into government or polity members, in jail, or dead. In the white mind, blacks had won their struggle. Black militancy appeared a radical aberration and a proper target for the authorities. Moreover, new issues of war, economy, energy, ecology, and crime commanded attention and funds. A resurgent Republican party, meanwhile, had devalued the black vote and conceded it to the Democrats. Republican strategists had fashioned a new majority, minus blacks, by uniting southern white and northern ethnic voters.[98]

The civil rights movement was the creation of several vehicles that differed in style, philosophy, and membership. Anchored in the southern black community, these organizations appealed beyond the local polity to bring the pressure of northern groups and public opinion to bear on a receptive federal government. The members of the Student Nonviolent Coordinating Committee, steeped in integrationist ideals, prepared to put their bodies on the line to spur federal action and build black community resources. Confrontation with the economic and political powerlessness of blacks, southern repression, and the North's unwillingness to perceive civil rights as a moral issue radicalized SNCC cadre. Declining white interest and changing national priorities, as well, fed its radicalization. SNCC became isolated and, in isolation, more militant and racially conscious. Black power, an evolution rather than a break with the past, was viewed in the context of racial rioting and violence. Opinion makers revised their images of SNCC and sponsored public hostility and aggressive government action. Weak internally, SNCC could not long survive financial drain, repression, and internal dissension.

The sacrifices of SNCC and other civil rights groups bought change. State-sanctioned caste discrimination based on skin color that stripped blacks daily of dignity and self-worth had been overturned. New legislation guaranteed blacks the vote and a lever to create political change. The civil rights campaign was also directly responsible for launching other social movements. As role models or hands-on teachers of activism, black groups precipitated the women's, Chicano, native-American, gay rights, student, New Left, and antiwar movements of the 1960s and 1970s.

The post-SNCC careers of many of the cadre testify to the changes experienced individually and nationally. In the 1980s voters elected John Lewis to the House of Representatives, Marion Barry to the mayor's chair of Washington, D.C., Julian Bond to the Georgia State Legislature, and Charles Sherrod to the Albany, Georgia, city commission. Unita Blackwell became the first black woman mayor of a Mississippi town. President Jimmy Carter named Mary King as deputy director of the Action program. Cleve Sellers administered a federal unemployment project in North Carolina. Bob Moses and James Forman returned to graduate school to work on advanced degrees. Stokely Carmichael, now Kwame Toure, leads the All African Revolutionary party in quest of a united Africa.[99]

Success often hides what remains unfinished. In the 1960s, civil rights activists reached for another goal that eluded their grasp. Caste discrimination was vanquished, but the problems of class injustice proved more intractable. The "benign neglect" of the 1970s and the Reagan revolution of the 1980s ignored, and probably exacerbated, the unequal distribution of wealth and power in America. While the middle class expanded, nearly two-thirds of blacks remained below the poverty line in 1986. The 1970s and 1980s also witnessed the erosion of the black family, with two-thirds of black children born out of wedlock. An underclass of the socially disabled—tripling since the 1960s—inhabits the deteriorating ghettos of the North, West, and South. There, joblessness, drugs, and teenage pregnancy shackle the next generation to an unchanging future.[100]

Civil rights accomplishments, too, may be less far-reaching and more precarious than assumed. The influence of class on political behavior has led analysts to revise predictions of the impact of the voting rights victory. In the 1980s, less than one-half of eligible blacks vote. Blacks hold just 1 percent of all elective offices in the nation. Even gains by middle-class blacks reflect continuing discrimination. With two-thirds of black professionals and managers working for the federal government, the middle-class workplace remains a segregated environment. The white exodus to the suburbs has even fueled a resegregation in schools and housing. The present recalls the past. In 1968 the National Advisory Commission on Civil Disorders warned: "Our nation is moving toward two societies, one black and one white—separate and unequal."[101]

8

THE CAMPUS REVOLT:
THE BERKELEY FREE
SPEECH MOVEMENT

The employers will love this generation. They aren't going to press many grievances. They are going to be easy to handle. There aren't going to be any riots
CLARK KERR

You can't trust anybody over thirty.
JACK WEINBERG

At noon on 2 December 1964 five thousand University of California, Berkeley, students gathered for a free speech rally in the plaza before the Sproul Hall administration building. The students were tense, anticipating a showdown in a conflict that had waged for more than two months. Speaker after speaker condemned the administration's stubbornness and justified the student's demands. Mario Savio, a Free Speech Movement (FSM) leader, captured the moment with a call for civil disobedience:

There is a time when the operation of the machine becomes so odious, makes you so sick at heart, that you can't take part; you can't even passively take part; and you've got to put your bodies upon the gears and upon the wheels, upon the levers, upon all the apparatus and you've got to make it stop.[1]

One thousand men and women responded and began a mass sit-in of Sproul Hall. As they filed into the building, folk singer Joan Baez affirmed the students' identification with the civil rights movement as she sang "We Shall Overcome" and "Oh Freedom." At 3:05 AM the next morning police began arresting demonstrators. The arrests continued throughout the morning and into the afternoon. Meanwhile, FSM activists, with the permission of sympathetic faculty chairpersons, used academic offices and resources to organize a strike of classes to shut down the university.

These events were the climax of perhaps the most carefully documented social movement in American history. A spiral of action and reaction, charge and countercharge, had polarized the Berkeley campus during the 1964 fall semester. Oriented more to issues than ideology, students rejected university paternalism as an immoral infringement upon individual rights. Administration officials, as agents of campus authority, used resources to isolate the protest and limit its impact. Both sides acknowledged the moral influence of the faculty and pleaded for its approval. In this polity in microcosm, student challengers abandoned traditional paths, absorbed repression, and galvanized support to effect successfully decision making.

If the Free Speech Movement was unique to the University of California, student unrest was not. *Newsweek* accurately characterized the Berkeley struggle as the "Concord Bridge of the student rebellion."[2] Significant changes, accelerated at Berkeley, had altered the American campus environment. Amid structural and demographic transition there emerged, during the 1960s, issues of individual freedom, war and peace, and racism that touched students personally and highlighted the gap between the American promise and American reality. This interplay between long-range developments and immediate grievances offers an explanation for the decade's campus-based protest. In the chain reaction of 1960s protest, Berkeley activism was the prototype that aroused students' sense of efficacy as issues escalated beyond campus life. Berkeley, then, was a beginning.

THE "MULTIVERSITY" SETTING

With war's end in 1945, men and women resumed more normal lives and renewed dreams long deferred. The media's acclaim of family life and an expanding economy supported private decisions. The resulting "baby boom" of the 1940s and 1950s was one of the most significant demographic trends in recent American history. The birth rate escalated to rival Third World statistics and, by 1961, four of every ten Americans were under twenty years of age. This swelling generation, as it slowly came of age, required major societal adjustments. America accommodated the ballooning numbers of young people with more hospitals and schools, new housing and leisure facilities, and revised marketing strategies to attract consumer dollars.[3]

In the 1960s the first waves of the baby boom generation were ready for college. The increased demand for college education was a reflection of more than numbers. In the 1920s colleges had begun their transformation from upper-class preserves to middle-class institutions. Thus, while just over 4 percent of high school graduates had attended college in 1900, by 1968, 50 percent did so. Between 1963 and 1973 total enrollment at American colleges and universities doubled, from 4.7 million to 9.6 million students.[4]

Universities adapted to a changing environment. The number of institutions of higher learning reached twenty-four hundred in the 1960s, accompanied by a dramatic expansion of facilities, faculty, and administration. At the pinnacle of the educational structure were the "multiversities," which grew in response to new social and economic demands. Developed in partnership with the government, the military, and industry, the multiversity countered the illusion of ivory tower isolation. By the mid-twentieth century, colleges had abandoned their traditional role of training men and women to be proper gentlemen and ladies. Research and career-oriented, higher education now focused upon creating critical minds that could examine diverse viewpoints. To meet the needs of students and the nation, universities were tuned to staffing business, medical, legal, and educational bureaucracies.[5]

This expansion and change during the 1950s and 1960s occurred within a campus society that was highly stratified and segmented. Great disparities in power resulting from differences in age, rank, tenure, and reputation defined these campus strata. Despite changes and new functions, the university retained many traditional controls over student behavior. Operating *in loco parentis*, administrators assumed the authority of surrogate parents. Campus rules monitored living styles and restricted constitutional freedoms of speech, press, and assembly. Academic regulations strictly fixed requirements and courses of study. If the bounds were clearly marked and well known, the rule givers were not. Research absorbed faculty, who relinquished their role as models to guide and influence students. Administrators chose communication by directive, content to rule invisibly, from a distance. As President Clark Kerr of the University of California would realize, "students deserve a fair chance to participate appropriately in the making of rules and decisions, rather than being relegated to the position of dissenting to rules already enacted and decisions already proclaimed."[6]

The University of California at Berkeley set the mold for this new multiversity. The University of California system accepted the top one-eighth of high school applicants, and the Berkeley campus attracted the best of this elite. In 1964 the campus enrolled 27,500 students, a 60 percent increase over enrollment in 1953. Its faculty had achieved national and international distinction and included several Nobel Prize laureates. Faculty research and consultation had fused the university with the wider society. The Berkeley administration, similarly, was considered efficient, responsible, and worthy of emulation. Yet, the problems of mass education plagued Berkeley. Students complained of aloof faculty and remote administrators. Classes were large and impersonal. The university restricted students' rights. In particular, the Kerr Directives of 1959, which liberalized existing regulations, still forbade student government to address off-campus issues and tightened the monitoring of student government and organizations.[7]

A new activism The potential for campus activism was high at Berkeley and elsewhere in the 1960s. Even before the baby boomers reached campus, the nation had instilled in them a sense of common identity and self-confidence. Proclaiming them the best educated and brightest of all generations, America had adapted to its children. High expectations nurtured these young men and women, and they were prepared to accept the torch from their elders. Their sheer numbers alone, in a concentrated campus area, would fortify this generation's sense of power, destiny, and group identity. The campus, as an age ghetto, similarly fostered the growth of leadership and organization from within the peer group. Compared to their war-veteran predecessors, baby boomers were young and relatively free of financial and family responsibilities. Flexible schedules allowed time for activism in an environment where security forces were minimal and the risks of involvement low. Literate and sophisticated, these men and women had at their command the skills necessary to organize protest.[8]

Opportunity, however, does not guarantee successful mobilization. As the Students for a Democratic Society's Port Huron statement noted, the campus was "a place of private people."[9] Individualistic and geared to their studies in high-powered academic environments, students could not easily be persuaded to an activist course. The campus population, moreover, is transient; large numbers of men and women are reshuffled each year. Graduation takes the most experienced and knowledgeable, while newcomers with little commitment to campus change replace them. Intermittent vacations, examination periods, and the truncated academic year rob a protest of necessary momentum. Only the authorities maintain a continuous and permanent residence. Finally, to act, students have to perceive issues in personal terms. It is this understanding, said Berkeley activist Gerald Rosenfeld, that "finally wrenches you in some way from the accustomed routine of privateness, from the doubts and ambiguities and compromises, day in day out, of life in America . . . [then] it is possible . . . to know . . . which side you are on."[10]

The silence that pervaded American campuses in the 1950s ended first at Berkeley. In 1957 a coalition of liberal and radical students organized Toward

An Active Student Community to contest campus elections. Regrouping more permanently as SLATE, activists rallied classmates for an end to discrimination in fraternities and sororities, improvement in classroom instruction, fair wages for student workers, and abolition of compulsory military training. At the same time, they pressed students to take stands on capital punishment, the arms race, and de facto segregation in local housing. SLATE agitation resulted in a narrow victory in 1959, with members winning control of student government and naming a campus body president. The University of California responded to SLATE power with the Kerr Directives that gagged student government. Administrators also rejected SLATE's request to use campus facilities to organize support for fair-housing legislation. Meanwhile, SLATE circulated petitions and planned demonstrations against mandatory Reserve Officers' Training Corps (ROTC) courses. Seven thousand students on the Berkeley and Los Angeles campuses supported the effort. Their sense of efficacy rose sharply when the board of regents voted in 1962 to make military training voluntary.[11]

Despite the Kerr Directives against advocacy, SLATE directed its attention to off-campus issues. In May 1960 SLATE members participated in a vigil protesting the scheduled execution of convicted rapist Caryl Chessman. Two weeks later, the House Committee on Un-American Activities hearings into local communist influence drew SLATE protestors to San Francisco. Berkeley students picketed, chanted, and held sit-ins to disrupt the investigation. Police using clubs and high-pressure fire hoses to clear the building arrested over sixty men and women. The events of "Black Friday" shocked students. "Our eyes were opening," said Michael Rossman, "a mystification was breaking, we were beginning to see the acts of official America as ugly, wherever we looked."[12] At the end of the 1961 academic year, university officials stripped SLATE of its student organization status because its primary purpose was the advocacy of off-campus issues.[13]

Berkeley students, meanwhile, mobilized in support of the civil rights movement. They picketed the Berkeley and Oakland outlets of chain stores that resisted integration efforts in the South. In 1962 Students for Racial Equality collected food and money for southern blacks. University Friends of SNCC and Campus CORE also attracted recruits and participated in equal rights demonstrations.[14]

Certain sectors of the Berkeley community sustained the protest minority in the face of official disapproval. On the campus fringe in a complex network of bookstores, coffee shops, and gathering places, were several dissident subcultural groups. There were the "beats," for example, who had rejected middle-class life-styles and goals to achieve personal liberation through new identities, roles, and family patterns. Apolitical, they experimented with eastern religions, drugs, and sex to enhance individual autonomy. Also present were political radicals representing the many varieties of anarchism, socialism, and communism. Whether living within this subculture or not, Berkeley students were in close contact with the dissenters, which not only fostered the students' awareness and tolerance of unorthodoxy and radicalism but made them acceptable.[15]

Students were well aware of changing national currents. The inspiring rhetoric of a charismatic president sanctioned a new social consciousness. Reformist and optimistic, John Kennedy called the young to a higher commitment to community and nation. Many Berkeley students were already involved helping the poor in urban ghettos and migrant farm worker camps. The Berkeley campus supplied the Peace Corps with nearly eight hundred volunteers, twice as many as any other university. Campus activists, too, could easily see their protest as part of the authorized campaign to realize American ideals.[16]

Activism gradually replaced complacency at other universities too. Students built campus political parties at the University of Chicago, University of Michigan, Oberlin College, and Columbia University. Students of the University of Wisconsin, Madison, began the periodical *Studies on the Left* in 1959 and within three years twenty-seven other journals of dissent appeared on seventeen different campuses. Civil rights and reformist groups competed with the Young Socialist Alliance, the Young People's Socialist League, and the Dubois Club, affiliated with the Communist party, for student recruits. More loosely affiliated, thousands of college students in the North and West participated in civil rights boycotts and picketing.[17]

The Students for a Democratic Society (SDS), formed in 1960, was one of the more important groups to emerge at this time. A coalition of socialists, radicals, and liberals, it expanded from the University of Michigan to chapters at eleven colleges by 1962. SDS's reformist critique called upon young men and women to overcome alienation and take control of the institutions that governed their lives. Through participatory democracy, America's contradictions in wealth and power, foreign policy, and race would be addressed and solved. A waning of campus activism in 1963 led SDS to abandon its university base and write off students as agents of change. With SNCC as the model and a grant from the United Auto Workers, members turned to community organizing in northern cities. Although SDS planned a lengthy campaign, its absence from the campus would prove brief.[18]

In the early 1960s, on scattered campuses and among a minority, activism had revived. Students had expanded or created organizations while a growing communication network informed the diverse centers of protest activities. This new left core was diverse and ranged from liberals to unaffiliated radicals to orthodox Marxists. Yet the great majority of students remained unmoved and unmobilized. They retained their faith in authorities on campus and in the wider society. Before they could be roused from their academic burrows new issues clearly salient to their rights and lives had to emerge.

DISPUTED GROUND

The direction and pace of Berkeley protest changed in 1963. Raising the salience of racial justice, the civil rights movement turned students from campus-bound issues. Responses varied in intensity, but built into a growing activist involvement. Men and women increased their contributions to University Friends of SNCC, a financial conduit to the integration campaign in Mississippi. More people responded to local efforts to strike immediate targets of racism. Under the direction of Campus CORE and the community-wide Ad Hoc Committee Against Discrimination, Berkeley students picketed and held sit-ins to protest business hiring and promotion practices unfair to blacks. Civil disobedience led police to arrest hundreds of demonstrators in February and March 1964. Confrontation, however, brought results; restaurants, hotels, and supermarkets agreed to remove barriers to job advancement. This success fueled the activists' sense of accomplishment and commitment to change. In identification with the black struggle, they assumed a moral mantle and expanded the protest community. The internal communication and organizational net, meanwhile, tightened through personal contact and became more elaborate.[19]

Protest ebbed in Berkeley during the 1964 summer vacation, but students did not abandon their causes. Perhaps as many as sixty students volunteered for the Mississippi freedom summer campaign. Among them were Mario Savio and former SLATE chair Art Goldberg, both active in Berkeley civil rights efforts. But activism was not confined to the left wing. The candidacy of Barry Goldwater had ignited much enthusiasm among conservative students. With San Francisco the site of the 1964 Republican National Convention, they prepared to bask in their champion's victory. These men and women also laid plans to mobilize campus conservatives for the fall presidential campaign.[20]

Thus, the University of California, Berkeley, was a crucial staging area for the mobilization of resources whether for causes of the left, right, or center. Because university regulations prohibited advocacy, recruiting, and fund raising for off-campus action, activists set up tables in a twenty-six-by-ninety-foot strip of brick walkway at the intersection of Bancroft and Telegraph avenues. Here, straddling a main artery into the campus, they came in daily contact with thousands of students. Although a low wall, concrete posts, and flag poles suggested that the strip bordered university property, it was actually within campus grounds. Small metal plaques, embedded in the sidewalk, identified the area as campus property. Still, most students either believed the land belonged to the city of Berkeley or ignored the violation, and the university's inaction sanctioned these responses. Despite continuous violation, campus authorities did not enforce the regulation and left the activists' claims unchallenged.[21]

However, the growing intensity of mobilization along the strip in 1964 ended the acquiescence of the administration. Vice-Chancellor for Student Affairs Alex Sherriffs was particularly incensed about the disregard for university rules and decorum. Positioning himself as the guardian of campus order and image, he declared, "Frankly I had been exasperated with this excessive permissiveness."[22] Sherriffs appointed an ad hoc committee to consider the issue during the summer. The vice-chancellor and his committee viewed the problem solely in disciplinary terms and concurred in the necessity of upholding university regulations. At no time during decision making were the students consulted. On 14 September 1964 the dean of students sent letters to all campus organizations announcing the administration's decision to prohibit the students' use of its facilities to support or advocate off-campus political and social action. The organizations were given seven days to remove their tables from the strip.[23]

Confrontation   Representatives from eighteen student groups, including University Friends of SNCC, Campus CORE, the Dubois Club, the Young Socialist Alliance, the Young Republicans, the Young Democrats, and Students for Goldwater responded with the formation of the United Front.[24] If the administration perceived the matter as one of law enforcement, activists invested the dispute with far greater significance. Students argued that the ban was an immoral and illegal attack on their rights as American citizens. They accused the administration of summarily abolishing freedoms of speech and assembly without even consulting the governed and, more directly, of short-circuiting mobilization efforts by closing of the activists' resource base. Students believed that campus officials had succumbed to conservative pressure from the community to curb their activities. Prohibitions on advocacy, fund raising, and recruitment robbed them of the means to effect social and political change. The struggle for racial equality, particularly, appeared in jeopardy. Many agreed with Mike Rossman, who condemned administrative initiates for striking "at the organizational heart of the Civil Rights movement on campus."[25] According to Marty Roysher: "If we . . . cannot advocate joining SNCC, cannot raise money for SNCC, it doesn' make a damn bit of difference what we do on this campus. We're not going to be of any use to the people in Mississippi."[26] Moreover, Berkeley rules seemed arbitrary and anachronistic when compared to policies at other universities. Nearby Stanford University and San Francisco State University had already liberalized regulations concerning on-campus advocacy.[27]

On these principles, then, activists prepared to take a stand. This was especially true of those who, just a month before, had refused to submit to southern terrorism in Mississippi. Berkeley students would soon sing words bonding them in spirit and cause to those who sacrificed for justice in the South:

I'm going to put my name down, brother,
    where do I sign?
Sometimes you have to lay your body on
    the line.
We're going to make this campus free,
And keep it safe for democracy,
So, I'm going to put my name down.[28]

Starting on 20 September two hundred students proclaiming free speech picketed the Sproul Hall administration building while half that number conducted all-night vigils. Berkeley campus chancellor Edward Strong responded to the rising clamor. Misunderstanding or ignoring the impact of the ruling on student organizations, he contended that "The open forum policy of the University is being fully maintained. Any student or staff member is free to address a campus audience."[29] While refusing to yield on the issue, Strong did sanction the distribution of campaign literature advocating votes on off-campus issues and candidates. This concession further confused the question and prodded student charges of the administration's duplicity and capriciousness. President Kerr backed his chancellor and derided the protesters: "Their actions—collecting money and picketing—aren't high intellectual activity. . . . These actions are not necessary for the intellectual development of the students."[30]

United Front member organizations sought advantage through escalation. On 28 September, they declared that regaining what had been lost was no longer sufficient. The United Front's new stand rejected any limits on student free speech. The next day, they set up tables on the strip and within the campus. University police requested the removal of the tables and were ignored. On 30 September, University Friends of SNCC, CORE, SLATE, and the Young Socialists Alliance placed tables in front of Sproul Hall and openly challenged the ban on fund raising and advocacy. University officials took the names of the five students manning the tables and asked them to appear at the dean of students' office that afternoon to discuss disciplinary measures. More than five hundred students assembled at the dean's office at the appointed time with a petition signed by hundreds more claiming that they, too, had broken university regulations. Under the leadership of Mario Savio, Art Goldberg, and Sandor Fuchs, they demanded the same punishment as that to be meted out to the five students already cited. Chancellor Strong condemned the "small minority of students" and, at Kerr's suggestion, "indefinitely suspended" Savio, Goldberg, Fuchs, and the five activists.[31] Interestingly, under university regulations no such punishment existed nor could any disciplinary action be instituted until a faculty-student conduct committee had held a hearing. The protesters charged that the eight had been singled out as examples and declared a "crisis of legitimacy" on campus. On their part,

administrators bemoaned a "crisis of authority." The students remained in
the building until the early hours of the morning, when they disbanded to
prepare for a noon rally. Events had now entwined the issues of free speech
and the justice of administrative discipline.[32]

The administration planned a decisive response to contain the protest
and end the crisis. Fifteen minutes before the beginning of the noon free
speech rally, university officials and police confronted Campus Core's Jack
Weinberg, who manned a table in front of Sproul Hall. They ordered Weinberg, a civil rights activist and former graduate student, to leave campus and
arrested him when he refused. As Weinberg awaited a police car to take him
to jail, he seized the opportunity to make a speech. "I want to tell you about
this knowledge factory. . . . It seems that certain of the products are not
coming out to standard specifications. . . . [T]he university is trying to purge
these products so that they can once again produce for the industry exactly
what they specify."[33] Meanwhile, the arrival of the police car focused the
attention of the growing body of students gathering in Sproul Plaza for the
rally.[34]

If the arrest had been timed to intimidate the most students, it would
prove to have an unforseen result. A dozen students sat down in front and
in back of the police car, immobilizing it. Within minutes, others joined the
protest and the number of demonstrators reached two hundred, then five
hundred, and within an hour, three thousand. "This was a wrong," said a
freshman, "which had to be righted immediately because it would set a
precedent for denying more and more rights."[35] A graduate student in nuclear
engineering sat down because, "This was an unfair arrest, a major crisis for
student rights, an opportunity to assert our protest against coercion. . . . I
decided to participate immediately—bodies were needed. . . . Students have
the right of free speech."[36]

The appearance of the multiversity issue in the free speech protest
surprised few. The perceived curtailment of student rights renewed complaints of arbitrary administrators and the irrelevance of university education. An explicit statement of the problem had appeared on the eve of the
free speech controversy in a SLATE handout, "Letter to Undergraduates." The
letter rejected the university as an "impersonal factory" that was devoid of
moral content and gave allegiance to the status quo while neglecting students.
On the academic assembly line, according to the letter, students were trained,
not educated. "THE MULTIVERSITY IS NOT AN EDUCATIONAL CENTER,
BUT A HIGHLY EFFICIENT INDUSTRY: IT PRODUCES BOMBS, OTHER WAR
MACHINES, A FEW TOKEN 'PEACEFUL' MACHINES, AND ENORMOUS
NUMBERS OF SAFE, HIGHLY SKILLED, AND RESPECTABLE AUTOMA-
TONS TO MEET THE IMMEDIATE NEEDS OF BUSINESS AND GOVERN-
MENT." Student government, operated by "political castrates," offered no
means of redress. The only possible response was "OPEN, FIERCE, AND

THOROUGHGOING REBELLION ON THIS CAMPUS."[37] As the crisis evolved, the theme of alienation and the symbol of the knowledge factory gained greater currency. Protesters wore IBM cards announcing: "Student at UC, Do Not Fold, Bend, or Mutilate."[38] Still, the alienated remained a minority and the multiversity a secondary current of protest. Most students and protesters were satisfied with the quality of education they received at Berkeley. For them, the issue gained meaning as it related to their central demands for civil rights and constitutional liberties.[39]

The trapped police car became a prop in the protest drama. While Weinberg sat under arrest in the back seat, speakers mounted the roof of the car to address the crowd. Mario Savio enunciated the protesters' demands, adding the release of Weinberg and immunity for sit-in demonstrators to free speech and justice for the eight suspended students. The university administration rejected negotiations. President Clark Kerr denounced the protest and declared, "the rules will not be changed in the face of mob action."[40] Chancellor Edward Strong refused to talk with protest leaders until they ended the demonstration and released the car. "Freedom of speech by students on campus," he reiterated, "is not the issue. The issue is one presented by deliberate violations of University rules and regulations."[41] In response to the stalemate, students increased the pressure. During the midafternoon, they sat down on Sproul Hall steps and blocked entrances to the building. With neither side willing to back down, the siege continued into the night.[42]

The next day, 2 October, demonstrators remained locked around the police car. Many read *The Daily Californian*, the Berkeley campus newspaper, which rejected them as "a near mob" engaged in "irrational and rash challenges."[43] Administrators spent the morning huddled with representatives of local law enforcement agencies devising a police option to the protest. If the demonstration did not end by evening, riot police would clear the campus and arrest those refusing to disperse. At the same time, protest speakers counseled students on civil disobedience tactics and their legal rights.[44]

The impasse prompted action from a group still outside the conflict—the faculty. Members of the sociology, history, philosophy, economics, and political science departments interceded between students and administrators to spur negotiations. Their efforts brought the two sides together as police took up positions just beyond Sproul Plaza. At 7:15 PM, thirty-two hours after the siege began, Mario Savio climbed to the now-dented police car roof to announce a truce. Student leaders agreed to end their sit-in and refrain from illegal protest against university regulations. A university conduct committee would evaluate the duration of the suspensions of the eight student activists. Chancellor Strong pledged to appoint a committee representing every segment of the university community, including the demonstrators, to discuss and make recommendations about all aspects of political activity on campus. The police arrested Jack Weinberg but later freed him when the University

of California did not press charges. After demonstrators had accepted these
terms and released the car, university officials withdrew the police from
campus.[45]

TAKING STOCK

The agreement lowered the level of confrontation and opened channels for
discussion. A resolution of the dispute, however, was nowhere in sight. Each
side remained secure in the justice of its cause and its self-definition as
defender of principle. As a result, both the students and university officials
moved to gather resources, cultivate support, and bargain from positions of
strength.

The day after the signing of the truce, university administrators stressed
that they had conceded little and gained much. The rules remained un-
changed, the eight students were still suspended, and Weinberg had been
arrested and removed. They continued to maintain, as well, that the protesters were an aberrant and isolated group, unrepresentative of the campus
community. Berkeley, San Francisco, Oakland, and Los Angeles newspapers
echoed these charges, characterizing protesters as radicals and off-campus
agitators and hinting of Communist connections. Condemnations of the
demonstration from the Interfraternity Council, the Panhellenic Council, the
Association of Women Students, and four residence hall presidents seemed
to confirm official claims.[46]

The car siege enhanced the salience of the free speech issue for Berkeley
students. This was a cause whose immediacy they could hardly ignore.
Moreover, it was difficult not to identify with fellow students and friends
who spoke for the rights of all and were punished in their exercise. The
appearance of capitulation by the administration simultaneously kindled a
sense of efficacy and power. For Mario Savio and other civil rights activists,
events drew meaning from their association with the movement in the South:

> Last summer I went to Mississippi to join the struggle there for
> civil rights. This fall I am engaged in another phase of the same
> struggle, this time in Berkeley. . . . The same rights are at stake in
> both places—the right to participate as citizens in democratic soci-
> ety and the right to due process of law.[47]

On 3 October, the United Front reorganized as the Free Speech Movement
to absorb recruits and resources from outside the affiliated organizations.
Graduate students, independents, and members of campus religious groups
elected men and women to join sitting representatives on a sixty-person
executive committee. Heterogeneous in membership and ideology, the coali-

tion had united on an ad hoc basis in defense of common rights and against a mutual foe. The executive committee made FSM policy decisions but relied upon a twelve-member steering committee for implementation and daily direction. On the steering committee, power rested with CORE, SNCC, and other left-wing activists. University of California students, with the exception of Jack Weinberg, formed the committee. The majority of its members were Jewish, many with Old-Left family ties.[48]

The steering committee operated through a multitude of "work centrals" charged with the tasks of mobilization. These units were responsible for press relations, information gathering, picketing, manning tables, typing, leafleting, and telephone soliciting. The newsletter central published an FSM newspaper throughout the campaign to insure that the movement's version of events received wide circulation. Fund raisers gathered contributions to finance the effort from students, faculty, staff, and parents. Sensing the movement's significance, an archives central collected materials for historians. Still, integration was difficult and organization sometimes chaotic.[49]

Like any challenger seeking to effect a change in the rules, the Free Speech Movement had to mobilize resources and marshall them effectively to influence decision makers. As a coalition of diverse groups, the FSM built upon its constituents' networks of personnel and communication. Its focus on common interests and concrete issues rooted in basic American values helped it to avoid ideological conflicts. Early on, members realized that reform would not occur if its urgency was felt within just the small circle of campus activists. Free speech had to become the concern of large numbers of men and women. Only when these students offered their resources to the movement would it become a mass vehicle of widespread dissent. Broad support and the resulting power to disrupt were the critical bargaining chips capable of forcing polity members to act and authorities to consider the students' claims of influence.

The powers that be   The FSM mobilized on the University of California campus, an arena within an arena. The board of regents operated under state auspices as the ultimate authority of university policy. California's governors drew from the state's economic and social elite to appoint the board's twenty-four members for insulating sixteen-year terms. The direction of the regents was general and distant; policy implementation and even formation was left in the hands of the system's administrators. Through support, reform, co-optation, and repression, university officials balanced the different interests on campus. At their disposal were means of coercion ranging from suspension and dismissal to the employment of police forces. Only in times of acute crisis would the regents reassert their control and govern actively.[50]

Clark Kerr, president of the University of California system since 1958, administered this educational bureaucracy with the aid of chancellors and their staffs on the different campuses. A professor of industrial relations and former Berkeley campus chancellor during the 1950s. Kerr had specialized in bargaining and conflict resolution. He also had a reputation for liberalism, receiving the 1964 American Association of University Professors' Alexander Meiklejohn Award for his defense of academic freedom. Kerr's influence was felt most directly on the Berkeley campus. He exerted authority through Edward Strong, whom he appointed campus chancellor in 1961. A professor of philosophy, Strong lacked bureaucratic expertise and temperament and followed Kerr's lead with few misgivings.[51]

The most important university polity member for both authorities and challengers was the faculty. Professors possessed the moral and intellectual influence that gave them weight in decision making. In their intermediate position, they enjoyed direct access to administrators and students. A diversity of interests motivated faculty members. They feared disruption of the campus calm they needed to teach and do research, a concern that mirrored that of the administration. In educational and political areas, professors echoed students' needs, a reflection not only of their mentor status but of their liberal beliefs. At the same time, faculty had a self-interest in defending their academic freedom and prerogative of self-governance from administrative pressure. Antagonism and resentment were products of this sometimes adversarial relationship. Still, faculty power was difficult to marshal. Individualistic and divided by academic discipline, professors were not readily amenable to united action. They would take a stand only when they believed that university officials had blundered and lost control and that intervention would benefit their students and themselves.[52]

Less significant, but also holding polity member status, were fraternities, sororities, and the student government. Members of these groups had routine access to the university administration and gained its recognition and rewards. Officials, in turn, showcased this student population to denigrate the activists. Protesters, however, rejected the accepted student channels to influence, for the administration's embrace robbed such groups of their credibility. In addition, the student government represented only undergraduates, thus excluding 37 percent of the university population; the Free Speech Movement claimed leadership from its broader base on campus.[53]

Authorities and the free speech challenger competed for the allegiance of the unorganized student population. The FSM could not sustain a protest or prove its legitimacy unless it mustered students for rallies and demonstrations. Administrators, too, by deriding activists as a minority, made student support the measure of the protest's substance. The immediacy of events lessened the power of opinion makers to screen the images of the movement. Men and women experienced firsthand the actions of movement proponents and university officials and fashioned unmediated conceptions of the protest. As individuals and in groups, they calculated responses that took into account the tactics and goals of the FSM, a sense of common identity with the protesters, a responsibility to authority, and the risks of disobedience.

The power of the opinion-making public was more significant off-campus. Newspapers circulated the administration's case and rejected student protest. An opinion poll found three-quarters of California's population opposed to the Free Speech Movement. However, the outsiders' view played only a minor role in determining the alignment of students, faculty, and staff on campus. It would prove more significant later, when officials were held to account for their "abdication" to the demands of campus agitators and nonstudent radicals.[54]

A JOINING OF ADVERSARIES

During October and November, the confrontation entered a negotiating stage, each side engaged in posturing and intimidation strategies. Chancellor Strong's appointment of a study committee on campus political activity, representing students, faculty, and administration, provoked an immediate FSM outcry. Activists condemned Strong's "unilateral action" depriving them of a significant voice on the body as a violation of the spirit of the October 2 agreement. The issue consumed ten days before Strong named four FSM leaders to the committee. On 15 October the academic senate created the Heyman Committee to hear the cases of the eight suspended students and advise the chancellor on a disciplinary course.[55]

While the committees deliberated, the parties maneuvered for position. President Kerr continued to elicit community support. In one off-campus address he declared that a significant segment of the protest leadership was nonstudent and "sympathetic with the Communist Party and Communist causes."[56] The FSM rallied daily, repeatedly warning of a return to direct action if negotiation failed. Meanwhile, eighty-eight professors signed a petition supporting a Heyman Committee proposal to reinstate the suspended students pending the outcome of their hearings. Strong rejected their request. In such an atmosphere, mistrust deepened and further lessened chances for compromise.[57]

The study committee on campus political action met through October and into November without reaching agreement. While all participants eventually accepted the right of student groups to advocate and advance off-campus causes, they deadlocked on the university's authority to discipline protestors for unlawful acts that might result from these activities. FSM representatives feared that such administrative power would gut the equal rights struggle by disallowing civil disobedience tactics. The threat of university discipline was, they argued, a prior restraint that inhibited action and censored free speech. Regulations would also entangle students in a double-jeopardy bind.[58]

In a split that was tactical rather than ideological, the FSM leadership divided on a response to the impasse. SNCC and CORE activists pressed for immediate confrontation and a renewal of free speech demonstrations. Lacking reserves and dependent upon daily infusions of funds and recruits, these groups had suffered most during the protest moratorium. Direct action now would energize the free speech issue and revive the movement and their organizations. Demonstrations might also discredit Kerr and Strong and influence the board of regents, which had scheduled a meeting on the Berkeley campus for later in November. Representatives of more-established groups such as the Young Democrats, Young Republicans, and Young People's Socialist League counseled moderation and continued negotiations. Protest would unleash a wave of official repression perhaps resulting in mass expulsions. An unprovoked walkout, moreover, might ignite a student backlash against the movement. After long debate, the executive committee decided on a return to confrontation.[59]

On 9 November, FSM members violated university regulations en masse declaring: "Rights unexercised are lost."[60] Tables reappeared in Sproul Plaza and organizations again solicited funds and recruited for off-campus activities. Administration officials quickly compiled the names of those manning the tables. Protestors continued to violate university regulations in the days to follow. When officials did not return, the activists forwarded a list of over seven hundred names identifying those in defiance. Chancellor Strong ruled that the FSM's lifting of the moratorium breached the 2 October agreement and dissolved the committee on political action. Henceforth, the administration would resolve the free speech issue in consultation with the student government and academic senate, without FSM interference.[61]

Students outside the activist core rejected the renewal of resistance. Few appeared for a rally in support of the November offensive. While a majority continued to approve of FSM's goals, those accepting its tactics declined from 50 percent on November 2 to 14 percent on November 9.[62]

The release of the Heyman Committee report on 13 November temporarily stanched the FSM drain. The committee condemned the administration for singling out the eight students "almost as hostages" to intimidate the protest movement and for suspending them without a hearing. Declaring the violations not serious and hardly a sign of delinquency, members recommended that six of the eight students be reinstated as of the date of their suspensions. For leaders Mario Savio and Art Goldberg, the committee suggested six-week suspensions dating from 30 September to 16 November. Many in the student community interpreted the Heyman Committee's lenient recommendations as a faculty endorsement of the FSM. In the report's aftermath, student support of FSM goals and tactics climbed to 47 percent of the campus population. The report was less pleasing to the administration. Chancellor Strong shifted the issue, asking why "serious misconduct" since

30 September had not been investigated. He promised that "regular disciplinary procedures will prevail including the immediate filing of charges."[63] Perhaps his threat was ignored as official posturing or understood in the context of the recent violations, but few perceived the import of his intention to punish students involved in the car siege.[64]

On 20 November three thousand students rallied and marched to the site of the board of regents meeting. If they were expecting a hearing on their demands, the regents disappointed them. FSM leaders were admitted to the gathering but denied permission to speak. Instead, they watched as the regents rubber-stamped administration proposals. The regents approved Chancellor Strong's suggested penalties, heavier than the Heyman Committee recommendations, of suspending to date the eight accused students and keeping Savio and Goldberg on probation for the rest of the semester. The regents also revised university policy on student political activity. They designated certain areas, including the Bancroft-Telegraph strip, as sites to advocate, raise funds, and recruit, but only for lawful off-campus action. Finally, the board authorized new disciplinary proceedings for students accused of violating university regulations subsequent to 30 September.[65]

The regents' action demoralized the FSM leadership. The new rules followed administration suggestions exactly and again excluded students from participation in campus decision making. Rather than a favorable resolution to the conflict, activists could only look forward to, in Michael Rossman's words, "a long and bitter battle ahead."[66] The prospects cheered few. Coming after two months of agitation during which studies had received a low priority, activists were concerned about their academic status and "damned tired."[67] The regents' hard line on student discipline increased the jeopardy of those cited for recent violations. Moreover, the liberalization of regulations preempted the movement's goals and threatened to undercut seriously campus support.[68]

The FSM steering committee met nonstop for forty-eight hours to consider a future course. A divided vote launched a sit-in of Sproul Hall on 23 November. When only three hundred demonstrators responded, the committee reversed itself and aborted the protest. The FSM suffered another setback the following day when the academic senate defeated a motion supporting its program. As the campus disbanded for the Thanksgiving holiday, the FSM had reached low tide. Exhausted, unsure of direction, outmaneuvered, and losing favor, the Free Speech Movement faced demobilization.[69]

ENDGAME

The administration not only failed to capitalize upon FSM setbacks, but blundered so seriously that it revived the movement. Rather than allow time for the new regulations to pacify activism or the coming examination period and Christmas vacation to quiet protest, university officials initiated disciplinary proceedings against movement leaders. They sent letters to Mario Savio, Art Goldberg, Jackie Goldberg, and Brian Turner informing them of pending conduct hearings for their involvement in the seizure of the police car. The letters provoked an uproar on campus. Both students and faculty condemned the action as vindictive and arbitrary. The administration appeared consumed with revenge and bent upon destroying the conciliatory spirit of the Heyman Committee. The university had again decided to single out a few from thousands of participants for acts committed two months earlier. Students who had joined in the car siege felt a palpable sense of shared identity with the accused and rushed to their defense. Moreover, the regents' revisions had liberalized the very regulations the students had protested. Opposition to administration sanctions had fused with and rallied the campaign for free speech. Together, these currents rekindled a sense of injustice and commitment.[70]

Movement leaders mobilized quickly to take advantage of the situation. On 1 December, FSM speakers demanded that the university halt all disciplinary action and relinquish control over the content of free speech to civil authorities. They warned that failure to accede within twenty-four hours would spark a sit-in of Sproul Hall. The graduate coordinating council announced a meeting for that night to discuss a teaching assistants' strike in support of FSM demands. Aware of the FSM's building momentum, the pro-administration student senate pleaded with students to reject the strike call while urging university officials to dismiss charges against the accused. President Kerr, falling behind the pace of events, refused to bargain. His condemnation of the movement as "an instrument of anarchy and of personal aggrandizement" convinced few on campus.[71]

On 2 December, one thousand demonstrators marched into Sproul Hall and occupied its four floors. Into the evening they studied in "freedom schools," watched movies, played cards, and talked. Hundreds of Jewish students conducted a Hanukkah celebration. In the early morning hours, Chancellor Strong entered the building and went floor to floor asking students to disperse or face arrest. More than two hundred demonstrators followed his advice. Meanwhile, Alameda County district attorney Edwin Meese, later attorney general of the United States under President Ronald Reagan, coordinated police forces drawn from surrounding communities and ordered them to clear the building. Demonstrators went limp, causing the operation to drag on into the late afternoon of 3 December. The police arrested 773 men and women, many of whom were physically abused. In response, faculty members raised bail money and organized a car caravan to return the protesters to campus.[72]

Who was there?   Who formed the activist rank and file of the Free Speech Movement? Eighty-seven percent of the arrested were Berkeley students; men and women joined the Sproul Hall action in numbers proportional to their distribution on campus. Social sciences and humanities contributed most students to the cause, 50 percent and 20 percent of the protest total, respectively. The biological and physical sciences and fine arts added strong contingents. The proportion of activists in sophomore, junior, and senior classes approximated the wider campus population, with freshmen overrepresented and graduate students underrepresented. Not surprisingly, the average age of the FSM demonstrators was just under twenty-one years, almost two years younger than the campus mean. While more than one-half of the demonstrators carried a B average or better, there was no significant difference between their academic credentials and the grade point averages of other Berkeley students. One in four of the FSM protesters was a Jew, compared to a university Jewish population of just over 16 percent. Those listing no religious affiliation formed 50 percent of the arrested group, double their number for the university as a whole. Finally, the mothers and fathers of demonstrators held more advanced degrees than the parents of nonparticipants.[73]

Surveys of those involved in the car seizure offer additional information about the FSM activists. These samples of protesters indicate that social sciences and humanities majors formed the mainstay of the effort. Personal ties mediated involvement with 75 percent of those at the siege acquainted with at least four other demonstrators; one-half knew more than seven others. Also important to the protest was the off-campus radical milieu. Two-thirds of the demonstrators were apartment dwellers who lived on the fringes of the campus.[74]

From these data can be discerned the characteristics of the most activist members of the FSM. Social sciences' and humanities' students filled the ranks of the protest movement. Studying subjects that stressed analysis of social values and institutions rather than rote learning or business perspectives, these men and women applied their education in the streets. Off-campus residence heightened their critical perceptions and intensified their suspicion of university authorities. Personal ties, moreover, enhanced their awareness of the movement's activities and spurned their own participation. The involvement of Jewish students may be tied to community and family conditioning that taught the legitimacy and fostered tolerance of its radical subculture. Familiar with the left-wing critique, Jews had to overcome fewer barriers to protest.

Studies of 1960s' New Left activists complete this Berkeley case study. Observers describe protesters as individualistic high achievers, with a strong sense of social responsibility. Parents of participants had attained at least a college education and, in the home environment, fostered self-esteem, independence, and a humanistic and egalitarian orientation. Politically liberal and religiously Jewish or secular, they encouraged children to question and not merely accept authority and traditional beliefs. In this context, then, and not in permissive child-rearing or an "Oedipal" revolt of sons and daughters, may be discovered the roots of protest. In the 1960s events at home and abroad exposed this generation to the gap between the American dream and its reality. The actions of authorities helped strengthen the salience of issues, and the civil rights movement provided a catalyst. With peer group support and activist role models, the students developed an interpretation and a sense of efficacy. It was this vision of a better America, combined with the personal impact of events, that fired their activism.[75]

Resolution   A crowd estimated at between five and ten thousand men and women gathered outside Sproul Hall on 3 December and watched the police action. The mood was tense. "People were pressed shoulder to shoulder, chest to back," wrote an observer. "You could *feel* the breathing rates of people around you. As you craned to see between people, you became aware of a sea of outraged faces."[76] As the arrests continued, pickets raised signs announcing that the strike planned for 4 December had begun.[77]

Students were not alone in their outrage over the arrests. As the FSM rallied, eight hundred Berkeley professors met to consider the situation. The police presence on campus had united faculty factions in an assertion of power. In the face of the administration's bankruptcy and the impending strike, the faculty attempted to capture campus leadership and control of decision making. It overwhelmingly approved resolutions calling for the dismissal of campus disciplinary action against protesters and for the regents' retraction of the university's right to prosecute students for their off-campus political activities. The professors also named a council of department chairs to act on their behalf and press the administration and the regents for a resolution of the crisis in concert with these proposals.[78]

The student strike gathered strength as the department chairs caucused. With faculty approval, FSM members used department offices and supplies to hold meetings, mimeograph leaflets, and print posters. One hundred and fifty activists formed a telephone committee to call students and ask their support. Bolstering these efforts, faculty and teaching assistants dismissed their classes. A survey of classrooms indicated that the strike was 60 percent effective, with an estimated 10,500 Berkeley students picketing or participating in the boycott. At the same time, 8,000 students opposed the strike or ignored it.[79]

Efforts to mediate the conflict continued during the weekend of 5 and 6 December. Chancellor Strong's hospitalization for abdominal pains on 5 December brought President Kerr into direct negotiation with the department chairs. Both Kerr and the board of regents now realized that the police action had isolated the administration from its campus supporters and accelerated the challenger's mobilization. Faced with an expanding revolt and few control options, the authorities prepared to accept the faculty's leadership. Kerr, with board of regents consent, agreed to rescind the university's demand to prosecute students for off-campus political action and refrain from disciplinary measures against students for activities prior to 2 December. The chairs concurred with Kerr that the university retained the power to discipline students for activities after that date and allowed him a face-saving statement that the Sproul Hall sit-in had been "unwarranted." The agreement would be announced on 7 December before an assembly of students, faculty, and staff at the campus's Greek Theater. While these negotiations proceeded, a group of two hundred faculty members met to formulate a pro-FSM platform for presentation to the academic senate on 8 December.[80]

The seventh of December brought the "tragedy" of the Greek Theater. Before sixteen thousand men and women, Kerr reported the terms of his agreement with the faculty chairs. But his statement was a declaration rather than an attempt to open a dialogue with students. For many, Kerr's medium and message demonstrated the administration's continuing disregard for student opinion and input. Even more disastrous was an incident that occurred at the end of the gathering. After Kerr's speech, Mario Savio appeared on the stage and approached the microphone. Before Savio could speak, police grabbed and removed him. The silencing of Savio not only discredited the negotiated settlement but put into bold, symbolic relief the cause they championed. Ten thousand students jammed Sproul Plaza after the address and by acclamation rejected Kerr's proposals. They now looked to the academic senate, scheduled to meet the next day, for relief and affirmation.[81]

With three thousand students gathered outside, the Berkeley faculty debated a course of action. Proponents of the FSM's program condemned the administration for provoking and prolonging the crisis. Authorities had unconstitutionally and undemocratically restricted free speech rights for reasons that were unconvincing. Refusing to negotiate in good faith, university officials escalated the confrontation with ill-advised disciplinary measures, Red baiting, lies, and a resort to police. Only a decisive move could bring the crisis to an end and initiate a process of healing. On the other side, critics of the FSM also rebuked the administration, but for pursuing a policy of "appeasement." To them, movement activists had bypassed established channels of change, weakened the institutional authority of the university, and engaged in unjustified direct action. Demagogic and extremist, the FSM leadership exploited the free speech issue to disguise a thirst for power. For such men as sociologists Nathan Glazer and Seymour Lipset, the Berkeley crisis of authority became an important way station on their path to neo-conservatism.[82]

After three hours of debate, the professors approved the Free Speech Movement challenge. They resolved by a large majority that no disciplinary measures be taken against students for any previous activities, including the Sproul Hall sit-in and the university strike. The faculty also called upon university authorities to revise regulations to eliminate all restraints on the content of free speech. Finally, the assembly declared its intention to assume disciplinary responsibility for students engaged in political activities. For Savio, on his twenty-second birthday, the faculty's stand meant "our protest has been vindicated."[83] Also on 8 December SLATE was victorious in campus elections and gained control of the student government.[84]

The board of regents met four days later to acknowledge change and partially reassert its authority. The regents rejected the faculty claim of responsibility for student conduct and retained it within the administration's sphere. On free speech, the regents bowed to the student challenger and its faculty supporter: "The policies of the Regents do not contemplate that advocacy or content of speech shall be construed beyond the purview of the First and Fourteenth Amendments to the Constitution."[85] The board promised to review university regulations on the issue and make revisions. An emergency regents' meeting on 2 January 1965 continued the transition, naming an acting chancellor to replace Strong, who was on leave of absence to recuperate from his recent illness. Martin Meyerson, considered more sympathetic to student needs, the next day issued free speech guidelines consistent with the FSM's platform. The university even offered to provide voice amplification equipment to student activists.[86]

The three-month challenge of the FSM had succeeded. Activists had rallied polity members, student groups, and a majority of the unorganized campus community in support of its free speech goals and against authorities' reprisals. Conceding FSM power, the board of regents rewrote its rules and sacrificed Berkeley's chief executive officer. Student government rested in the hands of SLATE and the FSM. Maintaining a fragile coalition based on issues, the outsiders had resisted both preemption and repression. Now, a more receptive administration prepared to deal with the challenger-turned-polity-member.

CHANGING TIMES

The Free Speech Movement's stay within the inner circle of influence was brief and without effect. Yesterday's issues lost relevance in the changed, officially tolerant atmosphere. Dependent upon its constituent groups and an unreliable campus population, the FSM had not mined a continuing supply of resources. Organizational structure remained ad hoc, never designed to survive times of crisis. As Michael Rossman observed, "Who were 'members' of the FSM? No one ever knew, or defined what membership meant. . . . If a need for a function was clear enough, people puddled like rainfall to fill it."[87] Nor did the leadership, antibureaucratic in temperament and committed to their individual groups, have a self-investment in their expendable vehicle.

In January and February 1965 the FSM's executive and steering committees held no meetings and abandoned influence efforts to marshall all resources in defense of those arrested during the Sproul Hall sit-in. The trials ended in June with the courts punishing demonstrators for trespassing and resisting arrest with fines and jail terms. In 1967 Savio, Goldberg, and Weinberg began serving four-month sentences for their leadership roles in the demonstrations.[88]

Free speech was the core of the movement's appeal and, with victory, leaders could not muster the will or the means to plot a new course. Although the multiversity issue had symbolic meaning for participants, it was a peripheral concern eliciting little enthusiasm outside a small constituency. Thus, a majority of students welcomed Chancellor Meyerson's proposals to combat the alienation and anonymity felt by students, but would do little collectively to insure their success. In the May student elections, SLATE candidates ran on a platform advocating curriculum reforms, pass-fail grades, and teaching alternatives to the lecture format. Apathy greeted their campaign, and all but two SLATE activists suffered defeat.[89]

With loyalty to their own organizations primary and the free speech battle won, men and women abandoned the coalition of issues that was the FSM. Campus CORE renewed demonstrations in the San Francisco Bay Area to combat job discrimination. Others returned to campaigns against nuclear war, capitalism, and Republicans. The centrifugal force of conflicting interests was most obvious and dramatic in the separation of political and cultural activists. In March a few protesters, among them Art Goldberg, attempted to expand the free speech effort to include four-letter words. Again, authorities and activists clashed and several students were jailed and also subject to campus discipline. The FSM officially denied responsibility, withheld support, and confined its attention to the protection of students' due process rights. University staff member and socialist Hal Draper voiced the left-wing perspective: "The whole thing was a trivial incident involving a handful of students."[90] Rallies to drum up student support for the accused attracted small crowds, and the academic senate resolved by a large majority that the affair was a "willful flaunting of obscenity."[91] When Goldberg was dismissed and three students suspended, the campus remained quiet.[92]

On 26 April Mario Savio resigned from the movement. Three days later, the executive committee formally dissolved the FSM and created the Free Student Union. FSU activists conceived their new group as an industrial union prepared to bargain collectively for student rights. Berkeley students, however, did not recognize their class identity and failed to collect membership cards. Learning, teaching, and research had replaced activism for the majority of the FSM's student and faculty supporters. Yet the pursuit of grades and careers did not erase the FSM's effect. If confrontation had cultivated a radical consciousness in only a few, it had spawned a suspicion of authorities and heightened a sense of efficacy. In the escalation of the war in Vietnam, a new issue would impel men and women to action by appealing to their moral idealism and sense of personal jeopardy.[93]

The authorities also attempted to ascertain the meaning of events. The board of regents commissioned a committee to conduct a post mortem. The resulting Byrne Report defended the protesters, citing the moral basis of their challenge and the strong support they commanded on campus. The regents ignored its findings and recommendations. President Clark Kerr continued to view the confrontation from a social control perspective. "We fumbled, we floundered," he said, "and the worst thing is I still don't know how we should have handled it."[94] Conservatives refused to allow Kerr to escape punishment for his defeat. During the 1966 California governor's race, Republican candidate Ronald Reagan vowed to conduct a complete investigation and "clean up the university." The board of regents responded to Reagan's victory by dismissing Kerr in January 1967. Interestingly, the FSM's portrayal of the multiversity made an impression on Governor Reagan. In June 1969 he defended and promised relief for the men and women of a generation "being fed into the knowledge factory with no regard to their individualism, their aspirations, or their dreams."[95]

Jerry Rubin, future antiwar activist and cofounder of the Yippies, declared during the Sproul Hall sit-in:

> The War against Amerika
>   in the schools
>   and the streets
>   by white middle-class kids
>   thus commenced.[96]

As Rubin predicted, the FSM's ripples reached far beyond the Berkeley campus. For students across the nation, the free speech effort at Berkeley presented resistance as an option as it convinced men and women of their power to effect change through confrontation. Authorities were likewise impressed and moved to forestall protest by liberalizing regulations to allow students greater influence in educational decision making. As *in loco parentis* rules were relaxed, students gained greater freedom of action in their private lives. The Berkeley flare attracted the attention of Students for a Democratic

Society, whose members were frustrated by the faltering of their economic research and action projects in 1964 and 1965. Returning to campus, they offered their leadership and organization to a burgeoning anti–Vietnam War movement beginning to find its stride. Teach-ins, peace vigils, marches, and demonstrations escalated with the pace of war and subsumed the activities of both student and civil rights movements. Throughout the 1960s the university remained the center of protest, a result not only of the availability of resources but such war-related issues as academic ties to the military-industrial complex, CIA recruiting, ROTC training, and cooperation with Selective Service officials in determining student eligibility for the draft.[97]

In a separate, yet entwined, effort, cultural dissidents were redefining life-styles, sexual mores, and gender roles in a modern romanticism. "Tuning in, turning on, and dropping out" were the watchwords for individual transformation—the first step to social change. Free universities, underground newspapers, rock lyrics, and the traditional media spread the word and mood rapidly, and "flower children" and "hippies" entered the national consciousness.[98]

Even if only a minority of Americans of any generation participated, their efforts shaped a decade. Washington policy makers, while refusing to abandon their Vietnam crusade, did respond to domestic pressure with troop withdrawals and the gradual Vietnamization of the conflict. The antiwar protest also spurred the creation of a draft lottery that limited eligibility for service to a year. Such victories, however, defused protest and resulted in demobilization. For the majority, the sense of alienation was tied to the Vietnam War; few demonstrators envisioned a large-scale transformation of America's socioeconomic structure. Violence and a rhetoric of revolution similarly isolated radicals from the more moderate rank and file and facilitated government repression. Organizationally weak, the resistance could not survive the early 1970s. As the war wound down, feminism, ecology, gay rights, and other causes emerged to strip the antiwar movement of its remaining resources. Others turned inward. On an estimated three thousand communes, men and women pursued their image of the good society. Born-again Christianity, eastern religions, the human potential impulse, and careers offered alternative routes to self-actualization. Meanwhile, the media domesticated the counterculture, stripping it of its radical intentions.[99]

The American campus is quieter today. In a decade emphasizing mobility and wealth, students conform to impress corporate recruiters. Authorities have learned their lessons from the 1960s and are better prepared to derail protest. Even campus architecture, in its disruption of public space and gathering points, reflects the university's concern with social control. Yet this tranquility shields undercurrents that bear an eerie resemblance to patterns that last emerged in the early 1960s. The university in the 1980s witnessed protests against sexism, CIA recruiting, and American policy in Central

America. An anti-apartheid movement drew students on campuses throughout the United States and pressed administrators to divest holdings in
corporations operating in South Africa. Activists have also organized a nationwide alternative student press network that counted sixty affiliates in
1987. In February 1988 a national student convention attracted seven hundred participants from 130 schools in forty-one states. Thus, the activist core
has begun to mobilize. Whether men and women may be moved to action
depends upon its translation of a program of change into individual concerns.
With a Berkeley-like spark, student movement leaders may become the role
models to light the sense of efficacy that is the requisite fuel of protest.[100]

9

NEVER ANOTHER SEASON OF SILENCE: THE NATIONAL ORGANIZATION FOR WOMEN

In 1946 *Fortune* magazine surveyed popular attitudes about American women. The poll found that nearly two-thirds of men and one-half of women judged women to be less creative than men. Three-quarters of the women believed that men made the best lawyers and that women were better suited to be stenographers. One in four women would choose, if born again, to be male. In an understated conclusion, the editors declared: "Evidently, it is still to some slight degree a man's world, even in woman's mind."[1]

Compare these findings with poll results from the 1970s and 1980s. In a 1972 Harris Poll, nearly 75 percent of women agreed that "if women don't speak up for themselves and confront men on their real problems, nothing will be done."[2] Three years later, two-thirds of

We will not condemn another generation of American women to fight for the obvious.
ELEANOR SMEAL

What we are trying to do is change the world.
JANET CANTERBURY

polled women voiced support for efforts to enhance women's status. A *Psychology Today* readers' survey showed 65 percent of men and 61 percent of women in favor of women's liberation. In 1987 the Gallup organization found that over one-half of American women and 88 percent of those 18 to 29 years of age described themselves as "feminists."[3]

These survey data reflect the significant change in public opinion and in women's self-image that has occurred in the second half of the twentieth century. Under the impetus of war-driven need and postwar economic development, women's roles expanded and transformed the content of their lives. Whether in the work place or at home, women became increasingly aware of the conflict between America's promise and their own restricted opportunities. At the same time, women emerged from the civil rights, antiwar, and student movements trained for activist roles and sensitive to a sexism that scored even the most progressive sectors of American society. Changing life-styles decisions by both men and women regarding birth control, marriage, and family size also nourished a rejection of stereotypes and traditional beliefs.

An amalgam of groups collectively labeled "women's liberation" crystallized from the heightened awareness of social, cultural, political, and economic prejudice and developed along preexisting communication channels. With a variety of targets, tactics, and goals, women's clusters ranged from the local consciousness-raising group to reform associations, to radical-feminist communes. The most important member of the women's liberation coalition—in terms of influence, size, and stability—is the National Organization for Women. Focusing its challenge initially on bringing women into the male mainstream, NOW addressed the larger issues of sexual roles, family, and life-style by proposing an androgynous alternative to traditional conceptions. Authorities and established groups, made receptive by the civil rights movement to demands for equality, perceived NOW as a nonradical vehicle of American women and feminism as an idea whose time had come. Yet NOW's influence would prove temporary. An antifeminist backlash exposed NOW's weaknesses and controlled the meaning of confrontation. Continuing reform and declining salience cut the feminist constituency. Ironically, hard-fought victories would raise new barriers for women to surmount. In NOW's challenge can be seen both the ground women gained in securing their rights and the distance they have still to travel.

RISING OPPORTUNITIES

World War II was a critical event in the history of American women. Patriotism, labor shortages, and high-paying jobs drew women from the home and into the workplace in unprecedented numbers. Six and one-half million women responded to government appeals and filled previously male-dominated jobs as well as those traditionally done by women. By 1945 twenty million women or one-third of America's female population worked outside the home. The nature of the change, however, was more than the sum of numbers. Before the war, marriage and middle-class status removed most women from the job market; only the young, the unmarried, and black and immigrant minorities were employed. War reshaped the meaning of work and legitimized labor outside the home for middle-class, native-born wives and older women. Seventy-five percent of new war workers were married, and wives accounted for one-fourth of the female labor force by war's end. The media and the government had so normalized "Rosie the Riveter" that public opinion shifted from 80 percent in 1938 opposed to married women working to 60 percent in favor just four years later.[4]

The war emergency ended in 1945. Defense plants closed and war veterans gained preference in job placement. Despite public fears of job shortages, rising divorce rates, and spreading juvenile delinquency, women remained in the work force, and war-time employment trends accelerated. In 1960 more than 37 percent of women worked outside the home; in 1970, 43 percent; and in 1980, over 50 percent. Wives continued working; approximately one-third of married women were employed in 1960 and over one-half in 1980. In a related development, nearly one-fifth of women with children under the age of five years worked in 1960 and, by 1980, almost one-half.[5]

Work outside the home proved a catalyst for continuing change. Employment removed the blinders that kept women's sights restricted to home and family. In becoming members of the work force, women entered the cash nexus of the capitalist economy and earned the tokens essential for status in American society. Completion of work tasks and assignments translated into a heightened sense of accomplishment and self-worth. These achievements, in turn, challenged the stereotype of women as dependent and passive. Outside the family circle women could be seen as individuals rather than as their husbands' wives or their children's mothers. At the same time, women grew increasingly sensitive to workplace barriers that limited their growth and advancement.[6]

The expansion of women's economic sphere, however, produced no immediate transformation in their status, for employment continued to be seen in a traditional framework. Work was an extension of the primary roles of wife and mother that enabled the family to attain or maintain a middle-class life-style. Many would delay outside employment until children had entered school or were grown. Thus, women left the home for the benefit of others rather than in a self-fulfilling pursuit of career. "She works," wrote Laura Bergquist in *Look* magazine in 1956 "rather casually, . . . less toward a 'big career' than as a way of filling a hope chest or buying a new home freezer.

She gracefully concedes the top job rungs to men. . . . Marriage is still woman's main goal."[7]

In the 1940s and 1950s ideals of female selflessness and nurturing drew strength from a media celebration of domesticity. Described by Betty Friedan as the "feminine mystique," the doctrine of fulfillment through total involvement in family was a favorite subject of opinion makers. "Togetherness" became a national priority and meant that women were most content as homemakers living in the suburbs and caring for a husband and three or four children. Television shows, radio programs, films, magazines, and advertisements inundated the American woman with advice for catching a husband, being a good wife, remaining attractive, becoming a cleaning and cooking expert, and making children the center of her life. Clothing designers decreed that the stylish woman would be attired in fashions featuring long, full skirts, small waists, defined bust lines, and high heels. In a special issue on American women in 1956, *Life* magazine decreed escape from her prescribed role "unnatural," for the female was "driven by her primitive biological urge toward reproduction, toward homemaking and nurturing."[8] The media had little mercy for those who fought their instincts, characterizing the career woman as frustrated, sexually inadequate, masculinized, and in need of psychiatric attention. The message registered. A woman's age at her first marriage declined to twenty years in 1960, and the birth rate soared. "The program for 'good' girls of the 1950s," remembers Ginny Foat, "was closely prescribed and 'good' girls went along with the program. Suited for it or not, they got married, had babies, tried to keep their men happy, and hoped for the best."[9]

According to *Look* writer Russell Lynes: "There is no country in the world where women are treated with more deference, given such latitude, or pampered with more courtesy and devotion than in America."[10] For many women such a declaration had a hollow ring. Having achieved the goals society set, they could not ignore an awareness of lives unfulfilled. As educated as men and raised in a nation extolling individualism and drive, women felt the emptiness of a life bounded by husband and children and experienced, through them, vicariously. In the workplace other issues emerged. Pay inequality, gender segregation, and job discrimination shadowed the potential and mocked the initiative of women. *Newsweek* columnist Edwin Diamond, like many men, was puzzled: "She is dissatisfied with a lot that women of other lands can only dream of."[11]

Domestic and employment grievances were salient issues to women in the 1950s, but they could not alone spur activism. Discontent was experienced in isolation, conceived as a personal problem, and interpreted as a failure to be a proper wife, mother, or daughter. Women blamed themselves, felt guilty and depressed, and turned to a frenzied submersion in prescribed roles. Tranquilizers, sleep, consumerism, husbands' careers, and children's futures offered relief and meaning. Thus, while the 1950s had set into motion mobilizing opportunities, women were yet to see their personal lives within a wider context. So deep-seated and pervasive was the conditioning that made women see themselves as unequal, that many would not even recognize it. Rising consciousness awaited the 1960s when activists and events helped women tie the personal to a political and collective response.[12]

HIGHER CONSCIOUSNESS

The federal government inadvertently laid the foundation for the building of the movement. With his recent, narrow victory in mind, John Kennedy established in 1961 the President's Commission on the Status of Women. He charged the commissioners to examine the economic, social, and legal position of American women and make recommendations that would redress disparities and foster equal treatment. The commission's report, issued in 1963, reflected attitudes in transition. Members endorsed women's primary roles as "mothers and homemakers and society's stake in strong family life" and left unquestioned social stereotypes.[13] Yet they also bowed to the reality of an expanded sphere for women and pressed government and business to promote women's rights. The commission recommended that women be allowed equal access to educational institutions and insured opportunities similar to those granted men in hiring, job training, and promotion. It proposed passage of equal pay legislation for women and men engaged in similar occupations. In light of women's multiple roles, members invited business to offer its employees paid maternity leaves and government to expand child care services and supports. Reviews of federal and state statutes prompted commissioners to suggest repeal of laws limiting women's property, legal, and economic rights. Concurrently, the members rejected enactment of an equal rights amendment to the United States Constitution and supported instead the retention of legislative protections such as maximum hours and minimum wage for women. Their report concluded with a call to women to enter politics and end their invisibility at all levels of government.[14]

The Commission on the Status of Women's two-year effort produced more than a series of recommendations. Government attention legitimized women's complaints of sexual inequality and raised the salience of the issue to women. A body of evidence now existed to substantiate claims of discrimination, clarify targets, and justify additional action. President Kennedy provided official support for further effort when he formed in November 1963 the Interdepartmental Commission on the Status of Women and the Citizens' Advisory Council on the Status of Women. These groups, as internal and external government watchdogs, monitored progress and pressed for change. States followed in the federal wake and created their own commissions to address the problems of women at the local level. By 1967 all fifty states had organized government agencies to document sexual discrimination and recommend solutions. From these governmental bases of "woodwork feminists," networks grew to absorb women in labor unions, professions, private industry, the media, and universities. Conferences strengthened personal ties which, in turn, facilitated the exchange of visits, staff, and information. On common interests, through friendships, and with government resources, they erected the scaffolding critical to the construction of a movement.[15]

Betty Friedan's *The Feminine Mystique*, published in February 1963, accelerated these efforts by further energizing an awareness of women's subordinate status in American society. Confronting "the problem that has no name," Friedan rejected a feminine ideal steeped in biological determinism and promoting women's domestication. "In the second half of the twentieth century in America," she wrote, "woman's world was confined to her own body and beauty, the charming of a man, the bearing of babies." In the "comfortable concentration camp" of the suburban home, women had been rendered passive and obedient, reduced to pursuing fulfillment in male domination and maternal love. It was time for woman to reclaim her "forfeited self" and reassert control over her life. For many, Friedan voiced unspoken thoughts and redefined as collective grievances problems that they had internalized. She awakened women to a victimization that was as much a product of overt action as more subtle institutional practice. *The Feminine Mystique*, by defining the problem, fixing blame, and proposing a remedy, offered women an ideology. With sales of one million copies, the book focused the attention not only of unmobilized women, but of contenders, authorities, and members of the developing feminist network.[16]

From civil rights to women's rights   Like other causes in the 1960s, women's activism evolved in an environment conditioned by the civil rights movement. The aspirations and demands of blacks fed back into the minds of members of other disadvantaged groups and legitimized their rejection of socially prescribed places and roles. Civil rights advances spurred more than awareness, for they defined for attentive challengers the potential of mobilization. Similarly, the civil rights movement sensitized opinion makers, polity members, authorities, and the wider public to fresh protest. Having already yielded, however belatedly or reluctantly, authorities were more amenable to removing the more obvious legal and civil caste restraints from other minorities. As a model and path breaker, then, the black struggle facilitated the mobilization of future movements. More directly, the civil rights movement provided fellow challengers with activists trained in the leadership and organizational skills essential to successful encounters.[17]

The first fruits of the renewed interest in women's rights appeared in 1963 when the Congress enacted and President Kennedy signed the Equal

Pay Act for women and men engaged in interstate commerce. While it was the first piece of federal legislation to prohibit discrimination on the basis of sex, the law had little immediate impact because the great majority of American women worked in occupations filled primarily by women. The following year, Michigan congresswoman Martha Griffiths adroitly seized the 1964 civil rights bill as a means to couple women's rights to the momentum behind rights for blacks. She convinced her bemused colleagues to amend the measure's Title VII ban on discrimination by private employers and labor unions because of race, color, and religion to include "sex." On passage, the law created an Equal Employment Opportunity Commission (EEOC) to investigate charges of unfair treatment in hiring, firing, promotion, and pay and to issue findings.[18]

In 1965, President Lyndon Johnson advanced beyond the Civil Rights Act's targeting of overt discrimination and issued an executive order attacking more complex and deeply rooted institutional bias. This order required employers holding government contracts to redress past discrimination against minorities with "affirmative action" hiring and training programs. Despite a heightened awareness of bias against women, the president's order ignored sexual discrimination, making affirmative action a remedy for bias against race, color, religion, and national origin.[19]

In the absence of a mobilized constituency, the limits of federal reform, earned through the labor of another challenger, quickly became apparent. President Johnson appointed only one woman, who was also black, to serve on the commission. At the same time, EEOC members focused their attention and efforts on blacks' grievances and minimized complaints from white women. For the commission's first executive secretary, Title VII's prohibition against sexual bias was a "fluke," a provision "conceived out of wedlock."[20] Not only did commissioners refuse to take sex discrimination seriously, they ruled that consideration of Title VII's impact upon state laws regulating women in the workplace was beyond their jurisdiction; it was a matter for the courts. In April 1966 the EEOC published guidelines sanctioning newspapers' customary practice of segregating job want ads by sex.[21]

The stalemate on women's issues concerned the members of the "feminist underground" of official Washington, D.C. Catharine East of the Labor Department's Women's Bureau; Mary Eastwood, a Department of Justice attorney; and the EEOC's Aileen Hernandez and Richard Graham quickly concluded that no advances or even revisions were possible unless women mobilized to demand action. Graham conferred with leaders of the League of Women Voters and the American Association of University Women but found them reluctant to campaign for Title VII enforcement.[22]

Looking for a lightning rod to galvanize women, several approached Betty Friedan, a highly visible and prestigious advocate since the publication of *The Feminine Mystique*. Friedan was receptive, believing that a civil rights group tor women was necessary to stimulate change. Choosing the June 1966 national meeting of the State Commissions on the Status of Women as her opportunity, Friedan canvassed the delegates for support. Hers was a well-conceived move, for the gathering attracted women with shared interests, experiences, and expectations from all over the nation. Moreover, Friedan believed the women would be receptive to her plans because President Johnson's decision not to reappoint Richard Graham to the EEOC had intensified uneasiness and energized the women's rights issue. Friedan's initial overtures, however, were rebuffed. Led by Katharine Clarenbach of the Wisconsin State Commission, most rejected the mobilization of a movement in favor of continued effort within official channels. But when Clarenbach attempted to offer resolutions before the gathering urging Graham's reappointment and more vigorous work against sexual discrimination by the EEOC, she was ruled out of order. Convention organizers had decreed that discussion and study were the purposes of the gathering and denied it any power to claim influence. This silencing outraged many of the delegates and impressed upon them the meaning of second-class citizenship and the low priority assigned women's concerns. Progress, they realized, would continue at a glacial pace unless women acted in their own interests.[23]

The emergence of NOW Twenty-eight women, including Clarenbach, Friedan, and Eastwood, met to consider a response. Pledging five dollars each, they accepted an activist course. Friedan scribbled their goal on a napkin: "To take actions needed to bring women into the mainstream of American society, now, full equality for women, in fully equal partnership with men."[24] The group chose Clarenbach as its chief coordinator, established a temporary steering committee to plan a chartering convention, and prepared to sound the recruiting call through local networks.[25]

Six months later, on 29 and 30 October 1966, thirty-two women and men representing three hundred members in twelve states and the District of Columbia met to christen the National Organization for Women. In their statement of purpose NOW members vowed to combat prejudice and discrimination that denied women equal access to government, the professions, industry, and education. This cause, they argued, had become even more urgent in recent decades because of a growing constriction in opportunities. Pink-collar ghettos confined women to sex-segregated and low-paying clerical, sales, and factory jobs. Women had not only failed to breach such male strongholds as law and medicine, they had lost ground in the traditionally female fields of teaching and social work. Meanwhile, laws remained in force that restricted women in the exercise of their civil and property rights. NOW also targeted the media, promising to expunge the "false image" it created of women. To wait for government action would be to accelerate women's decline. By mobilizing, *now*, women could lay claim to constitutional guarantees of equality and insure the realization of their full potential as human beings.[26]

NOW's statement was more than a simple acceptance of male social, economic, and political models. Within the platform was a vision of androgyny that conceived significant change in the lives of both men and women. "WE BELIEVE that this nation has the capacity ... to innovate new social institutions which will enable women to enjoy the true equality of opportunity and responsibility." NOW rejected marriage and family as primarily woman's tasks—"hers to dominate, his to support"—and proposed a "true partnership"and an "equitable sharing of ... home, and children and of the economic burdens."[27] Sister Mary Joel Read spoke for many in NOW: "This movement centers around the possibility of being human."[28]

Annual conventions, where initially a one-member-one-vote rule operated, set general policy directions for the new organization. To implement their decisions, members elected Betty Friedan as NOW's president, a cabinet consisting of two vice presidents and a secretary-treasurer, and Katharine Clarenbach as chair of the twenty-member executive board. The first board socially and economically mirrored the membership; it consisted of university professors, business executives, professionals, labor union officers, and government officials. The six men sitting on the executive board, however, were overrepresented when compared to the less than 5 percent male contingent in the NOW rank and file. The NOW constitution, in addition, mandated a structure of financial, legal, membership, and public relations committees to manage the daily activities of the movement. To translate convention directives into practical action, the movement established task forces dealing with employment opportunities, legal and political rights, poor women, women in education, the family, and the image of women in the media.[29]

Resource shortages inhibited NOW's initial thrust. Lacking funds, office space, and staff, the movement could not erect a centralized base of operations or even effectively answer its mail. Ballast came from Clarenbach's Madison office at the University of Wisconsin, Continuing Education Division, which maintained organizational files and catalogued executive board minutes. In Detroit the Women's Committee of the United Auto Workers under Caroline Davis's direction provided printing, telephone, mailing, and record-keeping services. Executive board member and advertising executive Muriel Fox handled NOW's public relations from her New York City office while Betty Friedan's Manhattan apartment served as NOW's provisional headquarters.[30]

Living on borrowed means and with a 1967 budget of less than $7,000, NOW had little with which to build an organizational structure to the grass roots. Nor could movement leaders afford to spend time and energy away from their careers in mobilizing activities that demanded experiences and training they lacked. They depended heavily, at first, on the media and and personal contacts in professional and government networks to spread the word. Friedan supplemented these efforts with brief speaking forays outside New York City that brought her before scores of small, East Coast groups of potential recruits. Limited resources, then, dictated NOW's reliance on local and individual initiative. "When someone would get so impatient that she'd call long distance," remembered Friedan, "I'd make her the local NOW organizer—if she didn't sound too crazy. It was a chancy method, and the style of the women's movement in different cities varied enormously according to that initial self-appointed NOW organizer—nurse, secretary, colonel's lady, academic or embittered divorced housewife."[31] If unorthodox, NOW was able to establish a local base. By 30 October 1967 it counted twelve hundred members in fourteen chapters.[32]

Immediately, with the aid of feminist sympathizers in government, NOW requested action on women's issues. Leaders called upon President Lyndon Johnson to amend his affirmative action executive order prohibiting bias by government contractors to include sexual bias. NOW petitioned the EEOC to rescind its guidelines permitting the division of help-wanted ads by gender. The movement also joined women who brought grievances before the commission or sued in court to overturn state criminal and protective work laws that discriminated. By watchdogging enforcement of Title VII, testifying before congressional committees, providing information to administrators, picketing, and exposing problems to media attention, NOW gradually gained ground. In 1967 Johnson revised his affirmative action order in accord with NOW's recommendation, and the EEOC ruled against sexually segregated want ads. In early 1968 the EEOC agreed to decide on a case-by-case basis whether state laws were discriminatory and thus superceded by Title VII.[33]

These concessions, however, did not develop their own momentum or guarantee further change. Government agencies were hardly aggressive in discharging case backlogs, canceling contracts, issuing new guidelines, or modifying laws. If politicians were sensitive to equal rights questions and the existence of a potentially cohesive women's vote, they remained unconvinced of the urgency of feminism. According to Benjamin Minitz of the Justice Department's Civil Rights Division: "We respond to social turmoil. The fact that women have not gone into the streets is indicative that they do not take employment discrimination too seriously."[34] Reformist, respectable, and accepting of procedures, NOW had been given an official audience and advanced the cause. For more fundamental change at an accelerated pace, authorities and polity members would have to be convinced that NOW fronted a mass-based insurgency with the resources to effect its will.

WOMEN'S LIBERATION

Apart from and unknown to NOW members, a feminist groundswell was already building. Its catalysts were the women of the political Left whose campaigns against racism and capitalism had exposed the power of sexism even in radical circles. In the fall of 1964 Mary King and Casey Hayden had anonymously broached complaints of sexual discrimination in the Student Nonviolent Coordinating Committee. Their position paper decried SNCC's inability to transcend society's sexual stereotypes that led to the assignment of women activists to clerical and household chores. Their proximity to white prejudice and black suffering had raised the salience of their own subordination while the struggle had instilled in the women the skills and sense of efficacy to conquer their passivity. In rejecting their organization's "caste system," they argued that "Assumptions of male superiority are as widespread and deep-rooted and every much as crippling to the woman as the assumptions of white supremacy are to the Negro."[35]

King and Hayden sent this and a follow-up memo written in 1965 to forty women activists "across the spectrum of progressive organizing."[36] Women of the Students for a Democratic Society were particularly responsive, having been fitted with similar sexual straightjackets. Their experiences in SDS's economic research and action projects in northern ghettos had awakened them to their own strengths, the reality of male chauvinism, and the double burden of sex and class that poor women carried. "What happened," declared Marya Levensen, "was that a group of us who were women became much stronger. We learned how to deal with a lot of situations. We learned how to fight."[37] Caucusing apart from men, they crafted a feminist interpretation within a radical framework that conceived of women as a colonized people whose liberation would come through class struggle. The overthrow of capitalism would revolutionize the basic institutions of America and bring sexual equality and the transformation of sex roles. SDS men, however, dismissed the significance of the feminist critique. Vietnam and draft resistance consumed their attention—movements in which women could relate only through men and could assume only subordinate positions. In the face of SDS patriarchy and neglect, women looked to themselves for support, using their organizational training as a platform. Feminist discussion groups evolved in 1967 into new organizations such as Women's Radical Action Project in Chicago, Bread and Roses in Boston, and the Berkeley Women's Liberation Group. Independent bodies also appeared in Detroit, Toronto, and Gainesville.[38]

For other radical women, feminism became the central concern and not simply one of several revolutionary goals. Patriarchy in radical movements convinced them that capitalism was only a means to women's subordination and that men were the true agents of oppression. In a militant celebration of women, feminist radicals repudiated the male master class, marriage, and the traditional nuclear family. They denied the equation of lesbianism with deviancy and accepted those twice oppressed into their ranks. Abortion was an inalienable right, a recognition of a woman's exclusive control over her own body and life. Once women united in sisterhood they could effect their own liberation from a male-dominated society that aimed to degrade them as sex objects, breeders, and domestic servants. These ideas assumed organizational form in the late 1960s in such groups as New York Radical Women, the Redstockings, and the Women's International Terrorist Conspiracy from Hell (WITCH).[39]

To counter the conditioning to subordination that had become so ingrained as to be unquestioned, radical women met in small discussion groups to analyze the power of sexism. "Rapping on oppression" enabled them to dismiss self-perceptions of inadequacy for a thoroughgoing critique of the treatment of women in America. In relating the personal to the political and liberating themselves from stereotypes and guilt, women raised their consciousness of the enemy and formulated individual and collective responses to achieve redress. Consciousness raising, by focusing on common grievances and fostering bonds of empathy and loyalty, heightened salience and efficacy. Small groups proliferated within and without radical circles, exposing more and more women to a feminist analysis. In 1969 there were approximately forty consciousness-raising groups in the United States. A year later, New York City, Chicago, and San Francisco, alone, supported 125 such groups. Women supplemented these bodies with a feminist network of gathering spots and private spaces encompassing bookstores, child care co-ops, abortion counseling centers, health clinics, craft stores, and communes. Feminist scholars also built caucuses in academic disciplines and media corporations. The women's liberation movement, however, was more than its organized vehicles. According to Robin Morgan:

> This is not a movement one "joins." There are no rigid structures
> or membership cards. The Women's Liberation Movement exists
> where three or four friends or neighbors decide to meet regularly
> over coffee and talk about their personal lives. It also exists in the
> cell of women's jails, on the welfare lines, in the supermarkets, the
> factory, . . . the old ladies' home, the kitchen, the steno pool, the
> bed. It exists in your mind. . . . It is creating history, or rather,
> *herstory*.[40]

In response to these grass-roots activities, newspapers and magazines increased their coverage of women's issues. The media initially treated the "libbers" derisively, dismissing them as bra burners and man haters with frivolous demands. This picture changed in 1969 when opinion makers, pressed by feminists within their organizations, began to reconceptualize women's rights as legitimately within the tradition of American reform. The media were especially attracted to the flares of progress and praised the first women to breech the social, political, and occupational preserves of men. By 1970 media attention to women's liberation rivaled that given to Vietnam, inflation, and student demonstrations.[41]

Reinforcing and, in turn, influenced by feminist activism were important changes during the 1960s in sexual attitudes and behavior, marriage patterns, and family size. Approved by the Food and Drug Administration in 1960, the birth control pill relieved women of the fear of pregnancy and permitted them greater sexual freedom and control over their reproductive lives. In response to a greater sensitivity to birth defects generated by the thalidomide tragedies and a rubella epidemic in the early 1960s, Colorado became in 1967 the first state to liberalize its abortion laws. Women during the decade chose to marry at a later age than their older sisters. In 1971 one-half of all women twenty years of age were single, compared to one-third ten years before. By 1979 only 50 percent of women twenty to twenty-four years of age had married, as opposed to 70 percent in 1960. Delaying marriage reflected new attitudes toward work and career and a desire for self-enhancement. Medical technology, later marriage, and evolving priorities combined to influence birth rates and the average number of children per family decreased from nearly four in 1957 to under two in 1976. By 1972 American death and birth rates had balanced to create zero population growth. Divorce, concurrently, had become economically and socially more viable and doubled between 1963 and 1975. Social changes of this magnitude offered women opportunities to revise traditional sexual roles and society to reexamine stereotypes. Women and men also redefined their relationships before these new realities. In this fertile ground, feminist ideas and organizations could flourish while stimulating further change.[42]

For the woman-turned-feminist, activist options were limited. Consciousness-raising groups proved short-lived and difficult to move from a discussion to an action orientation. Radical feminism made many American women uncomfortable and attacks by opinion makers on the "libbers" increased their reluctance to affiliate. Nor could the radical feminists, scattered and localized, promise recruits structural permanence or short-term steps toward long-range goals. NOW, however, had a national organization in place, a media-sanctioned leadership, evidence of success, and proven access to authorities. Positioned as a viable vehicle for action, it was prepared to channel personal concerns related to educational and occupational discrimination, child care, rape, spousal abuse, and media stereotyping into reform. For those seeking to bridge the private to the public, to bolster personal growth with societal and institutional transformation, NOW was a logical choice.[43]

NOW evolves   In the midst of ferment, NOW would not remain as it was. Radical feminists had effectively argued the shortcomings of a conservative solution that concentrated only on finding places for women in male-oriented business and political institutions. Their support of abortion and lesbian rights broadened the definition of women's issues. Consciousness-raising groups expanded the feminist circle to include suburban housewives, students, and smaller numbers of clerical and factory workers. Confined to the home, juggling career and family responsibilities, or facing discrimination as nonprofessionals in pink-collar ghettos, they entered NOW with experiences and needs in sharp contrast to the movement's founders. This combination of outside pressure and inside change caused NOW to adjust and develop more fully the meaning of its challenge. The ramifications of an economic and political partnership with men would constitute a significant reordering of American life. So, too, would the creation of a sex-blind world free of all forms of prejudice and discrimination. Calls for sexual self-determination, an equitable sharing of family responsibilities, and liberation from traditional roles would point America toward an androgynous society.[44]

The evolution of NOW's ideology was gradual. At their 1967 convention, NOW members appealed to the major political parties to incorporate a bill of rights for women into their national platforms. In it, NOW restated support for equal access to jobs and education, tax deductions for home and child care expenses, and maternity leave for working mothers. Going beyond these planks, the movement proposed the creation of federally funded day-care centers, suggesting that nurturing was not solely a woman's task but a responsibility for all. NOW also championed the passage of the Equal Rights Amendment that decreed, "Equality of rights under the law shall not be denied or abridged . . . on account of sex." Finally, the organization included among women's rights unrestricted access to abortion and birth control information and devices. If a growing consensus of Americans accepted abortion for health reasons and to reduce birth rates, NOW members stepped out of the mainstream and pressed for recognition of a woman's right to reproductive self-determination. The third annual NOW convention would make abortion rights a high priority.[45]

There were other signs that NOW had moved beyond its original critique. In circulars used for college campus recruiting NOW expressed an expanding vision: "Organizing against discrimination may be the legs of a group, but developing new life styles as women and experiencing group solidarity are the life-blood that keep the collective individual moving and alive."[46] In 1970 delegates to NOW's fourth annual convention resolved that "the movement is aimed at changing not only discriminatory laws, but the entire concept of man as the bread-winning, decision-making head of household and women as his subordinate helpmate. It envisions a society where men and women would share equal opportunities for supporting their families and taking care of their children."[47] Learning from its environment, NOW later implemented consciousness-raising courses lasting ten to fifteen weeks to immerse new members in a feminist interpretation and bolster their sense of movement community. Orientation packets explained the consciousness-raising group: "[It will] show you the shared trends of oppression running through the lives of all women. It will show you how to work to free yourself and your sisters through feminist understanding and NOW action."[48]

NOW confronted the issue of lesbian rights in the early 1970s. Following intense and divisive debate, NOW members rejected expediency and opted for ideological consistency. Delegates to the 1971 annual convention passed a resolution recognizing a woman's "right to define and express her own sexuality and to choose her own lifestyle."[49] According to Aileen Hernandez, who replaced Betty Friedan as NOW president in 1970, "We need to free *all* our sisters from the shackles of a society which insists on viewing us in terms of sex."[50] In 1975 lesbian rights became a movement priority, as NOW pledged to work for the repeal of all laws that criminalized private sex acts between consenting adults. NOW's openness encouraged lesbians to join and integrate their cause into the larger women's rights agenda. Dedicated and energetic volunteers, they gained status and attained influence in decision making while maintaining a low profile to protect the movement's image. At the same time, NOW sympathizers in the media kept a public silence to reduce the organization's vulnerability.[51]

Movement splintering characterized NOW's first years. Radical feminists in the New York City chapter, NOW's largest and most active, decried the organization's hierarchical structure as oppressive and demanded a participatory democracy in which leadership alternated among members. Led by Ti-Grace Atkinson, who advocated a class analysis of women's oppression, communal child rearing, and the abolition of the nuclear family, radicals mutinied in 1968 and formed the October 17th Movement and later, the Feminists.[52]

Labor union members in NOW's right wing opposed initially the Equal Rights Amendment because they feared the loss of legislation that protected women in the workplace. The United Auto Workers' disapproval meant the withdrawal of clerical services which, in turn, briefly threw NOW into administrative and financial disorder. Professional women and businesswomen who had joined the movement to combat legal and economic discrimination rejected abortion rights as disruptive and tangential to NOW's original goals. Many resigned and reformed in the Women's Equality Action League (WEAL) targeting for attack educational and occupational inequality.[53]

The most vocal critic of NOW's changing course was Betty Friedan. Friedan railed against "female chauvinism" and "orgasm politics," convinced that such stances would force women and men into an adversarial relationship. Radicalism would repel authorities, polity members, and opinion mak-

ers and provide "good soil for fascist, demagogic appeals based on hatred."
She pleaded with NOW members to realize that "the new understanding that
women are developing must be channeled into political action, not into a
highly verbalized sexual emphasis with a lot of whining and wallowing."
NOW's recognition of lesbian rights intensified Friedan's alienation. She
raised the specter of the "lavender menace" wondering if it "was simply an
ideological mistake, fed by those long suppressed rages, or a calculated
diversion provoked by agent provocateurs within our ranks." In the mid-
1970s NOW factions turned their resources against one another, giving
opponents opportunities to mobilize and stop the advance of women's
rights.[54]

Thus, the women's liberation movement forced NOW members to reevaluate their aims and expand their vision of sexual equality. The emergence of
new activists and the replacement or departure of influential early joiners
facilitated this ideological change. Despite these shifts, the movement retained an image of respectability and responsibility. NOW members continued to pursue reform through acceptable channels. By the 1970s media
exposure and the achievement of short-term goals had expanded the bounds
of women's rights. Authorities and established groups had retained their
perception that the organization represented a potentially powerful mobilizing constituency that held women's issues salient. NOW activists, compared
to more radical feminists, appeared more desirable as partners in negotiations
and coalition building. Both NOW leaders and women's liberationists were
aware of their symbiotic relationship. "The more we talk about test-tube
babies," said one radical, "the more NOW can demand child care centers and
abortion repeal."[55] With a consistent ideology, flexible tactics, and a secure
image, NOW prepared to further women's causes.

EQUAL RIGHTS NOW

During the first half of the 1970s evidence of NOW's advance accumulated.
Personal ties and media publicity attracted recruits, raising movement membership from twelve hundred in 1967 to forty thousand women and men in
1974. During the same period NOW's fourteen chapters mushroomed into
seven hundred local organizations. While NOW recruited most of its members individually, in some instances local feminist groups were absorbed
intact.[56]

NOW broadened its thrust by forming ad hoc coalitions with other
feminist groups. Most notably, NOW initiated, organized, and coordinated a
National Women's Strike for Equality to mark the fiftieth anniversary of the
passage of the Suffrage Amendment to the Constitution. On 26 August 1970
thousands of women turned out for rallies, teach-ins, and marches in two

dozen cities across the nation to support abortion rights, twenty-four-hour child care centers, and equal opportunity. The effect of this visible demonstration of women's power was not lost on decision makers. Governor Nelson Rockefeller of New York State and Mayor John Lindsey of New York City issued proclamations endorsing women's rights. President Richard Nixon declared: "While we herald their great accomplishment, [the suffrage amendment] let us also recognize that women surely have a still wider role to play in the political, economic and social life of our country."[57] With an aura of legitimacy, activists maintained the pressure on authorities and polity members creating in July 1971 the National Women's Political Caucus. Overlapping NOW in membership and issues, the NWPC pledged to mobilize the feminist vote in election campaigns and lobby for abortion rights and the Equal Rights Amendment. In 1972 the NWPC successfully pressed the now-receptive Democratic and Republican parties to place women's rights planks in their platforms.[58]

NOW power grew because of increasing movement activity and resource accumulation at the grass roots. The organization chartered local chapters once they had recruited at least ten women and men; strong chapters included as many as five hundred members. The financial health of the movement was based upon membership dues that were divided between local and national levels. Meeting monthly, members tuned the NOW program to their individual community's needs, creating task forces to campaign for ordinances outlawing sexual discrimination, monitor school textbooks for sexism, lobby legislators for abortion reform, and educate their neighbors about women's rights. In different communities, movement women established centers that provided day care, counseled rape victims, and housed battered women.[59]

A sample of five hundred NOW activists offers a glimpse at the grass-roots membership in 1974. These NOW members were young: Over 50 percent were under the age of thirty, and 40 percent were between thirty and fifty. More than one-half of the women were married. Despite efforts to recruit minority women, only 10 percent of the sample were black or Hispanic. Two-thirds of the NOW members had earned college degrees, while nationally, this was true of less than one-fourth of women. Two-thirds of the NOW members worked full time compared to just under one-half of the American female population. For NOW women, education correlated with occupation: One in four enjoyed a professional career. Only 8 percent of the NOW sample held clerical jobs while 35 percent of all women worked in these positions. Additional contingents of NOW members were homemakers (20 percent) and students (14 percent). Young, white, educated, and affluent, these NOW members were neither socially nor economically representative of their American sisters.[60]

Relatively autonomous, local chapters developed their own projects with little direction from the national organization. "We operated," recalled one chapter leader, "on our own."[61] "National NOW," said another, "is something out there that I hear from once in a while; or that I read about in the papers."[62] While encouraging grass-roots creativity and flexibility, the absence of intervening bureaucratic levels made coordination and communication difficult. A lack of contact bred accusations that NOW leaders were "elitist" and "self-seeking." Estrangement was also felt laterally, for news of other NOW chapters, whether close by or far away, came only intermittently. To remedy its bureaucratic deficiencies, NOW enlisted directors for its East, South, Midwest, and West regions and entrusted them with integrating and organizing functions. However, the movement's growing but tight budgets of less than $50,000 in 1971 and under $100,000 in 1972 allocated no staff or secretarial support to activate these critical links in the chain of command.[63]

Rising public support for women's rights, reflecting the tide of grass-roots mobilization and a steady stream of favorable publicity, disguised NOW's structural weaknesses. According to a Louis Harris opinion poll in 1972, 48 percent of women supported efforts to raise women's status. Three years later, 65 percent of women approved of such activities. Also in 1975 Gallup pollsters found that 84 percent of American women assigned responsibility for improved conditions to feminist organizations. Laura Graeber, writing for *Mademoiselle*, declared: "It's chic to be in a women's group. . . . In 1975, women's rights are as American as, well, apple pie."[64]

In response to popular demand, and their perception of feminist strength, authorities accepted NOW's claims to influence with little apparent risk. By 1972 six of the eight goals listed in NOW's bill of rights had been at least partially achieved. Congress had passed legislation prohibiting sexual discrimination in job training and federally aided educational programs. It had authorized tax deductions for child care expenses. Congress also approved a bill creating a national child care program but it was vetoed by President Nixon. With no obvious price tag or organized opposition, the Equal Rights Amendment to the Constitution received bipartisan support and was dispatched with the president's signature for ratification by the states. Meanwhile, the Equal Employment Opportunities Commission had adopted a feminist perspective and treated sexual discrimination as seriously as racial inequality. The EEOC issued guidelines that supported maternity leave and pressed for redress in hiring, wages, and job opportunities. In other administrative action, the Internal Revenue Service facilitated NOW fund raising by exempting contributions from taxation. In 1973 the United States Supreme Court in its *Roe* v. *Wade* decision made abortion a matter between a woman and her physician. Within a decade and under feminist prompting, legislation, court decisions, executive orders, and administrative action had effected important changes in the status of women in America. NOW, as the chief proponent of reform, had gained recognition from the country's elite and its authorities. The challenger had become an accepted contender for power.[65]

THE ERA

Between 1972 and 1982, NOW and other feminist groups made ratification of the Equal Rights Amendment their highest priority. In one stroke, the ERA would wipe out scores of discriminatory federal and state statutes and regulations concerning property, criminal penalties, family, occupational restrictions, and military service. Its wording also shifted from the woman plaintiff to government authorities the burden of proving the injustice of unequal treatment. The amendment would insure the accomplishments of the reform and prevent their erosion in more conservative times. And, as a symbol of moral commitment, the ERA could energize women and men to redefine further their roles in American society.[66]

With congressional passage of the amendment, NOW shifted its focus from the national arena to the fifty state battlegrounds. This meant coordinating movement sectors, activating the neglected middle echelons, and intensifying grass-roots mobilization. These were not easy tasks. National NOW maintained offices in Washington, D.C., New York City, and Chicago to handle, respectively, legislative affairs, public relations, and administration. In 1973 NOW's budget stood at nearly $300,000, a significant increase over previous years but sufficient to fund only fifteen paid staff positions. NOW remained heavily dependent from top to bottom on volunteer help. In preparation for the ratification campaigns, NOW leaders divided the United States into nine regions and appointed directors and councils for each. Newly created state hierarchies linked the regional offices to local chapters. These administrative measures promised to facilitate horizontal and vertical communication, resource allocation, and control. With so many direct-mail and unaffiliated members, NOW moved to build its chapter strength. It distributed organizer kits to instruct activists in chapter building, media relations, and political pressure tactics. Supplementing internal action, NOW helped fashion an ERA coalition of over 450 organizations with a collective membership of more than fifty million women and men.[67]

The ratification campaigns would test NOW's claim to polity membership. Power in Washington, D.C., did not necessarily transfer to the states, where ERA forces had to unravel traditional group alignments and contend with the primacy of local issues. The advance of women's rights would also provoke mobilization by challengers, who commanded the strategic advantage. They could claim victory by concentrating all their resources in a few states and capturing a one-vote plurality in a single house of thirteen legislatures. Finally, if the campaigns proved lengthy, ERA proponents would have to confront the changing salience of the issues and changing polity patterns on both the state and national levels.[68]

NOW's initial concerns soon dissipated as twenty-two state legislatures, with minimal debate and in domino-like action, ratified the amendment in

1972. Easy victories with little resistance led NOW leaders to relax their efforts. They did not release resources to shore up organizational scaffolding, staff the middle levels of the command chain, or press for vigorous grass-roots canvassing. Their sense of security continued into 1973 when eight more legislatures approved the amendment, reducing the number needed for ratification to eight. The Gallup Poll, meanwhile, counted 78 percent of the American people in favor of the ERA.[69]

At the end of 1973 ratification momentum flagged sharply. In 1974 only three legislatures accepted the ERA, and proponents claimed just two more victories before 1978. Activists then won from Congress an extension of the ratification deadline until 1982, but no other state would join the pro-ERA ranks. Meanwhile, feminists failed to spark the cause and perhaps even stalled the ratification drive with unsuccessful campaigns to place ERA amendments in the state constitutions of New York, New Jersey, and Florida. While fighting for the deadline extension and driving for three more state victories, NOW also had to contend with legislatures trying to rescind their ratification votes. Other resources went to defend NOW against lawsuits brought by Missouri and Nevada challenging NOW's economic boycott of recalcitrant states.[70]

Critical to the course of ratification was the rise of a STOP-ERA movement. Launched by conservative activist Phyllis Schlafly, the resistance successfully altered the meaning of the amendment from a recognition of women's rights as American citizens to a radical attack on traditional values and the family. "Women's lib," Schlafly argued, "is a total assault on the role of the American woman as wife and mother and the family as the basic unit of society."[71] She warned that, under the ERA, men could deny financial sustenance to their families and be relieved of alimony and child support obligations. Sex-segregated prisons and rest rooms would be outlawed and rape laws declared unconstitutional. Critics also charged that the ERA legalized homosexuality and allowed gays to marry, adopt children, and teach in the schools. Ratification would, as well, subject women to the military draft and force them to serve in combat. The 1973 *Roe* v. *Wade* decision fed into the ratification fights and galvanized women and men in opposition to change. In the hands of the building opposition, the ERA became the shorthand symbol for homosexuality, sexual promiscuity, teenage pregnancy, divorce, abortion, and drug abuse.[72]

In all, more than 130 New Right and religious groups rallied to challenge ratification of the ERA, including the Eagle Forum, the American Conservative Union, Right to Life, the American Legion, Veterans of Foreign Wars, the Catholic Church, the Rabbinical Alliance of America, the Mormon Church, the Knights of Columbus, and the Moral Majority. Opponents concentrated their forces in the southern states, Illinois, Oklahoma, Utah, and Nevada and convinced legislators that the ERA spelled radical and unpopular change.

Politicians, similarly, were not persuaded that NOW had the clout either to punish or reward their votes. They even questioned NOW's permanence within their communities. Awakened to the power of the opposition and reluctant to take risks against it, lawmakers voted against change. "The movement," remarked NOW's Eleanor Smeal, "never realized the depth of the opposition."[73]

Stalemated   At this critical time, when resistance had begun to grow and the ERA was faltering, NOW turned against itself. In the mid-1970s attorney Karen DeCrow running on the slogan "Out of the Mainstream, into the Revolution" was elected as NOW's President.[74] DeCrow represented a growing consensus that wanted the movement to grow ideologically and expand its constituency. She called for more determined organizing among minorities, the poor, and working-class women. NOW would have to address concretely issues of job security, salary, welfare, child care, and the feminization of poverty. DeCrow also championed direct action demonstrations and sit-ins to complement more traditional means of gaining influence. These proposals, coming in the midst of dissension over lesbian rights and marking a shift in control from one generation to the next, factionalized the movement. Personal animosities sharpened ideological disagreements as different elements struggled for dominance. "There were power plays," wrote Ginny Foat, "and coups and counter coups."[75] Amid accusations of fraud and "since no one was able to trust anyone else in NOW," leaders hired the American Arbitration Association to police the organization's 1975 elections.[76] Dissension was not confined to the national level. In the Dade County, Florida, chapter, for example, early members felt bypassed on issues by a rising generation of activists. Rather than accept a new place in an evolving NOW, they split the chapter and worked independently for women's rights. According to Roxcy Bolton, the founder of Dade County NOW: "NOW left me, I didn't leave NOW."[77]

Factionalism eased in 1977 with the rise to leadership of Pittsburgh homemaker Eleanor Smeal. Less by eloquence than the strength of her personality and convictions, Smeal righted the movement and prodded NOW toward a new orientation. While maintaining its commitment to equal economic and educational opportunities, NOW moved to incorporate the demands of minority, elderly, and working-class women. It also proposed a bill of rights for homemakers, countering the perception that feminists disparaged these women as "victims or fools."[78] Under Smeal, the movement attempted to regain the initiative in the ERA ratification drive and to emphasize coalition building, door-to-door organizing, and mass marches and picketing. Her efforts attracted members and money. Between 1977 and 1982 NOW grew from 65,000 to more than 200,000 women and men, and its budgets increased from $700,000 to more than $8 million. The accumulation of resources brought NOW increased influence within the Democratic party. Delegates to the party's 1980 convention, one-half of whom were women, adopted platform planks that denied aid to candidates opposed to the ERA and approved federal funding of abortion for poor women. Said Smeal, "We have arrived in the Democratic Party."[79] Missouri delegate Frances Noonan, however, had a better sense of political possibilities: "The test is not here. . . . We're going back to Peoria and it won't play there."[80]

By 1980 opposition forces had stalemated the ERA drive. Feminist intensity also eroded in the wake of United States Supreme Court decisions supporting women's rights. Attuned to the environment, the justices expanded the equal protection clause of the Fourteenth Amendment and broadened their interpretation of Title VII, reversing nearly all laws and regulation for which the ERA had been proposed as a remedy. The most significant exception was the military draft, from which, in a popular decision, the Court excluded women in 1981. At the same time, state legislatures had revised rape, family, and property statutes in line with feminist demands. Several states had placed equal rights amendments in their constitutions. As progress was made and women felt a sense of individual, rather than collective, efficacy, the salience of feminism and the ERA declined. This was especially true for Americans coming of age after the rise of the women's rights movement. Thus, Catharine Simpson complained that younger women "accept its benefits, but God forbid they should make the ideological commitment. . . . Perhaps you can only be a good feminist over 30—you've been knocked around and you have a strong enough sense of sexual identity."[81]

The 1980 election delivered a crushing blow to the Democratic party and to NOW's hopes. Anti-ERA groups had moved into the Republican party in force. Convention delegates turned against feminism, removed the ERA from their platform, and called for a constitutional amendment outlawing abortion. Ronald Reagan's victory brought a slashing of social welfare programs and a relegation of affirmative action and antidiscrimination guidelines to the lowest priority. Even before the Republican return, Congress had restricted the conditions under which the federal government would fund abortions. Pro-choice advocates would lose even more ground under the Reagan administration. When time expired on the ERA extension there was little chance for another renewal. Supporters reintroduced the ERA in 1983 but were unable to obtain the two-thirds majority necessary for congressional passage. In the 1980s, with authorities pursuing a new agenda, NOW lost its influence and returned to the rank of challenger.[82]

PRESENT AND FUTURE

In the aftermath of the ERA's defeat and before an unresponsive Republican administration, NOW reevaluated its course. Judy Goldsmith, elected president when Smeal stepped down in 1982, believed that changed circumstances dictated a de-emphasis on controversial issues and public protest. NOW had to bolster its political resources before pressing again for reform. This meant registering women to vote, lobbying more intensely, and creating political action committees to fund pro-choice and feminist candidates and causes. Tapping the Democratic party as the vehicle to power, NOW brokered its support for influence. At the 1984 convention, NOW commanded a bloc of four hundred delegate votes and secured both a feminist platform and a woman on the national ticket. Its endorsement of Walter Mondale and Geraldine Ferraro broke a movement tradition of neutrality in presidential contests.[83]

The Reagan landslide denied Goldsmith's wisdom. So, too, did her failure to halt the breakup of the movement that had begun with the ERA's defeat. Judging NOW unnecessary or ineffective, members deserted and thinned the ranks by 25 percent to 150,000 women and men in 1985. Budget revenues were down significantly, and the organization was more than $1 million in debt. Setbacks provoked a bitter internal struggle, and Eleanor Smeal returned to reclaim NOW. Her victory called members "back to the streets" and signaled a revival of militancy and visible activism. In 1986 the movement sponsored a march on Washington, D.C., in support of abortion and reproductive rights. Activism continued under President Molly Yard, and in recent years the capital has witnessed mass demonstrations for gay and lesbian rights and against revision of the Roe v. Wade decision. NOW has not neglected its political focus. Movement operatives have engineered a "feminization of power" campaign to multiply the number of women's rights advocates in Washington and in city halls and state houses across the nation. The organization has also launched NOWNET, a computer network linking local chapters to national offices through the instant transmission of alerts and tactical bulletins. Approaching its twenty-fifth year of existence, NOW has stabilized, stanched its losses, and resumed the offensive.[84]

As NOW activists enter the 1990s, they can look back upon a quarter century of progress. Feminist action lowered the barriers that denied women equal access to educational and occupational opportunities. College-educated women entering such fields as law and medicine, especially, have made great strides. Through design or osmosis, feminism has raised the society's consciousness of sexism and succeeded in revising media images of women, child-rearing practices, school textbooks, and language habits. Abortion remains a viable alternative to an unwanted pregnancy, and women have achieved new freedoms in life-style and sexual behavior. Collectively, these changes have kindled within women a sense of their own power to escape traditional prohibitions and realize their dreams.[85]

Yet progress should not disguise women's unfinished agenda. Nor should it foster a belief that a victory gained is a right guaranteed. The list of women's issues is long. The ratification of the Equal Rights Amendment remains a NOW priority, both for symbolic reasons and for guarantees of full citizenship. Authorities, polity members, and challenging groups threaten abortion rights, and anti-abortion organizations have convinced doctors to stop performing, insurance companies from covering, and hospitals from permitting abortions. Recently, Operation Rescue has enlisted thousands in a nationwide civil disobedience campaign to close clinics. Homophobic reactions in the wake of the AIDS crisis lend credence to fears that gays and lesbians face a new repression. NOW task forces on image still protest the media's portrayals of women as sex objects and the scarcity of women in roles other than wife and mother. Unsympathetic government officials and an increasingly conservative Supreme Court demand increased vigilance to protect affirmative action programs. Women's advances in professional fields should not draw attention from the highest rungs of media, corporate, and educational power that still remain beyond women's grasp.[86]

Change also exposes new issues and demands creative solutions from NOW and other feminist groups. In the 1970s and 1980s the majority of American women have suffered a deterioration in economic condition and plunged to a level of security below that of their mothers. Revisions in family law concerning divorce, community property, and alimony have eliminated the guarantees married women traditionally possessed. In the first year after divorce, a man may expect his standard of living to rise 42 percent while a woman's economic status drops 73 percent. Women cannot easily compensate for these losses, for gains in the workplace have proved insufficient. Seventy-five percent of women work in low-status occupations in which three-quarters of the employees are female. This sexual segregation of labor, when combined with family responsibilities, discrimination, and subsequent differences in training and work experience, produce a wage gap that has left women with sixty-four cents for every dollar a male worker earns. In the wake of change, poverty has become feminized and two-thirds of all families headed by women have been unable to maintain a decent standard of living.[87]

Feminists have also begun to reassess the personal costs of work and career. Husbands have failed to assume household responsibilities, leaving wives the double burden of cleaning, cooking, and caring for their children in addition to holding full-time jobs. Unmarried women face a more basic dilemma. With career paths established according to male rhythms, women are forced to make choices between their personal and working lives. They must balance career opportunities against marriage and a running biological "clock." Fanning the concerns of single women, the media portray a "feminization of loneliness," warning that career orientation has lowered the chances for marriage and children.[88]

These diverse problems have stimulated a multifaceted response. While continuing to combat occupational segregation through affirmative action,

NOW has championed a solution to pay inequality based on "comparative worth," which proposes that the jobs of men and women be ranked according to the knowledge, skill, training, and effort required to perform them. People holding equivalent jobs would receive similar benefits; as a result, women's salaries would be equal to those of men's. NOW has also called upon decision makers to upgrade and fortify the status of homemakers. This proposal entails extending to homemakers Social Security and disability benefits, funding retraining programs, and recognizing the economic value of housework in marital property and divorce settlements. To aid working wives, NOW has reemphasized ideas overshadowed by its stands on the ERA, abortion, and lesbian rights: a federally funded, nationwide child-care system; eighteen-week, unpaid, family leave for birth, sickness, or other emergencies, with protection against job loss; increased child-care benefits; and greater flexibility in the hours and conditions of work.[89]

With these insights into the reality of women's lives, coupled with a vision of equal treatment, NOW offers Americans a formula to advance the country closer to an androgynous society. Seasoned activists are preparing for the next stage of their challenge in an organization better coordinated and more firmly rooted in the local community than ever before. As energizing events create opportunities and link individual concerns to collective grievances, the uncommitted feminist majority will move toward mobilization. Polity and media sympathizers can quicken the pace by adding their voices and resources to the cause. In such an environment, authorities will be hard-pressed to deny the necessity and justice of change.

10

THE CHALLENGERS' LEGACY

Those who study social movements follow roads-less-travelled. The majority of Americans ignore the collective path to power, either pursuing influence through prescribed channels or dismissing it as beyond their grasp. The media are attracted to the flashes of history—the cataclysmic events or technological breakthroughs that dramatize the social, economic, and political transformation to which ordinary men and women are captive. For too long, scholars have heard only the voices of presidents and congress leaders and have ignored the local players.

The overview of twentieth-century social movements presented here reflects a different perception of history and society. All of these movements—the Anti-Saloon League, the Industrial Workers of the World, the Ku Klux

Think Globally, Act Locally
BUMPER STICKER

218

Klan, the Communist party, the John Birch Society, the Student Nonviolent Coordinating Committee, the Free Speech Movement, and the National Organization for Women—were created by men and women who mobilized resources from established groups, authorities, challengers, and the rank and file. Welded into a collective force, the members of these vehicles acted to redress real grievances of individuals and the community. They stood in tight embrace with their environments while jockeying for control of their image and the flow of events. In degree rather than kind, they differed from more conventional contenders. Rooted in the daily rhythm of life, these social movements were the tools of common people trying to shape the present and realize the future.

MOVEMENT MEMBERS

The social movements we discussed were not spontaneous undertakings of the impatient. Men and women built their protest upon an existing base. Churches, unions, political parties, fraternal lodges, business associations, campus bodies, and government-sponsored commissions provided challengers with members and the names of potential recruits, among other resources. Activists first drew followers by using the communication and organizational networks to which they already had access. After thoroughly working these channels, they looked to the media to spread their message.

Joining a movement was hardly a random decision. Community attitudes, organizational ties, and family background and interaction influenced the choice. Sufficient evidence exists to suggest a continuing crossgenerational commitment to activism that links the century's succession of left- and right-wing challengers. A combination of social responsibility and self-interest impelled participation, as is true of involvement in more conventional associations. Like traditional groups, movements offer members intellectual and social support in addition to ideological direction. Marginal men and women seeking escape from freedom or a cure for personal problems may turn to challengers as they do to established organizations, but they will play only minor roles.

The organizers of our eight movements were middle class, educated, primarily male, usually native born, and well-connected to community groups. This description fits leaders in poor people's movements like the Industrial Workers of the World and the Student Nonviolent Coordinating Committee as well. Whites rose to leadership positions and exerted a strong influence, even in SNCC and other minority movements. Cadre, in turn, united a heterogeneous rank and file, forging alliances across religious, racial, class, and gender lines. The Anti-Saloon League and Ku Klux Klan attracted a multiclass and multidenominational following. The Communist party blended immigrants and native-born, the working and the middle classes. The John Birch Society and the National Organization for Women, middle- and upper-middle-class in complexion, counted sizable blue-collar and ser- vice-worker minorities. Diverse in issue orientations, the membership of the Berkeley Free Speech Movement was demographically most homogeneous. Finally, from a supportive subculture, the number of Jewish-Americans in our protest groups was disproportionate to their numbers in the wider society. They formed an important contingent within the leadership and the rank and file of the Communist party, SNCC, the FSM, and NOW.

The eight examples, while not a random sample of twentieth-century American social movements, reflect that universe's class, gender, racial, political, social, regional, and organizational contours. Blending sociology's conceptualization with history's sensitivity to time and place yields a method of analyzing past, present, and future movements and offers evidence to help answer critical and unresolved questions: How have movements changed over the century's course? Why do some movements succeed; why do others fail?

THE PROTEST PRESENT

Many have described the passing of activism in the 1980s. In this view, national leaders rarely challenged Americans to rise above their smallest intentions. Instead, they easily coaxed the nation into a celebration of the status quo and the satisfaction of material desires. The media, meanwhile, reduced their vigilance and relaxed in the glow of prosperity. Matters of race, class, gender, and environment were not pressing to the majority; redress could wait the coming of official action in President Bush's "kinder, gentler nation." In such a time, movement memberships lapsed, resources evapo- rated, and authorities and elite groups raised the barriers to influence.

These reports of the demise of activism, however, are greatly exaggerated. In fact, the 1980s witnessed considerable movement activity, whether as extensions of past mobilizations or in the form of resurgent and even new protest. In the 1980s, left-wing, center, and right-wing groups built and bolstered their resource bases to empower present challenges and to prepare for future opportunities.

For example, conflict over abortion, beginning in the wake of *Roe* v. *Wade* in 1973, increased in intensity during the 1980s. Pro-choice activists massed in "counterterrorist" actions to repel pro-life demonstrators. Identifying with the civil rights movement, anti-abortion protesters employed civil disobedi- ence tactics to shut down clinics, fill the jails, and clog court calendars. The Supreme Court's review of its 1973 decision promises to transfer the issue to state polities and bring increased mobilization there to effect legislation.

London-based Amnesty International, founded in 1961, made significant membership strides during the 1980s. By the end of the decade, it claimed more than 800,000 members in 150 nations and a $15 million budget. Organized in a "network of caring," members gather in local groups to work for the release of prisoners of conscience and against torture and the death penalty. Gay rights activists continue their efforts to combat violence against homosexuals, repeal state sodomy laws, and end social and economic discrimination. Greenpeace initiated confrontations in defense of the environment, attracting great media attention. In a multi-issue campaign for the "ecological integrity of the planet," Greenpeace cadre work for nuclear-free seas; the safety of whales, seals, and endangered species; the elimination of toxic wastes; and the protection of the world's rain forests.[1]

Just before the end of the Reagan administration, the New Right challenge receded before scandals ensnaring televangelists. Guilt by association infected the religious right and losses in viewers and members meant decreasing funds. Sympathetic authorities, effusive in their verbal support, did little concretely to redress concerns. Thus, issues of abortion, sexual morality, pornography, drugs, and school prayer remain on the New Right agenda. If some vehicles and leaders have been discredited and the salience of some issues diminished, the institutional base of conservative political action committees, think tanks, organizations, press, and corporate and political sponsors remains intact.

Further to the right are the seventeen thousand members of the Aryan Nations, the American Nazi Party, the Ku Klux Klan, the Arm of the Lord, the White Aryan Resistance, the Covenant, and more than fifty other splinter groups. In the late 1980s, these organizations recruited "skinhead" gang members to their campaign against blacks, Jews, Asians, Hispanics, and gays. With heads shaved and their black jackets adorned with Nazi paraphernalia, these teenagers have contributed to a surge in violence that in 1988 produced four deaths, three dozen assaults, and vandalism against scores of churches and synagogues. Local and state authorities have responded with increased surveillance and arrests. The federal government has also moved swiftly to suppress the radical right. After federal agents infiltrated white supremacist groups, the Justice Department filed charges against 150 activists and gained convictions in one-third of the cases. In action reminiscent of the repression of the Communist party in the 1950s, prosecutors charged fourteen radical right leaders with conspiracy to overthrow the federal government. Their acquittal in 1988 came only after the movement's heavy expenditures of time, money, and energy.[2]

Past activists and causes have also reemerged in the 1980s. In 1987, 1960s' radicals Russell Banks, Abbie Hoffman, Phil Berrigan, and William Kunsler joined 250 other activists in advocating the creation of a "new grass-roots organization to resist government policy." Said Kunsler, "It is time to stop being good Germans."[3] Many who heard the call, having continued their involvement in labor, peace, gay, and women's causes, were prepared to answer. Opposition to American policy in Central America mirrors the antiwar demonstrations of the 1960s. Singing "Give Peace A Chance," activists have been arrested en masse for blockading induction centers and trains carrying military supplies. In a related effort, the Sanctuary Movement, rooted to a church base, acts to aid refugees fleeing the Central American battlegrounds. Authorities have moved quickly to stall these challengers. Between 1981 and 1985 Federal Bureau of Investigation agents monitored the Committee in Solidarity with the People of El Salvador, the United Auto Workers, and the National Council of Churches to uncover proof of Communist influence and terrorist links. In addition, they photographed demonstrators, recorded license plate numbers, and opened files on one hundred movement activists. The Immigration and Naturalization Service hired informants to join the Sanctuary Movement and gather evidence for prosecution. In 1985 courts convicted eight activists of violating immigration laws. The American Peace Test revived antinuclear activism of the 1950s and 1960s. In 1988 and 1989 Nevada demonstrations to "reclaim the test site," police arrested thousands for trespassing and blocking roads in a show of civil disobedience. Nuclear power plants, as well, have been the sites of protests in the 1980s.[4]

College students returned to protests against racism, sexism, homophobia, Pentagon-funded research, and Central American policy. Nationwide agitation against apartheid in South Africa prodded administrators to divest university holdings in companies doing business with that country. Students staged sit-ins to pressure officials to accelerate the recruitment of minority students and faculty and to rescind tuition hikes. During the second half of the 1980s, evidence of a rising tide of racial and religious prejudice, both on- and off-campus, has hastened mobilization efforts against bigotry. In a campaign reminiscent of the Free Speech Movement's challenge to administration paternalism, the students of Gallaudet University in Washington, D.C., demanded "deaf power" and a voice in campus decision making. They boycotted classes, marched, and conducted vigils to protest the selection of a hearing president and the underrepresentation of deaf people on the university's board of directors. Their action had effect. The president resigned before "this extraordinary social movement of deaf people," and a deaf professor later assumed the office.[5] The federal government appropriated additional funds for Gallaudet University, and student enrollment increased. Chants of "deaf power" kindled a new sense of pride for the deaf, not only on campus but far beyond its confines. Perhaps predicting future mobilizations, Gallaudet's new president, I. King Jordan, declared: "We are recognizing the right of every disabled person to have unlimited goals and expectations."[6]

Animal rights groups, tracing their roots back to the nineteenth century, to organizations like the American Anti-Vivisection Society, revived the battle against the exploitation by humans of other species. Organizations like Trans-Species Unlimited, People for the Ethical Treatment of Animals, and the Animal Liberation Front have proposed legislation regulating treatment of animals in farm "factories," bans on the use of animals in product-safety tests and scientific laboratories, and war on the fur industry. In addition to lobbying and letter writing, activists have vandalized and set fire to labs and freed caged animals. These actions have generated extensive media coverage and intensified opposition from the scientific community and its allies in government.[7]

Events of the 1980s have provoked new movements as well. Most important is the AIDS protest, a response to the deaths of nearly fifty thousand men and women during the decade and the bleak future awaiting many more. Health care practitioners and gay activists, spearheaded by the AIDS Coalition To Unleash Power (ACT UP), seek "to seize control of our own treatment."[8] Demanding access to experimental drugs and a streamlining of the government's drug-approval process, thousands of demonstrators laid siege to the Food and Drug Administration headquarters, and hundreds were arrested. At the same time, as the baby boom generation ages, issues of health care and the elderly will grow more important and may elicit a series of new protest movements.[9]

CHANGE AND CONTINUITY

A review of twentieth-century American social movements reveals a variety of changes over time. These changes suggest an evolutionary process rather than series of sharp breaks with the past. As activists have adopted tactical means that gained greater public acceptance, they have also conceived innovative ways to graft new technologies onto traditional tasks. Additionally, a trend toward the professionalization of protest has important implications for challengers. As the electronic media's influence has grown, movement leaders have become better tuned to its power to shape images. Finally, a broader constituency has claimed the social movement as a viable vehicle of protest.

Since the 1960s, an increasing number and variety of movements have chosen to use civil disobedience to gain power. The civil rights movement, with media support, conditioned the American public to view nonviolent direct action as a confrontation between right and wrong, justice and injustice. Granted legitimacy as a challenging tactic, it drew additional energy from a growing sensitivity to the need to protect civil liberties. Later activists also incorporated civil disobedience into their arsenals because, in the aftermath of racial change, it was a proven success. Contrast, for example, the public's tolerance since the 1960s with its reaction to the Industrial Workers of the

World's free speech campaigns at the beginning of the century. Although complicated by Wobbly rhetoric and an outcast image, Americans equated civil disobedience with law breaking and anarchy. The link between nonviolent direct action and defiance of authority was unbroken and called for drastic repressive measures.

As civil disobedience has become more tolerated, so too has protest movement activity in general. Except in regard to far-Right challengers, the popular conception of protest groups as symptoms of social distress and psychopathology has weakened. The experiences of the 1960s have helped bring about this change in perceptions. Many, through friends and relatives, had direct contact with movement members and sympathized with their protest. Also, two decades have dulled antagonism with understanding or, at the least, a truce has replaced anger and confrontation. The media's reinterpretation of the 1960s—its celebration of the civil rights movement and transformation of the Vietnam War from patriotic crusade to personal tragedy—has diluted the bitterness. The generation of scholars who came of age in the 1960s treat protesters of both left and right wings as rational men and women. The influence of these scholars influences, in turn, the generation still in the classroom. It may be that the public acceptance of dissent is a temporary phenomenon, possible because current movements are either considered less threatening than past mobilizations or are occurring under democratic banners in distant nations.

The more things change . . .   Because they have taken advantage of technological innovations and changing laws, it has been easier for movement activists to mobilize resources and maintain their organizations. For example, groups across the ideological spectrum use direct mailing not only for fund raising from within but to gather contributions from sympathizers. Direct mail also supplements other channels of information, providing members with current reports from the leadership and bolstering morale with a sense of the movement's forward and constant motion. "It is the advertising medium of the underdog," wrote conservative Richard Viguerie. "It allows organizations or causes not part of the mainstream or not popular to get funded."[10] Challenging groups have also adapted easily to the computer. Not only do movements use computers to keep records more efficiently, they have effectively exploited them to tighten the chains of command and to speed communication. Local leaders and even the rank and file can, with a personal computer and modem, tie into a movement's bulletin boards that provide ideological information, action calls, tactical updates, and news about other chapters. Amnesty International's "urgent action network" links members all over the world and is capable of spurring avalanches of letters in support of imprisoned men and women. Aryan Nations runs LibertyNet to expose the

Jewish conspiracy and ZOG, the Zionist Occupation Government in Washington D.C. The American Peace Test's PEACENET builds its members' sense of purpose and community by thickening communication ties. High-tech developments, then, promise activists the potential of coordinating their movement's resources in pursuit of national and even international goals, with response time cut to a minimum.

Movement theorists John McCarthy and Mayer Zald have found, in certain protest movements, a growing "bureaucratization of social discontent" since the 1960s.[11] They describe some recent movements, unlike their predecessors, that operate with small or nonexistent membership bases and draw resources from a "conscience constituency" rather than a rank and file. Contacted by direct mail, subscribers to such groups as Greenpeace and the Committee for the Survival of a Free Congress are asked to make financial pledges and to leave all other movement tasks to a professional staff. Informed of activities through internal channels or the media, "members" of these movements thus have no meetings to attend. Continued involvement translates into paying annual membership fees or, perhaps, checking names in elections for selected slates of national officers. Full-time, professional activists, often trained in government programs like the Peace Corps and VISTA, work in the name of their supporters, not through them. Unlike the cadre of the Anti-Saloon League and the Communist party, their loyalty is to goals and programs and not to an organization. Career and family considerations may lead these men and women to switch their allegiance from one movement to another.[12]

This important trend, however, has deep historical roots. Movements with small memberships under professional leadership appeared during the Progressive Era at the beginning of the century. In the 1030s the Highlander Folk School and Saul Alinsky's Industrial Areas Foundation began organizing workshops and training professional cadre for community organizing. The Communist party created an elaborate indoctrination process with strict courses of study for its full-time personnel. Also, the twists and turns of challenge have led many past leaders to abandon protest organizations for more promising vehicles. The ASL and the KKK were movements that relied heavily on "conscience constituencies" for votes and funds. The great majority of men and women recruited into protest groups, then and now, are invisible members who provide little more than their annual dues. Still, these "spokesmen" movements, acting as proxies for a larger, silent public, will become an increasingly significant wing of the protest community in the future.[13]

In the nineteenth century, protest movements were usually not "news"—print journalists confined themselves to coverage of politics, diplomacy, war, crime, and social events. Protest groups responded by purchasing printing machines that would bring their messages before the public. In the twentieth century, this relationship changed, and media and movements gradually became entwined. The Anti-Saloon League, at the century's turn, was thus a movement in transition relying on both an extensive internal printing plant and non-ASL magazines and newspapers to publish protest appeals and news. By the 1920s Klan and other movement leaders understood the importance of public relations and were well aware of the media and their image-making and image-breaking potential. Nor is withdrawal from the relationship possible. Suspicious of a communist-infiltrated media, the John Birch Society attempted to offer members an informational alternative that merged well with its educational thrust. But, as the society's history has shown, the opinion-makers' power could not be ignored. The interaction between media and movements grew even more intense with television's coming of age. Sensitive to this new opinion force, movement activists have adjusted to the medium's insatiable appetite for the novel, the visual, and the dramatic. They are attuned to news schedules, competition between the press and networks, and reporters' thirst for authoritative sources.[14]

The stakes of the "media dance" are high. Television coverage may confer legitimacy on a movement and enhance its credibility by mirroring widespread, popular discontent or, perhaps, by creating this impression. These images will, in turn, influence the reactions of authorities, polity members, and other challenging groups. Media attention can raise rank-and-file morale and facilitate resource building by carrying the movement's case before large, unmobilized audiences. Such a hearing is vital to movements without extensive memberships. But if the rewards are great, so too are the risks. Silence or negative coverage may sap a movement's energy and prepare the ground for repression. Because the camera transforms activists into instant media stars, it may exacerbate internal tensions and encourage dissension. Also, news deadlines, the demand for knowledgeable informants, and the centralization of network facilities favor hierarchical and national protest groups over decentralized organizations. Regardless of the type of movement, however, efforts to manipulate the media will continue to consume much time and effort.[15]

Long-term change in this century has also broadened the constituency of social movements. As educational opportunities and facilities expanded, large numbers of young people with similar aspirations and vulnerabilities found themselves in close quarters. Students on some campuses, as early as the 1930s, realized the potential of protest in a relatively risk-free environment. The Communist party and its front organizations were especially receptive to student recruits. Students as protesters became even more visible in the 1960s, when they populated such groups as SNCC, the Free Speech Movement, SDS, and Young Americans for Freedom, among others. In contrast was the absence of students as cadre or rank and file in the ASL, the IWW, and the Klan. The continuation of student protests in the 1980s shows that involvement was not simply a demographic quirk of the baby boom generation. Skinheads and the teenage members of Aryan Nations, neo-Nazi groups, and Ku Klux Klan organizations suggest too that youthful activism is not limited to campuses.

Women have accounted for a significant section of the volunteer work force of social movements throughout American history. Their continued subordination, even in the civil rights movement, the New Left, and the antiwar movements in the 1960s helped birth modern feminism. Refusing to retreat in the 1970s and 1980s, they demanded and won entrance into the leadership of nonfeminist protest organizations. Future research will certainly focus upon gender-related changes in movements' decision making, organization, image making, and challenging tactics.

. . . The more they stay the same   Even more telling than these changes are the patterns of continuity that tightly link past and present challengers. For all of the movements, long-term social, economic, and political transformations shape opportunities for protest by affecting the distribution of resources and the relationships of contenders for power with authorities and with one another. Short-term electoral shifts on national, state, and community levels also act significantly, but briefly, to adjust the balance of resources, the possibilities of building coalitions, and the receptivity of authorities to the needs of polity members and challengers. Within this environment of groups and individuals occur incidents that put into bold relief the implications of broad change. The appearance of the saloon "menace," crime waves, sit-in demonstrations, and campus edicts enhance the salience of issues and generate attention, concern, and outrage. Men and women with and without organizational ties question their allegiance to leaders who are powerless to ameliorate conditions or who refuse measures of redress.

If discontent is to have an effect beyond an immediate time and place, an activist core is necessary. Men and women anchored in existing groups with an established communications net must offer to harness and channel grievances. Organizers must provide skills, a vehicle for mobilizing resources, and a program identifying enemies and suggesting solution. Linking their listeners' self interest to visions of better times, they stoke a sense of efficacy in order to build defiance. Thus did Big Bill Haywood, John Galen Locke, Robert Welch, Stokely Carmichael, Mario Savio, and Eleanor Smeal take the reins of leadership, delegate responsibilities, allocate resources, and make tactical and strategic choices. Power came to them as representatives of the people, representatives who could speak, think, and act within the experiences and expectations of their followers.

However, opportunity and organization do not equate with influence. Nor do the maintenance and momentum of a movement occur in a vacuum. The protest environment encompasses friends and foes, both powerful and powerless, inside and outside government. Challengers must maneuver carefully, weighing options of disruption or cooperation and selecting coalition partners who offer the most benefits without bringing heavy debts. Authorities, with their power to grant influence, offer resources, and activate repression, demand a movement's constant attention. The public definition of a movement is continually contested. In a disadvantaged position, leaders vie for control of the movement's image, acknowledging the power of the media and the weight Americans give to opinion makers and authorities. The challenger's words and deeds are thus only one element in an image-making equation that also includes government position papers and press leaks, the quality and quantity of media coverage, and the stances of established groups. From opinion makers, direct observation, and discussions with friends and family, people calculate this equation and figure personal risks and rewards. Their solution will form a decision to join, support, oppose, or remain neutral in the face of challenge.

The challenge of a social movement is always fragile: It is prone to disintegration and faces a brief window of success. Influence demands resource risks and media gambles, which expose the movement to embarrassment, error, repression, and defeat. Miscalculation, media neglect, shifts in issue salience, electoral change, and even the appearance of failure may stimulate members and supporters to abandon the cause. In continuous combat with stronger groups and determined authorities, the challenger can not afford any disruption of resources or expenditure of time and money in defense and retreat.

As the ASL, the Klan, and NOW demonstrate, acceptance is no guarantee of stability or lasting influence. To be successful in elite circles, movements must abandon their challenger perspective and effect new means of competition. As negotiation replaces confrontation, management and bureaucratic skills are more highly rewarded than powers of agitation. Even goals must evolve to accommodate shifting circumstances. The movement's leaders will not have time to adjust to these new demands, for they will be distracted by other emergencies. Many of the rank and file will have departed when success was achieved, and supporters will have turned to other causes. In this situation, activists will have to experiment with innovative methods to replace lost resources. At the same time, polity members will battle one another for authorities' attention, testing their competitor's right to remain among the privileged. Joining a political coalition, another means to influence, may also enhance the movement's vulnerability because of America's frequent electoral shifts. Finally, and ironically, the former challenger may have to implement defensive strategies to counter a protest against *its* program.

CHALLENGING OUTCOMES

William Gamson's *The Strategy of Social Protest* is the most comprehensive and sophisticated study of the experiences of American challenging groups. From the more than five hundred movements that appeared between 1800 and 1945, Gamson randomly selected fifty-three for in-depth analyses of protest strategies and careers. He characterized a challenger as completely successful if it achieved its stated goals and was accepted as the representative of the people and the interests it championed. He assigned a movement partial success if it achieved preemption (benefits without recognition) or cooptation (recognition without benefits). If it gained neither, the movement "collapsed."[16]

From his sample, Gamson concluded that bureaucratically organized movements with centralized chains of command are moderately more successful than those lacking such an organizational makeup. A "modest advantage" goes to challenging groups that press for single-issue, limited reform rather than programs with many goals that project the displacement of opponents. This finding confirms Roberta Ash Garner's observation that movements with a broad range of demands appear more threatening and thus encourage greater resistance. The sponsorship or support of polity members is another ingredient to the successful outcome of a protest. Historical context, Gamson continued, also affects a movement's course. Events like war and depression aid movements that began mobilizing before the onset of the crisis. Violence, too, brings rewards, as unruly movements advance beyond more law-abiding contenders. Movement size is less a factor in predicting outcomes, but larger groups more often achieve at least minimal acceptance.[17]

According to Gamson, 58 percent of his sample was successful: They achieved preemption, cooptation, or reform and acceptance. Preempted and coopted movement activists, however, might question their inclusion among the victors: Did *they* believe that the battle was lost but the war won? Are the means to challenge as important as the ends? In any case, issue-poaching authorities and polity members often redefine protesters' claims and control the extent of change, robbing advocates of legitimacy and efficacy. For example, the government-sponsored Loyal League of Loggers and Lumbermen enacted an eight-hour workday and a minimum wage, outmaneuvering the Wobblies and smothering the Commonwealth of Toil in the Pacific Northwest. Also illustrative, was the fate of the civil rights movement in San Antonio, Texas, during the 1960s. City officials there evaded controversy until pressured to react, often failed to acknowledge the existence of pressure, and in the end delivered the minimum response. This policy of gradualism and control undercut black activists who sought to accelerate the pace of desegregation. The government's strategy, said the NAACP's Reverend Claude

Black, was "to give it to you and not give it to you. It is a pattern that has made it most difficult to develop the kind of unity that you need in the black community in order to develop the opposition. Any time you give people in desperate conditions a glimmer of hope, you defuse them."[18] Rather than emerging from the period united and determined to press for further reforms, blacks remained divided and complacent. "To have done it the way we had wanted it done," remarked student activist William Donoughue, "would have been a demonstration of power and strength. And power and strength are the only common denominators understood in this community."[19]

The incorporation of challengers as groups or individuals within elite and government circles may also sap a protest's vitality. VISTA and War on Poverty programs and corporate affirmative action helped drain the organizing and decision-making cores of dissenting groups. Nor does inclusion guarantee the implementation of change or its continuing thrust; it may even shackle future mobilization efforts and protest options. Cooptation, then, might better be analyzed as an official strategy to silence through inclusion rather than a challenger's breakthrough to influence.[20]

Success and failure, moreover, are not absolutes. Policy gains may last for long periods or face immediate short-circuiting. Recognition and its loss are constant occurrences for some groups, while others are positioned more securely. Electoral change, shifting resources and polity members' jockeying for position create an ebb and flow to influence which, in turn, affects a group's fortunes and the reception to its program. A time dimension must refine judgments concerning the outcome.

With these qualifications, Gamson's measures of protest achievement provide a framework to analyze the protest careers of the eight movements we have considered. Movements were judged successful if they at least partially fulfilled their goals through their own efforts or their entrance into the polity no matter how brief, translated into new practices and rules. By these criteria, members of the Anti-Saloon League, the Ku Klux Klan, the Student Nonviolent Coordinating Committee, the Free Speech Movement, and the National Organization for Women waged winning campaigns. The FSM won recogniton, but lacked the will, program, and resources to exploit it. The Industrial Workers of the World, the Communist party, and the John Birch Society neither achieved acceptance nor obtained new benefits. Note that even the most successful of the movements could not lay claim to a long-term polity membership or full and secure policy gains.

Four critical variables   Four interrelated variables, none alone sufficient, were critical to each movement's fate: polity members' responses, image, authorities' stance, and organizational structure. Most significant in the histories of the victors was the support of powerful sponsoring groups. Consistent with Gamson's findings, formal and informal alliances with churches, political parties, and opinion makers brought the ASL, the KKK, SNCC, the FSM, and NOW valuable resources that facilitated their efforts. The IWW and the Communist party not only lacked such support, they often faced repression and strategies of cooptation and preemption. Communists and John Birchers might infiltrate polity members, but their influence was personal and not rooted in an affiliation with protest. Varying in influence over time and space, sponsors were hardly identical. It was critical for challengers to select wisely among supporters and remain tuned to resource and electoral shifts.

Public perceptions of a movement, the work of many hands, were also critical to outcomes. Successful movements grounded themselves in American values and popular traditions. If they represent the challenge as one that commands widespread support, is necessary, and is based on well-documented grievances, opinion makers and activists can fashion an image of protest as moral and reasonable. Defeated movements, on the other hand, were tagged as radical, irresponsible, risky, or lacking salience. Elite group members and authorities, taking advantage of war-time concerns, crafted the IWW into a tool of German imperialism and an enemy within. A continually changing line, an immigrant and Jewish character, and foreign entanglement raised the impression that the Communist party was dangerous, un-American, and worthy of repression. The John Birch Society, out of touch with prevailing opinion in the 1960s and governed by men given to leveling reckless charges, wore an extremist brand. One of the factors in SNCC's eclipse was a public reinterpretation of the meaning of its challenge.[21]

Considerations of image suggest that a movement's size, while easily quantifiable, explains little without reference to context. Opinion polls, press coverage, and television cameras can create an aura of a movement's power and immediacy and the impression of a supportive public mood. Also, a focus on a movement's size ignores those who aid protest with money and votes but reject formal membership. Attempts to discern the role of numbers also fails to acknowledge the variety of American polities. A movement of ten thousand members may be judged ineffectual in a national arena, but of great significance within the University of California system or in contests at community and state levels. Thus, assessments of the significance of size on outcomes must take into account the protest group's relationship to other contenders, the level at which the challenge is mounted, and perceptions of movement strength.

Similarly, violence can best be understood as it relates to image. The mere occurrence of violence is secondary to the manner in which it is perceived. For example, opinion makers, and through them ordinary people, judged Klan violence as a reasonable and necessary means to protect citizens and their property from lawbreakers and minorities. They accepted the Klan's posturing as a guardian of the interests of the Protestant community, able to act when authorities had failed. The Wobblies, victims rather than victimizers, were nevertheless stigmatized as violent because they posed a threat to the established order. Even in the absence of violence, IWW verbal militancy created in the public mind a fear of turmoil and cultivated a negative image and hostility. Throughout the twentieth century, Americans have exhibited more tolerance for challenger violence directed against "outsiders" than against authorities or established groups. Rather than an independent variable, violence, in relation to its target and its goal, becomes another element in the formation of image.

Are outcomes related to the number of planks in a protest platform or to perceptions of the degree of change demanded? Our eight movements demonstrate how difficult it is to identify protests as single- or multiple-issue organizations. The Anti-Saloon League, at first glance, appears to have had a single goal. Yet the movement always looked beyond the saloon target to prohibition and abstinence and the eradication of the problems associated with drink. Likewise, characterizing SNCC or NOW as movements for equality is simplistic and distorting. Even the Free Speech Movement carried more than a single issue. A division based on the number of issues also neglects differences between short- and long-range aims and ignores the evolution of a program. Finally, activists like those in the ASL may disguise more divisive goals by emphasizing compatible demands thus deceiving not only followers but future scholars.

A focus on overall image allows us to overcome these surrounding issues. Do authorities, elite contenders, and opinion makers view the proposals of a challenger as moderate and reformist, or do they rule them out of order as drastic and revolutionary? These definitions, too, depend on time, place, and target. The ASL, the Klan, SNCC, and NOW were able to displace opponents who were minorities or weakened polity members considered un-American, lawless, or reactionary. The IWW, the John Birch Society, and the Communist party were regarded as too radical, having chosen confrontation with strongly established elite groups, opinion makers, or government itself. Attention, then, to the perceived meaning of protest proposals rather than to their number avoids semantic difficulties and addresses historical context.

Movement histories highlight the part authorities play in the protest process. Often acting in tandem with favored contenders, or at their request, government officials have ignored, facilitated, and suppressed activists. SNCC's career, from infusions of foundation aid at the prompting of the Kennedy administration to COINTELPRO, demonstrates the impact of an official response. So does the disruption of the IWW and the Communist party through infiltration, arrest, and trial. The ASL and the Klan, on the other hand, entwined with authorities, and support of their protest agendas became an official act of government. If activists and analysts must include a government's stance in their protest scenarios, the FSM case sheds light on the mediating role of key polity members. Events at Berkeley separated authorities from the faculty, their prime campus supporter. Official action in the face of faculty disapproval created a governing crisis that weakened the legitimacy of administrators and forced concessions. Government may be determined to protect and defend the status quo, but success is a result of more than its will.

Characterizations of a movement as centralized and bureaucratic or decentralized and informal must take into account more than written constitutions or organizational blueprints. The IWW's clear divisions of labor and chain of command did not reflect its segmented nature and grass-roots leadership. Without adequate funding, even the most complex structure remains a hollow shell. Different tactics, goals, and spheres of operation undermine the application of a single, correct organizational formula. Instead of clearly affirming either centralization and bureaucratization or decentralization as the most effective means to influence, the case studies suggest a middle road. The most highly disciplined challengers—the Anti-Saloon League, the Communist party, and the John Birch Society—achieved mixed results. So, too, did the most decentralized movements—SNCC and the IWW. The Klan, the FSM, and NOW combined central direction and coordination with autonomy of local and constituent groups. Rather than appearing as an outside force, protest became, in leadership, message, and image, a community creation. Nor did local emphasis sacrifice a wider perspective. This diversified command structure, by facilitating the accumulation of and promoting the image of widespread protest power, enhanced a challenger's chances for gaining influence.[22]

No structure insulated a movement from factionalism. All of the groups experienced internal dissension either in their challenging phase or polity membership phase. Additional research is needed to measure more carefully the impact of varying intensities of factionalism and its appearance at different stages in a protest movement's career.

The movements' histories offer no obvious conclusions about the independent influence of war and economic depression on the success or failure of their challenge. Investigators must yet show how these factors influenced the course of movements by moving beyond the simple temporal juxtaposition of protest and crisis. Perhaps by studying the historical context, answers may be found in changing group and personal priorities, issue salience, resource opportunities, and coalition options. In a similar vein, the appearance of challengers is instrumental in provoking new protests. Movements may serve as role-model catalysts that legitimize dissent while offering resources to emerging contenders. The multiplication of challengers might dilute resources for repression or cause authorities to revise their strategies of social control and confront only the relatively more threatening movements. Many protest vehicles, with similar goals, can harass opponents in different ways and along a broader front. Common ends may also generate competition for attention, funds, and members, seriously undermining protest. Likewise, resource competition from nonrelated movements could erode support and similarly weaken challenging efforts.

Thus, the responses of elite groups, image, authorities' position, and organizational structure are the key variables in the success and failure of challenge. Each represents a spectrum of possibilities, the sum of internal and external forces. Change over time is inherent in the individual factors and characterizes their interplay as well. In this interaction may be discerned the path of protest in twentieth-century America.

PLURALISM REVISED

What do the results of Gamson's study and the histories of our eight movements tell us about the permeability of the American system? Over one-half of Gamson's sample of challenging groups were successful. Even when the preempted and coopted are excluded, 38 percent still registered gains. Of the eight movements considered here, five achieved some measure of victory. On their face, the numbers are impressive. Social movements, it seems, operating outside prescribed channels, innovating means of challenge, and combating more established contenders, can make decision makers listen and respond. These results should not, however, mask the quality of the victories. Gains were fragile, acceptance was brief, and benefits minimal and easily lost. The ASL's twenty-seven-year challenge earned it a little over a decade of influence. Klan power was erased in less than three years. SNCC advances, made in alliance with other civil rights groups, proved more enduring yet reflect an agenda only half fulfilled. As the 1980s end, NOW battles to maintain its eroding, partial gains. Only free speech on campus remains secure. The IWW, the Communist party, and the John Birch Society, defeated and bypassed, inhabit the periphery.[23]

A study of social movements in America suggests that we revise the pluralist interpretation of our society. Perceptions of the system's openness are situational, dependent upon time and power position. Government is hardly a neutral referee mediating disinterestedly among contenders. Furthermore, violence may be useful in challenge—it is certainly effective when employed by authorities and polity members for suppressing protest. Nor is accepting prescribed procedures a protection or a guarantee of access to decision makers. According to William Gamson, "A member of the polity may need to wheel and deal, but a challenger should be prepared to stand and fight. . . . The appropriate image . . . is more a fight with few holds barred than it is a contest under well-defined rules."[24] SNCC's John Lewis echoed Gamson's observation: "When you play the game and go by the rules, you still can lose, if you don't have the resources, if you're going to disrupt the natural order of things."[25]

This focus on the outcome of the group masks another level of analysis— the impact of protest on the individual. Movements are more than their tangible programs. Allegiance raises the consciousness of individuals and affects their values, beliefs, and behavior beyond the protest vehicle. But how and to what extent does participation in a protest touch dreams, self-esteem, knowledge, skills, and an awareness of people and society? Like a stone thrown into a pond, the movement's impact may ripple through interpersonal, family, and economic relationships and reemerge in visions of individual and social possibilities. Without uncovering these "intangible benefits," the study of social movements remains incomplete.[26]

Activists enter the last decade of the twentieth century with positions on issues already staked out and resource reservoirs filling. Broad social, economic, and political transformations frame the protest environment and adjust the balance of power among challengers, established groups, and authorities. Energizing events such as economic setbacks, foreign adventures, or ecological disaster may shift and concentrate attention, raising and lowering opportunities for dissent. The activists of the 1990s, as did their predecessors, must convince men and women of their power in common and the viability of protest. Personal experiences and individual grievances must merge to generate collective efforts at amelioration. As in the past, protesters will have to steer a course to influence by taking into account polity-member responses, image making, the position of authorities, and their means of organizing. A study of the success and failure of previous challenges may not only offer direction but identify the shoals ahead.

NOTES

CHAPTER 1: AN INTRODUCTION TO SOCIAL MOVEMENTS

1. Roberta Ash Garner, *Social Movements in America* (Chicago: Rand McNally, 1977), pp. 1–2, 7–8; John Wilson, *Introduction to Social Movements* (New York: Basic Books, 1973), pp. 4, 8–13; William A. Gamson, *The Strategy of Social Protest* (Homewood, Ill.: Dorsey Press, 1975), pp. 91–93.

2. Wilson, *Introduction to Social Movements*, pp. 90–96, 108–10, 124–30; Anthony Oberschall, *Social Conflict and Social Movements* (Englewood Cliffs, N.J.: Prentice-Hall, 1973), pp. 178–84.

3. Under this rubric I refer to models based on theories of mass society, status inconsistency, collective behavior, and relative deprivation. All stress the impact of societal strain and disruption on the psychological state of the individual. A movement, these theorists agree, results from a union of men and women in search of cognitive or social stability. For further discussion of the commonality of these specific approaches, see Doug McAdam, *Political Process and the Development of Black Insurgency, 1930–1970* (Chicago: University of Chicago Press, 1982), pp. 6–12.

4. Erich Fromm, *Escape from Freedom* (New York: Holt, Rinehart, 1941), pp. 131–32.

5. Fromm, *Escape from Freedom*, pp. 19–23, 37–43, 134, 217, 256–57; Fromm, *The Sane Society* (New York: Holt, Rinehart, 1955), p. 237.

6. Eric Hoffer, *The True Believer: Thoughts on the Nature of Mass Movements* (New York: Harper & Row, 1951), p. 39.

7. Ibid., p. 82. For more on the personalities of potential movement recruits from a similar perspective, see T.W. Adorno, et al., *The Authoritarian Personality* (New York: Harper & Row, 1950).

8. William Kornhauser, *The Politics of Mass Society* (New York: Free Press, 1959), p. 33.

9. Kornhauser, *Politics of Mass Society*, pp. 32–60 passim; Neil Smelser, *Theory of Collective Behavior* (New York: Free Press, 1962), pp. 8, 16, 72, 79, 81–82, 117.

10. Kornhauser, *Politics of Mass Society*, pp. 43–44, 220 (quote); Philip Selznick, *The Organizational Weapon* (Glencoe, Ill.: Free Press, 1952), pp. 282, 293; Robert Nisbet, *The Quest for Community: A Study in the Ethics of Order and Freedom* (New York: Oxford University Press, 1953), p. 34.

11. Nisbet, *The Quest for Community*, p. 198.

12. Hoffer, *The True Believer*, p. 23.

13. Hannah Arendt, *The Origins of Totalitarianism*, rev. ed. (New York: Meridian, 1966), pp. 323–24.

14. Seymour Lipset, *Political Man: The Social Bases of Politics* (Garden City, N.Y.: Doubleday, 1959), p. 178.

15. Michael Harrington, "Foreword," in Ron E. Roberts and Robert M. Kloss, *Social Movements: Between the Balcony and the Barricade* (St. Louis: Mosby, 1974), p. v.

16. Gamson, *The Strategy of Social Protest*, p. 134; Ash, *Social Movements*, p. 2; McAdam, *Political Process*, p. 20; J. Craig Jenkins, "Resource Mobilization Theory and the Study of Social Movements," *Annual Review of Sociology* 9 (1983): p. 528; Ralph H. Turner, "Collective Behavior and Resource Mobilization as Approaches to Social Movements: Issues and Continuities," in Louis Kriesberg, ed., *Research in Social Movements, Conflicts and Change* vol. 4 (Greenwich, Conn.: JAI Press, 1981): pp. 9–10; Oberschall, *Social Conflict*, p. 24.

17. Richard E. Rubenstein, *Rebels in Eden: Mass Political Violence in the United States* (Boston: Little, Brown, 1970), pp. 40–42; Oberschall, *Social Conflict*, pp. 334–35; Gamson, *Strategy of Social Protest*, p. 142.

18. Oberschall, *Social Conflict*, p. 29.

19. Michael Schwartz, *Radical Protest and Social Structure: The Southern Farmers' Alliance and Cotton Tenancy, 1880–1890* (New York: Academic Press, 1976), p. 135.

20. Schwartz, *Radical Protest*, pp. 135, 137, 142–44, 182–83; Oberschall, *Social Conflict*, pp. 25, 28–29.

21. Jenkins, "Resource Mobilization Theory," pp. 528, 530–32; McAdams, *Political Process*, pp. 20–21, 181; John D. McCarthy and Mayer N. Zald, "Resource Mobilization and Social Movements: A Partial Theory," *American Journal of Socialogy* 82 (May 1977): 1214–16.

22. Oberschall, *Social Conflict*, p. 125.

23. Oberschall, *Social Conflict*, pp. 111, 125, 135, 161–64; William Gamson, Bruce Fireman, and Steven Rytina, *Encounters with Unjust Authorities* (Chicago: Dorsey Press, 1982), p. 8.

24. Charles Tilly, *From Mobilization to Revolution* (Reading, Mass.: Addison–Wesley, 1978), p. 52.

25. Charles Tilly, "Does Modernization Breed Revolution?" *Comparative Politics* 5 (April 1973): p. 18; Tilly, *From Mobilization to Revolution*, pp. 52–53.

26. Tilly, *From Mobilization to Revolution*, pp. 54–57, 84, 229–30.

27. McAdam, *Political Process*, p. 30; Wilson, *Introduction to Social Movements*, pp. 226–30.

28. McAdam, *Political Process*, pp. 27–29; Tilly, *From Mobilization to Revolution*, pp. 153, 179.

29. Gary T. Marx, "External Efforts to Damage or Facilitate Social Movements: Some Patterns, Explanations, Outcomes, and Complications," in Mayer Zald and John D. McCarthy, eds., *The Dynamics of Social Movements: Resource Mobilization, Social Control, and Tactics* (Cambridge, Mass.: Winthrop, 1979), pp. 97–107; Tilly, *From Mobilization to Revolution*, pp. 100, 106; Garner, *Social Movements in America*, pp. 12–14.

30. Gamson, *Strategy of Social Protest*, pp. 28–37.

31. Melvyn Dubofsky, *We Shall Be All: A History of the Industrial Workers of the World* (Chicago: Quadrangle Books, 1969), p. 246.

32. Frances Fox Piven and Richard Cloward, *Poor People's Movements: Why They Succeed, How They Fail* (New York: Pantheon, 1977), pp. 3–7, 12; McAdams, *Political Process*, pp. 2, 48, 59.

33. Todd Gitlin, *The Whole World Is Watching: Mass Media in the Making and Unmaking of the New Left* (Berkeley: University of California Press, 1980), pp. 3–4, 12, 27.

CHAPTER 2: THE DEATH OF JOHN BARLEYCORN: THE ANTI-SALOON LEAGUE

1. Peter Odegard, *Pressure Politics: The Story of the Anti-Saloon League* (New York: Columbia University Press, 1928), p. 43.

2. Norman H. Clark, *The Dry Years: Prohibition and Social Change in Washington* (Seattle: University of Washington Press, 1965), p. 66.

3. Norman Clark, *Deliver Us from Evil: An Interpretation of American Prohibition* (New York: Norton, 1976), p. 18.

4. Robert Smith Bader, *Prohibition in Kansas: A History* (Lawrence, Kans.: University Press of Kansas, 1986), p. 7.

5. Alice Felt Tyler, *Freedom's Ferment* (New York: Harper & Bros., 1962), pp. 308–13; Clark, *Deliver Us*, pp. 14–18, 45–48; Bader, *Prohibition*, pp. 7–8; K. Austin Kerr, *Organized for Prohibition: A New History of the Anti-Saloon League* (New Haven, Conn.: Yale University Press, 1985), pp. 16–17.

6. Tyler, *Freedom's Ferment*, pp. 322–29, 347–48; Bader, *Prohibition*, pp. 9–14; Clark, *Deliver Us*, pp. 45–49.

7. Bader, *Prohibition*, p. 109; Kerr, *Organized for Prohibition*, pp. 44–49, 56–61, 64–65, 73; Jack S. Blocker, Jr., *Retreat from Reform: The Prohibition Movement in the United States, 1890–1913* (Westport, Conn.: Greenwood Press, 1976), pp. 39, 68–77, 112.

8. Kerr, *Organized for Prohibition*, pp. 14–15, 19.

9. Kerr, *Organized for Prohibition*, pp. 15, 21–23; Perry R. Duis, *The Saloon: Public Drinking in Chicago and Boston, 1880–1920* (Urbana, Ill.: University of Illinois Press, 1983), pp. 17–21; Alfred D. Chandler, Jr., *The Invisible Hand: The Managerial Revolution in American Business* (Cambridge, Mass.: Belknap Press, 1977), p. 256; George Kibbe Turner, "Beer and the City Liquor Problem," *McClure's Magazine* 33 (September 1909): p. 36.

10. Kerr, *Organized for Prohibition*, p. 12; Duis, *The Saloon*, p. 44.

11. Duis, *The Saloon*, pp. 25–26, 34, 40, 49, 52, 68; Clark, *Deliver Us*, pp. 4, 50; Kerr, *Organized for Prohibition*, pp. 23–24; Jon M. Kingsdale, "The Poor Man's Club: Social Functions of the Urban Working-Class Saloon," in Elizabeth and Joseph Pleck, *The American Man* (Englewood Cliffs, N.J.: Prentice-Hall, 1980), p. 259.

12. Kingsdale, "The Poor Man's Club," pp. 257–58; Clark, *Dry Years*, p. 61.

13. Kingsdale, "The Poor Man's Club," p. 261; Clark, *Dry Years*, pp. 55–57; Duis, *The Saloon*, pp. 68–72; Thomas J. Noel, "The Immigrant Saloon in Denver," *Colorado Magazine*, 54 (Summer 1977): pp. 216–18.

14. Kerr, *Organized for Prohibition*, p. 24; Duis, *The Saloon*, pp. 89, 101–102, 233–34; Clark, *Deliver Us*, pp. 2, 61; Clark, *The Dry Years*, pp. 57–61.

15. Bader, *Prohibition*, pp. 118–19, 121.

16. Odegard, *Pressure Politics*, p. 7.

17. Kerr, *Organized for Prohibition*, pp. 77–78.

18. Ibid, p. 79; Odegard, *Pressure Politics*, p. 9.

19. Odegard, *Pressure Politics*, pp. 4–5; Kerr, *Organized for Prohibition*, pp. 80–86, 88.

20. Odegard, *Pressure Politics*, pp. 5–6; Kerr, *Organized for Prohibition*, pp. 75–76.

21. Kerr, *Organized for Prohibition*, pp. 66, 76, 81–82, 115–19; Odegard, *Pressure Politics*, pp. 8–12, 14–15.

22. Odegard, *Pressure Politics*, pp. 73–76, 118; Kerr, *Organized for Prohibition*, pp. 81, 122–23, 125–26, 151–55; Blocker, *Retreat from Reform*, p. 158; Clark, *Deliver Us*, p. 113.

23. Kerr, *Organized for Prohibition*, pp. 92–94; Odegard, *Pressure Politics*, pp. 13, 22; Frank P. Stockbridge, "The Church Militant Against the Saloon," *The World's Work* 26 (October 1913): pp. 709–10.

24. Odegard, *Pressure Politics*, pp. 18, 20, 190–95; Kerr, *Organized for Prohibition*, pp. 93–94; Clark, *Dry Years*, p. 82; Stockbridge, "The Church Militant," p. 71; Harry M. Chalfant, "The Anti-Saloon League—Why and What?" American Academy of Political and Social Science, *Annals* 109 (1923): p. 282.

25. Frank C. Lockwood, "The Anti-Saloon League," *The Independent* 65 (30 July 1908): p. 243.

26. "A Slugger of John Barleycorn," *Literary Digest* 48 (10 January 1914): p. 76.

27. Kerr, *Organized for Prohibition*, p. 127.

28. Ibid., pp. 96–97, 119; James H. Timberlake, *Prohibition and the Progressive Movement, 1900–1920* (Cambridge, Mass.: Harvard University Press, 1963), p. 136; Bader, *Prohibition*, pp. 129, 192.

29. Kerr, *Organized for Prohibition*, p. 120; Blocker, *Retreat from Reform*, pp. 8–12, 33; Robert E. Wenger, "The Anti-Saloon League in Nebraska Politics, 1898–1910," *Nebraska History* 52 (Fall 1971): pp. 271–72.

30. Odegard, *Pressure Politics*, p. 16; Kerr, *Organized for Prohibition*, pp. 73, 83, 134, 159; Blocker, *Retreat from Reform*, pp. 139–42, 176, 185, 187.

31. Clark, *Deliver Us*, pp. 104–105.

32. Timberlake, *Prohibition and the Progressive Movement*, pp. 4–7, 34–37; Odegard, *Pressure Politics*, p. 6.

33. Clark, *Deliver Us*, pp. 57, 60–62, 65–66; Odegard, *Pressure Politics*, pp. 43–44, 62; Timberlake, *Prohibition and the Progressive Movement*, p. 58; Clark, *Dry Years*, pp. 60, 67.

34. Odegard, *Pressure Politics*, p. 60.

35. Ibid., p. 39.

36. Timberlake, *Prohibition and the Progressive Movement*, p. 44.

37. Ibid., p. 47.

38. Ibid., pp. 40–47, 52–55.

39. Ibid., pp. 67–68, 77, 81, 84–85, 89, 97, 105–106; Kerr, *Organized for Prohibition*, p. 8; Clark, *Dry Years*, p. 76.

40. Odegard, *Pressure Politics*, p. 39.

41. Gilman M. Ostrander, *The Prohibition Movement in California, 1848–1933* (Berkeley: University of California Publications in History, 1957), p. 66.

42. Timberlake, *Prohibition and the Progressive Movement*, pp. 102, 112–113, 118–119, 121; Kingsdale, "The Poor Man's Club," p. 270.

43. Timberlake, *Prohibition and the Progressive Movement*, pp. 52, 156–57.

44. Ibid., p. 145.

45. Blocker, *Retreat from Reform*, p. 164.

46. Kerr, *Organized for Prohibition*, p. 3.

47. Ibid., p. 94.

48. Odegard, *Pressure Politics*, p. 95.

49. Earnest H. Cherrington, *The Evolution of Prohibition in the United States of America* (Westerville, Ohio: American Issue Publishing Company, 1920), pp. 255–57, 289–91; Timberlake, *Prohibition and the Progressive Movement*, pp. 149, 154; Kerr, *Organized for Prohibition*, p. 124.

50. Blocker, *Retreat from Reform*, p. 238; Odegard, *Pressure Politics*, p. 18; Timberlake, *Prohibition and the Progressive Movement*, p. 150.

51. Odegard, *Pressure Politics*, pp. 258, 264–65.

52. Kerr, *Organized for Prohibition*, pp. 24–34, 160–61, 182–84; Odegard, *Pressure Politics*, pp. 98–99.

53. Odegard, *Pressure Politics*, pp. 249–50, 252, 256–57; Timberlake, *Prohibition and the Progressive Movement*, p. 164.

54. Kerr, *Organized for Prohibition*, pp. 187–88, 141–42, 147–50.

55. Odegard, *Pressure Politics*, pp. 153, 163; Timberlake, *Prohibition and the Progressive Movement*, p. 166; Bader, *Prohibition*, p. 190; Cherrington, *Evolution of Prohibition*, pp. 341–49.

56. Odegard, *Pressure Politics*, pp. 68–70; Kerr, *Organized for Prohibition*, pp. 200–202; Timberlake, *Prohibition and the Progressive Movement*, pp. 174, 178–79; Bader, *Prohibition*, p. 190.

57. *Constitution of the United States*.

58. Kerr, *Organized for Prohibition*, pp. 204–207.

59. Charles Merz, *The Dry Decade* (Garden City, New York: Doubleday, 1931), pp. 57–59, 67, 329; Ostrander, *Prohibition Movement in California*, p. 162; David E. Kyvig, *Repealing National Prohibition* (Chicago: University of Chicago Press, 1979), p. 31.

60. Kerr, *Organized for Prohibition*, pp. 145–46, 209–210, 215–221, 240–41.

61. Ibid., pp. 211–15, 242, 246–48.

62. Ibid., p. 247.

63. Ibid., pp. 249, 251; Kyvig, *Repealing*, pp. 98–99. For more on the transformation of the Democratic party, see David Burner, *Politics of Provincialism: The Democratic Party in Transition, 1918–1932* (Cambridge, Mass.: Harvard University Press, 1986).

64. Clark, *Deliver Us*, p. 200; Kyvig, *Repealing*, pp. 43, 45, 49, 78, 83, 88, 93.

65. Kyvig, *Repealing*, pp. 46–47, 50–52, 72–73, 118, 121, 123.

66. Kerr, *Organized for Prohibition*, pp. 258, 260, 273–74; Kyvig, *Repealing*, pp. 103, 116, 133, 147, 156–58, 171–72, 182.

67. *New York Times;* 11 December 1933, p. 4; 26 August 1935, p. 11; 8 December 1935, IV, p. 7; Clark, *Dry Years*, pp. 252–53; George Gallup, *The Gallup Poll: Public Opinion, 1935–1971* (New York: Random House, 1972), pp. 44, 549, 1991.

68. Edward W. Desmond, "Out in the Open," *Time* 130 (30 November 1987): pp. 81, 83.

CHAPTER 3: ONE BIG UNION:
THE INDUSTRIAL WORKERS OF THE WORLD

1. Industrial Workers of the World, *Proceedings of the Founding Convention* (New York: Merit Publishers, 1969), p. 1.

2. All headings in this chapter are from *Songs of the Workers: To Fan the Flames of Discontent* 35th ed. (Chicago: Industrial Workers of the World, 1987), pp. 4, 5, 14, 18, 26, 27, 30, 34, 36, 46.

3. George Brown Tindall, *America: A Narrative History*, vol. 2, 2nd ed. (New York: W. W. Norton & Co., 1988), pp. 796–97. See also, Stephen

Thernstrom, *The Other Bostonians: Poverty and Progress in the American Metropolis, 1880–1970* (Cambridge, Mass.: Harvard University Press, 1973).

4. Mark Wyman, *Hard Rock Epic: Western Miners and the Industrial Revolution, 1860–1910* (Berkeley: University of California Press, 1979), pp. 6–12, 19, 29; Melvyn Dubofsky, *We Shall Be All: A History of the Industrial Workers of the World* (Chicago: Quadrangle, 1969), pp. 19, 22–23, 27, 29.

5. James W. Byrkit, *Forging the Copper Collar: Arizona's Labor-Management War of 1901–1921* (Tucson: University of Arizona Press, 1982), p. 30; Wyman, *Hard Rock Epic*, pp. 86, 96–98, 105, 109, 113–14, 119–22, 125, 145; Brian Shovers, "The Perils of Working in the Butte Underground: Industrial Fatalities in the Copper Mines, 1880–1920," *Montana, The Magazine of Western History*, 37 (Spring 1987): pp. 26–28, 32–34.

6. Dubofsky, *We Shall Be All*, p. 128; Robert L. Tyler, *Rebels of the Woods: The I.W.W. in the Pacific Northwest* (Eugene: University of Oregon Press, 1967), pp. 5–7; Joseph R. Conlin, *At the Point of Production: The Local History of the I.W.W.* (Westport, Conn.: Greenwood Press, 1981), p. 98.

7. Dubofsky, *We Shall Be All*, p. 294; Ralph Chaplin, *Wobbly: The Rough and Tumble Story of an American Radical* (Chicago: University of Chicago Press, 1948), p. 144.

8. Dubofsky, *We Shall Be All*, pp. 230, 264; Anne H. Tripp, *The I.W.W. and the Paterson Silk Strike of 1913* (Urbana: University of Illinois Press, 1986), pp. 19, 213; Robert A. Goldberg, *Back to the Soil: The Jewish Farmers of Clarion, Utah and Their World* (Salt Lake City, University of Utah Press), p. 31.

9. Goldberg, *Back to the Soil*, pp. 31–32; Sidney Lens, *Radicalism in America* (New York: Crowell, 1969), p. 218; Robert Justin Goldstein, *Political Repression in Modern America: From 1870 to the Present* (Cambridge, Mass.: Schenkman, 1978), p. 66.

10. Byrkit, *Forging the Copper Collar*, pp. 31–32, 72, 102; Wyman, *Hard Rock Epic*, pp. 186, 189, 205, 248; Shovers, "Perils," pp. 28–29.

11. Bruno Ramirez, *When Workers Fight: The Politics of Industrial Relations in the Progressive Era, 1898–1916* (Westport, Conn.: Greenwood Press, 1978), p. 213.

12. Tindall, *America*, pp. 805–807.

13. David A. Shannon, *The Socialist Party of America: A History* (Chicago: Quadrangle Books, 1955), pp. 1, 5–7; Joseph R. Conlin, *Bread and Roses Too: Studies of the Wobblies* (Westport, Conn.: Greenwood, 1969), p. 119.

14. Migratory workers who carried their bedding and clothing in a small bundle.

15. Dubofsky, *We Shall Be All*, pp. 34–35, 37–39, 66–67, 71–72.

16. Ibid., pp. 40–55, 56, 68–69, 71, 74–75.

17. Ibid., p. 76; Paul F. Brissenden, *The I.W.W.: A Study of American Syndicalism* (New York: Columbia University Press, 1919), pp. 54, 56–62; Proceedings, pp. 82–83.

18. *Proceedings*, pp. 3–7; Brissenden, *The IWW*, pp. 62–63; Dubofsky, *We Shall Be All*, p. 78.

19. Dubofsky, *We Shall Be All*, pp. 81–82; Brissenden, *The IWW*, pp. 67–68, 71, 74–75.

20. *Proceedings*, p. 247.

21. Brissenden, *The IWW*, pp. 96–98, 108; *Proceedings*, pp. 299–300, 445, 495.

22. *Proceedings*, p. 495.

23. Brissenden, *The IWW*, pp. 98–101; *Proceedings*, pp. 447, 454–55, 458–59, 468.

24. Brissenden, *The IWW*, p. 108; Fred Thompson and Patrick Murfin, *The I.W.W., Its First Seventy Years, 1905–1975* (Chicago: Industrial Workers of the World, 1976), p. 23; Dubofsky, *We Shall Be All*, pp. 105–106.

25. Leland W. Robinson, "Social Movement Organizations in Decline: A Case Study of the I.W.W. " (Ph.D. dissertation, Northwestern University, 1973), p. 35.

26. Joyce L. Kornbluh, ed., *Rebel Voices: An I.W.W. Anthology* (Ann Arbor: University of Michigan Press, 1964), p. 36.

27. Robinson, "Social Movement," pp. 7–18; David A. Carter, "The Industrial Workers of the World and the Rhetoric of Song," *Quarterly Journal of Speech* 66 (December 1980): pp. 368–69, 371; Dubofsky, *We Shall Be All*, pp. 152–58; Kornbluh, *Rebel Voices*, p. 12.

28. Kornbluh, *Rebel Voices*, p. 36.

29. Stewart Bird, Dan Georgakas, and Deborah Shaffer, *Solidarity Forever: An Oral History of the IWW* (Chicago: Lake View Press, 1985), pp. 3–5; Kornbluh, *Rebel Voices*, p. 174.

30. *Proceedings*, p. 152.

31. Bird, *Solidarity Forever*, p. 5; Brissenden, *The IWW*, p. 93.

32. Bird, *Solidarity*, p. 7; Conlin, *Bread*, pp. 26–30; Dubofsky, *We Shall Be All*, pp. 164–65.

33. Bird, *Solidarity*, p. 10.

34. Dubofsky, *We Shall Be All*, pp. 158–62; Kornbluh, *Rebel Voices*, pp. 37, 38; Conlin, *Bread*, pp. 104–5; Thompson, *The I.W.W.*, pp. 81, 86, 87.

35. Dubofsky, *We Shall Be All*, p. 94.

36. Brissenden, *The IWW*, pp. 65, 114–18; Dubofsky, *We Shall Be All*, pp. 93–94, 106–108.

37. Dubofsky, *We Shall Be All*, pp. 96–105, 115–17; Brissenden, *The IWW*, pp. 173–75.

38. Dubofsky, *We Shall Be All*, pp. 95–96, 109, 112; Brissenden, *The IWW*, pp. 136–38.

39. Dubofsky, *We Shall Be All*, pp. 96, 110, 113–14, 134–39; William D. Haywood, *Bill Haywood's Book: The Autobiography of William D. Haywood* (New York: International Publishers, 1929), pp. 202–203.

40. Brissenden, *The IWW*, p. 211; Dubofsky, *We Shall Be All*, pp. 131–32.

41. Bird, *Solidarity*, p. 150.

42. Kornbluh, *Rebel Voices*, p. 209.

43. Dubofsky, *We Shall Be All*, p. 142.

44. Bird, *Solidarity*, p. 147.

45. Dubofsky, *We Shall Be All*, pp. 142–43; Kornbluh, *Rebel Voices*, p. 190.

46. Dubofsky, *We Shall Be All*, pp. 121–22, 125–30; Tyler, *Rebels*, p. 56; Thompson, *The I.W.W.*, p. 35.

47. Brissenden, *The IWW*, pp. 183, 207; Dubofsky, *We Shall Be All*, pp. 122–25.

48. Sidney Lens, *The Labor Wars: From the Molly Maguires to the Sitdowns* (Garden City, N.Y.: Doubleday, 1973), pp. 159–63; Dubofsky, *We Shall Be All*, pp. 198–209, 210–19.

49. Philip S. Foner, *Fellow Workers and Friends: I.W.W. Free-Speech Fights as Told by Participants* (Westport, Conn.: Greenwood Press, 1981), p. 17.

50. Bird, *Solidarity*, pp. 7–8; Dubofsky, *We Shall Be All*, pp. 173–79, 184, 197; Foner, *Fellow Workers*, pp. 12, 16–18, 21; Conlin, *Bread*, pp. 68–76.

51. Brissenden, *The IWW*, p. 226.

52. Foner, *Fellow Workers*, p. 77.

53. John Clendenin Townsend, *Running the Gauntlet: Cultural Sources of Violence Against the I.W.W.* (New York: Garland Press, 1986), p. 196.

54. Aileen S. Kraditor, *The Radical Persuasion, 1890–1917: Aspects of the Intellectual History and the Historiography of Three American Radical Organizations* (Baton Rouge: Louisiana State University Press, 1981), pp. 102–103; Townsend, *Running the Gauntlet*, pp. 192–193; Brissenden, *The*

IWW, p. 325; Shannon, *The Socialist Party*, pp. 72, 77–78; William Preston, Jr., *Aliens and Dissenters: Federal Suppression of Radicals, 1903–1933* (Cambridge, Mass.: Harvard University Press, 1963), pp. 48–49.

55. "Menace of the I.W.W.," *New York Times Magazine*, 2 September 1917, sec. 6, p. 8.

56. Townsend, *Running the Gauntlet*, p. 205; Foner, *Fellow Workers*, p. 13; Bird, *Solidarity*, p. 143; Peter Filene, *Him, Her, Self: Sex Roles in Modern America* (New York: Harcourt Brace Jovanovich, 1974), pp. 78, 94.

57. Bird, *Solidarity*, p. 40.

58. Robinson, "Social Movement," p. 44; Elizabeth Gurley Flynn, *The Rebel Girl: An Autobiography, My First Life (1906–1926)* (New York: International Publishers, 1955), p. 102; Bird, *Solidarity*, p. 92.

59. Robinson, "Social Movement," p. 313; Kraditor, *Radical Persuasion*, pp. 12, 18, 20.

60. Brissenden, *The IWW*, pp. 267, 334.

61. Dubofsky, *We Shall Be All*, pp. 227–41; Haywood, *Bill Haywood's Book*, pp. 247–48; Kornbluh, *Rebel Voices*, pp. 158–60.

62. Dubofsky, *We Shall Be All*, pp. 241–55; Tripp, *I.W.W.*, p. 28.

63. Dubofsky, *We Shall Be All*, p. 260.

64. Tripp, *I.W.W.*, p. 34; Dubofsky, *We Shall Be All*, p. 255.

65. Tripp, *I.W.W.*, pp. 154–56; Dubofsky, *We Shall Be All*, pp. 264–84.

66. Tripp, *I.W.W.*, pp. 210–35.

67. Dubofsky, *We Shall Be All*, pp. 256–58, 286–87; Bird, *Solidarity*, pp. 177–78.

68. Tripp, *I.W.W.*, pp. 179–85, 198–200; Steve Golin, "Defeat Becomes Disaster: The Paterson Strike of 1913 and the Decline of the IWW," *Labor History* 24 (Spring 1983): pp. 228–33, 238–44; Flynn, *Rebel Girl*, pp. 214–16; Dubofsky, *We Shall Be All*, pp. 221–33.

69. Goldstein, *Political Repression*, p. 240; Bird, *Solidarity*, pp. 8, 32–34; Dubofsky, *We Shall Be All*, pp. 314–19, 343–46; Brissenden, *The IWW*, p. 339.

70. Preston, *Aliens*, p. 60.

71. Preston, *Aliens*, pp. 64–69; Goldstein, *Political Repression*, p. 101; Brissenden, *The IWW*, pp. 345, 380–82, 384; Kornbluh, *Rebel Voices*, pp. 127, 306; Foner, *Fellow Workers*, pp. 184–95.

72. *Proceedings*, p. 269; Preston, *Aliens*, pp. 88–89; Dubofsky, *We Shall Be All*, pp. 354–57; Haywood, *Bill Haywood's Book*, p. 294.

73. Dubofsky, *We Shall Be All*, p. 377.

74. "Industrial Workers Who Won't Work," *Literary Digest* 55 (28 July 1917): p. 20.

75. Haywood, *Bill Haywood's Book*, p. 299; Kornbluh, *Rebel Voices*, p. 233; Robinson, "Social Movement," p. 55; Townsend, *Running the Gauntlet*, p. 199; Byrkit, *Forging the Copper Collar*, p. 251 (quote). For a sampling of opinion makers' attitudes see, "What the I.W.W. Black Cat and Wooden Shoe Emblems Mean," *Literary Digest* 61 (19 April 1919): pp. 70–75; "Treason Must Be Made Odious," *North American Review* 206 (October 1917): pp. 513–17; Lewis Allen Browne, "Bolshevism in America," *The Forum* 59 (June 1918): pp. 703–17; John A. Fitch, "Sabotage and Disloyalty," *Survey* 39 (13 October 1917): pp. 35–36; "The I.W.W. Develops into a National Menace," *Current Opinion* 63 (September 1917): pp. 153–54; "The I.W.W. As an Agent of Pan-Germanism," *World's Work* 36 (October 1918): pp. 581–82.

76. Kornbluh, *Rebel Voices*, p. 325.

77. Dubofsky, *We Shall Be All*, pp. 407, 433; Preston, *Aliens*, pp. 118–49; Goldstein, *Political Repression*, pp. 110–13, 117–18, 126.

78. Byrkit, *Forging the Copper Collar*, p. 192.

79. Preston, *Aliens*, pp. 103–105; Tyler, *Rebels*, pp. 102–15, 121, 127–36, 148–53; Goldstein, *Political Repression*, pp. 125–29; Haywood, *Bill Haywood's Book*, p. 301; Byrkit, *Forging the Copper Collar*, pp. 1–3, 160–86; Philip Taft, "The Bisbee Deportation," *Labor History* 13 (Winter 1972): p. 22.

80. Golstein, *Political Repression*, p. 146; Kornbluh, *Rebel Voices*, p. 322; Tyler, *Rebels*, pp. 156, 161, 166, 176; Robinson, "Social Movement," p. 57.

81. Conlin, *Bread*, pp. 141–42 (quote).

82. Dubofsky, *We Shall Be All*, pp. 457, 461–62, 465–66; Robinson, "Social Movement," pp. 66, 68, 71, 81; Thompson, *The I.W.W.*, pp. 150–51.

83. Chaplin, *Wobbly*, p. 298.

84. Haywood, *Bill Haywood's Book*, p. 360.

85. John P. Diggins, *The American Left in the Twentieth Century* (New York: Harcourt Brace Jovanovich, 1973), p. 89.

86. Haywood, *Bill Haywood's Book*, pp. 360–62; Conlin, *Bread*, p. 147; Tyler, *Rebels*, pp. 206–12; Theodore Draper, *The Roots of American Communism* (New York: Viking Press, 1957), p. 318; Chaplin, *Wobbly*, pp. 285–98, 314, 337–38, 350; Bird, *Solidarity*, pp. 160–61; Thompson, *The I.W.W.*, pp. 136–37; Dubofsky, *We Shall Be All*, pp. 463–65. Bill Haywood died in the Soviet Union in 1928. In tribute, his ashes were placed in the Kremlin wall.

87. Robinson, "Social Movement," pp. 79–80, 85–91; Thompson, *The I.W.W.*, p. 156.

88. Thompson, *The I.W.W.*, pp. 145–202, 206, 210; Robinson, "Social Movement," pp. 111, 193, 196–98, 211, 215, 218; "Again the Wobblies," *Time* 47 (1 April 1946): p. 24; "The Union That Never Died," *Newsweek* (24 September 1984): pp. 16–17; *Industrial Worker*, November 1987, January–November 1988.

CHAPTER 4: INVISIBLE EMPIRE: THE KNIGHTS OF THE KU KLUX KLAN

1. Winfield Jones, *Story of the Ku Klux Klan* (Washington, D.C.: American Newspaper Syndicate, 1921), p. 59.

2. U.S. Congress, House Committee on Rules, *Hearings on the Ku Klux Klan*, 67th Cong., 1st sess. (1921), pp. 32–34, 148; William G. Shepherd, "Ku Klux Koin," *Collier's* 82 (21 July 1928): p. 39.

3. David M. Chalmers, *Hooded Americanism: The History of the Ku Klux Klan* (New York: Franklin Watts, 1981), p. 26.

4. Ibid., pp. 22–27.

5. Charles C. Alexander, *The Ku Klux Klan in the Southwest* (Lexington: University of Kentucky Press, 1966), pp. 9–10.

6. Ibid., pp. 9–10; Chalmers, *Hooded Americanism*, p. 38.

7. Alexander, *Klan in the Southwest*, p. 29.

8. Ibid., p. 30.

9. Robert A.Goldberg, *Hooded Empire: The Ku Klux Klan in Colorado* (Urbana: University of Illinois Press, 1981), p. 7. Unless otherwise noted, the source of material for the rest of this chapter is *Hooded Empire*.

10. Chalmers, *Hooded Americanism*, pp. 39, 40, 88, 144, 175, 216, 218, 236, 237, 260; Kenneth T. Jackson, *The Ku Klux Klan in the City, 1915–1930* (New York: Oxford University Press, 1967), pp. 96, 237, 239.

11. Arnold Rice, *The Ku Klux Klan in American Politics* (Washington, D.C.: Public Affairs Press, 1962), p. 4.

12. Chalmers, *Hooded Americanism*, pp. 100–106; Jackson, *Klan in the City*, pp. 12–16.

13. *Kloran* (Atlanta: Knights of the Ku Klux Klan, n.d.), p. 26.

14. Philip Jenkins, "The Ku Klux Klan in Pennsylvania, 1920–1940," *Western Pennsylvania Historical Quarterly* 69 (April 1986): 130.

15. Robert A. Goldberg, "The Ku Klux Klan in Madison, 1922–1927," *Wisconsin Magazine of History* 58 (Autumn 1974): pp. 31–44; Chalmers, *Hooded Americanism*, p. 152; Alexander, *Klan in the Southwest*, p. 31; Shawn Lay, *War, Revolution and the Ku Klux Klan: A Study of Intolerance*

in a Border City (El Paso: Texas Western Press, 1985), pp. 57–62; Richard Melching, "The Activities of the Ku Klux Klan in Anaheim, California, 1923–1925," *Southern California Quarterly* 56 (Summer 1974): pp. 175–79.

16. Representative occupations for each category are:

> *High nonmanual* banker, businessman (sufficient property), clergyman, lawyer, physician, teacher
> *Middle nonmanual* accountant, businessman (small), farm owner (small), manager of a business
> *Low nonmanual* bookkeeper, foreman, office clerk, salesman
> *Skilled* baker, brick mason, butcher, carpenter, furrier, machinist, painter, tailor
> *Semiskilled and service* apprentice, barber, cook, driver, factory operative, janitor, policeman, waiter
> *Unskilled* laborer, porter

17. Jackson, *Klan in the City*, pp. 62, 119, 120.

18. Chalmers, *Hooded Americanism*, pp. 202–11.

19. Ibid., pp. 200, 215.

20. The transparency of the Internal Revenue Service's investigation is suggested by the results of the probe. In 1935 the U.S. Board of Tax Appeals ruled that Locke had not shielded income and was, in fact, entitled to a tax refund on monies previously paid.

21. Jackson, *Klan in the City*, pp. 186, 209–11; Goldberg, "Klan in Madison:" p. 44.

22. Alexander, *Klan in the Southwest*, pp. 234, 238, 241; Chalmers, *Hooded Americanism*, pp. 291, 300, 304, 322; Wyn Craig Wade, *Fiery Cross: The Ku Klux Klan in America* (New York: Simon & Schuster, 1987), pp. 273–75.

23. Chalmers, *Hooded Americanism*, pp. 325, 332–33, 335–36, 348–49; Wade, *Fiery Cross*, pp. 300, 309–10, 324, 351.

24. George Gallup, *The Gallup Poll: Public Opinion, 1935–1971* (New York: Random House, 1972), p. 1977; Chalmers, *Hooded Americanism*, pp. 387, 398–99, 432; Wade, *Fiery Cross*, pp. 361–64.

25. Wade, *Fiery Cross*, pp. 368–75, 383–84, 397.

26. Ibid., pp. 391, 394–96; Jesse Kornbluh, "The Woman who beat the Klan," *New York Times Magazine*, 1 November 1987, sec. 6, 26–39; "Going After the Klan," *Newsweek* 107 (23 February 1987): 29; *Salt Lake Tribune*, 6 November 1987.

CHAPTER 5: THROW OFF YOUR CHAINS: THE COMMUNIST PARTY

1. Theodore Draper, *American Communism and Soviet Russia: The Formative Period* (New York: Viking Press, 1960), p. 9.

2. Ibid., p. 302.

3. Robert K. Murray, *Red Scare: Study in National Hysteria, 1919–1920* (Minneapolis: University of Minnesota Press, 1955), pp. 9, 15, 71, 78; Draper, *American Communism*, p. 16.

4. David Shannon, *The Socialist Party of America: A History* (Chicago: Quadrangle, 1955), pp. 128, 131, 133; Theodore Draper, *The Roots of American Communism* (New York: Viking Press, 1957), p. 57; Draper, *American Communism*, pp. 13, 17.

5. Shannon, *Socialist Party*, pp. 132, 138; Draper, *Roots*, pp. 32, 138, 144, 156, 158–59, 191.

6. Draper, *Roots*, pp. 164–68, 173–76, 179–81, 190; Nathan Glazer, *The Social Basis of American Communism* (New York: Harcourt, Brace & World, 1961), pp. 38–39.

7. Murray, *Red Scare*, pp. 34, 41, 167.

8. Ibid., p. 63.

9. Ibid., p. 186.

10. William E. Leuchtenburg, *The Perils of Prosperity, 1914–32* (Chicago: University of Chicago Press, 1958), p. 71; Murray, *Red Scare*, pp. 58, 73–75, 92–93.

11. Murray, *Red Scare*, p. 219.

12. Leuchtenburg, *Perils of Prosperity*, pp. 77–78; Murray, *Red Scare*, pp. 192–94, 196, 210–11, 213–17, 235; Draper, *Roots*, pp. 203–4.

13. Draper, *Roots*, pp. 205, 207, 226, 272, 391; William Z. Foster, *Pages from a Worker's Life* (New York: International Publishers, 1939), p. 232.

14. Harvey Klehr, *The Heyday of American Communism: The Depression Years* (New York: Basic Books, 1984), p. 4.

15. Draper, *Roots*, pp. 261–70, 338–40, 356–57, 394; Draper, *American Communism*, pp. 124 (quote), 125, 207.

16. Draper, *Roots*, pp. 268–70, 276, 349; Draper, *American Communism*, pp. 25–26, 43–48, 75, 174, 215.

17. Draper, *American Communism*, p. 188.

18. Ibid., pp. 83–86, 96–97, 102, 105–11, 113–14, 119.

19. Draper, *Roots*, p. 186; Klehr, *Heyday*, pp. 6–7; Glazer, *Social Basis*, pp. 50–51; James Weinstein, *Ambiguous Legacy: The Left in American Politics* (New York: New Viewpoints, 1975), pp. 44–46; Al Richmond, *A Long View*

from the Left: Memoirs of an American Revolutionary (Boston: Houghton Mifflin, 1973), pp. 142–43; Paul Lyons, *Philadelphia Communists, 1936–1956* (Philadelphia: Temple University Press, 1982), pp. 51–54; Draper, *American Communism*, pp. 155–56, 158, 160–61.

20. Glazer, *Social Basis*, pp. 43, 47; Draper, *American Communism*, p. 191.

21. Glazer, *Social Basis*, pp. 52, 60–62; Draper, *American Communism*, pp. 187–88, 193.

22. Draper, *American Communism*, pp. 248–50, 260, 278–81, 296–97, 306, 307–11, 392, 398–414, 423–29; Glazer, *Social Basis*, p. 65.

23. Bert Cochran, *Labor and Communism: The Conflict That Shaped American Unions* (Princeton: Princeton University Press, 1977), pp. 30–39; Draper, *American Communism*, pp. 290, 378.

24. "No One Has Starved," *Fortune* 6 (September 1932): pp. 23–24; Irving Bernstein, *The Lean Years: A History of the American Worker, 1920–1933* (Boston: Penguin, 1966), pp. 254–57, 293, 301, 307, 316, 331–32; Arthur M. Schlesinger Jr., *The Age of Roosevelt: The Crisis of the Old Order, 1919–1933* (Boston: Houghton Mifflin, 1957), pp. 174, 250–251; *New York Times*, 6 March 1931, p. 11; Remley J. Glass, "Gentlemen, the Corn Belt!" *Harper's Magazine* 167 (July 1933): pp. 201, 207–8; Leuchtenburg, *Perils of Prosperity*, pp. 248–49, 253.

25. Bernstein, *Lean Years*, pp. 422, 432–34; Frances Fox Piven and Richard Cloward, *Poor People's Movements: Why They Succeed, How They Fail* (New York: Pantheon, 1977), pp. 48–49; *New York Times*, 21 January 1931, p. 1, 26 February 1931, p. 2.

26. Weinstein, *Ambiguous Legacy*, pp. 47–49; Cochran, *Labor and Communism*, p. 43; Klehr, *Heyday*, pp. 49 (quote), 52–53, 65, 90.

27. Bernstein, *Lean Years*, pp. 426–28; Piven and Cloward, *Poor People's Movements*, pp. 50–51, 68; Klehr, *Heyday*, pp. 12–14; Roy Rosenzweig, "Organizing the Unemployed: The Early Years of the Great Depression," *Radical America* 10 (July-August 1976): pp. 38, 40–41, 44; Cochran, *Labor and Communism*, pp. 43–44, 50, 60, 63.

28. John P. Diggins, *The American Left in the Twentieth Century* (New York: Harcourt, Brace, Jovanovich, 1973), p. 122.

29. Sidney Hook, "Breaking with the Communists—A Memoir," *Commentary* 77 (February 1984): p. 51; Klehr, *Heyday*, pp. 74, 79–80.

30. Glazer, *Social Basis*, pp. 92–93, 100, 101; Cochran, *Labor and Communism*, pp. 74–75; Klehr, *Heyday*, pp. 118–21, 132–33.

31. Klehr, *Heyday*, pp. 167, 170, 202.

32. Ibid., p. 190.

33. Ibid., p. 370; Weinstein, *Ambiguous Legacy*, pp. 77–78.

34. Klehr, *Heyday*, p. 23.

35. Draper, *Roots*, pp. 307–9; Joseph R. Starobin, *American Communism in Crisis, 1943–1957* (Cambridge, Mass.: Harvard University Press, 1972), p. 52; Maurice Isserman, *Which Side Were You On?: The American Communist Party During the Second World War* (Middletown, Conn.: Wesleyan University Press, 1982), p. 5; Klehr, *Heyday*, pp. 87, 171.

36. Klehr, *Heyday*, pp. 186–89, 190, 195–97.

37. Ibid., p. 222.

38. Ibid., pp. 205–9, 222, 252–65.

39. Ibid., p. 225; Isserman, *Which Side*, p. 19; Irving Bernstein, *The Turbulent Years: A History of the American Worker, 1933–1941* (Boston: Houghton Mifflin, 1970), pp. 400–404, 782–83.

40. Klehr, *Heyday*, pp. 223–40; Daniel Bell, *Marxian Socialism in the United States* (Princeton, N.J.: Princeton University Press, 1967), p. 145; Cochran, *Labor and Communism*, pp. 95–98.

41. Starobin, *American Communism in Crisis*, pp. 37–39; Lyons, *Philadelphia Communists*, p. 135; Cochran, *Labor and Communism*, p. 136; Glazer, *Social Basis*, p. 124.

42. Klehr, *Heyday*, pp. 101, 309–17, 321, 350–53; Junius Irving Scales and Richard Nickson, *Cause at Heart: A Former Communist Remembers* (Athens: University of Georgia Press, 1986), p. 173; Draper, *American Communism*, p. 185; David Shannon, *The Decline of American Communism: A History of the Communist Party of the United States Since 1945* (New York: Harcourt Brace, 1959), pp. 83–84.

43. Klehr, *Heyday*, pp. 365–66, 375–76, 305–7.

44. Glazer, *Social Basis*, pp. 100, 114, 116; Klehr, *Heyday*, pp. 164, 270, 275, 378–80.

45. Klehr, *Heyday*, p. 367; Bell, *Marxian Socialism*, p. 14; Shannon, *Decline*, pp. 74–75; Harvey Klehr, *Communist Cadre: The Social Background of the American Communist Party Elite* (Stanford: Stanford University Press, 1978), pp. 5–8.

46. Cochran, *Labor and Communism*, p. 12.

47. Michael Francis Urmann, "Rank and File Communists and the CIO," (Ph.D. dissertation, University of Utah, 1981), p. 160.

48. Lyons, *Philadelphia Communists*, pp. 20, 24–25, 44–47; Scales, *Cause at Heart*, pp. 69, 191; Urmann, "Rank and File," p. 169; Richmond, *Long View*, p. 70.

49. Lyons, *Philadelphia Communists*, 10; Glazer, *Social Basis*, p. 190.

50. Klehr, *Heyday*, p. 163; Glazer, *Social Basis*, pp. 130–40, 188; Lyons, *Philadelphia Communists*, pp. 28–29; Arthur Liebman, *Jews and the Left* (New York: John Wiley & Sons, 1979), pp. 26–29, 134, 206, 280, 310, 355.

51. Urmann, "Rank and File," p. 181.

52. Liebman, *Jews and the Left*, pp. 501–3; Lyons, *Philadelphia Communists*, pp. 29, 32–33, 38.

53. Glazer, *Social Basis*, pp. 170–81, 185; Weinstein, *Ambiguous Legacy*, pp. 87–91; Klehr, *Heyday*, pp. 324–48; Klehr, *Communist Cadre*, pp. 54–64, 66; Pettis Perry, *The Communist Party: Vanguard Fighter for Peace, Democracy, Security, Socialism* (New York: New Century Publishers, 1953), pp. 16, 51–52. See also, Mark Naison, *Communists in Harlem During the Depression* (New York: Grove Press, 1983).

54. Lyons, *Philadelphia Communists*, pp. 61–64, 88; *Party Organizer* 8 (1935): pp. 18–32; Klehr, *Heyday*, p. 155.

55. Lyons, *Philadelphia Communists*, p. 69.

56. Urmann, "Rank and File," p. 198.

57. Liebman, *Jews and the Left*, pp. 307–10.

58. Klehr, *Communist Cadre*, p. 86; Klehr, *Heyday*, pp. 154–58; Cochran, *Labor and Communism*, p. 12; Liebman, *Jews and the Left*, pp. 533–35.

59. Isserman, *Which Side*, pp. 18, 32–34, 40–43; Klehr, *Heyday*, pp. 390, 395–99, 405.

60. Isserman, *Which Side*, pp. 37–38, 44, 47, 49, 50–52, 70–71, 76, 87; Klehr, *Heyday*, pp. 402–3; Cochran, *Labor and Communism*, pp. 165–66; George Gallup, *The Gallup Poll: Public Opinion, 1935–1971* (New York: Random House, 1972), pp. 192, 199, 245; Scales, *Cause at Heart*, p. 84; Peter Steinberg, *The Great "Red Menace": United States Prosecution of American Communists, 1947–1952* (Westport, Conn.: Greenwood, 1984), pp. 11–13; Michal R. Belknap, *Cold War Political Justice: The Smith Act, the Communist Party, and American Civil Liberties* (Westport, Conn.: Greenwood, 1977), pp. 9, 18, 24–27.

61. Klehr, *Heyday*, p. 384; Lyons, *Philadelphia Communists*, pp. 139–41; Scales, *Cause at Heart*, pp. 93–94; Urmann, "Rank and File," pp. 161, 162, 170.

62. Isserman, *Which Side*, pp. 103–4, 119, 124–26, 148, 152, 180; Cochran, *Labor and Communism*, p. 211.

63. John Lewis Gaddis, *The United States and the Origins of the Cold War, 1941–1947* (New York: Columbia University Press, 1972), p. 38.

64. Isserman, *Which Side*, pp. 120, 127–29, 131–32, 138, 143, 145, 167, 174; Gaddis, *The United States and the Origins of the Cold War*, pp. 33–36,

47–48, 56; Starobin, *American Communism in Crisis*, pp. 24–25; Shannon, *Decline*, p. 3.

65. Isserman, *Which Side*, p. 213.

66. Ibid., pp. 139, 145–46, 179, 185–203, 214–20, 229–34, 241–43; Cochran, *Labor and Communism*, pp. 229–30; Starobin, *American Communism in Crisis*, pp. 78–81.

67. Shannon, *Decline*, pp. 47, 186–88, 219–20, 232; Steinberg, *Great "Red Menace,"* pp. 20–31, 186; Belknap, *Cold War Political Justice*, pp. 42–44.

68. Belknap, *Cold War Political Justice*, pp. 6–7.

69. Steinberg, *Great "Red Menace,"* pp. 126–27, 191; Shannon, *Decline*, p. 190; Gallup, *Gallup Poll*, pp. 594, 639, 640, 690, 736, 752, 863, 874, 1191; Belknap, *Cold War Political Justice*, p. 43.

70. Richmond, *Long View*, pp. 296–98, 302, 308, 314, 326–27; Belknap, *Cold War Political Justice*, pp. 47, 51–52, 58, 79–81, 141–42, 152–58, 188–89, 197; Shannon, *Decline*, pp. 196–97; Steinberg, *Great "Red Menace,"* pp. 232, 247, 251.

71. Steinberg, *Great "Red Menace,"* pp. 146, 209–210; Athan Theoharis, *Spying on Americans: Political Surveillance from Hoover to the Huston Plan* (Philadelphia: Temple University Press, 1978), pp. 44–55.

72. Steinberg, *Great "Red Menace,"* pp. 43–44; Cochran, *Labor and Communism*, pp. 153–55, 267–70, 290–92, 304–12, 330–31; Shannon, *Decline*, pp. 102–4, 216–18; F. S. O'Brien, "The 'Communist-Dominated' Unions in the United States Since 1950," *Labor History* 9 (Spring 1968): pp. 184–206.

73. Starobin, *American Communism in Crisis*, p. 123.

74. Steinberg, *Great "Red Menace,"* pp. 67–68, 82–87, 134–36; Cochran, *Labor and Communism*, pp. 299–303; Glazer, *Social Basis*, p. 126; Starobin, *American Communism in Crisis*, pp. 123–28, 174–85; Shannon, *Decline*, pp. 41–44, 114, 122, 131–36, 164–81.

75. Steinberg, *Great "Red Menace,"* pp. 211–13, 225; Shannon, *Decline*, pp. 228–30, 244–47; Scales, *Cause at Heart*, pp. 221–23; Starobin, *American Communism in Crisis*, pp. 198–200.

76. Starobin, *American Communism in Crisis*, pp. 5–6, 219–23; Belknap, *Cold War Political Justice*, pp. 192–97; Steinberg, *Great "Red Menace,"* pp. 149–53, 193, 230, 262–64; Scales, *Cause at Heart*, pp. 224, 231, 258–59; Isserman, *Which Side*, pp. 247–48.

77. Starobin, *American Communism in Crisis*, pp. 9–17; Liebman, *Jews and the Left*, pp. 522, 592–95; Shannon, *Decline*, pp. 107–10, 251–52.

78. Belknap, *Cold War Political Justice*, p. 190.

79. Isserman, *Which Side*, p. 250.

80. Liebman, *Jews and the Left*, p. 518.

81. Scales, *Cause at Heart*, p. 302.

82. Richmond, *Long View*, pp. 364–65, 368–73, 380; Shannon, *Decline*, pp. 272, 284, 287–96, 303–8; Steinberg, *Great "Red Menace,"* pp. 265–73; Starobin, *American Communism in Crisis*, pp. 6–7; Maurice Isserman, *If I Had a Hammer . . . The Death of the Old Left and the Birth of the New Left* (New York: Basic Books, 1987), pp. 15, 19, 23, 30.

83. Belknap, *Cold War Political Justice*, p. 205; Shannon, *Decline*, pp. 324–33, 346–60; Isserman, *If*, pp. 25–29.

84. Arthur Herzog, "A Specter Haunts the American Communist Party," *New York Times*, 25 October 1964, sec. 6, p. 62.

85. *New York Times:* 6 June 1961, pp. 1; 16–17; 1 December 1961, p. 7; 20 March 1962, p. 14; 18 October 1962, p. 16; 30 May 1963, p. 7; 18 December 1963, p. 1; 27 December 1963, p. 22; 9 June 1964, p. 1; 11 June 1964, p. 32; 6 November 1964, p. 8; 10 January 1965, pp. 1, 24; 26 February 1965, pp. 1, 11; 23 March 1965, p. 25; 16 November 1965, pp. 1, 34; 3 April 1967, p. 1; 8 April 1967, p. 30; Theoharis, *Spying*, pp. 135–38; Frank Donner, "Let Him Wear a Wolf's Head: What the FBI Did to William Albertson," *The Civil Liberties Review* 3 (April-May 1976): pp. 12–15.

86. *New York Times:* 14 December 1959, p. 19; 3 January 1964, p. 26; 26 September 1964, p. 11; 24 February 1966, pp. 1, 2; 26 February 1966, p. 9; 23 June 1966, p. 3; 25 June 1966, p. 14; 27 June 1966, pp. 1, 4; 2 September 1969, p. 95.

87. Ibid., 5 July 1968, p. 14; 27 February 1981, p. 2.

88. Ibid., 28 June 1975, p. 34; Richmond, *Long View*, pp. 394–96.

89. NBC, "Donahue Show," 12 January 1988.

90. *New York Times:* 26 September 1964, p. 11; 21 April 1965, p. 6; 22 June 1966, p. 4; 23 June 1966, p. 3; 19 February 1972, p. 13; 21 February 1972, p. 11; 25 August 1979, p. 6; 27 February 1981, p. 2; "A Communist in America," *Newsweek* 103 (27 February 1984): p. 9.

CHAPTER 6: BRIDGING MCCARTHYISM AND REAGANISM: THE JOHN BIRCH SOCIETY

1. William H. Chafe and Harvard Sitkoff, *A History of Our Times: Readings on Postwar America* (New York: Oxford University Press, 1987), p. 65; Robert Griffith, *The Politics of Fear: Joseph R. McCarthy and the Senate* (Lexington: University of Kentucky Press, 1970), p. 49.

2. Seymour Lipset and Earl Raab, *The Politics of Unreason: Right-Wing Extremism in America, 1790–1970* (New York: Harper & Row, 1970), p. 218.

3. Griffith, *Politics of Fear*, p. 89.

4. Ibid., pp. 14–17, 29, 53, 132, 139.

5. David M. Oshinsky, *A Conspiracy So Immense: The World of Joe McCarthy* (New York: Free Press, 1983), pp. 92–96; Griffith, *Politics of Fear*, p. 143; Dewey W. Grantham, *Recent America: The United States Since 1945* (Arlington Heights, Ill.: Harlan Davidson, 1987), pp. 17–36.

6. Griffith, *Politics of Fear*, p. 46; Grantham, *Recent America*, pp. 59–69.

7. Griffith, *Politics of Fear*, pp. 43–48; Grantham, *Recent America*, pp. 69–71; William H. Chafe, *The Unfinished Journey: America Since World War II* (New York: Oxford University Press, 1986), p. 105.

8. Chafe, *Unfinished Journey*, p. 98.

9. Griffith, *Politics of Fear*, p. 52.

10. Ibid., p. 11.

11. Chafe, *Unfinished Journey*, p. 98.

12. Griffith, *Politics of Fear*, pp. 115–16.

13. Michael M. Miles, *The Odyssey of the American Right* (New York: Oxford University Press, 1980), p. 142; Michael Paul Rogin, *The Intellectuals and McCarthy: The Radical Specter* (Cambridge, Mass.: MIT Press, 1967), pp. 232–36, 239, 243, 247; Nelson W. Polsby, "Toward an Explanation of McCarthyism," *Political Studies* 8 (October 1960): pp. 258, 263; George Gallup, *The Gallup Poll: Public Opinion, 1935–1971* (New York: Random House, 1972), p. 1296.

14. Griffith, *Politics of Fear*, pp. 187, 198; Rogin, *Intellectuals and McCarthy*, pp. 250–59.

15. Griffith, *Politics of Fear*, pp. 213–16, 243–63, 270, 302–305, 318–19; Oshinsky, *Conspiracy*, pp. 503–505.

16. Arnold Forster and Benjamin Epstein, *Danger on the Right* (New York: Random House, 1965), p. 18; Eckard V. Toy, Jr., "Ideology and Conflict in American Ultra-Conservatism" (Ph.D. dissertation, University of Oregon, 1965), pp. 232, 237–38, 241–42; Robert H. W. Welch, Jr., *The Blue Book of the John Birch Society* (Belmont, Mass.: Western Islands, 1961), p.1.

17. Robert Welch's lecture was printed as *The Blue Book* and became an important part of each member's introduction into the movement.

18. Welch, *Blue Book*, p. 93.

19. Ibid., pp. 9, 18–28, 33, 59–64, 104, 141; J. Allen Broyles, *The John Birch Society: Anatomy of a Protest* (Boston: Beacon Press, 1966), pp. 12, 17, 102–112, 118; Toy, "Ideology and Conflict," p. 234.

20. Robert H. W. Welch, Jr., *What Is the John Birch Society?* (Belmont, Mass.: Western Islands, 1981), p. 4.

21. Jonathan Martin Kolkey, *The New Right, 1960–1968: With Epilogue, 1969–1980* (Lanham, Md.: University Press of America, 1983), pp. 105–107; Lipset and Raab, *Politics of Unreason,* pp. 264–66; Broyles, *John Birch Society,* pp. 127–29; Welch, *What Is the John Birch Society?,* p. 4.

22. Welch, *Blue Book,* pp. 121, 129, 158, 159, 161; Forster and Epstein, *Danger on the Right,* p. 22; Barbara Stone, "The John Birch Society of California" (Ph.D. dissertation, University of Southern California, 1968), pp. 45–49.

23. Welch, *Blue Book,* pp. 163–65; Stone, "The John Birch Society," pp. 40–44, 66–67.

24. Welch, *Blue Book,* pp. 76–94, 107–110, 167, 174.

25. Broyles, *John Birch Society,* pp. 20–21. For more on John Birch see, Robert H. W. Welch, Jr., *The Life of John Birch: In the Story of One American Boy, the Ordeal of His Age* (Belmont, Mass.: Western Islands, 1954).

26. Broyles, *John Birch Society,* p. 28; Welch, *Blue Book,* unpaged.

27. Robert Welch personally delivered a copy of this manuscript to Barry Goldwater in Phoenix, Arizona. Goldwater read the manuscript and was unconvinced. He pleaded with Welch not to publish it: "I thought he would harm his cause if he printed the book." Barry M. Goldwater, *With No Apologies: The Personal and Political Memoirs of United States Senator Barry M. Goldwater* (New York: William Morrow & Company, 1979), p. 119.

28. Forster and Epstein, *Danger on the Right,* p. 42. Compare quotations in *Danger on the Right* with those toned down in subsequent editions of *The Politician.* For example, see Robert H. W. Welch, Jr., *The Politician* (Belmont, Mass.: Western Islands, 1963), pp. 5–6, 277–79.

29. Broyles, *John Birch Society,* pp. 7, 31; Forster and Epstein, *Danger on the Right,* pp. 40–42.

30. Broyles, *John Birch Society,* pp. 4, 27.

31. California Legislature, *Twelfth Report of the Senate Fact-Finding Subcommittee on Un-American Activities,* 1963, p. 16; Forster and Epstein, *Danger on the Right,* pp. 120–21, 177–83; Toy, "Ideology and Conflict," pp. 237–38, 241, 247, 251, 256–60.

32. Daniel Bell, "The Dispossessed," in Bell, ed., *The New American Right* (Garden City, N.Y.: Doubleday-Anchor, 1964), p. 5.

33. Bell, "The Dispossessed," pp. 5–6, 8; Forster and Epstein, *Danger on the Right,* pp. 47–49; Broyles, *John Birch Society,* pp. 132–33.

34. California Senate *Report*, pp. 4, 16, 20, 33; Stone, "Birch Society of California," pp. 22–24; Forster and Epstein, *Danger on the Right*, p. 39; Broyles, *John Birch Society*, p. 46; Welch, *Blue Book*, p. 175.

35. Kolkey, *New Right*, pp. 32–35, 102, 113–18.

36. Barry M. Goldwater, *The Conscience of a Conservative* (Shepherdsville, Ky.: Victor Publishing Company, 1960), p. 22. See also pages 24, 69, 87, 89.

37. Barry M. Goldwater, *Why Not Victory: A Fresh Look at American Foreign Policy* (New York: Macfadden Books, 1962), p. 169.

38. Kolkey, *New Right*, p. 82.

39. Ibid., p. 79.

40. Ibid., p. 77.

41. William A. Rusher, *The Rise of the Right* (New York: William Morrow and Company, 1984), p. 63.

42. Goldwater, *With No Apologies*, p. 99.

43. Toy, "Ideology and Conflict," p. 36; Welch, *Blue Book*, p. 111; Kolkey, *New Right*, p. 209.

44. Forster and Epstein, *Danger on the Right*, pp. 3–4, 217; Alan F. Westin, "The Deadly Parallels: Radical Right and Radical Left," *Harper's Magazine* 224 (April 1962): p. 31.

45. Broyles, *John Birch Society*, p. 103; Forster and Epstein, *Danger on the Right*, pp. 24–25; Toy, "Ideology and Conflict," p. 243; Lipset and Raab, *Politics of Unreason*, p. 322.

46. Ira Rohter, "Radical Rightists: An Empirical Study" (Ph.D. dissertation, Michigan State University, 1967), pp. 173–74; Gerald Schomp, *Birchism Was My Business* (New York: MacMillan and Company, 1970), p. 23.

47. Broyles, *John Birch Society*, pp. 83–84, 92; Stone, "Birch Society of California," p. 68.

48. Toy, "Ideology and Conflict," p. 248; Stone, "Birch Society of California," p. 165; Frederick W. Grupp, Jr., "Social Correlates of Political Activists: The John Birch Society and the A.D.A." (Ph.D. dissertation, University of Pennyslvania, 1968), pp. 224, 263, 294–95, 297–98; California Senate, *Report*, p. 12.

49. California Senate, *Report*, p. 13.

50. Thomas Storke, "How Some Birchers Were Birched," *New York Times Magazine*, 10 December 1961, sec. 6, pp. 9, 101; *New York Times:* 9 March 1961, p. 12; 31 March 1961, p. 10.

51. *Time* 77 (10 March 1961): p. 22.

52. *Los Angeles Times*, 12 March 1961.

53. "New Lord High Executioner?," *America* 105 (22 July 1961): p. 537.

54. Young, "Danger on the Right," p. 7.

55. *Time* 77 (7 April 1961): p. 19.

56. *New York Times*, 8 April 1961, p. 13; George Barrett, "Close-up of the Birchers' Founder" *New York Times Magazine*, 14 May 1961, sec. 6, pp. 13, 89, 91, 92; "The John Birch Society: Patriotic or Irresponsible, it is subject of controversy," *Life* 50 (12 May 1961): p. 124–30; *Newsweek* 57 (10 April 1961): p. 38 (24 April 1961): pp. 43–44; Chester Morrison, "The Man Behind the John Birch Society," *Look* 25 (26 September 1961): pp. 23–27; Stephen M. Young, "Danger on the Right," *Saturday Evening Post* 235 (13 January 1962): pp. 6–7; Athan Theoharis, *Spying on Americans: Political Surveillance from Hoover to the Huston Plan* (Philadelphia: Temple University Press, 1978), pp. 156–166.

57. William F. Buckley, Jr., "The Uproar," *National Review* 10 (22 April 1961): pp. 241, 242, 243.

58. "The Question of Robert Welch," *National Review* 12 (13 February 1962): pp. 84, 88.

59. *National Review* 12 (27 February 1962): p. 140.

60. Gallup, *The Gallup Poll*, pp. 1715, 1756; *National Review* 12 (27 February 1962): pp. 140, 143; *Time* 79 (16 February 1962): p. 23.

61. *The John Birch Society: Twenty-Five Years of Responsible Leadership* (Belmont, Mass.: John Birch Society, 1983), p. 5.

62. Broyles, *John Birch Society*, p. 68.

63. California Senate *Report*, p. 61.

64. Stone, "California Birch Society," pp. 54, 57–58; California Senate *Report*, pp. 53–54; Miles, *Odyssey*, p. 248.

65. Lipset and Raab, *Politics of Unreason*, pp. 270–71; Arnold Forster and Benjamin Epstein, *The Radical Right: Report on the John Birch Society and Its Allies* (New York: Vintage, 1967), p. 185; Grupp, "Social Correlates," p. 70; Rusher, *Rise of the Right*, p. 121.

66. Rusher, *Rise of the Right*, p. 167.

67. Gallup, *Gallup Poll*, p. 1896; Forster and Epstein, *Radical Right*, p. 187; *Los Angeles Times*, 27 September 1964.

68. Miles, *Odyssey*, p. 297. See also, Theodore H. White, *The Making of the President, 1964* (New York: Atheneum, 1965).

69. Forster and Epstein, *Radical Right*, pp. 92, 195–203; Stone, "California Birch Society," p. 26.

70. *John Birch Society: Twenty-Five Years*, pp. 17–25, 29; California Senate *Report*, p. 41; Lipset and Raab, *Politics of Unreason*, pp. 310, 312, 315;

James W. Byrkit, *Forging the Copper Collar: Arizona's Labor-Management War of 1901–1921* (Tucson, University of Arizona Press, 1982), p. 8.

71. Grupp, "Social Correlates," pp. 5, 8, 53, 69, 98, 101, 105, 178, 180, 197, 299, 301–304; Stone, "California Birch Society," pp. 62, 64, 89, 94, 101, 102, 159, 163.

72. Schomp, *Birchism*, p. 12.

73. *New York Times*, 6 April 1961, p. 16; Alan F. Westin, "The John Birch Society: 'Radical Right' and 'Extreme Left' in the Political Context of Post World War II," in Bell, *The Radical Right*, p. 260; Lipset and Raab, *Politics of Unreason*, p. 262; Forster and Epstein, *Radical Right*, p. 113.

74. Lipset and Raab, *Politics of Unreason*, p. 267; Forster and Epstein, *Radical Right*, pp. 96, 99; Robert H. W. Welch, Jr., *The New Americanism: And Other Speeches and Essays* (Belmont, Mass.: Western Islands, 1966), pp. 199, 203 (quote); Kolkey, *New Right*, pp. 160–61.

75. Welch, *Blue Book*, p. 162.

76. *New York Times*, 7 March 1965, p. 72; 28 July 1965, p. 71; 30 October 1965, p. 23; 27 March 1966, p. 78; 10 May 1966, p. 30; Forster and Epstein, *Radical Right*, pp. 140–44; Interview with John McManus, Belmont, Massachusetts, 3 December 1987.

77. Welch, *New Americanism*, pp. 125–36, 149, 171–74; Robert H. W. Welch, Jr., "The Truth in Time," *American Opinion* 9 (November 1966): pp. 1–8, 38; McManus interview.

78. Rohter, "Radical Rightists," p. 222.

79. Welch, "Truth in Time," p. 21.

80. Welch, *New Americanism*, pp. 158–70.

81. Fletcher Knebel, "The GOP Attacks the John Birch Society," *Look* 29 (28 December 1965): p. 74.

82. Forster and Epstein, *Radical Right*, p. 146.

83. Knebel, "GOP Attacks," p. 74.

84. *Newsweek* 65 (27 December 1965): p. 26; Gallup, *Gallup Poll*, p. 1977.

85. Forster and Epstein, *Radical Right*, pp. 83, 131–33, 137; Lipset and Raab, *Politics of Unreason*, pp. 265–66; *New York Times*, 28 August 1966, p. 68; 18 January 1967, p. 36; James Phelan, "Mutiny in the Birch Society," *Saturday Evening Post* 240 (8 April 1967): pp. 21–22, 25.

86. *New York Times*, 8 December 1968, pp. 1, 74 (quote); *American Opinion* 9–12 (1966–1969).

87. *New York Times*, 3 March 1968, p. 42; McManus interview; *Birch Society: Twenty-Five Years*, p. 7.

88. For a more complete discussion of the New Right, its origins, personalities, and organizations see, Kolkey, *New Right;* Alan Crawford, *Thunder on the Right: The 'New Right' and the Politics of Resentment* (New York: Pantheon, 1980); Miles, *Odyssey;* Peter Steinfels, *The Neoconservatives: The Men Who Are Changing America's Politics* (New York: Simon & Schuster, 1979); John S. Saloma III, *Ominous Politics: The New Conservative Labyrinth* (New York: Hill and Wang, 1984); Gillian Peele, *Revival and Reaction: The Right in Contemporary America* (New York: Oxford University Press, 1984).

89. Jerry Falwell, "Introduction," to Richard A. Viguerie, *The New Right: We're Ready to Lead* (Falls Church, Va.: The Viguerie Company, 1980), unpaged.

90. McManus interview; *New York Times*, 11 January 1974, p. 34; Loch Johnson, "Frank Church and the Birchers," *Nation* 219 (19 October 1974): pp. 358–60.

91. John McManus, *The Insiders* (Belmont, Mass.: John Birch Society, 1983), pp. 27, 32, 41; McManus interview.

92. Crawford, *Thunder on the Right*, p. 133; McManus interview.

93. Charles R. Armour, "Year-End Report to our Membership," *Bulletin* No. 334 (Feburary 1987): pp. 3–4; *New York Times:* 8 January 1985, p. B6; 1 September 1986, p. 24.

94. McManus interview.

CHAPTER 7: "WE SHALL NOT BE MOVED": THE STUDENT NONVIOLENT COORDINATING COMMITTEE

1. All headings in this chapter are from Guy and Candie Carawan, eds., *We Shall Overcome!: Songs of the Southern Freedom Movement* (New York: Oak Publications, 1963), pp. 14, 44–45, 60–61, 84, 86–87, 88–89, 91, 93, 106, 111.

2. Frances Fox Piven and Richard Cloward, *Poor People's Movements: Why They Succeed, How They Fail* (New York: Pantheon, 1977), pp. 186–89; Harvard Sitkoff, *The Struggle for Black Equality, 1954–1980* (New York: Hill and Wang, 1981), pp. 4–12.

3. Jack Bloom, *Class, Race and the Civil Rights Movement* (Bloomington: Indiana University Press, 1987), pp. 63–66; Doug McAdam, *Political Process and the Development of Black Insurgency* (Chicago: University of Chicago Press, 1982), pp. 75–78; Harry C. Dillingham and David F. Sly, "The Mechanical Cotton-Picker, Negro Migration, and the Integration Movement," *Human Organization* 25 (Winter 1966): pp. 348–49; Piven and Cloward, *Poor People's Movements*, pp. 182, 190–92; Aldon D. Morris, *The*

Origins of the Civil Rights Movement: Black Communities Organizing for Change (New York: Free Press, 1984), p. 6; Anthony Oberschall, *Social Conflict and Social Movements* (Englewood Cliffs, N.J.: Prentice-Hall, 1973), p. 209.

4. Morris, *Origins*, pp. 1–2; Piven and Cloward, *Poor People's Movements*, pp. 189–90; Louis E. Lomax, *The Negro Revolt* (New York: Harper & Row, 1962), pp 68–69; Oberschall, *Social Conflict*, pp. 209–10, 213; McAdam, *Political Process*, pp. 97–98.

5. Piven and Cloward, *Poor People's Movements*, pp. 195–98; McAdam, *Political Process*, pp. 79–81, 157.

6. Bloom, *Class*, pp. 83–85; Doug McAdam, "The Decline of the Civil Rights Movement," in Jo Freeman, ed., *Social Movements of the Sixties and Seventies* (New York: Longman, 1983), pp. 306–7; Piven and Cloward, *Poor People's Movements*, pp. 198–202, 214–15, 217, 220; McAdam, *Political Process*, pp. 81–82, 86.

7. Bloom, *Class*, p. 90; Oberschall, *Social Conflict*, p. 206; Piven and Cloward, *Poor People's Movements*, p. 207; McAdam, *Political Process*, p. 84.

8. Piven and Cloward, *Poor People's Movements*, pp. 182, 203–5; Morris, *Origins*, pp. 3–4; McAdam, *Political Process*, pp. 127–29.

9. Morris, *Origins*, pp. 4–6, 9–11, 15; McAdam, *Political Process*, pp. 87–90; Jo Freeman, "On the Origins of Social Movements," in Freeman, ed., *Social Movements*, pp. 10–12; Oberschall, *Social Conflict*, pp. 221–22.

10. Morris, *Origins*, pp. 16, 40, 43.

11. Morris, *Origins*, pp. 12–16, 76–77, 83–92, 129–35, 193. For more on the Congress of Racial Equality see, August Meier and Elliott Rudwick, *CORE: A Study in the Civil Rights Movement, 1942–1968* (New York: Oxford University Press, 1973).

12. Bloom, *Class*, pp. 108, 152; Lomax, *Negro Revolt*, p. 75; Piven and Cloward, *Poor People's Movements*, pp. 211–12.

13. Sitkoff, *Struggle*, pp. 65–66; Bloom, *Class*, pp. 98–99, 101, 108–10; McAdam, *Political Process*, pp. 144–45.

14. Oberschall, *Social Conflict*, pp. 217–19.

15. Lomax, *Negro Revolt*, pp. 74–75, 78; Bloom, *Class*, p. 134; Sitkoff, *Struggle*, p. 67; Morris, *Origins*, pp. 188, 193–94.

16. Morris, *Origins*, pp. 195–202, 212–13; Clayborne Carson, *In Struggle: SNCC and the Black Awakening of the 1960s* (Cambridge, Mass.: Harvard University Press, 1981), pp. 9–15; McAdam, *Political Process*, pp. 250–51; Donald R. Matthews and James W. Prothro, *Negros and the New Southern Politics* (New York: Harcourt, Brace & World, 1966), pp. 412–18. See also,

Robert A. Goldberg, "Racial Change on the Southern Periphery: The Case of San Antonio, Texas, 1960–1965," *Journal of Southern History* 49 (August 1983): pp. 349–74.

17. Cleveland Sellers with Robert Terrell, *The River of No Return: The Autobiography of a Black Militant and the Life and Death of SNCC* (New York: William Morrow & Company, 1973), p. 18.

18. Howard Zinn, *SNCC: The New Abolitionists* (Boston: Beacon Press, 1965), p. 17.

19. Jack Newfield, *The Education of Jack Newfield* (New York: St. Martin's Press, 1980), p. 167.

20. Bloom, *Class*, p. 161.

21. Zinn, *SNCC*, p. 18; Bloom, *Class*, p. 157; Oberschall, *Social Conflict*, p. 226.

22. James Forman, *The Making of Black Revolutionaries* (Washington, D.C.: Open Hand Publications, 1985), pp. 215–16; Morris, *Origins*, pp. 215–17; Carson, *In Struggle*, p. 20; Zinn, *SNCC*, pp. 32–33.

23. Carson, *In Struggle*, pp. 20–22, 24; Sellers, *River*, p. 34; Zinn, *SNCC*, pp. 19–20; Morris, *Origins*, pp. 174–78, 218.

24. David J. Garrow, *Bearing the Cross: Martin Luther King, Jr., and the Southern Christian Leadership Conference* (New York: William Morrow & Company, 1986), p. 132; Carson, *In Struggle*, pp. 22–23; Emily Schottenfeld Stoper, "The Student Nonviolent Coordinating Committee: The Growth of Radicalism in a Civil Rights Organization" (Ph.D. dissertation, Harvard University, 1968), pp. 169–71; Sellers, *River*, p. 35.

25. Morris, *Origins*, pp. 219–21; Carson, *In Struggle*, pp. 19, 25–26; Forman, *Making*, pp. 218–19; McAdam, *Political Process*, p. 253; Zinn, *SNCC*, p. 36.

26. Carson, *In Struggle*, pp. 27–31; Forman, *Making*, pp. 219, 423; Zinn, *SNCC*, p. 37.

27. Meier and Rudwick, *CORE*, pp. 135–158; James Peck, *Freedom Ride* (New York: Grove Press, 1962), pp. 88–101; Carson, *In Struggle*, pp. 33–34.

28. Carson, *In Struggle*, pp. 34–36; Zinn, *SNCC*, pp. 45–54.

29. McAdam, *Political Process*, p. 253; Carson, *In Struggle*, pp. 37–38; Sellers, *River*, pp. 46–47; Allen J. Matusow, "From Civil Rights to Black Power: The Case of SNCC, 1960–1966," in Barton J. Bernstein and Alan J. Matusow, eds., *Twentieth Century America: Recent Interpretations* (New York: Harcourt, Brace, 1972), pp. 498–99.

30. Steven F. Lawson, *Black Ballots: Voting Rights in the South, 1944–1969* (New York: Columbia University Press, 1976), p. 279.

31. Garrow, *Bearing the Cross*, pp. 162–63; Lomax, *Negro Revolt*, pp. 232–33; Lawson, *Black Ballots*, pp. 261–66.

32. Piven and Cloward, *Poor People's Movements*, pp. 225–27, 231–32; Theodore C. Sorensen, *Kennedy* (New York: Harper & Row, 1965), pp. 478–79; McAdam, *Political Process*, pp. 157–58.

33. Sorensen, *Kennedy*, p. 471.

34. Zinn, *SNCC*, p. 204; Lawson, *Black Ballots*, pp. 255, 259–60; Piven and Cloward, *Poor People's Movements*, pp. 227–29; Bruce Miroff, *Pragmatic Illusions: The Presidential Politics of John F. Kennedy* (New York: McKay, 1976), pp. 223–70.

35. Morris, *Origins*, p. 239; Carson, *In Struggle*, pp. 39–42.

36. Piven and Cloward, *Poor People's Movements*, p. 234; Oberschall, *Social Conflict*, pp. 210–11.

37. Carson, *In Struggle*, pp. 26, 41, 45–47, 49; Zinn, *SNCC*, pp. 58, 62–68, 72.

38. Carson, *In Struggle*, pp. 48–50, 54; Zinn, *SNCC*, pp. 68–70, 74–77.

39. Interview with Unita Blackwell, Salt Lake City, Utah, 19 January 1988; Zinn *SNCC*, pp. 79–84; Mary King, *Freedom Song: A Personal Story of the 1960s Civil Rights Movement* (William Morrow & Company, 1987), p. 35.

40. Zinn, *SNCC*, pp. 82, 85–86, 88–91; Carson, *In Struggle*, pp. 79–81.

41. Carson, *In Struggle*, p. 83; Zinn, *SNCC*, pp. 192, 195–96, 198–201; Lawson, *Black Ballots*, pp. 279–82, 287.

42. Zinn, *SNCC*, pp. 223–31.

43. King, *Freedom Song*, pp. 7–8.

44. Carson, *In Struggle*, pp. 56–58, 74–75; Zinn, *SNCC*, pp. 123–37, 145–46.

45. Garrow, *Bearing the Cross*, pp. 175–76; Morris, *Origins*, pp. 241–42.

46. Carson, *In Struggle*, pp. 60–62; Morris, *Origins*, pp. 243–48.

47. David J. Garrow, *Protest at Selma: Martin Luther King, Jr., and the Voting Rights Act of 1965* (New Haven, Conn.: Yale University Press, 1978), pp. 2–3; Piven and Cloward, *Poor People's Movements*, pp. 241–44, 246; Sorensen, *Kennedy*, pp. 495–97.

48. Garrow, *Bearing the Cross*, pp. 166–67, 423; Carson, *In Struggle*, pp. 62–65, 85.

49. Zinn, *SNCC*, pp. 3, 9–10; Forman, *Making of Black Revolutionaries*, p. 304; Carson, *In Struggle*, pp. 69–71, 90; King, *Song*, pp. 35, 274.

50. Carson, *In Struggle*, pp. 50, 66–68; Stoper, "Student Nonviolent Coordinating Committee," pp. 121–22; Forman, *Making of Black Revolutionaries*, pp. 423–24.

51. Carson, *In Struggle*, pp. 93–95; Garrow, *Bearing the Cross*, pp. 281–83.

52. Garrow, *Bearing the Cross*, p. 296.

53. Theodore H. White, "Power Structure, Integration, Militancy, Freedom Now!" *Life* 55 (29 November 1963): pp. 86, 87.

54. Carson, *In Struggle*, pp. 96–98; Zinn, *SNCC*, pp. 250–51.

55. Carson, *In Struggle*, pp. 108–10.

56. Zinn, *SNCC*, pp. 183, 186, 188; Carson, *In Struggle*, pp. 98–100, 112, 121.

57. King, *Song*, p. 520; Carson, *In Struggle*, pp. 101, 107–8.

58. Elizabeth Sutherland, ed., *Letters from Mississippi* (New York: McGraw-Hill, 1965), p. 35; Carson, *In Struggle*, pp. 117, 119.

59. Sutherland, *Letters*, p. 149.

60. Sellers, *River*, p. 106.

61. Sitkoff, *Struggle*, p. 177.

62. Sutherland, *Letters*, p. 203.

63. Mary Aicken Rothschild, *A Case of Black and White: Northern Volunteers and the Southern Freedom Summer, 1964–1965* (Westport, Conn.: Greenwood, 1982), p. 179.

64. Sutherland, *Letters*, pp. 3, 5–6, 58–59; Gary Marx and Michael Useem, "Majority Involvement in Minority Movements: Civil Rights, Abolition, and Untouchability," *Journal of Social Issues*, 27 (1971): pp. 85–86, 90, 92, 96–97, 100.

65. Sitkoff, *Struggle*, pp. 181–84; Blackwell interview; Matusow, "From Civil Rights," pp. 505–6; Carson, *In Struggle*, pp. 124–26.

66. King, *Song*, p. 523.

67. Sellers, *River*, p. 111.

68. Carson, *In Struggle*, pp. 127–29; 137–39; Forman, *Making of Black Revolutionaries*, pp. 395–96; Stoper, "Student Nonviolent Coordinating Committee," pp. 124–28.

69. Carson, *In Struggle*, p. 140.

70. Bloom, *Class*, p. 194.

71. Carson, *In Struggle*, p. 155.

72. Carson, *In Struggle*, pp. 133–35, 137–47, 155; Forman, *Making of Black Revolutionaries*, pp. 413–14, 420–22, 424–25; King, *Song*, pp. 443–55. For more on SNCC and feminism see Chapter 9.

73. Sellers, *River*, p. 130; Carson, *In Struggle*, pp. 149–50, 173–74; Blackwell interview.

74. Carson, *In Struggle*, pp. 157–59; Sitkoff, *Struggle*, pp. 187–88.

75. Sitkoff, *Struggle*, pp. 188–97; Carson, *In Struggle*, pp. 153, 162–65, 170; King, *Song*, p. 514.

76. Piven and Cloward, *Poor People's Movements*, pp. 252–54.

77. "Waving the Red Flag," *Newsweek* 65 (12 April 1965): p. 30.

78. Oberschall, *Social Conflict*, pp. 207–8; Sitkoff, *Struggle*, pp. 200–3; McAdam, "Decline," pp. 308–12; McAdam, *Political Process*, pp. 159, 201; George Gallup, *The Gallup Poll: Public Opinion 1935–1987* (New York: Random House, 1986), pp. 1933, 1934.

79. McAdam, *Political Process*, pp. 183–84, 228; Carson, *In Struggle*, p. 261.

80. Stoper, "Student Nonviolent Coordinating Committee," pp. 18–19, 53; King, *Song*, pp. 518–19; McAdam, "Decline," p. 304.

81. Blackwell interview.

82. Carson, *In Struggle*, pp. 162–63, 184–88, 191, 201–3; Matusow, "From Civil Rights," p. 512.

83. Sellers, *River*, p. 166.

84. *New York Times:* 7 June 1966, pp. 1, 26; 9 June 1966, pp. 1, 33; 17 June 1966, pp. 1, 33; Garrow, *Bearing the Cross*, pp. 481–87; Sitkoff, *Struggle*, pp. 209–10, 213.

85. Stokely Carmichael and Charles V. Hamilton, *Black Power: The Politics of Liberation in America* (New York: Vintage, 1967), p. 44.

86. Ibid., pp. 34, 37, 43, 47, 54; Stokely Carmichael, "What We Want," *New York Review of Books* 7 (22 September 1966): pp. 5–6, 8.

87. "Waving the Red Flag," *Newsweek*: p. 31.

88. "The New Racism," *Time* 88 (1 July 1966): p. 11.

89. "Backlash," *Saturday Evening Post* 238 (10 September 1966): p. 88.

90. *Newsweek* 68 (19 September 1966): p. 32.

91. Garrow, *Bearing the Cross*, p. 489; Bloom, *Class*, pp. 209–10; Carson, *In Struggle*, pp. 219–20, 224. See also, Lerone Bennett, Jr., "SNCC: Rebels With A Cause," *Ebony* 20 (July 1965): pp. 146–53; Andrew Kopkind, "New Radicals in Dixie," *New Republic* 152 (10 April 1965): pp. 13–16; Gene Roberts, "The Story of Snick: From 'Freedom High' to 'Black Power'," *New York Times Magazine*, 25 September 1966, sec. 6, pp. 27–29, 119–20, 122, 124, 126, 128.

92. Forman, *Making of Black Revolutionaries*, pp. 471–72; Carson, *In Struggle*, pp. 225–26, 234, 262 (quote).

93. "SNCC and the Jews," *Newsweek* 70 (28 August 1967): p. 22.

94. Carson, *In Struggle*, pp. 196–98, 236–38, 240–41, 267–69, 296; Sellers, *River*, pp. 193–94, 203.

95. Forman, *Making of Black Revolutionaries*, p. 504.

96. Carson, *In Struggle*, pp. 244–49, 251–53, 256, 288–90, 297–98; Sellers, *River*, pp. 241, 257–59; *New York Times*, 10 May 1973, p. 12.

97. Sellers, *River*, pp. 184, 207; Carson, *In Struggle*, pp. 278–85, 292–93, 296–98; Forman, *Making of Black Revolutionaries*, pp. 527–37.

98. Alphonso Pinkney, *The Myth of Black Progress* (New York: Cambridge University Press, 1984), pp. 19–21; Sellers, *River*, pp. 253–54; McAdam, *Political Process*, pp. 185–88, 195–97.

99. Carson, *In Struggle*, pp. 305–6; King, *Song*, pp. 535–36.

100. Morris, *Origins*, p. 289; Sitkoff, *Struggle*, pp. 229, 234–36; *New York Times*, 17 January 1988, sec. 4, p. 1 and 11 September 1988, p. 4; Andrew Hacker, "American Apartheid," *New York Review of Books* 34 (3 December 1987): pp. 26–33; "Black and White in America," *Newsweek* 91 (7 March 1988): pp. 20, 21, 43.

101. Sitkoff, *Struggle*, pp. 231–34; Pinkney, *Myth*, pp. 171, 177; *Salt Lake Tribune*, 7 March 1988; *Report of the National Advisory Commission on Civil Disorders* (New York: Bantam Books, 1968), p. 1.

CHAPTER 8: THE CAMPUS REVOLT:
THE BERKELEY FREE SPEECH MOVEMENT

1. Max Heirich, *The Beginning: Berkeley, 1964* (New York: Columbia University Press, 1968), pp. 199–200.

2. *Newsweek*, 108 (15 October 1984): p. 92.

3. Landon Y. Jones, *Great Expectations: America and the Baby Boom Generation* (New York: Coward, McGann, and Geoghegan, 1980), pp. 1, 39, 398.

4. Todd Gitlin, *The Whole World Is Watching: Mass Media in the Making and Unmaking of the New Left* (Berkeley: University of California Press, 1980), p. 239; Jones, *Great Expectations*, pp. 90–94.

5. Wini Breines, *Community and Organization in the New Left, 1962–1968: The Great Refusal* (New York: Praeger, 1982), pp. 99–101; Clark Kerr, "The Frantic Race to Remain Contemporary," in Michael V. Miller and Susan Gilmore, eds., *Revolution at Berkeley: The Crisis in American Education* (New York: Dell Publishing Co., 1965), pp. 5, 14–17, 24; Clark Kerr, "Uses of the University," in Immanuel Wallerstein and Paul Starr, eds., *The University Crisis Reader: The Liberal University Under Attack*, vol. 1 (New York: Random House, 1971), pp. 80–86.

6. Anthony Oberschall, *Social Conflict and Social Movements* (Englewood Cliffs, N.J.: Prentice-Hall, 1973), p. 277; Carl Davidson, "The Multiversity: Crucible of the New Working Class," in Wallerstein and Starr, eds., *The University Crisis Reader*, vol. 1, pp. 188–90, 194–97; Bruce Payne, David Walls, and Jerry Berman, "Theodicy of 1984: The Philosophy of Clark Kerr," in Mitchell Cohen and Dennis Hale, eds., *The New Student Left: An Anthology* (Boston: Beacon Press, 1966), pp. 235–36; Max Heirich, *Beginning*, pp. 14–15; Clark Kerr, "Student Dissent and Confrontational Politics," in Julian Foster and Durward Long, eds., *Protest! Student Activism in America* (New York: William Morrow & Company, 1970), p. 10.

7. Irwin Unger, *The Movement: A History of the American New Left, 1959–1972* (New York: Dodd, Mead & Co., 1974), p. 64; Heirich, *Beginning*, pp. 7–9; Sheldon S. Wolin and John H. Schaar, "The Abuses of the Multiversity," *New York Review of Books* 12 (11 March 1965): pp. 352–53; James Cass, "What Happened at Berkeley," *Saturday Review* 48 (16 January 1965): 67; Verne A. Stadtman, *The University of California, 1869–1968* (New York: McGraw-Hill, 1970), pp. 435–36.

8. E. Joseph Shoben, Jr., "The Climate of Protest," in Foster and Long, eds., *Protest*, pp. 555–56; Theodore Roszak, *The Making of a Counter Culture: Reflections on the Technocratic Society and Its Youthful Opposition* (Garden City, N.Y.: Doubleday, 1969), pp. 27–28; Seymour Martin Lipset, *Rebellion in the University* (Chicago, University of Chicago Press, 1976), pp. 35–36, 262.

9. "The Port Huron Statement," in Ronald Lora, ed., *America in the '60s: Cultural Authorities in Transition* (New York: John Wiley & Sons, 1974), p. 265.

10. Charles Perrow, "The Sixties Observed," in Mayer N. Zald and John D. McCarthy, eds., *The Dynamics of Social Movements: Resource Mobilization, Social Control, and Tactics* (Cambridge, Mass.: Winthrop Publishers, 1979), pp. 193, 198; Irving Louis Horowitz and William H. Friedland, *The Knowledge Factory: Student Power and Academic Politics in America* (Chicago: Aldine Publishing Co., 1970), pp. 85–86; Paul Jacobs and Saul Landau, *The New Radicals: A Report with Documents* (New York: Random House, 1966), pp. 213–14.

11. Heirich, *Beginning*, pp. 29–31, 35–37; David Horowitz, *Student: The Political Activities of Berkeley Students* (New York: Ballantine, 1962), pp. 18–20; Hal Draper, *Berkeley: The New Student Revolt* (New York: Grove Press, 1965), pp. 88–90; Michael Rossman, *Wedding Within the War* (New York: Doubleday, 1971), 30, 85–86; W. J. Rorabaugh, "The Berkeley Free Speech Movement," in James L. Rawls, ed., *New Directions in California History* (New York: McGraw-Hill, 1988), p. 335; Max Heirich and Sam

Kaplan, "Yesterday's Discord," in Seymour Martin Lipset and Sheldon Wolin, eds., *The Berkeley Student Revolt: Facts and Interpretations* (Garden City, N.Y.: Anchor Press, 1965), pp. 18–21.

12. Rossman, *Wedding*, p. 34.

13. Heirich and Kaplan, "Yesterday's Discord," p. 22; Heirich, *Beginning*, pp. 38–42; Horowitz, *Student*, pp. 68–82; Rossman, *Wedding*, p. 86; Unger, *The Movement*, pp. 45–46.

14. Rossman, *Wedding*, pp. 50–51.

15. Roszak, *Making*, pp. 66, 82, 206, 236–37; Horowitz and Friedland, *Knowledge Factory*, p. 87; Unger, *The Movement*, pp. 17–18; Heirich, *Beginning*, pp. 20–23; Henry May, "The Student Movement at Berkeley: Some Impressions," in Lipset and Wolin, eds., *Berkeley Student Revolt*, p. 455.

16. Christopher Lasch, *The Culture of Narcissism: American Life in an Age of Diminishing Expectations* (New York: Norton, 1979), p. 257; Kenneth Kenniston, "Sources of Student Discontent," in Edward E. Sampson and Harold A. Korn, eds., *Student Activism and Protest* (San Francisco: Jossey-Bass, 1970), pp. 163–64; Stadtman, *University*, pp. 439–40.

17. Frederick W. Obear, "Student Activism in the Sixties," in Foster and Long, eds., *Protest*, p. 15.

18. Maurice Isserman, *If I Had a Hammer... : The Death of the Old Left and the Birth of the New Left* (New York: Basic Books, 1987), pp. 202–4, 208, 213–14, 218–19; Armand L. Mauss, "The Lost Promise of Reconciliation: New Left vs. Old Left," *Journal of Social Issues* 27 (1971): 3–14; Richard Flacks, "The Liberated Generation: An Exploration of the Roots of Student Protest," *Journal of Social Issues* 23 (July 1967): 56–57; Richard Flacks, "The New Left and American Politics After Ten Years," *Journal of Social Issues* 27 (1971): 21–23, 25–26; Unger, *The Movement*, pp. 52–61; Wini Breines, *Community*, pp. 97, 123–26; James Miller, *"Democracy Is in the Streets:" From Port Huron to the Siege of Chicago* (New York: Simon & Schuster, 1987), pp. 184–89. For more on SDS, see Kirkpatrick Sale, *SDS* (New York: Random House, 1973).

19. Unger, *The Movement*, pp. 47–48; Hal Draper, *Berkeley:* pp. 23–24; Rossman, *Wedding*, pp. 88–89; Heirich, *Beginning*, pp. 43–45.

20. Rorabaugh, "Berkeley," p. 336; Heirich, *Beginning*, p. 50.

21. Rorabaugh, "Berkeley," p. 334; Heirich, *Beginning*, pp. 27–29; Terry F. Lunsford, *The "Free Speech" Crisis at Berkeley, 1964–1965: Some Issues for Social and Legal Research* (Berkeley: University of California Press, 1965), p. 4.

22. Heirich, *Beginning*, p. 51.

23. Rorabaugh, "Berkeley," pp. 335–36; Heirich, *Beginning*, pp. 50–51, 53–54, 56–57.

24. Conservatives would later withdraw from the coalition. While maintaining support for free speech, they felt powerless to effect movement decision making and rejected direct-action means that violated university regulations.

25. Rossman, *Wedding*, p. 89.

26. Heirich, *Beginning*, p. 93.

27. Lunsford, *"Free Speech Crisis,"* p. 4; Heirich, *Beginning*, p. 65, 295; Max Heirich, *The Spiral of Conflict, Berkeley, 1964* (New York: Columbia University Press, 1971), p. 200; Rossman, *Wedding*, p. 89.

28. "(I'm Going to) Put My Name Down," in Hal Draper, ed., "The FSM Papers" (Berkeley, Microfilm, 1965?).

29. Heirich, *Beginning*, p. 72.

30. Heirich, *Beginning*, pp. 71–72; Lipset and Wolin, eds., *Berkeley Student Revolt*, pp. 103, 105, 106.

31. Lipset and Wolin, *Berkeley Student Revolt*, p. 109.

32. Heirich, *Beginning*, pp. 77–78, 87; Lipset and Wolin, eds., *Berkeley Student Revolt*, pp. 107–10.

33. Draper, *Berkeley*, p. 40.

34. Lunsford, *"Free Speech Crisis,"* p. 5; Heirich, *Beginning*, pp. 102–3.

35. Heirich, *Beginning*, p. 112.

36. Lipset and Wolin, *Berkeley Student Revolt*, p. 111; Heirich, *Beginning*, pp. 104–6, 110, 112.

37. Bradford Cleaveland, "A Letter to Undergraduates," in Lipset and Wolin, eds., *Berkeley Student Revolt*, pp. 66–75.

38. Jacobs and Landau, eds., *New Radicals*, p. 216.

39. Horowitz and Friedland, *Knowledge Factory*, pp. 13–14; Heirich, *Spiral*, pp. 194–95; Draper, *Berkeley*, pp. 153–55; Lipset and Wolin, *Berkeley Student Revolt*, pp. 209–16; Paul Lauter and Florence Howe, *The Conspiracy of the Young* (New York: World Publishing Co., 1971), pp. 85–86.

40. Draper, *Berkeley*, p. 51.

41. Lipset and Wolin, eds., *Berkeley Student Revolt*, p. 114.

42. Heirich, *Beginning*, pp. 114–15, 121.

43. Lipset and Wolin, eds., *Berkeley Student Revolt*, pp. 115–16.

44. Draper, *Berkeley*, p. 55; Lipset and Wolin, eds., *Berkeley Student Revolt*, pp. 116–17.

45. Draper, *Berkeley*, pp. 52–56; Heirich, *Beginning*, pp. 121–22, 135, 137, 139–44.

46. Heirich, *Beginning*, p. 123; Colin Miller, "The Press and the Student Revolt," in Miller and Gilmore, eds., *Revolution*, pp. 314–15, 318, 320–22.

47. Draper, *Berkeley*, p. 179.

48. Draper, ed., "FSM Papers," pp. 161–65, 340–41; Heirich, *Beginning*, p. 146; Calvin Trillin, "Letter from Berkeley," pp. 273–75, John Searle, "The Faculty Resolution," p. 103 in Miller and Gilmore, eds., *Revolution*; Rorabaugh, "Berkeley," p. 341; Lewis S. Feuer, *The Conflict of Generations: The Character and Significance of Student Movements* (New York: Basic Books, 1969), p. 423.

49. *FSM Newsletter*, 2 November 1964; Draper, *Berkeley*, pp. 61–63; Heirich, *Beginning*, p. 303.

50. Draper, *Berkeley*, pp. 215–19.

51. A. H. Raskin, "The Berkeley Affair: Mr. Kerr vs. Mr. Savio and Co.," in Lipset and Wolin, eds., *Berkeley Student Revolt*, 426; Rorabaugh, "Berkeley," pp. 333–34.

52. Heirich, *Spiral*, pp. 220–22; 264, 338.

53. Draper, "FSM Papers," pp. 166–67; Stadtman, *University*, pp. 453–55.

54. Trillin, "Letter," p. 266.

55. Lipset and Wolin, eds., *Berkeley Student Revolt*, pp. 122–25, 129–31.

56. Ibid., p. 161.

57. Heirich, *Beginning*, pp. 159–62, 164; Lipset and Wolin, eds., *Berkeley Student Revolt*, pp. 128, 132.

58. Heirich, *Beginning*, p. 157.

59. Lipset and Wolin, eds., *Berkeley Student Revolt*, pp. 141–42, 145; Draper, *Berkeley*, pp. 73–79; Heirich, *Beginning*, pp. 172–73.

60. Lipset and Wolin, eds., *Berkeley Student Revolt*, p. 205.

61. Draper, *Berkeley*, pp. 80–84; *FSM Newsletter*, 2, 17 November 1964; Lipset and Wolin, eds., *Berkeley Student Revolt*, pp. 143–44, 149.

62. Draper, *Berkeley*, pp. 82–84; Heirich, *Beginning*, p. 169.

63. Lipset and Wolin, eds., *Berkeley Student Revolt*, pp. 147–48.

64. Heirich, *Beginning*, p. 178; Draper, *Berkeley*, p. 85.

65. Lipset and Wolin, eds., *Berkeley Student Revolt*, pp. 154–55, 560–74; Draper, *Berkeley*, pp. 85–88.

66. Heirich, *Beginning*, p. 183.

67. Draper, *Berkeley*, p. 90.

68. Ibid., pp. 89–90.

69. Lipset and Wolin, eds., *Berkeley Student Revolt*, pp. 158–59; Heirich, *Beginning*, pp. 188–92.

70. Draper, *Berkeley*, pp. 95–96; Heirich, *Beginning*, pp. 193–94.

71. Lipset and Wolin, eds., *Berkeley Student Revolt*, pp. 161–63, 246.

72. Heirich, *Beginning*, pp. 198–202; Draper, ed., "FSM Papers," p. 490; Rorabaugh, "Berkeley," p. 340.

73. Watts and Whittaker, "Free Speech Advocates," 53–54.

74. Heirich, *Spiral*, pp. 208–10, 212–13, 348; Glen Lyonns, "The Police Car Demonstration: A Survey of Participants," pp. 519–30, Robert H. Somers, "The Mainsprings of the Rebellion: A Survey of Berkeley Students in November, 1964," 530–57 in Lipset and Wolin, eds., *Berkeley Student Revolt.*

75. Leonard L. Baird, "Who Protests: A Study of Student Activists," pp. 123–33; Richard Flacks, "Who Protests: The Social Bases of the Student Movement," pp. 134–57 in Foster and Long, eds., *Protest!;* Flacks, "Liberated Generation," pp. 55, 60, 65–72; Feuer, *Conflict*, pp. 488, 514, 524.

76. Heirich, *Beginning*, p. 207.

77. Draper, ed., "FSM Papers," p. 398; Heirich, *Beginning*, p. 216.

78. Lipset and Wolin, eds., *Berkeley Student Revolt*, pp. 166–68, 173–74.

79. Heirich, *Beginning*, pp. 213, 215–16, 218, 227; Heirich, *Spiral*, pp. 345, 347, 350–51.

80. Lipset and Wolin, eds., *Berkeley Student Revolt*, pp. 174–76; Draper, *Berkeley*, pp. 117–18.

81. Heirich, *Beginning*, pp. 221–26.

82. Lipset and Wolin, eds., *Berkeley Student Revolt*, pp. 252–64, 267–80, 285–303; Draper, ed., "FSM Papers," pp. 179–80; Sidney Hook, "Academic Freedom and the Rights of Students," pp. 39–40, Searle, "Faculty Resolution," pp. 96–98, Trillin, "Letter," p. 262, James F. Petras and Michael Shute, "Berkeley '65," pp. 208–14 in Miller and Gilmore, eds., *Revolution.*

83. Lipset and Wolin, eds., *Berkeley Student Revolt*, p. 182.

84. Heirich, *Beginning*, pp. 209–12; Searle, "Faculty Resolution," pp. 92–93; *FSM Newsletter*, 10 December 1964.

85. Heirich, *Beginning*, p. 248.

86. Lipset and Wolin, *Berkeley Student Revolt*, pp. 194, 197–98, 579–80; Heirich, *Beginning*, pp. 248–50.

87. Breines, *Community*, p. 29.

88. Draper, *Berkeley*, pp. 137–38; Stadtman, *University*, pp. 472–73; Heirich, *Beginning*, pp. 252–53; *New York Times*, 1 July 1967, p. 21.

89. Lipset and Wolin, *Berkeley Student Revolt*, pp. 581, 584; Draper, ed., "FSM Papers"; Lipset, *Rebellion*, pp. 63–64.

90. Draper, *Berkeley*, pp. 142–43.

91. Lunsford, *"Free Speech Crisis,"* p. 12.

92. Unger, *The Movement*, pp. 76–79; Heirich, *Beginning*, pp. 256–62; Draper, *Berkeley*, pp. 140–47.

93. Draper, *Berkeley*, p. 148; Draper, "Free Speech Papers"; *Los Angeles Times:* 24 March 1982; 12 June 1988. The career paths of the Berkeley activists have been diverse. Mario Savio left Berkeley without receiving a degree. He later enrolled at San Francisco State University and graduated in 1984. Art Goldberg attended law school at Rutgers University and now serves as a "people's" lawyer in Los Angeles. Bettina Aptheker is the coordinator of Feminist Studies at the University of California, Santa Cruz. Michael Rossman remained in Berkeley where he teaches in a Montessori School. Jack Weinberg organizes steel workers in Gary, Indiana.

94. Lipset and Wolin, *Berkeley Student Revolt*, p. 430.

95. Draper, *Berkeley*, pp. 151–52, 234–37; Heirich, *Beginning*, pp. 273–74, 277; Stadtman, *University*, pp. 483, 487, 492; A. H. Raskin, "Where it all Began—Berkeley, 5 Years Later, Is Radicalized, Reaganized, Mesmerized," *New York Times Magazine*, 11 January 1970, sec. 6, p. 85.

96. Jerry Rubin, *DO It: Scenarios of the Revolution* (New York: Simon & Schuster, 1970), p. 23.

97. Flacks, "New Left," pp. 30–31; Horowitz and Friedland, *Knowledge Factory*, pp. 50–59; Unger, *The Movement*, pp. 80–85; Lipset, *Rebellion*, pp. 43–46, 65–67.

98. Allen J. Matusow, *The Unraveling of America: A History of Liberalism in the 1960s* (New York: Harper & Row, 1984), pp. 305–6; Jones, *Great Expectations*, pp. 121–34.

99. Unger, *The Movement*, pp. 201–8; Anthony Oberschall, "The Decline of the 1960s Social Movements," in Louis Kriesberg, ed., *Research in Social Movements, Conflicts and Change* vol. 1 (Greenwich, Conn.: JAI Press, 1978), pp. 277–83.

100. Morris Dickstein, "Columbia Recovered," *New York Times Magazine*, 15 May 1988, sec. 6, p. 68; *The Nation* 246 (26 March 1988): pp. 405–36.

CHAPTER 9: NEVER ANOTHER SEASON OF SILENCE: THE NATIONAL ORGANIZATION FOR WOMEN

1. "The *Fortune* Survey: Women in America," *Fortune* 34 (August 1946): pp. 6, 8, 10, 14.

2. Barbara Deckard, *The Women's Movement: Political, Socioeconomic, and Psychological Issues* (New York: Harper & Row, 1979), p. 361.

3. Ibid., pp. 361, 407; *Psychology Today* 5 (March 1972): p. 63; "The Feminization of Power" (Washington, D.C.: Fund for the Feminist Majority, 1988).

4. William H. Chafe, *The American Woman: Her Changing Social, Economic, and Political Roles, 1920–1970* (New York: Oxford University Press, 1972), pp. 135–48; Jo Freeman, *The Politics of Women's Liberation: A Case Study of an Emerging Social Movement and Its Relation to the Policy Process* (New York: McKay, 1975), pp. 21–22.

5. Chafe, *American Woman*, pp. 175–84; Sara Rix, ed., *The American Woman, 1987–88: A Report in Depth* (New York: Norton, 1987), p. 107.

6. Chafe, *American Woman*, p. 251.

7. Chafe, *American Woman*, pp. 190–93; Laura Bergquist, "A New Look at the American Woman," *Look* 20 (16 October 1956): pp. 35, 40.

8. "On Modern Marriage," *Life* 41 (24 December 1956): p. 110.

9. Betty Friedan, *The Feminine Mystique* (New York: Norton, 1963), pp. 14–22, 29–31, 37–54; Betty Friedan, *"It Changed My Life": Writings on the Women's Movement* (New York: Random House, 1985), pp. 48–50, 62; Glenda Riley, *Inventing the American Woman: A Perspective on Women's History* (Arlington Heights, Ill.: Harlan Davidson, 1986), pp. 238–40; Ginny Foat with Laura Foreman, *Never Guilty, Never Free* (New York: Random House, 1985), p. 18.

10. *Look* (16 October 1956): p. 54.

11. Edwin Diamond, "Young Wives," *Newsweek* 55 (7 March 1960): p. 57.

12. Riley, *Inventing*, pp. 241–42; William H. Chafe, "The Paradox of Progress," in Jane E. Friedman and William G. Shade, eds., *Our American Sisters: Women in American Life and Thought* (Lexington, Mass.: D.C. Heath, 1982), pp. 568–69; Friedan, *Feminine Mystique*, pp. 54, 172, 226, 241.

13. Judith Hole and Ellen Levine, *Rebirth of Feminism* (New York: Quadrangle, 1971), p. 24.

14. Ibid., pp. 19–24, 435–40.

15. Cynthia E. Harrison, "A 'New Frontier' for Women: The Public Policy of the Kennedy Administration," *Journal of American History* 67 (December 1980): pp. 643–45; Freeman, *Politics*, pp. 52–53, 226, 228.

16. Friedan, *Feminine Mystique*, pp. 30, 31, 226, 351, passim.

17. Freeman, *Politics*, p. 229.

18. Harrison, "New Frontier," 642; Hole and Levine, *Rebirth*, pp. 28–31; Evans, *Personal Politics*, p. 17.

19. Hoyt Gimlin, ed., *The Women's Movement: Achievements and Effects* (Washington, D.C.: Congressional Quarterly Inc., 1977), pp. 30–31.

20. Freeman, *Politics*, p. 54.

21. Mary Frances Berry, *Why the ERA Failed: Politics, Women's Rights, and the Amending Process of the Constitution* (Bloomington: Indiana University Press, 1986), p. 61; Hole and Levine, *Rebirth*, p. 35.

22. Sara Evans, *Personal Politics: The Roots of Women's Liberation in the Civil Rights Movement and the New Left* (New York: Alfred Knopf, 1979), pp. 18–19; Friedan, *"It,"* pp. 77–78, 80.

23. Eleanor Humes Haney, *A Feminist Legacy: The Ethics of Wilma Scott Heide and Company* (Buffalo, N.Y.: Margaretdaughters, Inc., 1985), p. 85; Friedan, *"It,"* pp. 80–83; Levine and Hole, *Rebirth*, pp. 82–83.

24. Friedan, *"It,"* p. 83.

25. Ibid., pp. 83–84; Aileen C. Hernandez and Letitia Sommers, *NOW: The First Five Years, 1966–1971* (np., nd.), p. 2; Haney, *Legacy*, p. 56.

26. Friedan, *"It,"* pp. 87–91; Levine and Hole, *Rebirth*, p. 85.

27. Friedan, *"It,"* pp. 90–91.

28. Gayle Yates, *What Women Want: The Ideas of the Movement* (Cambridge, Mass.: Harvard University Press, 1975), p. 46; *New York Times*, 22 November 1966, p. 44.

29. Friedan, *"It,"* pp. 95–96; Hernandez and Sommers, *NOW*, p. 3.

30. Freeman, "A Model for Analyzing the Strategic Options of Social Movement Organizations," in Jo Freeman, *Social Movements of the Sixties and Seventies* (New York: Longman, 1983), pp. 195–97; Freeman, *Politics*, pp. 73–75.

31. Freidan, *"It,"* p. 96.

32. Freeman, *Politics*, pp. 56, 91.

33. Ibid., pp. 75–77, 191–92; Yates, *What*, p. 44; Friedan, *"It,"* pp. 92–95; Deckard, *Women's Movement*, pp. 169–71; Hole and Levine, *Rebirth*, pp. 32–36, 41–43, 87–88.

34. Freeman, *Politics*, p. 79.

35. Evans, *Personal Politics*, pp. 38–40, 43, 46, 52–53, 57, 61, 67–80, 84–87, 99–100; Mary Aickin Rothschild, "White Women Volunteers in the Freedom Summers: Their Life and Work in a Movement for Social Change," *Feminist Studies* 5 (Fall 1979): 478–83, 488; Mary King, *Freedom Song: A Personal Story of the 1960s Civil Rights Movement* (New York: William Morrow, 1987), pp. 443, 450, 457–60, 568, 571, 573.

36. King, *Song*, p. 456.

37. Evans, *Personal Politics*, p. 143.

38. Ibid., pp. 466–68; Freeman, *Politics*, pp. 56–59, 61, 68; Yates, *What*, pp. 6–10; Evans, *Personal Politics*, pp. 105–24, 139–43, 145–55, 168–73, 181–90, 198–211.

39. Yates, *What*, pp. 8–9, 77–86, 97–100; Hole and Levine, *Rebirth*, pp. 136–39.

40. Hole and Levine, *Rebirth*, pp. 125–26; Hester Eisenstein, *Contemporary Feminist Thought* (Boston: G.K. Hall and Co., 1983), pp. 35–40; Leslie B. Tanner, ed., *Voices from Women's Liberation* (New York: New American Library, 1970), pp. 238–253; Maren Carden, *The New Feminist Movement* (New York: Russell Sage Foundation, 1974), pp. 64–71; Robin Morgan, *The Sisterhood Is Powerful: An Anthology of Writings from the Women's Liberation Movement* (New York: Random House, 1970), p. xxxvi.

41. Freeman, *Politics*, pp. 148–49; Monica B. Morris, "The Public Definition of a Social Movement: Women's Liberation," *Sociology and Social Research* 57 (July 1973): 527–35.

42. Judith M. Bardwick, *In Transition: How Feminism, Sexual Liberation, and the Search for Self-Fulfillment Have Altered Our Lives* (New York: Holt, Rinehart & Winston, 1979), pp. 59, 81–84, 88, 119; Chafe, "Paradox," pp. 574–76; Gimlin, ed., *Women's Movement*, pp 3–5, 8, 33, 114–15.

43. Freeman, *Politics*, pp. 105, 117; Interview with Penny Gardner, Miami, Florida, January 31, 1988; Carden, *New Feminist Movement*, pp. 23–24.

44. Carden, *New Feminist Movement*, pp. 106–7; Freeman, *Politics*, p. 85.

45. Hole and Levine, *Rebirth*, pp. 88, 289.

46. Carden, *New Feminist Movement*, p. 106.

47. *New York Times*, 23 March 1970, p. 32.

48. Freeman, *Politics*, p. 86; Judy MacLean, "N.O.W.," *Socialist Revolution* 6 (July-September 1976): pp. 45–46; Dade County NOW "Orientation Packet," pp. 4, 12, in the author's possession.

49. Deckard, *Women's Movement*, p. 343.

50. Hole and Levine, *Rebirth*, p. 94.

51. Freeman, *Politics*, pp. 99, 100, 134–36; Carden, *New Feminist Movement*, pp. 113–16; Deckard, *Women's Movement*, pp. 340–43; Ryan Jones, "Lesbian Rights in the National Organization for Women: Activism Within an Established Social Movement," term paper, University of Utah, 1989, in the author's possession.

52. Hole and Levine, *Rebirth*, pp. 90, 142–45; Freeman, *Politics*, pp. 81–82.

53. Friedan, *"It,"* pp. 106–7; Hole and Levine, *Rebirth*, pp. 88–89.

54. Friedan, *"It,"* pp. xiv, 112, 161, 163, 175, 244–45; *New York Times*, 19 July 1972, p. 43.

55. Hole and Levine, *Rebirth*, p. 92.

56. Interview with Dr. Janet Canterbury, Miami, Florida, February 2, 1988; Telephone interview with Charlotte Gaines, Miami, Florida, February 3, 1988; Gardner interview; Freeman, *Politics*, pp. 86–87. Members could decide to affiliate with a local chapter or maintain a mail membership directly with National NOW.

57. *New York Times*, 27 August 1970, p. 30.

58. Freeman, *Politics*, pp. 83–85; Deckard, *Women's Movement*, pp. 335–36, 361; *New York Times*, 27 August 1970, pp. 1, 30; Gardner interview; Interview with Doris Denison, Miami, Florida, February 1, 1988.

59. Interview with Roxcy Bolton, Miami, Florida, January 31, 1988; Dade County NOW "Orientation Packet"; MacLean, "NOW," pp. 46–47; Carden, *New Feminist Movement*, pp. 112–13; *Miami Herald*, 25 January 1980; *Miami Herald*, 2 September 1974.

60. Freeman, *Politics*, p. 91; *San Antonio Star*, 25 March 1979; Denison interview; Carden, *New Feminist Movement*, pp. 19–21, 29–30; 184–85.

61. Denison interview.

62. Carden, *New Feminist Movement*, p. 121.

63. Bolton interview; Deckard, *Women's Movement*, pp. 466, 468; Hernandez and Sommers, *NOW*, p. 9; Freeman, *Politics*, pp. 88–90; Carden, *New Feminist Movement*, pp. 119–21.

64. *New York Times*, 24 March 1972, p. 36; George Gallup, *The Gallup Poll: Public Opinion, 1972–1977* (Wilmington, Del.: Scholarly Resources, 1978), pp. 693–96; Deckard, *Women's Movement*, pp. 361, 407; Laura Graeber, "The Women's Movement: Too Much of a Good Thing?" *Mademoiselle* 81 (August 1975): p. 42.

65. Freeman, *Politics*, pp. 171, 184–86, 202, 217–18, 237.

66. Jane J. Mansbridge, *Why We Lost the ERA* (Chicago, University of Chicago Press, 1986), p. 42; Hole and Levine, *Rebirth*, pp. 58–67; Yates,

What, pp. 55–58; "ERA Countdown Campaign," in Penny Gardner Papers, private collection, Miami, Florida.

67. Freeman, *Politics*, pp. 83, 88, 91, 100; *National NOW Times* (September 1978).

68. Berry, *Why*, pp. 64–65; Elizabeth Pleck, "Failed Strategies; Renewed Hope," in Joan Hoff-Wilson, *Rights of Passage: The Past and Future of ERA* (Bloomington: Indiana University Press, 1986), p. 115.

69. Berry, *Why*, pp. 65, 68; Pleck, "Failed," pp. 108–9; Mansbridge, *Why We Lost*, pp. 4, 10; *New York Times*, 17 December 1972, p. 90; Gallup, *Gallup Poll*, p. 375.

70. Mansbridge, *Why We Lost*, pp. 13–14; *National NOW Times*, (September 1978); Berry, *Why*, pp. 67, 70; *New York Times*, 5 November 1975, pp. 1, 13 November 1977, pp. 1, 5 March 1978, p. 24.

71. Mansbridge, *Why We Lost*, p. 104.

72. Berry, *Why*, pp. 66, 69; Pleck, "Failed," pp. 111, 114; Mansbridge, *Why We Lost*, pp. 5–6, 13, 20–23, 116–17; Deckard, *Women's Movement*, pp. 180–82.

73. Pamela Johnson Conover and Virginia Gray, *Feminism and the New Right: Conflict over the American Family* (New York: Praeger, 1983), pp. 2–10, 68–93; Berry, *Why*, p. 82. See Chapter 6 for more on the New Right.

74. *New York Times*, 27 October 1974, p. 8.

75. Foat, *Never*, p. 204.

76. Haney, *Legacy*, p. 128.

77. Foat, *Never*, pp. 147, 192–93; *New York Times*, 26 May 1974, pp. 35, 27, October 1974, pp. 8, 28, October 1975, p. 15, 15 November 1975, pp. 1, 12; "Womenswar," *Time* 106 (1 December 1975): 55; Freeman, *Politics*, pp. 95–98; Friedan, *"It,"* pp. 369–73; MacLean, "NOW," pp. 40–43; Bolton interview; Interview with Fran Malone, Miami, Florida, February 3, 1988.

78. Dr. Joyce Brothers, "Women's Lib Backlash," *Good Housekeeping* 175 (September 1972): p. 54.

79. "Never Underestimate . . . ," *Newsweek* 96 (25 August 1980): p. 27.

80. *National NOW Times* (March 1979); Deckard, *Women's Movement*, p. 373; "Never Underestimate," p. 27.

81. Mansbridge, *Why We Lost*, pp. 2, 45–47, 50, 60; Berry, *Why*, pp. 86–87, 99–100; Deckard, *Women's Movement*, pp. 145–46, 161–63; *New York Times*, 15 November 1977, p. 46.

82. Deckard, *Women's Movement*, pp. 385–87, 413; Zillah Eisenstein, "Antifeminism in the Politics and Election of 1980," *Feminist Studies* 7

(Summer 1981): 190, 194; *New York Times:* 10 October 1981, p. 18; 12 October 1981, sec. II, p. 9; 25 June 1982, pp. 1, 12, 13.

83. *New York Times:* 5 July 1984, p. 10; 9 October 1982, p. 23; 11 October 1982, sec. II, p. 6; 1 October 1983, p. 12.

84. "Warrior for Women's Rights," *US News and World Report,* 100 (24 March 1986): p. 11; Foat, *Never,* p. 207; Gardner interview; Canterbury interview; *Wall Street Journal,* 5 September 1985; *New York Times:* 8 June 1985, p. 48; 19 July 1985, p. 8; 13 June 1986, p. 19; 1 December 1986, p. 18; *Washington Post:* 14 July 1985; 24 July 1985; *National NOW Times* (July-August 1987, September-October-November 1987).

85. Riley, *Inventing,* pp. 251–52, 255, 257; Gimlin, ed., *Women's Movement,* pp. 43–50, 57.

86. *National NOW Times* (Winter 1987, May-June 1988, July-August-September 1988, October-November-December 1988); Letter from Molly Yard to NOW members, 1988; Priority Message from Molly Yard to NOW Members, 1989; *New York Times,* 24 January 1989, p. 1; *Salt Lake Tribune,* 7 Feburary 1988; Rix, ed., *American Woman,* p. 240.

87. Dorothy Wickenden, "What Now?" *New Republic,* 194 (5 May 1986): pp. 19, 21; Deckard, *Women's Movement,* pp. 91–97; Riley, *Inventing,* p. 258; Sylvia Ann Hewlett, *A Lesser Life: The Myth of Women's Liberation in America* (New York: William Morrow & Co., 1986), pp. 14, 49, 55, 57, 60, 62, 71, 75–82.

88. *Salt Lake Tribune,* 20 January 1988; *New York Times,* 8 December 1988, p. 28; "Feminist Identity Crisis," *Newsweek* 107 (31 March 1986): pp. 58–59; *Wall Street Journal,* 30 October 1984; "Too Late for Prince Charming?" *Newsweek* 107 (2 June 1986): pp. 54–58.

89. "Feminization of Power;" *New York Times,* 29 April 1985, sec. II, p. 11; *National NOW Times* (Winter 1987); *Los Angeles Times,* 21 August 1986.

CHAPTER 10: THE CHALLENGERS' LEGACY

1. *Salt Lake Tribune:* 14 February, 12 October 1988; 11 and 30 April, 1 May 1989; *Amnesty Action,* September/October 1986, January/February 1988; Philip Jordan, "Amnesty International," term paper, University of Utah, 1989, in the author's possession, pp. 2–3, 6, 8, 12.

2. *Salt Lake Tribune:* 11 June 1987; 26 November 1988; "Going After the Klan," *Newsweek* 111 (23 February 1987): p. 29; "Intelligence Report," Klanwatch Project of the Southern Poverty Law Center (February 1989); *Atlanta Journal and Constitution,* 2 January 1989; *USA Today,* 9 November 1988; Jill Dunyon, "Aryan Nations" (Honors thesis, University of Utah, 1988), in the author's possession; "Curbing the Hatemongers," *Newsweek*

112 (19 September 1988): p. 29; *Great Falls Tribune*, 2 January 1988; *New York Times:* 28 February 1988, p. 27; 27 March 1988, p. 9; *Salt Lake Tribune*, 8 April 1988.

3. *Salt Lake Tribune*, 20 May 1987.

4. *Los Angeles Times*, 19 March 1988; *Salt Lake Tribune*, 6 June, 15 September, 17 and 18 October 1988; 16 April 1989; "Going After Dissidents," *Newsweek* 112 (8 February 1988): p. 29; Britt Welsh, "The American Peace Test" (Term paper, University of Utah, 1986) in the author's possession.

5. *Salt Lake Tribune*, 12 March 1988.

6. *Salt Lake Tribune;* 16, 18, 20 February, 7 March, 22 October 1988; 16 and 21 April, 5 May 1989; *New York Times:* 21 February 1988, sec. IV, p. 6; 20 November 1988, p. 26; Jon Weiner, "Racial Hatred on Campus," *Nation* 248 (27 Feburary 1989): pp. 260, 262: Oliver Sacks, "The Revolution of the Deaf," *New York Review of Books* 35 (2 June 1988): pp. 23, 27, 28; Lou Ann Walker, "'I Know How to Ask for What I Want,'"*Parade Magazine* (23 April 1989): pp. 4–6.

7. "Of Pain and Progress," *Newsweek* 112 (26 December 1988): pp. 50–54; *Salt Lake Tribune*, 4 April 1989; Venessa Pierce, "On Animal Rights," (Term paper, University of Utah, 1989), in the author's possession.

8. Mark Gevisser, "AIDS Movement Seizes Control," *Nation* 247 (19 December 1988): pp. 677–80.

9. *Salt Lake Tribune*, 12 October 1988.

10. Richard A. Viguerie, *The New Right: We're Ready to Lead* (Falls Church, Va.: The Viguerie Company, 1980), p. 124.

11. John D. McCarthy and Mayer N. Zald, *The Trend of Social Movements* (Morristown, N.J.: General Learning Press, 1973), p. 3.

12. Ibid., pp. 13–21, 24.

13. J. Craig Jenkins, "Resource Mobilization Theory and the Study of Social Movements," *Annual Review of Sociology* 9 (1983): p. 533; Donald C. Reitzes and Dietrich C. Reitzes, "Alinsky's Legacy: Current Applications and Extensions of his Principles and Strategies," in Louis Kriesberg, ed., *Research in Social Movements, Conflicts and Change* 6 (Greenwich, Conn.: JAI Press, 1984), pp. 40, 43–44.

14. Richard B. Kielbowicz and Clifford Scherer, "The Role of the Press in the Dynamics of Social Movements," in Louis Kriesberg, ed., *Research in Social Movements, Conflicts and Change* 9 (Greenwich, Conn.: JAI Press, 1986), pp. 71, 74–75, 77.

15. Ibid., pp. 81, 84–87. See also, Ralph H. Turner, "The Public Perception of Protest," *American Sociological Review* 34 (December 1969): 815–31.

16. William Gamson, *The Strategy of Social Protest* (Homewood, Ill.: Dorsey Press, 1975), pp. 19–20, 28–29, 31–37.

17. Ibid., pp. 43, 46, 49, 51, 79, 87, 95, 101, 108, 128; Roberta Ash Garner, *Social Movements in America* (Chicago: Rand McNally, 1977), p. 12.

18. Robert A. Goldberg, "Racial Change on the Southern Periphery: The Case of San Antonio, Texas, 1960–65," *Journal of Southern History* 49 (August 1983): p. 354.

19. Ibid., 373.

20. Jenkins, "Resource Mobilization Theory," p. 544.

21. Turner, "Public Perception," pp. 815–16, 818–19, 820.

22. Jenkins, "Resource Mobilization Theory," pp. 539, 542; Doug McAdam, "The Decline of the Civil Rights Movement," in Jo Freeman, ed., *Social Movements of the Sixties and Seventies* (New York: Longman, 1983), pp. 301–2.

23. Gamson, *Strategy*, p. 37.

24. Ibid., p. 142.

25. Ibid., pp. 141–42; Clayborne Carson, *In Struggle: SNCC and The Black Awakening of the 1960s* (Cambridge, Mass.: Harvard University Press, 1981), p. 127.

26. Jenkins, "Resource Mobilization Theory," p. 544.

BIBLIOGRAPHY

This bibliography is divided into ten sections corresponding to the book's ten chapters. In addition to references already cited in the footnotes, each section will list other secondary sources that give further background and information about the topic and period.

1. AN INTRODUCTION TO SOCIAL MOVEMENTS

Adorno, Theodore W.; Frenkel-Brunswik, Else; Levinson, Daniel J.; Sanford, R. Nevitt. *The Authoritarian Personality.* New York: Harper & Row, 1950.

Arendt, Hannah. *The Origins of Totalitarianism.* Revised ed. New York: Meridian, 1966.

Cameron, William. *Modern Social Movements: A Sociological Outline.* New York: Random House, 1966.

Cantril, Hadley. *The Psychology of Social Movements.* New York: John Wiley, 1941.

Dahl, Robert. *Who Governs?* New Haven: Yale University Press, 1961.

_____. *Pluralist Democracy in the United States: Conflict and Consent.* Chicago: Rand McNally, 1967.

Dubofsky, Melvyn. *We Shall Be All: A History of the Industrial Workers of the World.* Chicago: Quadrangle, 1969.

Evans, Sara, and Boyte, Harry C. *Free Spaces: The Sources of Democratic Change in America.* New York: Harper & Row, 1986.

Fogelson, Robert A. *Violence as Protest: A Study of Riots and Ghettos.* Garden City, New York: Doubleday, 1971.

Foss, Daniel A., and Larkin, Ralph. *Beyond Revolution: A New Theory of Social Movements.* South Hadley, Mass.: Bergin and Garvey, 1986.

Freeman, Jo, ed. *Social Movements of the Sixties and Seventies.* New York: Longman, 1983.

Fromm, Erich. *Escape from Freedom.* New York: Rinehart, 1941.

_____. *The Sane Society.* New York: Rinehart, 1955.

Gamson, William A. *Power and Discontent.* Homewood, Ill.: Dorsey, 1968.

_____. *The Strategy of Social Protest.* Homewood, Ill.: Dorsey, 1975.

_____. Fireman, Bruce, and Rytina, Steven. *Encounters with Unjust Authority.* Homewood, Ill.: Dorsey, 1982.

Garner, Roberta Ash. *Social Movements in America.* Chicago: Rand McNally, 1977.

Gitlin, Todd. *The Whole World Is Watching: Mass Media in the Making and Unmaking of the New Left.* Berkeley: University of California Press, 1980.

Gurr, Ted Robert. *Why Men Rebel.* Princeton: Princeton University Press, 1970.

Gusfield, Joseph R., ed. *Protest, Reform and Revolt: A Reader in Social Movements.* New York: John Wiley, 1970.

Heberle, Rudolf. *Social Movements: An Introduction to Political Sociology.* New York: Appleton-Century-Crofts, 1951.

Hoffer, Eric. *The True Believer: Thoughts on the Nature of Social Movements.* New York: Harper & Row, 1951.

Jenkins, J. Craig. "Resource Mobilization Theory and the Study of Social Movements." *Annual Review of Sociology* 9 (1983): 527–53.

Kornhauser, William. *The Politics of Mass Society.* New York: Free Press, 1959.

Lang, Kurt, and Lang, Gladys. *Collective Dynamics.* New York: Crowell, 1961.

Lipset, Seymour Martin. *Political Man: The Social Bases of Politics.* Garden City, N.Y.: Doubleday, 1959.

Lofland, John. *Protest: Studies of Collective Behavior and Social Movements.* New Brunswick, N.J.: Transaction Books, 1985.

Marx, Gary T. "External Efforts to Damage or Facilitate Social Movements: Some Patterns, Explanations, Outcomes, and Complications." In Mayer D. Zald and John D. McCarthy, eds. *The Dynamics of Social Movements: Resource Mobilization, Tactics and Social Control.* Cambridge, Mass.: Winthrop, 1979: 94–125.

McAdam, Doug. *Political Process and the Development of Black Insurgency, 1930–1970.* Chicago: University of Chicago Press, 1982.

McCarthy, John D., and Zald, Mayer D. "Resource Mobilization and Social Movements: A Partial Theory." *American Journal of Sociology* 82 (May 1977): 1212–41.

McLaughlin, Barry, ed. *Studies in Social Movements: A Social Psychological Perspective.* New York: Free Press, 1969.

Nisbet, Robert. *The Quest for Community: A Study in the Ethics of Order and Freedom.* New York: Oxford University Press, 1953.

Oberschall, Anthony. *Social Conflict and Social Movements.* Englewood Cliffs, N.J.: Prentice-Hall, 1973.

Piven, Frances Fox, and Cloward, Richard. *Poor People's Movements: Why They Succeed, How They Fail.* New York: Pantheon, 1977.

Roberts, Ron E., and Kloss, Robert M. *Social Movements: Between the Balcony and the Barricade.* St. Louis: Mosby, 1974.

Rubenstein, Richard E. *Rebels in Eden: Mass Political Violence in the United States.* Boston: Little, Brown, 1970.

Schwartz, Michael. *Radical Protest and Social Structure: The Southern Farmers' Alliance and Cotton Tenancy, 1880–1890.* New York: Academic Press, 1976.

Selznick, Philip. *The Organizational Weapon.* Glencoe, Ill.: Free Press, 1952.

Smelser, Neil J. *Theory of Collective Behavior.* New York: Free Press, 1963.

Tilly, Charles. "Does Modernization Breed Revolution?" *Comparative Politics* 5 (April 1973): 425–47.

_____. *From Mobilization to Revolution.* Reading, Mass.: Addison-Wesley, 1978.

Toch, Hans. *The Social Psychology of Social Movements.* Indianapolis: Bobbs-Merrill, 1965.

Turner, Ralph H. "Collective Behavior and Resource Mobilization as Approaches to Social Movements: Issues and Continuities." In Louis

Kriesberg, ed. *Research in Social Movements, Conflicts and Change* 4 Greenwich, Conn.: JAI, 1981: 1–24.

_____. "The Public Perception of Protest." *American Sociological Review* 69 (December 1969): 815–31.

Turner, Ralph H., and Killian, Lewis M. *Collective Behavior.* 2nd ed. Englewood Cliffs, N.J.: Prentice-Hall, 1972.

Useem, Michael. *Protest Movements in America.* Indianapolis: Bobbs-Merrill, 1975.

Wilson, John. *Introduction to Social Movements.* New York: Basic Books, 1973.

Zald, Mayer N., and McCarthy, John D., eds. *The Dynamics of Social Movements: Resource Mobilization, Social Control, and Tactics.* Cambridge, Mass.: Winthrop, 1979.

2. THE DEATH OF JOHN BARLEYCORN: THE ANTI-SALOON LEAGUE

Abrams, Richard M. *The Burdens of Progress, 1900–1929.* Glenville, Ill.: Scott, Foresman & Co., 1978.

Allen, Frederick Lewis. *Only Yesterday: An Informal History of the 1920's.* New York: Harper & Row, 1931.

Bader, Robert Smith. *Prohibition in Kansas: A History.* Lawrence: University Press of Kansas, 1986.

Blocker, Jack S., Jr. *Retreat from Reform: The Prohibition Movement in the United States, 1890–1913.* Westport, Conn.: Greenwood, 1976.

Burner, David. *Politics of Provincialism: The Democratic Party in Transition, 1918–1932.* Cambridge, Mass.: Harvard University Press, 1986.

Chandler, Alfred D., Jr. *The Visible Hand: The Managerial Revolution in American Business.* Cambridge, Mass.: Belknap, 1977.

Clark, Norman. *Deliver Us from Evil: An Interpretation of American Prohibition.* New York: W.W. Norton and Co., 1976.

_____. *The Dry Years: Prohibition and Social Change in Washington.* Seattle: University of Washington Press, 1965.

Duis, Perry, R. *The Saloon: Public Drinking in Chicago and Boston, 1880–1920.* Urbana: University of Illinois Press, 1983.

Gusfield, Joseph R. *Symbolic Crusade: Status Politics and the American Temperance Movement.* Urbana: University of Illinois Press, 1963.

Hicks, John D. *Republican Ascendancy, 1921–1933.* New York: Harper & Row, 1960.

Hofstadter, Richard. *The Age of Reform.* New York: Alfred A. Knopf, 1955.

Isaac, Paul E. *Prohibition and Politics: Turbulent Decades in Tennessee, 1885–1920.* Knoxville: University of Tennessee Press, 1965.

Kerr, K. Austin. *Organized for Prohibition: A New History of the Anti-Saloon League.* New Haven, Conn.: Yale University Press, 1985.

Kingsdale, Jon M. "The Poor Man's Club: Social Functions of the Urban Working-Class Saloon." In Elizabeth and Joseph Pleck. *The American Man.* Englewood Cliffs, N.J.: Prentice-Hall, 1980: 257–83.

Kyvig, David E. *Repealing National Prohibition.* Chicago: University of Chicago, 1979.

_____. "Sober Thoughts: Myths and Realities of National Prohibition After Fifty Years." In David E. Kyvig. *Law, Alcohol, and Order: Perspectives on National Prohibition.* Westport, Conn.: Greenwood, 1985: 3–20.

Leuchtenburg, William E. *The Perils of Prosperity, 1914–1932.* Chicago: University of Chicago Press, 1958.

Merz, Charles. *The Dry Decade.* Garden City, N.Y.: Doubleday, 1931.

Noel, Thomas J. "The Immigrant Saloon in Denver." *Colorado Magazine* 54 (Summer 1977): 201–19.

Odegard, Peter. *Pressure Politics: The Story of the Anti-Saloon League.* New York: Columbia University Press, 1928.

Ostrander, Gilbert M. *The Prohibition Movement in California, 1848–1933.* Berkeley: University of California Publications in History, 1957.

Rorabaugh, W. J. *The Alcoholic Republic: An American Tradition.* New York: Oxford University Press, 1979.

Sellers, James B. *The Prohibition Movement in Alabama, 1702–1943.* Chapel Hill: University of North Carolina Press, 1943.

Schlesinger, Arthur M., Jr. *The Crisis of the Old Order, 1919–1933.* Boston: Houghton Mifflin, 1957.

Sinclair, Andrew. *Prohibition: The Era of Access.* Boston: Little, Brown & Co., 1962.

Timberlake, James H. *Prohibition and the Progressive Movement, 1900–1920.* Cambridge, Mass.: Harvard University Press, 1963.

Tyler, Alice Felt. *Freedom's Ferment.* New York: Harper & Bros., 1962.

Wenger, Robert E. "The Anti-Saloon League in Nebraska Politics, 1898–1910." *Nebraska History* 52 (Fall 1971): 267–92.

Whitener, Daniel J. *Prohibition in North Carolina, 1715–1945.* Chapel Hill: University of North Carolina Press, 1946.

3. ONE BIG UNION: THE INDUSTRIAL WORKERS OF THE WORLD

Bird, Stewart.; Georgakas, Dan.; and Shaffer, Deborah. *Solidarity Forever: An Oral History of the IWW.* Chicago: Lakeview Press, 1985.

Brissenden, Paul F. *The I.W.W.: A Study of American Syndicalism.* New York: Columbia University Press, 1919.

Burbank, Garin. *When Farmers Voted Red: The Gospel of Socialism in the Oklahoma Countryside, 1910–1924.* Westport, Conn.: Greenwood, 1976.

Byrkit, James W. *Forging the Copper Collar: Arizona's Labor-Management War of 1901–1921.* Tucson: University of Arizona Press, 1982.

Conlin, Joseph R. *At the Point of Production: The Local History of the IWW.* Westport, Conn.: Greenwood, 1981.

——————. *Bread and Roses Too: Studies of the Wobblies.* Westport, Conn.: Greenwood, 1969.

Daniel, Cletus E. "In Defense of the Wheatland Wobblies: A Critical Analysis of the IWW in California." *Labor History* 19 (Fall 1978): 485–509.

Diggins, John P. *The American Left in the Twentieth Century.* New York: Harcourt Brace Jovanovich, 1973.

Draper, Theodore. *The Roots of American Communism.* New York: Viking Press, 1957.

Dubofsky, Melvyn. *We Shall Be All: A History of the Industrial Workers of the World.* Chicago: Quadrangle, 1969.

Ficken, Robert E. "The Wobbly Horrors: Pacific Northwest Lumbermen and the Industrial Workers of the World, 1917–1928." *Labor History* 24 (Summer 1983): 325–41.

Filene, Peter. *Him, Her, Self: Sex Roles in Modern America.* New York: Harcourt, Brace, Jovanovich, 1974.

Foner, Philip S. *Fellow Workers and Friends: I.W.W. Free-Speech Fights as Told by Participants.* Westport, Conn.: Greenwood, 1981.

——————. *History of the Labor Movement in the United States.* Vol. 4: *The Industrial Workers of the World, 1905–1917.* New York: International Publishers, 1965.

Goldberg, Robert A. *Back to the Soil: The Jewish Farmers of Clarion, Utah and Their World.* Salt Lake City: University of Utah Press, 1986.

Goldstein, Robert Justin. *Political Repression in Modern America: From 1870 to the Present.* Cambridge, Mass.: Schenkman, 1978.

Golin, Steve. "Defeat Becomes Disaster: The Paterson Strike of 1913 and the Decline of the IWW." *Labor History* 24 (Spring 1983): 233–48.

Green, James R. "Comments on the Montgomery Paper." *Journal of Social History* 7 (Summer 1974): 530–35.

_____. *Grass-Roots Socialism: Radical Movements in the Southwest, 1895–1943.* Baton Rouge: Louisiana State University Press, 1978.

Gutfeld, Arnon. *Montana's Agony: Years of War and Hysteria, 1917–1921.* Gainesville: University of Florida Press, 1979.

Hays, Samuel. *The Response to Industrialism.* Chicago: University of Chicago Press, 1957.

Kornbluh, Joyce L., ed. *Rebel Voices: An I.W.W. Anthology.* Ann Arbor: University of Michigan Press, 1964.

Kraditor, Aileen S. *The Radical Persuasion, 1890–1917: Aspects of the Intellectual History and the Historiography of Three American Radical Organizations.* Baton Rouge: Louisiana State University Press, 1981.

Laslett, John H. M., and Lipset, Seymour Martin, eds. *Failure of a Dream? Essays in the History of American Socialism.* Garden City, N.Y.: Anchor, 1974.

Lens, Sidney. *The Labor Wars: From the Molly Maguires to the Sitdowns.* Garden City, N.Y.: Doubleday, 1973.

_____. *Radicalism in America.* New York: Crowell, 1969.

Miles, Dione, ed. *Something in Common—An IWW Bibliography.* Detroit: Wayne State University Press, 1986.

Montgomery, David. "The 'New Unionism' and the Transformation of Workers' Consciousness in America, 1909–22." *Journal of Social History* 7 (Summer 1974): 509–29.

_____. "Workers' Control of Machine Production in the Nineteenth Century." *Labor History* 17 (Fall 1976): 485–509.

Murray, Robert K. *Red Scare: A Study in National Hysteria, 1919–1920.* Minneapolis: University of Minnesota Press 1955.

Preston, William Jr. *Aliens and Dissenters: Federal Suppression of Radicals, 1903–1933.* Cambridge, Mass.: Harvard University Press, 1963.

_____. "Shall This Be All?: U.S. Historians Versus William D. Haywood." *Labor History* 11 (Summer 1971): 435–53.

Ramirez, Bruno. *When Workers Fight: The Politics of Industrial Relations in the Progressive Era, 1898–1916.* Westport, Conn.: Greenwood, 1978.

Robinson, Leland W. "Social Movement Organizations in Decline: A Case Study of the I.W.W." Ph.D. dissertation, Northwestern University, 1973.

Shannon, David A. *The Socialist Party of America: A History.* Chicago: Quadrangle, 1955.

Shovers, Brian. "The Perils of Working in the Butte Underground: Industrial Fatalities in the Copper Mines, 1880–1920." *Montana, The Magazine of Western History* 37 (Spring 1987): 26–39.

Taft, Philip. "The Bisbee Deportation." *Labor History* 13 (Winter 1972): 3–40.

————. "The Federal Trials of the IWW." *Labor History* 3 (Winter 1962): 57–91.

Thernstrom, Stephen. *The Other Bostonians: Poverty and Progress in the American Metropolis, 1880–1970.* Cambridge, Mass.: Harvard University Press, 1973.

Thompson, Fred, and Murfin, Patrick. *The I.W.W., Its First Seventy Years, 1905–1975.* Chicago: Industrial Workers of the World, 1976.

Tindall, George Brown. *America: A Narrative History.* 2 vols. 2nd ed. New York: W.W. Norton & Co., 1988.

Townsend, John Clendenin. *Running the Gauntlet: Cultural Sources of Violence Against the I.W.W.* New York: Garland, 1986.

Tripp, Anne H. *The I.W.W. and the Paterson Silk Strike of 1913.* Urbana: University of Illinois Press, 1986.

Tyler, Robert L. *Rebels of the Woods: The I.W.W. in the Pacific Northwest.* Eugene: University of Oregon Press, 1967.

Weinstein, James. *Ambiguous Legacy: The Left in American Politics.* New York: New Viewpoints, 1975.

Wiebe, Robert H. *The Search for Order.* New York: Hill and Wang, 1967.

Wyman, Mark. *Hard Rock Epic: Western Miners and the Industrial Revolution, 1860–1910.* Berkeley: University of California Press, 1979.

4. INVISIBLE EMPIRE: THE KNIGHTS OF THE KU KLUX KLAN

Abbey, Sue Wilson. "The Ku Klux Klan in Arizona, 1921–1925." *Journal of Arizona History* 14 (Spring 1973): 10–30.

Alexander, Charles. *The Ku Klux Klan in the Southwest.* Lexington: University of Kentucky Press, 1966.

Cates, F. Mark. "The Ku Klux Klan in Indiana Politics: 1920–1925." Ph.D. dissertation, Indiana University, 1970.

Chalmers, David. *Hooded Americanism: The History of the Ku Klux Klan.* New York: Franklin Watts, 1981.

Davis, John Augustus. "The Ku Klux Klan in Indiana, 1920–1930: An Historical Study." Ph.D. dissertation, Northwestern University, 1966.

Gerlach, Larry. *Blazing Crosses in Zion.* Logan: Utah State University Press, 1983.

Goldberg, Robert A. *Hooded Empire: The Ku Klux Klan in Colorado.* Urbana: University of Illinois Press, 1981.

_____. "The Ku Klux Klan in Madison, 1922–1927." *Wisconsin Magazine of History* 58 (Autumn 1974): 31–44.

Harrell, Kenneth Earl. "The Ku Klux Klan in Louisiana, 1920–1930." Ph.D. dissertation, Louisiana State University, 1966.

Higham, John. *Strangers in the Land.* New Brunswick: Rutgers University Press, 1955.

Jackson, Kenneth T. *The Ku Klux Klan in the City, 1915–1930.* New York: Oxford University Press, 1967.

Jenkins, Philip. "The Ku Klux Klan in Pennsylvania, 1920–1940." *Western Pennsylvania Historical Magazine* 69 (April 1986): 121–37.

Jenkins, William D. "The Ku Klux Klan in Youngstown, Ohio: Moral Reform in the Twenties." *The Historian* 41 (November 1978): 76–93.

Jones, Winfield. *Story of the Ku Klux Klan.* Washington, D.C.: American Newspaper Syndicate, 1921.

Kirschner, Don S. *City and Country: Rural Responses to Urbanization in the 1920s.* Westport, Conn.: Greenwood, 1970.

Lay, Shawn. *War, Revolution and the Ku Klux Klan: A Study of Intolerance in a Border City.* El Paso: Texas Western Press, 1985.

Lipset, Seymour Martin, and Raab, Earl. *The Politics of Unreason: Right-Wing Extremism in America, 1790–1970.* New York: Harper & Row, 1970.

Loucks, Emerson H. *The Ku Klux Klan in Pennsylvania: A Study in Nativism.* Harrisburg: Telegraph Press, 1936.

Mecklin, John Moffatt. *The Ku Klux Klan: A Study of the American Mind.* New York: Russell and Russell, 1924.

Melching, Richard. "The Activities of the Ku Klux Klan in Anaheim, California, 1923–1925." *Southern California Quarterly 56* (Summer 1974): 175–96.

Miller, Robert Moats. "A Note on the Relationship between the Protestant Churches and the Revived Ku Klux Klan." *Journal of Southern History* 22 (August 1956): 355–68.

Moseley, Clement Charlton. "Invisible Empire: A History of the Ku Klux Klan in Twentieth Century Georgia." Ph.D. dissertation, University of Georgia, 1968.

_____. "The Political Influence of the Ku Klux Klan in Georgia, 1915–1925." *Georgia Historical Quarterly* 57 (Summer 1973): 235–55.

Rambow, Charles. "The Ku Klux Klan in the 1920s: A Concentration on the Black Hills." *South Dakota History* 4 (Winter 1973): 63–81.

Rice, Arnold. *The Ku Klux Klan in American Politics.* Washington, D.C.: Public Affairs Press, 1962.

Safianow, Allen. "Konklave in Kokomo." *The Historian* 50 (May 1988): 329–347.

Snell, William R. "Fiery Crosses in the Roaring Twenties: Activities of the Revived Klan in Alabama, 1915–1930." *Alabama Review* 23 (October 1970): 256–76.

Thornbrough, Emma Lou. "Segregation in Indiana during the Klan Era of the 1920's." *Mississippi Valley Historical Review* 47 (March 1961): 594–617.

Toy, Eckard V., Jr. "The Ku Klux Klan in Tillamook, Oregon." *Pacific Northwest Quarterly* 53 (April 1962): 60–64.

Wade, Wyn Craig. *The Fiery Cross: The Ku Klux Klan in America.* New York: Simon and Schuster, 1987.

Wald, Kenneth D. "The Visible Empire: The Ku Klux Klan as an Electoral Movement." *Journal of Interdisciplinary History* 11 (Autumn 1980): 217–34.

Weaver, Norman Frederic. "The Knights of the Ku Klux Klan in Wisconsin, Indiana, Ohio, and Michigan." Ph.D. dissertation, University of Wisconsin-Madison, 1954.

5. THROW OFF YOUR CHAINS: THE COMMUNIST PARTY

Abscarian, Gilbert. "Romantics and Renegades: Political Defection and the Radical Left." *Journal of Social Issues* 27 (1971): 123–39.

Belknap, Michal R. *Cold War Political Justice: The Smith Act, the Communist Party, and American Civil Liberties.* Westport, Conn.: Greenwood, 1977.

Bell, Daniel. *Marxian Socialism in the United States.* Princeton: Princeton University Press, 1967.

Bernstein, Irving. *The Lean Years: A History of the American Worker, 1920–1933.* Boston: Penguin Books, 1966.

_____. *Turbulent Years: A History of the American Worker, 1933–1941.* Boston: Houghton Mifflin, 1970.

Cochran, Bert. *Labor and Communism: The Conflict That Shaped American Unions.* Princeton: Princeton University Press, 1977.

Daniels, Roger. *The Bonus March: An Episode of the Great Depression.* Westport, Conn.: Greenwood, 1971.

Diggins, John P. *The American Left in the Twentieth Century.* New York: Harcourt Brace Jovanovich, 1973.

Donner, Frank. "Let Him Wear a Wolf's Head: What the FBI Did to William Albertson." *The Civil Liberties Review* 3 (April-May, 1976): 12–22.

Draper, Theodore. *American Communism and Soviet Russia: The Formative Period.* New York: Viking Press, 1960.

——————. "The Popular Front Revisited." *New York Review of Books* 32 (30 May 1985): 44–50.

——————. *The Roots of American Communism.* New York: Viking Press, 1957.

Gaddis, John Lewis. *The United States and the Origins of the Cold War, 1941–1947.* New York: Columbia University Press, 1972.

Garraty, John A. "Unemployment During the Great Depression." *Labor History* 17 (Spring 1976): 133–59.

Glazer, Nathan. *The Social Basis of American Communism.* New York: Harcourt Brace and World, 1961.

Gornick, Vivian. *The Romance of American Communism.* New York: Basic Books, 1977.

Hook, Sidney. "Breaking with the Communists—A Memoir." *Commentary* 77 (February 1984): 47–53.

Howe, Irving, and Coser, Louis. *The American Communist Party.* New York: Praeger, 1962.

Isserman, Maurice. *If I Had a Hammer. . . : The Death of the Old Left and the Birth of the New Left.* New York: Basic Books, 1987.

——————. "The 1956 Generation: An Alternative Approach to the History of American Communism." *Radical History* 14 (March–April, 1980): 43–51.

——————. "Three Generations: Historians View American Communism." *Labor History* 26 (Fall 1985): 517–45.

——————. *Which Side Were You On?: The American Communist Party During the Second World War.* Middletown, Conn.: Wesleyan University Press, 1982.

Jacobson, Phyllis. "Seeing Red, White and Blue: The 'Americanization' of the Communist Party." *New Politics* 1 (Summer 1986): 152–71.

Klehr, Harvey. *Communist Cadre: The Social Background of the American Communist Party Elite.* Stanford, Calif.: Stanford University Press, 1987.

_____. *The Heyday of American Communism: The Depression Decade.* New York: Basic Books, 1984.

Leuchtenburg, William E. *Franklin D. Roosevelt and the New Deal, 1932–1940.* New York: Harper & Row, 1963.

_____. *The Perils of Prosperity, 1914–1932.* Chicago: University of Chicago Press, 1958.

Liebman, Arthur. *Jews and the Left.* New York: John Wiley & Sons, 1979.

Lyons, Paul. *Philadelphia Communists, 1936–1956.* Philadelphia: Temple University Press, 1982.

Murray, Robert K. *Red Scare: Study in National Hysteria, 1919–1920.* Minneapolis: University of Minnesota Press, 1955.

Naison, Mark. *Communists in Harlem During the Depression.* New York: Grove Press, 1983.

O'Brien, F.S. "The 'Communist-Dominated' Unions in the United States Since 1950." *Labor History* 9 (Spring 1968): 184–209.

Piven, Frances Fox, and Cloward, Richard. *Poor People's Movements: Why They Succeed, How They Fail.* New York: Pantheon, 1977.

Rosenzweig, Roy. "Organizing the Unemployed: The Early Years of the Great Depression." *Radical America* 10 (July–August 1976): 37–60.

Schlesinger, Arthur M. Jr. *The Age of Roosevelt: The Crisis of the Old Order, 1914–1933.* Boston: Houghton Mifflin, 1957.

Shannon, David. *The Decline of American Communism: A History of the Communist Party of the United States Since 1945.* New York: Harcourt Brace Jovanovich, 1959.

_____. *The Socialist Party of America: A History.* Chicago: Quadrangle Books, 1955.

Shover, John. *Cornbelt Rebellion.* Urbana: University of Illinois Press, 1965.

Starobin, Joseph R. *American Communism in Crisis, 1943–1957.* Cambridge, Mass.: Harvard University Press, 1972.

Steinberg, Peter. *The Great "Red Menace:" United States Prosecution of American Communists, 1947–1952.* Westport, Conn.: Greenwood, 1984.

Terkel, Studs. *Hard Times: An Oral History of the Great Depression.* New York: Pantheon, 1970.

Theoharis, Athan. *Spying on Americans: Political Surveillance from Hoover to the Huston Plan.* Philadelphia: Temple University Press, 1978.

Urmann, Michael Francis. "Rank and File Communists and the CIO." Ph.D. dissertation, University of Utah, 1981.

6. BRIDGING MCCARTHYISM AND
REAGANISM: THE JOHN BIRCH SOCIETY

Bell, Daniel, ed. *The New American Right*. Garden City, New York: Doubleday-Anchor, 1964.

Broyles, J. Allen. *The John Birch Society: Anatomy of a Protest*. Boston: Beacon Press, 1966.

Chafe, William H. *The Unfinished Journey: America Since World War II*. New York: Oxford University Press, 1986.

Crawford, Alan. *Thunder on the Right: The 'New Right' and Politics of Resentment*. New York: Pantheon, 1980.

Forster, Arnold, and Epstein, Benjamin. *Danger on the Right*. New York: Random House, 1965.

_____. *The Radical Right: Report on the John Birch Society and Its Allies*. New York: Vintage, 1967.

Goldwater, Barry M. *The Conscience of a Conservative*. Shepherdsville, Kentucky: Victor Publishing Company, 1960.

_____. *Why Not Victory: A Fresh Look at American Foreign Policy*. New York: Macfadden Books, 1962.

Grantham, Dewey W. *Recent America: The United States Since 1945*. Arlington Heights, Ill.: Harlan Davidson, 1987.

Griffith, Robert. *The Politics of Fear: Joseph R. McCarthy and the Senate*. Lexington: University of Kentucky Press, 1970.

Gottfried, Paul, and Fleming, Thomas. *The Conservative Movement*. Boston: Twayne Publishers, 1988.

Grupp, Frederick W., Jr. "Social Correlates of Political Activists: The John Birch Society and the A.D.A." Ph.D. dissertation, University of Pennsylvania, 1968.

Hofstadter, Richard. *The Paranoid Style in American Politics and Other Essays*. New York: Vintage, 1964.

Kolkey, Jonathan Martin. *The New Right, 1960–1968: With Epilogue, 1969–1980*. Lanham, Md.: University Press of America, 1983.

Lipset, Seymour, and Raab, Earl. *The Politics of Unreason: Right-Wing Extremism in America, 1790–1970*. New York: Harper & Row, 1970.

Miles, Michael W. *The Odyssey of the American Right*. New York: Oxford University Press, 1980.

Oshinsky, David M. *A Conspiracy So Immense: The World of Joe McCarthy*. New York: Free Press, 1983.

Peele, Gillian. *Revival and Reaction: The Right in Contemporary America.* New York: Oxford University Press, 1984.

Polsby, Nelson W. "Toward an Explanation of McCarthyism." *Political Studies* 8 (October 1960): 250–71.

Ribuffo, Leo P. *The Old Christian Right: The Protestant Far Right from the Great Depression to the Cold War.* Philadelphia: Temple University Press, 1983.

Rogin, Michael Paul. *The Intellectuals and McCarthy: The Radical Specter.* Cambridge, Mass.: MIT Press, 1967.

Rohter, Ira. "Radical Rightists: An Empirical Study." Ph.D. dissertation, Michigan State University, 1967.

Rusher, William A. *The Rise of the Right.* New York: William Morrow & Company, 1984.

Saloma, John S. *Ominous Politics: The New Conservative Labyrinth.* New York: Hill and Wang, 1984.

Schrecker, Ellen W. *No Ivory Tower: McCarthyism in the Universities.* New York: Oxford University Press, 1986.

Steinfels, Peter. *The Neoconservatives: The Men Who Are Changing America's Politics.* New York: Simon & Schuster, 1979.

Stone, Barbara. "The John Birch Society of California." Ph.D. dissertation, University of Southern California, 1968.

Theoharis, Athan. *Spying on Americans: Political Surveillance from Hoover to the Huston Plan.* Philadelphia: Temple University Press, 1978.

Toy, Eckard V., Jr. "Ideology and Conflict in American Ultra-Conservatism, 1945–1960." Ph.D. dissertation, University of Oregon, 1965.

Trow, Martin. "Small Businessmen, Political Tolerance, and Support for McCarthyism." *American Journal of Sociology* 64 (1958): 270–81.

Vahan, Richard. *The Truth About the John Birch Society.* New York: Macfadden Books, 1962.

Viguerie, Richard A. *The New Right: We're Ready to Lead.* Falls Church, Virginia: Viguerie Co., 1980.

White, Theodore H. *The Making of the President, 1964.* New York: Atheneum, 1965.

Wolfinger, Raymond E.; Wolfinger, Barbara Kaye; Prewitt, Kenneth; and Rosenhack, Sheilah. "America's Radical Right: Politics and Ideology." In David E. Apter, ed. *Ideology and Discontent.* Glencoe, Ill.: Free Press, 1964.

7. "WE SHALL NOT BE MOVED": THE STUDENT NONVIOLENT COORDINATING COMMITTEE

Bloom, Jack. *Class, Race and the Civil Rights Movement.* Bloomington: Indiana University Press, 1987.

Carson, Clayborne. *In Struggle: SNCC and the Black Awakening of the 1960s.* Cambridge, Mass.: Harvard University, 1981.

Chafe, William H. *Civilities and Civil Rights: Greensboro, North Carolina and the Black Struggle for Freedom.* New York: Oxford University Press, 1980.

Dillingham, Harry C., and Sly, David F. "The Mechanical Cotton-Picker, Negro Migration, and the Integration Movement." *Human Organization* 25 (Winter 1966): 344–51.

Eagles, Charles W., ed. *The Civil Rights Movement in America.* Jackson: University Press of Mississippi, 1985.

Freeman, Jo, ed. *Social Movements of the Sixties and Seventies.* New York: Longman, 1983.

Garrow, David J. *Bearing the Cross: Martin Luther King, Jr., and the Southern Christian Leadership Conference.* New York: William Morrow and Company, 1986.

_____. *Protest at Selma: Martin Luther King, Jr., and the Voting Rights Act of 1965.* New Haven, Conn.: Yale University Press, 1978.

Geschwender, James A., ed. *The Black Revolt: The Civil Rights Movement, Ghetto Uprisings, and Separatism.* Englewood Cliffs, New Jersey: Prentice Hall, 1971.

Goldberg, Robert A. "Racial Change on the Southern Periphery: The Case of San Antonio, Texas, 1960–1965." *Journal of Southern History* 49 (August 1983): 349–74.

Hacker, Andrew. "American Apartheid." *New York Review of Books* 34 (3 December 1987): 26–33.

Lawson, Steven F. *Black Ballots: Voting Rights in the South, 1944–1969.* New York: Columbia University Press, 1976.

Lewis, Anthony. *Portrait of a Decade: The Second American Revolution.* New York: Random House, 1964.

Lomax, Louis E. *The Negro Revolt.* New York: Harper & Row, 1962.

Marx, Gary, and Useem, Michael. "Majority Involvement in Minority Movements: Civil Rights, Abolition, and Untouchability." *Journal of Social Issues* 27 (1971): 81–104.

Matthews, Donald R., and Prothro, James W. *Negroes and the New Southern Politics.* New York: Harcourt, Brace & World, 1966.

Matusow, Allen J. "From Civil Rights to Black Power: The Case of SNCC, 1960–1966." In Barton J. Bernstein and Allen J. Matusow, eds. *Twentieth Century America: Recent Interpretations.* New York: Harcourt, Brace, 1972.

McAdam, Doug. *Political Process and the Development of Black Insurgency, 1930–1970.* Chicago: University of Chicago Press, 1982.

Meier, August and Rudwick, Elliott. *CORE: A Study in the Civil Rights Movement, 1942–1968.* New York: Oxford University Press, 1973.

Miroff, Bruce. *Pragmatic Illusions: The Presidential Politics of John F. Kennedy.* New York: McKay, 1976.

Morris, Aldon D. *The Origins of the Civil Rights Movement: Black Communities Organizing for Change.* New York: Free Press, 1984.

Morrison, Joan and Robert K. *From Camelot to Kent State: The Sixties Experience in the Words of Those Who Lived It.* New York: Times Books, 1987.

Myers, Frank E. "Civil Disobedience and Organizational Change: The British Committee of 100." *Political Science Quarterly* 86 (March 1971): 92–112.

Newfield, Jack. *A Prophetic Minority.* New York: New American Library, 1966.

_____. *The Education of Jack Newfield.* New York: St. Martin's Press, 1984.

Oberschall, Anthony. *Social Conflict and Social Movements.* Englewood Cliffs, N.J.: Prentice-Hall, 1973.

Pinkney, Alphonso. *The Myth of Black Progress.* New York: Cambridge University Press, 1984.

Piven, Frances Fox, and Cloward, Richard. *Poor People's Movements: Why They Succeed, How They Fail.* New York: Pantheon, 1977.

Rogers, Kim Lacy. "Oral History and the History of the Civil Rights Movement." *Journal of American History* 75 (September 1988): 567–76.

Rothschild, Mary Aickin. *A Case of Black and White: Northern Volunteers and the Southern Freedom Summers, 1964–1965.* Westport, Conn.: Greenwood, 1982.

Silberman, Charles E. *Crisis in Black and White.* New York: Vantage, 1964.

Sitkoff, Harvard. *The Struggle for Black Equality, 1954–1980.* New York: Hill and Wang, 1981.

Sorensen, Theodore C. *Kennedy.* New York: Harper & Row, 1965.

Stoper, Emily Schottenfeld. "The Student Nonviolent Coordinating Committee: The Growth of Radicalism in a Civil Rights Organization." Ph.D. dissertation, Harvard University, 1968.

Sutherland, Elizabeth, ed. *Letters from Mississippi.* New York: McGraw-Hill, 1965.

Theoharis, Athan. *Spying on Americans: Political Surveillance from Hoover to the Huston Plan.* Philadelphia: Temple University Press, 1978.

Westin, Alan F., ed. *Freedom Now!: The Civil-Rights Struggle in America.* New York: Basic Books, 1964.

Zinn, Howard. *SNCC: The New Abolitionists.* Boston: Beacon Press, 1965.

8. THE CAMPUS REVOLT: THE BERKELEY FREE SPEECH MOVEMENT

Anderson, Walt, ed. *The Age of Protest.* Pacific Palisades, Calif.: Goodyear Publishing Co., 1969.

Astin, Alexander W.; Astin, Helen S.; Bayer, Alan E.; and Bisconti, Ann S. *The Power of Protest: A National Study of Student and Faculty Disruptions with Implications for the Future.* San Francisco: Jossey-Bass, 1975.

Altbach, P., and Kelly, D. *American Students: A Selected Bibliography.* Lexington, Mass.: D.C. Heath, 1973.

Breines, Wini. *Community and Organization in the New Left, 1962–1968: The Great Refusal.* New York: Praeger, 1982.

_____. "Whose New Left?" *Journal of American History* 75 (September 1988): 528–45.

Cohen, Mitchell, and Hale, Dennis, eds. *The New Student Left: An Anthology.* Boston: Beacon Press, 1966.

Draper, Hal. *Berkeley: The New Student Revolt.* New York: Grove Press, 1965.

Feuer, Lewis S. *The Conflict of Generations: The Character and Significance of Student Movements.* New York: Basic Books, 1969.

Flacks, Richard. "The Liberated Generation: An Exploration of the Roots of Student Protest." *Journal of Social Issues* 23 (July 1967): 52–75.

_____. "The New Left and American Politics After Ten Years." *Journal of Social Issues* 27 (1971): 21–34.

Foster, Julian, and Long, Durward, eds. *Protest! Student Activism in America.* New York: William Morrow & Co., 1970.

Gitlin, Todd. *The Whole World Is Watching: Mass Media in the Making and Unmaking of the New Left.* Berkeley: University of California Press, 1980.

Goodman, Mitchell. *The Movement Toward a New America.* Philadelphia: Pilgram Press, 1970.

Heirich, Max. *The Beginning: Berkeley, 1964.* New York: Columbia University Press, 1968.

————. *The Spiral of Conflict, Berkeley, 1964.* New York: Columbia University Press, 1971.

Horowitz, Helen Lefkowitz. "The 1960s and the Transformation of Campus Cultures." *History of Education Quarterly* 26 (Spring 1986): 1–38.

Horowitz, Irving Louis, and Friedland, William H. *The Knowledge Factory: Student Power and Academic Politics in America.* Chicago: Aldine Publishing Co., 1970.

Isserman, Maurice. *If I Had a Hammer . . . : The Death of the Old Left and the Birth of the New Left.* New York: Basic Books, 1987.

Jacobs, Paul, and Landau, Saul, eds. *The New Radicals: A Report with Documents.* New York: Random House, 1966.

Jones, Landon Y. *Great Expectations: America and the Baby Boom Generation.* New York: Coward, McGann, and Geoghegan, 1980.

Lasch, Christopher. *The Culture of Narcissism: American Life in an Age of Diminishing Expectations.* New York: Norton, 1979.

Lauter, Paul, and Howe, Florence. *The Conspiracy of the Young.* New York: World Publishing Co., 1971.

Liebman, Arthur. *Jews and the Left.* New York: John Wiley and Sons, 1979.

Lipset, Seymour Martin. *Rebellion in the University.* Chicago: University of Chicago Press, 1976.

————, and Wolin, Sheldon, eds. *The Berkeley Student Revolt: Facts and Interpretations.* Garden City, New York: Anchor, 1965.

Lora, Ronald, ed. *America in the '60s: Cultural Authorities in Transition.* New York: Wiley, 1974.

Lunsford, Terry F. *The "Free Speech" Crisis at Berkeley, 1964–1965: Some Issues for Social and Legal Research.* Berkeley: University of California Press, 1965.

Matusow, Allen J. *The Unraveling of America: A History of Liberalism in the 1960s.* New York: Harper & Row, 1984.

Mauss, Armand L. "The Lost Promise of Reconciliation: New Left vs. Old Left." *Journal of Social Issues* 27 (1971): 1–20.

Miller, James. *"Democracy Is in the Streets": From Port Huron to the Siege of Chicago.* New York: Simon & Schuster, 1987.

Miller, Michael V., and Gilmore, Susan, eds. *Revolution at Berkeley: The Crisis in American Education.* New York: Dell, 1965.

Oberschall, Anthony. *Social Conflict and Social Movements.* Englewood Cliffs, N.J.: Prentice-Hall, 1973.

_____. "The Decline of the 1960s Social Movements." In Louis Kriesberg, ed., *Research in Social Movements, Conflicts and Change.* Vol. 1. Greenwich, Conn.: JAI Press, 1978.

Otten, C. Michael. *University Authority and the Student: The Berkeley Experience.* Berkeley: University of California Press, 1970.

Perrow, Charles. "The Sixties Observed." In Mayer N. Zald and John D. McCarthy, eds. *The Dynamics of Social Movements: Resource Mobilization, Social Control, and Tactics.* Cambridge, Mass.: Winthrop Publishers, 1979.

Rapoport, Roger, and Kirshbaum, Laurence J. *Is the Library Burning?* New York: Random House, 1969.

Rorabaugh, W. J. "The Berkeley Free Speech Movement." In James L. Rawls, ed. *New Directions in California History.* New York: McGraw-Hill, 1988.

Roszak, Theodore. *The Making of a Counter Culture: Reflections on the Technocratic Society and Its Youthful Opposition.* Garden City, N.Y.: Doubleday, 1969.

Sale, Kirkpatrick. *SDS.* New York: Random House, 1973.

Sampson, Edward E., and Korn, Harold A. *Student Activism and Protest.* San Francisco: Jossey-Bass, 1970.

Stadtman, Verne A. *The University of California, 1868–1968.* New York: McGraw-Hill, 1970.

Unger, Irwin. *The Movement: A History of the American New Left, 1959–1972.* New York: Dodd, Mead and Co., 1974.

Wallerstein, Immanuel, and Starr, Paul, eds. *The University Crisis Reader.* 2 vols. New York: Random House, 1971.

Watts, William, and Whittaker, David. "Free Speech Advocates at Berkeley." *Journal of Applied Behavioral Science* 2 (January–March, 1966): 41–62.

9. NEVER ANOTHER SEASON OF SILENCE: THE NATIONAL ORGANIZATION FOR WOMEN.

Bardwick, Judith M. *In Transition: How Feminism, Sexual Liberation, and the Search for Self-Fulfillment Have Altered Our Lives.* New York: Holt, Rinehart & Winston, 1979.

Berry, Mary Frances. *Why ERA Failed: Politics, Women's Rights, and the Amending Process of the Constitution.* Bloomington: Indiana University Press, 1986.

Carden, Maren. *The New Feminist Movement.* New York: Russell Sage Foundation, 1974.

Chafe, William H. *The American Woman: Her Changing Social, Economic, and Political Roles, 1920–1970.* New York: Oxford University Press, 1972.

_____. *Women and Equality: Changing Patterns in American Culture.* New York: Oxford University Press, 1977.

Cohen, Marcia. *The Sisterhood: The True Story of the Women Who Changed the World.* New York: Simon and Schuster, 1988.

Conover, Pamela Johnson, and Gray, Virginia. *Feminism and the New Right: Conflict over the American Family.* New York: Praeger, 1983.

Deckard, Barbara. *The Women's Movement: Political, Socioeconomic, and Psychological Issues.* New York: Harper & Row, 1979.

Eisenstein, Hester. *Contemporary Feminist Thought.* Boston: G.K. Hall and Co., 1983.

Eisenstein, Zillah. "Antifeminism in the Politics and Election of 1980." *Feminist Studies* 7 (Summer 1981): 187–205.

Evans, Sara. *Personal Politics: The Roots of Women's Liberation in the Civil Rights Movement and the New Left.* New York: Alfred Knopf, 1979.

Freeman, Jo. *The Politics of Women's Liberation: A Case Study of an Emerging Social Movement and Its Relation to the Policy Process.* New York: McKay, 1975.

_____. *Social Movements of the Sixties and Seventies.* New York: Longman, 1983.

Friedman, Jane E., and Shade, William G., eds. *Our American Sisters: Women in American Life and Thought.* Lexington, Mass.: D.C. Heath, 1982.

Gimlin, Hoyt, ed. *The Women's Movement: Achievements and Effects.* Washington, D.C.: Congressional Quarterly Inc., 1977.

Haney, Eleanor Humes. *A Feminist Legacy: The Ethics of Wilma Scott Heide and Company.* Buffalo, N.Y.: Margaretdaughters, Inc., 1985.

Harrison, Cynthia E. "A 'New Frontier' for Women: The Public Policy of the Kennedy Administration." *Journal of American History* 67 (December 1980): 630–46.

Hewlett, Sylvia Ann. *A Lesser Life: The Myth of Women's Liberation in America.* New York: William Morrow & Co., 1986.

Hoff-Wilson, Joan. *Rights of Passage: The Past and Future of the ERA.* Bloomington: Indiana University Press, 1986.

Hole, Judith, and Levine, Ellen. *Rebirth of Feminism.* New York: Quadrangle, 1971.

Kaledin, Eugenia. *Mothers and More: American Women in the 1950s.* Boston: Twayne, 1984.

MacLean, Judy. "N.O.W." *Socialist Revolution* 6 (July–Sept. 1976): 39–50. University of Chicago Press, 1986.

Mansbridge, Jane J. *Why We Lost the ERA.* Chicago: University of Chicago Press, 1986.

Morgan, Robin, ed. *The Sisterhood Is Powerful: An Anthology of Writings from the Women's Liberation Movement.* New York: Random House, 1970.

Morris, Monica B. "The Public Definition of a Social Movement: Women's Liberation." *Sociology and Social Research* 57 (July 1973): 526–43.

Petchesky, Rosalind Pollack. "Antiabortion, Antifeminism, and the Rise of the New Right." *Feminist Studies* 7 (Summer 1981): 206–46.

Riley, Glenda. *Inventing the American Woman: A Perspective on Women's History.* Arlington Heights, Ill.: Harlan Davidson, 1986.

Rix, Sara, ed. *The American Woman, 1987–88: A Report in Depth.* New York: Norton, 1987.

Rothschild, Mary Aickin. "White Women Volunteers in the Freedom Summers: Their Life and Work in a Movement for Social Change." *Feminist Studies* 5 (Fall 1979): 466–495.

Tanner, Leslie B., ed. *Voices from Women's Liberation.* New York: New American Library, 1970.

Tedin, Kent L.; Brady, David W.; Buxton, Mary E.; Gorman, Barbara M.; and Thompson, Judy L. "Social Background and Political Differences Between Pro- and Anti-ERA Activists." *American Political Quarterly* 5 (July 1977): 395–408.

Ware, Cellestine. *Woman Power: The Movement for Women's Liberation.* New York: Tower Publishers, 1970.

Yates, Gayle. *What Women Want: The Ideas of the Movement.* Cambridge, Mass.: Harvard University Press, 1975.

10. THE CHALLENGERS' LEGACY

Boyte, Harry C. *The Backyard Revolution: Understanding the New Citizen Movement.* Philadelphia: Temple University Press, 1980.

Brill, Harry. *Why Organizers Fail: The Story of a Rent Strike.* Berkeley: University of California Press, 1971.

Carson, Clayborne. *In Struggle: SNCC and the Black Awakening of the 1960s.* Cambridge, Mass.: Harvard University Press, 1981.

Curry, Richard O. *Freedom at Risk: Secrecy, Censorship, and Repression in the 1980s.* Philadelphia: Temple University Press, 1989.

Gamson, William A. *The Strategy of Social Protest.* Homewood, Ill.: Dorsey, 1975.

Garner, Roberta Ash. *Social Movements in America.* Chicago: Rand McNally, 1977.

Gitlin, Todd. *The Whole World Is Watching: Mass Media in the Making and Unmaking of the New Left.* Berkeley: University of California Press, 1980.

Goldberg, Robert A. "Racial Change on the Southern Periphery: The Case of San Antonio, Texas, 1960–65." *Journal of Southern History* 49 (August 1983): 349–74.

Kielbowicz, Richard B., and Scherer, Clifford. "The Role of the Press in the Dynamics of Social Movements." In Louis Kriesberg, ed. *Research in Social Movements, Conflicts and Change* 9 Greenwich, Conn.: JAI, 1986: 71–96.

McAdam, Doug. "The Decline of the Civil Rights Movement." In Jo Freeman, ed. *Social Movements of the Sixties and Seventies.* New York: Longman, 1983.

McCarthy, John, and Zald, Mayer. *The Trend of Social Movements in America: Professionalization and Resource Mobilization.* Morristown, N.J.: General Learning Corp., 1973.

Reitzes, Donald C., and Reitzes, Dietrich C. "Alinsky's Legacy: Current Applications and Extensions of His Principles and Strategies." In Louis Kriesberg, ed. *Research in Social Movements, Conflicts and Change* 6 Greenwich, Conn.: JAI, 1984: 31–55.

Turner, Ralph H. "The Public Perception of Protest." *American Sociological Review* 34 (December 1969): 815–31.

INDEX

AIDS Coalition to Unleash Power, 223
Alcohol, 40
  consumption, 18, 19–20, 21
  industry, 21–23, 29
Alinsky, Saul, 225
America for Jesus, 138
American Anti-Vivisection Society,
  222–223
American Association of University
  Women, 199
American Coalition of Patriotic Societies, 124
American Conservative Union, 212
American Crusaders, 69
American Federation of Labor, 10, 29,
  44–45
  and Communist party, 94, 96, 97, 98,
    100, 101, 103, 111–114
  and Industrial Workers of the World,
    45, 47, 48, 51–52
American Freedom Coalition, 137
American Labor Union, 46, 47, 48
American League for Peace and
  Democracy, 104, 107

American Legion, 62, 94, 108, 126, 212
American Medical Association, 10, 30
American Nazi Party, 221, 227
American Peace Test, 222, 225
American Security Council, 139
American Society for the Promotion of
  Temperance, 20
American Student Union, 104, 107
American Veterans Committee, 104
Americans for Constitutional Action,
  124
Amnesty International, 220–221, 224
Anderson, Sherwood
  and Communist party, 100
Animal Liberation Front, 223
Anti-Defamation League, 90
Anti-Saloon League, 16, 228, 230, 234
  appeals and ideology, 19, 22–23, 26,
    28–30, 33, 35, 232
  demobilization, 39
  dissension, 36
  funding of, 25, 27, 39
  goals, 31, 32, 35, 39

Anti-Saloon League (*continued*)
  government response to, 27, 32, 34–35,
    37, 38, 232–233
  image, 26, 27–28, 30–31, 32, 34, 37,
    38–39, 225, 232
  and immigrants, 30, 33, 34, 37
  leadership, 23–26, 27, 34, 36–37, 225
  membership, 25–26, 219, 225, 227
  and opinion-making public, 26, 28, 30,
    231
  opposition to, 35–36
  organizational structure, 24–25, 32–33,
    233
  origins, 23–24
  polity member response to, 24, 25–26,
    29, 30, 33–34, 37–38, 231
  and progressive movements, 27
  tactics, 30–32, 34–35, 36–37, 39
Aptheker, Bettina, 273 n93
Arendt, Hannah, 5, 6
Arm of the Lord, 221
Armour, Charles, 139
Aryan Nations, 90, 221, 224–225, 227
Association Against the Prohibition
  Amendment, 38
Atkinson, Ti-Grace, 207
Authorities. *See* Government

Baby Boom Generation, 168–169
Baez, Joan, 168
Baker, Ella, 148–149, 152
Baker, Purley, 26
Baker, Ray Stannard
  and Industrial Workers of the World,
    57
Banks, Russell, 221
Barry, Marion, 149, 153, 165
Benson, Ezra Taft, 125
Bergquist, Laura, 195
Berkeley Free Speech Movement. *See* Free
  Speech Movement
Berkeley Women's Liberation Group, 203
Berrigan, Phil, 221
Birch Society. *See* John Birch Society
Birth of a Nation, 67
Black, Claude, 229–230
Black Panthers, 164
Blacks, 73, 75–76
  and affirmative action, 199
  and Communist party, 97, 100, 104,
    106, 109, 112, 113
  community organizations, 145
  economic mobility, 143
  and John Birch Society, 121–122, 125,
    131, 133
  and Ku Klux Klan, 65–66, 70, 89
  migration, 143–144

political power, 144, 166
  poverty, 165–166
  in rural South, 152
  and segregation, 142–144
Blackwell, Unita, 160, 165
Bliss, Ray
  and John Birch Society, 134
Bohn, Frank
  and Industrial Workers of the World, 47
Bolton, Roxcy, 213
Bond, Julian, 165
Bread and Roses, 203
Brophy, Frank Cullen, 132
Brophy, William, 132
Browder, Earl, 100, 108, 109
  biography, 102
  and Industrial Workers of the World,
    62
Brown, H. Rap, 164
*Brown v. Board of Education of Topeka,
  Kansas*, 144, 146, 147
Buckley, William F.
  and John Birch Society, 128–129
Bush, George, 220
  and John Birch Society, 138

Campus CORE, 171, 173, 174, 175, 176,
    179, 182, 189.
  See also Congress of Racial Equality
Canterbury, Janet, 193
Cardinal Mindszenty Foundation, 124
Carmichael, Stokely, 162–163, 164, 165,
    227
Casey, William
  and John Birch Society, 138
Catholic Abstinence League, 27
Catholics, 32, 37, 69, 73, 77, 84, 87, 119,
    137, 212
  and John Birch Society, 121, 128, 131,
    132–133, 140
  and Ku Klux Klan, 69–70, 74, 75, 76,
    77, 78, 86, 90
Chamber of Commerce, 108
Chaney, James, 158
Charney, George, 113
"Cheers", 19
Civil Rights Movement
  in Alabama, 160
  in Albany, 154–55
  competition within, 155
  evolution of, 160–162, 164–166
  and Freedom Rides, 150
  impact of, 198
  leadership of, 145, 146–147, 148–149
  March on Washington, 156
  in Mississippi, 150, 152–154, 156–159,
    162

Civil Rights Movement (*continued*)
and opinion-making public, 146, 147, 161
origins, 142–147
outcomes, 165–166
and riots, 161
in San Antonio, 229–230
and sit-in demonstrations, 147–148
and Vietnam, 161
and white resistance, 146, 152, 153–155, 158
and women, 158–159, 160, 194, 198–199, 203.
See also Congress of Racial Equality; Martin Luther King, Jr.; National Association for the Advancement of Colored People; Southern Christian Leadership Conference; Student Nonviolent Coordinating Committee
Clarenbach, Katharine, 200, 201
Clarke, Edward, 66–67, 71
Cloward, Richard, 12
Colorado Apostolate, 75
Comer, James, 71
Commission on the Status of Women, 197–198
Committee in Solidarity with the People of El Salvador, 222
Committee for the Survival of a Free Congress, 137, 139, 225
Communist Labor party, 93, 96
Communist Party of America, 87, 119, 120, 171, 172, 181, 221, 230, 234
appeals and ideology, 91–92, 93, 96, 99–100, 101–102, 104, 105–107, 108, 112, 114
demobilization, 112–114
dissension, 93, 98, 111–114, 115
funding, 94, 95, 104
government response to, 92, 94–95, 108, 109, 110–111, 114, 232
image, 92, 94–96, 98, 100, 101, 103–104, 105, 107, 108–110, 115, 232
and indoctrination, 95–96, 104, 107
leadership, 93, 96, 97–98, 102, 104–105, 111, 112–113, 225
membership, 92, 93, 95, 96–97, 98, 101, 103, 104–107, 108, 109, 113, 114, 115, 219–220, 226
and New Left, 106, 114–115
and opinion-making public, 92, 94, 100, 109, 111, 231
organizational structure, 96, 97–98, 102, 104, 112–113, 233
origins, 92–95

polity members response to, 94, 102–103, 108, 109, 111–112, 231
and Soviet Union, 92, 95–96, 97, 98, 101–102, 104, 107–109, 113, 114
tactics, 95, 96–99, 100, 101–103, 106–109, 112, 114
and violence, 94, 108, 110
Communist Political Association, 109
Congress of Industrial Organizations, 63
and Communist party, 103, 111–112
Congress of Racial Equality, 146, 147, 151, 153, 164
and Freedom Rides, 150, 151
and Student Nonviolent Coordinating Committee, 155
Connor, Bull, 155
Conservative Caucus, 137, 139
Council of Federated Organizations, 153
Council on Foreign Relations
and John Birch Society, 138
Counterculture, 171–172, 191
Covenant, 221
Cushing, Richard Cardinal
and John Birch Society, 132

Davis, Caroline, 201
De Caux, Len, 63
De Crow, Karen, 213
Debs, Eugene, 45, 47, 48, 52
DeLeon, Daniel, 47, 48, 52, 53
Democratic party, 37, 38
and blacks, 144, 146, 151, 161, 164
and Communist party, 102–103, 111, 112
and Ku Klux Klan, 82–84, 85
and National Organization for Women, 214, 215
and Student Nonviolent Coordinating Committee, 157–159
and women, 209, 214
Diamond, Ed, 196
Dirksen, Everett
and John Birch Society, 135
Donoughue, William, 230
Dos Passos, John
and Communist party, 100
Draper, Hal, 189–190
Dreiser, Theodore
and Communist party, 100
Dubois Club, 172, 174
Dupont, Irenee, 37
Dupont, Lammont, 37
Dupont, Pierre, 37

Eagle Forum, 137, 138, 212
East, Catharine, 199
Eastwood, Mary, 199, 200

Eisenhower, Dwight D.
  and blacks, 144
  and John Birch Society, 123, 131
Equal Employment Opportunities
  Commission, 199, 202, 210–211.
  See also Government
Equal Rights Amendment, 210, 211–215,
  216, 217
  opposition to, 212–215.
  See also National Organization for
    Women
Etheridge, Paul S., 65
Ettor, Joseph, 50, 53, 57, 59
Evans, Hiram Wesley, 71, 84, 86, 88
Evans, Rowland, 161
Everest, Wesley, 41, 62

Falwell, Jerry, 137
Farmer, James, 159
Farmer-Labor party, 96
Federal Bureau of Investigation, 222
  and Communist party, 108, 111, 114
  and John Birch Society, 128
  and Ku Klux Klan, 89
  and Student Nonviolent Coordinating
    Committee, 151, 153, 159, 163,
    164, 232.
  See also Government
The Feminine Mystique, 198, 200
Feminists, 207
Ferraro, Geraldine, 215
Flynn, Elizabeth Gurley, 53, 57, 59, 63
Foat, Ginny, 196, 213
Ford, Gerald
  and John Birch Society, 135
Ford, James, 100, 102
Forman, James, 156, 162, 165
Foster, William, 96, 98, 100, 102, 109,
  113, 114
  and Industrial Workers of the World,
    63
Fox, Muriel, 201
Free Speech Movement, 222, 230, 234
  appeals and ideology, 167–168,
    174–175, 176–177, 178–179,
    181–182, 184, 185–186, 189, 232
  creates Free Student Union, 189
  demobilization, 183, 189–190
  dissension, 189–190, 269 n24
  funding, 179, 182, 185
  government response to, 168, 175–178,
    179–185, 187–189, 190
  image, 168, 178, 180–184, 187–188, 189
  impact of, 190–191
  leadership, 175, 179, 183, 184, 189
  membership, 179, 180, 185–187, 189,
    220, 227
  and opinion-making public, 168, 177,
    178, 180–181, 231
  organizational structure, 179, 189, 233
  origins, 168–174
  polity member response to, 168, 177,
    178, 180, 181, 182–188, 189, 231,
    233
  tactics, 167–168, 175–178, 180–188
  and violence, 171, 185, 187.
  See also Students
Freedom Rides, 150, 151
Friedan, Betty, 196, 207
  criticizes lesbianism, 208
  organizes National Organization for
    Women, 200–201, 202
  publishes *The Feminine Mystique*, 198
Fromm, Erich, 4–5
Fuchs, Sandor, 175

Gallaudet University, 222
Gamson, William, 8, 9, 11, 229–230, 231,
  234–235
Garner, Roberta Ash, 2, 229
Gay Rights, 221
General Motors, 10
Giovannitti, Arturo, 53, 57
Gitlow, Benjamin, 93
Glazer, Nathan, 187
Goldberg, Art, 175, 182, 184, 273 n93
  dismissed, 190
  jailed, 189
  leads demonstration, 175
  in Mississippi, 173
  and obscenity, 189
Goldberg, Jackie, 184
Goldsmith, Judy, 214–215
Goldwater, Barry, 116, 125, 126, 135, 159
  political campaign, 129–131, 173
  and Robert Welch, 129, 257 n27
Gompers, Samuel, 51
Good Templars, 27
Goodman, Andrew, 158
Government, 8, 10, 12, 14, 16, 231
  and blacks, 142–143, 144, 146
  and Civil Rights Movement, 150–152,
    153, 158, 159
  role of, 9
  strategies of, 11, 221–223, 228–230,
    232–233, 234
  and students, 169–171, 173–174,
    179–180, 190–192
  and women, 197–200, 214.
  See also individual movements
Graeber, Laura, 210
Graham, Richard, 199, 200
Greenpeace, 221, 225
Griffiths, Martha, 199

Hagerty, Thomas, 50
Haig, Alexander
    and John Birch Society, 138
Hall, Gus, 114, 115
Hall, W. L., 47
Hanson, Ole, 94
Harkness, Edward, 37
Harrington, Michael, 7
Hayden, Casey, 154, 203
Haywood, William D., 51, 52, 53, 56, 57,
    58, 61, 227
    and Communist party, 62
    and Western Federation of Miners, 47
Hernandez, Aileen, 199, 207
Hicks, Granville
    and Communist party, 100
Highlander Folk School, 225
Hitler, Adolf, 4, 101
Hoffer, Eric, 5, 6
Hoffman, Abbie, 221
Hook, Sidney
    and Communist party, 100
Hoover, J. Edgar, 94, 114, 125
Hughes, Langston
    and Communist party, 100

Immigrants, 32, 73, 84, 87–88
    and Communist party, 93, 98, 101, 104
    and Ku Klux Klan, 69–70, 75, 78
Immigration and Naturalization Service,
    222.
    See also Government
Industrial Areas Foundation, 225
Industrial Workers of the World, 91, 132,
    230, 234
    appeals and ideology, 41–50, 55, 56,
        57–58, 60, 64
    and Communist party, 63
    demobilization, 62–63
    dissension, 52–53, 59, 63
    funding, 49, 59, 60
    government response to, 42, 52, 54–56,
        58, 60–63, 229, 232
    image, 48–49, 51, 52, 55–57, 60–62,
        64–65, 231, 232
    leadership, 47, 48, 49, 52–54, 56, 59, 219
    membership, 48, 51, 54, 57, 58, 59, 60,
        63, 64, 227
    and opinion-making public, 55, 61, 64,
        231
    organizational structure, 48, 49, 52, 53,
        57, 59, 64, 233
    origins, 41, 46–48
    polity member response to, 42, 49,
        51–52, 54–56, 58–62, 64, 231
    tactics, 49–52, 54–55, 57–60, 224
    and violence, 50, 51, 55

Industrialization, 21, 42–43
Internal Revenue Service, U.S.
    and Anti-Saloon League, 37
    and Communist party, 114
    and Ku Klux Klan, 86, 88, 249 *n*20
    and National Organization for Women,
        211
    and Student Nonviolent Coordinating
        Committee, 163.
    See also Government
International Workers Order, 104

Jenner, William, 119
Jewish Society of Americanists, 133
Jews, 32, 38, 69, 73, 77, 84, 87, 137, 221
    and Aryan Nations, 225
    and Communist party, 105–106, 113,
        114
    and Free Speech Movement, 179, 184,
        185–186
    and John Birch Society, 121, 132, 133,
        135, 140
    and Ku Klux Klan, 69–70, 74–77, 86
    and social movements, 220
    Student Nonviolent Coordinating
        Committee, 149, 155, 158,
        163–164
John Birch Society, 230, 234
    appeals and ideology, 117, 118–122,
        125–127, 129, 130, 134–135, 138,
        139
    demobilization, 135–136, 138–139
    dissension, 135–136
    funding, 122, 130, 133, 139
    government response to, 128, 129
    image, 117, 129–132, 135, 138–140,
        225, 232
    and indoctrination, 122, 127
    leadership, 121–124, 126, 132, 135, 139
    membership, 120–121, 124, 127, 128,
        129–133, 136, 139, 220
    and New Right, 117, 137, 138, 139
    and opinion-making public, 128–129,
        131, 136, 140
    organizational structure, 122, 124–125,
        127, 130–131, 133, 139, 233
    origins, 117–123
    polity member response to, 117, 124,
        125–126, 128–129, 131, 134–135,
        140, 231
    and Reagan administration, 138–139
    tactics, 122, 126–127, 130–131, 133,
        135, 141.
    See also New Right; Goldwater, Barry
Johnson, Lyndon, 164, 200
    and affirmative action, 199, 202
Jones, E. F., 25

Jones, Mother, 46
Jordan, I. King, 222
Justice Department, U.S., 221
  and Civil Rights Movement, 151
  and Communist party, 94–95, 111, 114
  and Industrial Workers of the World,
    61
  and John Birch Society, 128
  and National Organization for Women,
    202.
  See also Government

Kennedy, John F.
  and Student Nonviolent Coordinating
    Committee, 150–152, 154, 156
  and students, 172
  and women, 197, 198–199
Kennedy, Robert, 128
  and Freedom Rides, 150
  and Student Nonviolent Coordinating
    Committee, 150–152
Kerr, Clark, 167, 169, 182, 187, 190
  biography, 179–180
  criticizes Free Speech Movement, 175,
    177, 181, 184
  dismissed, 190
  and faculty, 187
  at Greek Theater, 187
  on outcome, 190
King, Martin Luther Jr., 142, 151, 159
  in Albany, 155
  in Birmingham, 155
  and Black Power, 162–163
  death of, 164
  forms Southern Christian Leadership
    Conference, 146
  in Selma, 160
  and Student Nonviolent Coordinating
    Committee, 148, 149, 155, 159
King, Mary, 159, 165, 203
Kirk, Russell
  and John Birch Society, 129
Knights of Columbus, 75, 212
Knights of the Ku Klux Klan, 37, 65–66,
    94, 116, 121, 146, 150, 221, 228, 230,
    234
  appeals and ideology, 66, 68–70, 73–76,
    78, 82, 88, 90
  in Colorado, 72, 78
  demobilization, 85–89, 90
  in Denver, 72, 73–77
  dissension, 71, 85–86, 87, 89–90
  funding, 67, 83
  government response to, 67, 73–74, 77,
    84–87, 88–90, 232–233
  image, 65–67, 73, 77, 82, 85–87, 89, 90,
    225, 231–232

leadership, 66–67, 70–73, 76, 81–82, 88
  membership, 66, 67, 69, 70, 72, 74, 76,
    78–82, 88, 89, 92, 225, 227
  and opinion-making public, 67, 74, 76,
    88, 231
  organizational structure, 67, 70–72, 76,
    82–83, 233
  origins, 67–68, 73
  polity member response to, 73–74,
    82–85, 88, 231
  tactics, 70, 77, 78, 82–84, 85, 87–89
  and violence, 66, 77, 84, 89, 90,
    231–232
Kornhauser, William, 5, 6
Ku Klux Klan. *See* Knights of the Ku Klux
  Klan
Kunsler, William, 221
Kynett, A. J., 18

Lafayette, Bernard, 160
LaFollette, Robert, 97
Leadership, 2, 8, 9, 10
  role of, 15, 219, 225, 227–228.
  See also individual movements
League of American Writers, 104, 107
League of Women Voters, 199
Lenin, Nicolai, 63, 91, 94, 106, 121
Levensen, Marya, 203
Lewis, John, 147, 162, 234
  at March on Washington, 156
  Student Nonviolent Coordinating
    Committee chair, 156
Lewis, John L., 103, 147
Lindsey, John, 209
Lipset, Seymour, 5, 6
  and Free Speech Movement, 187
Little, Frank, 53, 62
Liuzzo, Viola, 89
Locke, John Galen, 70, 76, 85, 86, 227
  biography, 73
Lovestone, Jay, 93, 98
Loyal Legion of Loggers and Lumbermen,
    62, 229
Lynes, Russell, 196

MacDonald, Larry, 139
McDonald, Daniel, 47
McCall, H. C., 71
McCarthy, John, 225
McCarthy, Joseph, 110, 117–118,
    119–120, 123
McCarthyism. *See* Red Scare: second.
McDew, Charles, 149–151, 153, 156
McKissick, Floyd, 162
McManus, John, 139
Malcolm X, 160
Manion, Clarence, 126

Matthews, Mark, 19
Meese, Edwin, 184
Membership, 3–4, 6–7, 9, 11, 219–220, 225, 226–227, 231.
  See also individual social movements
Meredith, James, 162
Meyerson, Martin, 188, 189
Miller, Jack, 56
Minitz, Benjamin, 202
Minute Men of America, 86–87, 121
Mississippi Freedom Democratic Party, 157–159
Mondale, Walter, 215
Moral Majority, 137, 212
  and Ku Klux Klan, 90
Morgan, Robin, 204
Mormon Church, 212
Morton, Thruston
  and John Birch Society, 134
Moses, Bob, 141, 147, 152–153, 154, 160, 165
Moyer, Charles, 47, 52

National Advisory Commission on Civil Disorders, 166
National Association for the Advancement of Colored People, 90, 104, 153, 163, 164, 230
  and Black Power, 163
  and government, 151
  membership, 144–146
  origins, 145
  and sit-in demonstrations, 147
  and Student Nonviolent Coordinating Committee, 155
National Association of Manufacturers, 10, 94, 120, 123
National Christian Action Coalition, 137
National Council of Catholic Men, 75
National Council of Churches, 222
National Founders' Association, 94
National Negro Congress, 104
National Organization for Women, 228
  appeals and ideology, 194, 200–201, 205–207, 211, 213, 214, 216–217, 232
  demobilization, 194, 213–215
  dissension, 207–208, 213–214, 215
  funding, 201, 202, 207, 209, 210, 211, 214, 215
  government response to, 194, 197–198, 202–203, 208, 210–212, 214–215, 216
  image, 202, 205–206, 208–211, 215, 232
  leadership, 200–202, 207, 208, 210, 212–214, 215
  membership, 200, 201, 202, 206, 207, 208–210, 214, 215, 220, 277 *n*56
  and opinion-making public, 205, 208, 210, 231
  organizational structure, 201–202, 207, 209–212, 233
  origins, 194–200
  outcomes, 194, 210–211, 214, 216–217, 230, 234
  polity member response to, 194, 201, 205, 207–209, 213–216, 231
  tactics, 202, 207, 209–212, 213–216.
    See also Women; Women's Liberation Movement
National Student Association, 148
National Women's Political Caucus, 209
New Left
  demobilization, 191
  membership profile, 186
  and women, 194, 203–204, 227.
    See also Communist party; Free Speech Movement
New Right, 221
  appeals, 136–139
  and Equal Rights Amendment, 136
  and John Birch Society, 117, 138, 139
  and Ku Klux Klan, 90
  organizational structure, 137
  origins, 136–137
  and Republican party, 138
  and tactics, 138
New York Radical Women, 204
Nixon, Richard, 119, 129, 135, 136, 209, 210
Noonan, Francis, 214
Novak, Robert, 161

Oberlin Temperance Alliance, 23–24
Oberschall, Anthony, 8, 9, 11
Operation Rescue, 216
Opinion-making public
  and social movement image, 16, 224, 225, 229, 231–232
  and women, 193, 195–196
  and women's liberation movement, 205.
    See also individual movements; Polity Members

Palmer, A. Mitchell, 94–95
People for the Ethical Treatment of Animals, 223
Pfaff, Henry, 55
Piven, Frances Fox, 12
Plessy v. *Ferguson*, 142–143, 144
Pluralism, 6–7
The Politician, 123, 128, 130, 257 *n*27

Polity Members, 14, 219, 222–224, 228,
229, 231–232
definition of, 9–10
tactics, 10, 12
tests of membership, 10, 228–229.
See also individual social movements;
Opinion-Making Public; Tilly,
Charles
Pro-Decency, 137
Progressive party, 112, 144
Prohibition party, 20, 27, 30

Rabbinical Alliance of America, 212
Rabinowitz, Matilda, 53
Raskob, John, 37
Read, Mary Joel, 201
Reagan, Ronald
administration of, 138–139
dismisses Kerr, 190
and multiversity, 190
and New Right, 221
and Robert Welch, 125–126,
134–135
and women, 214
Reagon, Cordell, 154
Red Scare
first, 61, 92–95
second, 109–110, 117–120
Redstockings, 204
Reed, John, 93
Republican party, 110
and Anti-Saloon League, 37, 38
and blacks, 144, 146, 164
and John Birch Society, 126–127,
129–131, 132–136
and Ku Klux Klan, 82–84, 85
and Second Red Scare, 119–120
and women, 209, 214–215
Richmond, Al, 114
Right to Life, 137, 212
Rockefeller, Nelson, 209
Roe v. Wade, 210, 213, 215, 220
Rosenberg, Julius and Ethel, 110
Rosenfeld, Gerald, 170
Rossman, Michael, 172, 174, 183, 189, 273
n93
Rousselet, John, 135
Royal Riders of the Red Robe, 69
Roysher, Marty, 174
Rubin, Jerry, 190
Russell, Howard, 23–24, 26
Ruthenberg, Charles, 93, 98

Sabin, Charles, 37
St. John, Vincent, 41, 53, 61
Saloons. See Alcohol; industry
Sanctuary Movement, 222

Savio, Mario, 167–168, 178, 188, 227, 273
n93
disciplined, 175, 182, 184
at Greek Theater, 187
jailed, 189
leads demonstration, 175, 177
in Mississippi, 173
resigns, 189
Scales, Junius, 113
Schafly, Phyllis, 212
Schomp, Gerald, 132
Schwartz, Michael, 8
Schwerner, James, 158
Sellers, Cleveland, 147, 158, 159, 165
Sherman, Charles, 47
Sherriffs, Alex, 174
Sherrod, Charles, 152, 154, 160, 165
Simmons, William J., 66, 67, 71, 73
Simons, A. M., 47, 52
Simpson, Catharine, 214
Sit-in demonstrations, 142, 147–148
as energizing event, 147–148
and students, 149
Skinheads, 221, 227
SLATE, 175, 176
defeated, 189
election victories, 171, 188
formed, 171
Smeal, Eleanor, 215, 227
quoted, 193, 213
as leader, 213–214, 215
Smelser, Neil, 5, 6
Smith, Clarence, 47
Smith, Ruby Doris, 147
Social Movements
in 1980s, 220–223
appeals and ideology, 2–7, 8, 14–15,
229, 232
and classical theorists, 4–7, 236 n3
continuity in, 227–229
definition, 2–4
dissension, 233
and energizing events, 15, 227, 235
evolution of, 223–227
image, 12, 15–16, 224, 225, 228,
231–232
joining of, 12–15, 16, 219
mobilization model of, 12–16, 219,
227–229
organizational structure, 2, 3, 8–9, 15,
224–225, 229, 233
origins, 4–5, 13–14, 227, 235
outcomes, 11, 229–235
and resource mobilization theorists,
7–12
and resources, 8–10
as role models, 233

Social Movements (*continued*)
  sample of, 16, 220
  tactics, 3–4, 7, 10–11, 223–225,
     228–229
  and violence, 7, 10, 229, 231–232.
  See also Government; individual social
     movements; Leadership;
     Membership; Opinion-Making
     Public; Polity Members
Socialist party, 42, 45, 61, 91, 99, 100, 102
  and Communist party, 93–94, 97, 99
  and Industrial Workers of the World,
     48, 50–51, 52–53, 56
Sons of Temperance, 27
Sorensen, Theodore, 151
Southern Christian Leadership
     Conference, 142, 147, 151, 153
  in Albany, 155
  organized, 146
  in Selma, 160
  and Student Nonviolent Coordinating
     Committee, 148–149, 155
Southern Poverty Law Center, 90
Stalin, Joseph, 98, 106, 108, 113, 120
Steffens, Lincoln
  and Industrial Workers of the World,
     57
  and Communist party, 100
Stembridge, Jane, 149
Stephenson, David, 71, 84, 87
Steunenberg, Frank, 51
Stop-ERA, 137, 138, 212
Storke, Thomas, 128
The Strategy of Social Protest, 211–230.
  See also Gamson, William
Strong, Edward, 178, 180, 182, 184
  hospitalized, 187
  negotiates, 181
  opposes activism, 175, 177
  replaced, 188
  and student misconduct, 183
Student Nonviolent Coordinating
     Committee, 171, 173, 174, 230,
     234
  appeals and ideology, 142, 149,
     152–154, 156, 162–163, 232
  demobilization, 160–164
  dissension, 157–161, 163
  funding, 149, 150, 151, 153, 156, 157,
     163, 164, 173
  government response to, 142, 150–156,
     158–159, 161, 163–164, 232–233
  image, 141, 150, 161, 163–165, 232
  and Martin Luther King, Jr., 148–149,
     154–155, 159
  leadership, 142, 147, 149–150, 153,
     155–156, 219

membership, 150, 154, 155–156, 157,
     159, 160, 227
  and opinion-making public, 142, 156,
     159, 161, 163, 231
  organizational structure, 142, 149–150,
     152, 155–156
  origins, 142–149
  polity member response to, 142,
     153–155, 157, 159, 162, 164, 231
  tactics, 149–150, 152–154, 156–160,
     162
  and Vietnam, 162
  and violence, 150, 153, 158, 164
  and women, 203.
  See also Blacks; Civil Rights
     Movement; Freedom Rides; Sit-in
     Demonstrations
Students, 168, 226
  and activism, 170–173
  and Civil Rights Movement, 168,
     171–175, 178
  and multiversity, 169–170
  in 1980s, 191–192, 222
  form United Front, 174
  and Vietnam, 190–191
Students for a Democratic Society, 148,
     226
  impact of Free Speech Movement on,
     191
  organizes, 172
  Port Huron Statement, 170
  program, 172
  and women, 203
Students for Goldwater, 174, 270 *n*24
Students for Racial Equality, 171
Studies on the Left, 172
Supreme Court, U.S.
  and abortion, 220
  and blacks, 142–143, 144, 150
  and women's rights, 214, 216.
  See also Roe v. *Wade*

Taft, Robert, 119
Temperance movement
  history of, 20–23
Tesca, Carlo, 53, 58, 59
Thomas, Norman, 99, 100
Tilly, Charles
  social movement model, 9–11
Toward an Active Student Community,
     170–171
Tower, John
  and John Birch Society, 129
Trade Union Unity League, 101
Trans-Species Unlimited, 223
Tridon, Andre, 49
The True Believer, 5

Truman, Harry
and blacks, 144
and communism, 110–111
Turner, Bryan, 184
Tyler, Elizabeth, 66–67, 71

United Auto Workers, 222
and National Organization for Women, 201
and Students for a Democratic Society, 172
University of California, 169–170, 171
as protest staging area, 173–174
University Friends of SNCC, 171, 173, 174, 175, 179, 182
Urban League, 104, 163

Varney, Harold, 62
Veterans of Foreign Wars, 108, 212
Viguerie, Richard, 224

Wallace, Henry, 112
Weinberg, Jack, 167, 179, 273 n93
arrested, 176–177, 178
jailed, 189
Welch, Robert, 125–129, 132–133, 138, 140, 227, 257 n27
biography, 120, 123–124
criticized, 128–129
death of, 139
and Insiders, 134–135
organizes John Birch Society, 120–124
quoted, 116
on Ronald Reagan, 138–139
Western Federation of Miners, 46–48
and Industrial Workers of the World, 47, 52–54
Weyl, Walter
and Industrial Workers of the World, 57
White Aryan Resistance, 221
White Citizens Council, 89, 146
White, Theodore, 156

Wilkins, Roy, 163
Women
attitudes about, 193–196, 210
and civil rights movement, 158–160, 194, 198–199, 203
and New Left, 194, 203–204, 227
in the 1980s, 216–217
and sex roles, 205
and social movements, 227
and Student Nonviolent Coordinating Committee, 160
and women's liberation movement, 194
in the work force, 195–196
and World War II, 194–195
Women's Christian Temperance Union, 20, 27, 30
Women's Equality Action League, 207–208
Women's International Terrorist Conspiracy from Hell, 204
Women's Liberation Movement, 194, 203–206
impact on National Organization for Women, 206–208
and opinion-making public, 205.
See also Women; National Organization for Women
Women's Organization for National Prohibition Reform, 38
Women's Radical Action Project, 203

Yard, Molly, 215
Yeagley, J. Walter, 114
Young Americans for Freedom, 139, 226
Young Communist League, 104
Young Democrats, 174, 182
Young People's Socialist League, 172, 182
Young Pioneers, 104
Young Republicans, 174, 182
Young Socialist Alliance, 172, 174, 177
Young, Whitney, 163

Zald, Mayer, 225
Zellner, Bob, 153